The Internet Resource Quick Reference

Que Quick Reference Series

Book introduction and part introductions by William A. Tolhurst

Part III by Mary Ann Pike

The Internet Resource Quick Reference

Copyright © 1994 by Que® Corporation.

All rights reserved. Printed in the United States of America. No part of this book may be used or reproduced in any form or by any means, or stored in a database or retrieval system, without prior written permission of the publisher except in the case of brief quotations embodied in critical articles and reviews. Making copies of any part of this book for any purpose other than your own personal use is a violation of United States copyright laws. For information, address Que Corporation, 201 W. 103rd Street, Indianapolis, IN 46290.

Library of Congress Catalog No.: 94-65146

ISBN: 1-56529-748-2

This book is sold *as is*, without warranty of any kind, either express or implied, respecting the contents of this book, including but not limited to implied warranties for the book's quality, performance, merchantability, or fitness for any particular purpose. Neither Que Corporation nor its dealers or distributors shall be liable to the purchaser or any other person or entity with respect to any liability, loss, or damage caused or alleged to be caused directly or indirectly by this book.

96   95   94   4   3   2   1

Interpretation of the printing code: the rightmost double-digit number is the year of the book's printing; the rightmost single-digit number, the number of the book's printing. For example, a printing code of 94-1 shows that the first printing of the book occurred in 1994.

All terms mentioned in this book that are known to be trademarks or service marks have been appropriately capitalized. Que cannot attest to the accuracy of this information. Use of a term in this book should not be regarded as affecting the validity of any trademark or service mark.

Publisher
David P. Ewing

Director of Publishing
Michael Miller

Director of Acquisitions and Editing
Corinne Walls

Publishing Manager
Lisa A. Bucki

Product Director
Steven M. Schafer

Production Editor
Susan Shaw Dunn

Copy Editors
J. Christopher Nelson
Susan Ross Moore

Technical Assistance
John Wile

Book Designer
Amy Peppler-Adams

Indexers
Charlotte Clapp
Jennifer Eberhardt

Production Team
Angela Bannan, Kim Cofer, Karen Dodson,
Stephanie Gregory, Carla Hall, Linda Quigley, Bob LaRoche,
Joy Dean Lee, Caroline Roop, Becky Tapley,
Mary Beth Wakefield, Donna Winter

Composed in *Stone Serif* and *MCPdigital* by Que Corporation.

Table of Contents

Introduction 1

Part I: The USENET News Group List.......................5

Part II: Publicly Accessible Mailing List 149

Part III: Host Resource Guide 379

Part IV: Special Internet Connections List 425

Part V: The Inter-Network Mail Guide 443

Index 461

Introduction

The Internet is fast becoming an essential information "appliance" for businesses and professionals. It is also a medium for casual exchange of opinions and discussion of topics ranging from TV shows to music to martial arts. More than 150 million "pages" of information per day flow through the Internet. Millions of computers and tens of millions of users participate in it every day.

One of the greatest challenges, even for an experienced Internet user, is locating the information you need. Whether it be for scientific research, self-education, or simple entertainment, the Internet offers an astounding and intimidating number of sources from which to draw. For example, is there a place within the Internet where you can obtain infrared satellite weather images of the East Coast? Or are you looking for a source that can provide the text of recent U.S. Supreme Court decisions?

On a more recreational level, suppose that you have developed a recent interest in motorcycling. As a newcomer to the sport (novices are generally referred to as *newbies* in the Internet jargon), you might have questions like "Where can I get rider training?" or "What experiences have other riders had with maintenance of the model I'm considering buying?" Such information is readily available, only if you could find its source.

Lacking any direction to the contrary, Internet newbies often resort to two approaches:

- They boldly send messages to others in an attempt to find a lead on where such information might be archived or discussed.

- They simply "cruise" around the Internet, searching for clues as to the whereabouts of a potential source.

These approaches can be very inefficient, however. Isn't there a better way to find what you're looking for, saving time and connect charges? Fortunately, a number of selfless individuals within the Internet community compile and maintain lists of various resources available to you as an Internet user. This book has collected several of the more popular of these on-line "roadmaps" into a single, easy-to-use reference to support your search for the information you need.

Who Should Buy This Book?

The Internet Resource Quick Reference will be of greatest value to current members of the Internet community who are familiar with the basics of its operation, including file transfer via ftp and remote host connection via telnet. If you aren't currently an Internet user or aren't familiar with such topics as ftp and telnet, consider acquiring a book that tells you how to access the Internet and to use its many tools and utilities. One such book is Que's *Using the Internet*, Special Edition, which also includes most of the information given here in its own section devoted to Internet resources.

On-Line Sources for the Lists

All the source material for *The Internet Resource Quick Reference* is available on-line from the following groups or individuals:

- The *USENET News Group List*, published by David Lawrence (tale@uunet.uu.net), is periodically posted to the following USENET news groups:

    news.lists
    news.group

```
news.announce.newusers
news.announce.newgroups
news.answers
```

- The *Publicly Accessible Mailing List*, published by Stephanie da Silva (arille@taronga.com) and Chuq Von Rospach (chuq@apple.com), is periodically updated and posted to the following USENET news groups:

  ```
  news.lists
  news.answers
  news.announce.groups
  ```

- The *Special Internet Connections* list, published by Scott Yanoff, is available via anonymous ftp from csd4.csd.uwm.edu. Or you can use the finger utility on Mr. Yanoff's account name (yanoff@csd4.csd.uwm.edu) to get information about other ways of acquiring it.

- The *Inter-Network Mail Guide*, also published by Scott Yanoff, is available from the same source as the Special Internet Connections list.

Each list is reprinted in the parts that follow, including a short introduction to the contents and organization of each list. Armed with this Quick Reference, you will be able to move through the maze of Internet information sources to find what you want quickly and efficiently.

> **Note**
>
> The materials used for *The Internet Resource Quick Reference* were the latest available before going to press. But the Internet is a very dynamic entity, changing and expanding literally every day. If you don't find a listing for your topic of interest, or a listed source has changed or no longer exists, you may want to consider downloading the most recent copy from the net.
>
> If you encounter any inconsistencies or omissions in the material presented in this book, send an Internet e-mail message to
>
> > mlmiller@phcp.win.net

Part I
The USENET News Group List

One of the most valuable resources the Internet has to offer is the mother of all bulletin board systems: USENET. USENET consists of many smaller areas, called *news groups*, each dedicated to a specific topic of interest. You can think of the news groups that make up USENET as being an electronic equivalent of a small-town barber shop or general store: a place for people with common interest to meet and exchange ideas, opinions, and other information. The biggest difference is that USENETville has thousands of "barber shops," each with a "sign" that says what topic is being discussed.

How the USENET Group List Is Organized

A recent count of the number of widely available news groups topped 2,500. Many more have regional or local circulation. With so many news groups to choose from, and more being added literally every day, some basic organization has to be applied to the USENET groups if participants can hope to find the area that addresses their topic of interest. Fortunately, USENET uses a hierarchical structure for group names that helps you narrow your search quickly. The USENET group list is organized in the same manner.

Major News Group Categories

News groups are set up into eight major categories:

Category	Description
alt	"Alternative" discussion on a wide variety of topics
comp	Computer-related information and discussion
sci	Science news and information
misc	The ubiquitous "all other" category
news	Issues concerning USENET itself
rec	Recreational activities such as golf and motorcycling
soc	Topics of interest for students of sociology and psychology
talk	USENET's version of talk radio

Note

Some of the alt news groups have names and discuss topics that are of questionable taste, while others are just benignly humorous. In general, alt news groups should not be taken too seriously. Fitting the style of the alt news groups themselves, the descriptions given in the list for many alt news groups are of a lighthearted, tongue-in-cheek style.

A number of other news group categories also exist for specific interest areas. The more popular of these include the following:

Category	Description
bionet	Groups of interest for biologists.
bit	Redistribution of BITNET LISTSERV mailing lists.
biz	Product announcements, enhancements, etc.
clari	ClariNet commercial news service.
gnu	GNU project of the Free Software Foundation.
hep	Groups of interest for high-energy physics researchers.
ieee	Groups distributed by the Institute of Electrical and Electronics Engineers.
inet	Alternative means for distribution of high-volume groups. Names are preceded with (inet) to distinguish from normal distribution.
info	Redistribution of University of Illinois mailing lists.
k12	Groups of interest for teachers of grades kindergarten through 12.
relcom	Groups of interest for Russian language readers.
u3b	Groups of interest for AT&T 3B computer users.
vmsnet	Groups of interest for DEC VAX/VMS users.

Listings Within a Category

Within each main category, news group names are listed alphabetically and hierarchically. Consider the following example:

```
comp.speech             Research & applications in
                        speech science & technology.
comp.std.c              Discussion about C language
                        standards.
comp.std.c++            Discussion about C++ language,
                        library, standards.
comp.std.internat       Discussion about international
                        standards.
comp.std.misc           Discussion about various
                        standards.
comp.std.mumps          Discussion for the X11.1
                        committee on Mumps. (Moderated)
comp.std.unix           Discussion for the P1003
                        committee on UNIX. (Moderated)
comp.std.wireless       Examining standards for wire-
                        less network technology.
                        (Moderated)
comp.sw.components      Software components and related
                        technology.
```

In this case, all the news groups listed are part of the comp main category and are within a subcategory dedicated to computer-related standards labeled std. The std subcategory comes after comp.speech and before comp.sw.components. Within the std subcategory, the news groups are listed alphabetically, starting with comp.std.c and ending with comp.std.wireless.

Notice that some news groups listed in the example have (Moderated) at the end of their descriptions. In these news groups, a moderator examines all postings before disseminating them via USENET. The examination isn't done to censor viewpoints, but rather to make sure that the messages posted to this group are appropriate for its participants. This is most often done for news groups that tailor themselves to scientists, researchers, or fellow professionals of a given field.

> **Note**
>
> Although the following list has come directly from the Internet, some descriptions have been edited for content and consistency.

News Group	Description
alt.1d	One-dimensional imaging.
alt.3d	Three-dimensional imaging.
alt.abortion.inequity	Paternal obligations of failing to abort unwanted child.
alt.abuse.recovery	Helping victims of abuse to recover.
alt.activism	Activities for activists.
alt.activism.d	A place to discuss issues in alt.activism.
alt.activism.death-penalty	For people opposed to capital punishment.
alt.adoption	For those involved with or contemplating adoption.
alt.aldus.pagemaker	Don't use expensive user support; come here instead.
alt.alien.visitors	Space Aliens on Earth! Abduction! Gov't Cover-Up!
alt.amateur-comp	Discussion and input for Amateur Computerist Newsletter.
alt.angst	Anxiety in the modern world.
alt.answers	As if anyone on alt has the answers. (Moderated)
alt.appalachian	Appalachian region awareness, events, and culture.

(continues)

News Group	Description
alt.aquaria	The aquarium (and related topics) as a hobby.
alt.archery	Robin Hood had the right idea.
alt.architecture	Building design/construction and related topics.
alt.architecture.alternative	Non-traditional building designs.
alt.artcom	Artistic community, arts, and communication.
alt.asian-movies	Movies from Hong Kong, Taiwan, and the Chinese mainland.
alt.astrology	Twinkle, twinkle, little planet.
alt.atheism	Godless heathens.
alt.atheism.moderated	Focused Godless heathens. (Moderated)
alt.autos.antique	Discussion of all facets of older automobiles.
alt.autos.rod-n-custom	Vehicles with modified engines and/or appearance.
alt.backrubs	Lower...to the right...aaaah!
alt.barney.dinosaur.die.die.die	There's enough hatred of Barney for everyone!
alt.basement.graveyard	Another side of the do-it-yourself movement.
alt.bbs	Computer BBS systems and software.
alt.bbs.ads	Ads for various computer BBSs.
alt.bbs.allsysop	SysOp concerns of all networks and technologies.

News Group	Description
alt.bbs.first-class	The First-Class Mac GUI BBS.
alt.bbs.internet	BBSs that are hooked up to the Internet.
alt.bbs.lists	Postings of regional BBS listings.
alt.bbs.pcboard	Technical support for the PCBoard BBS.
alt.bbs.pcbuucp	The commercial PCBoard gateway, PCB-UUCP.
alt.bbs.wildcat	WILDCAT! BBS from Mustang Software, Inc.
alt.beer	Good for what ales ya.
alt.best.of.internet	It was a time of sorrow, it was a time of joy.
alt.bigfoot	Dr. Scholl's gone native.
alt.binaries.multimedia	Sound, text, and graphics data rolled in one.
alt.binaries.pictures	Additional volume in the form of huge image files.
alt.binaries.pictures.d	Discussions about picture postings.
alt.binaries.pictures.erotica	Gigabytes of copyright violations.
alt.binaries.pictures.erotica.blondes	Copyright violations featuring blondes.
alt.binaries.pictures.erotica.d	Discussing erotic copyright violations.
alt.binaries.pictures.erotica.female	Copyright violations featuring females.
alt.binaries.pictures.erotica.male	Copyright violations featuring males.

(continues)

News Group	Description
alt.binaries.pictures.erotica.orientals	Copyright violations featuring Asians.
alt.binaries.pictures.fine-art.d	Discussion of the fine-art binaries. (Moderated)
alt.binaries.pictures.fine-art.digitized	Art from conventional media. (Moderated)
alt.binaries.pictures.fine-art.graphics	Art created on computers. (Moderated)
alt.binaries.pictures.fractals	Cheaper just to send the program parameters.
alt.binaries.pictures.misc	Have we saturated the network yet?
alt.binaries.pictures.supermodels	Yet more copyright violations.
alt.binaries.pictures.tasteless	Ecchh, that last one was *sick*....
alt.binaries.pictures.utilities	Posting of picture-related utilities.
alt.binaries.sounds.d	Sounding off.
alt.binaries.sounds.misc	Digitized audio adventures.
alt.binaries.sounds.music	Music samples in MOD/669 format.
alt.bitterness	No matter what it's for, you know how it'll turn out.
alt.bogus.group	A paradox for its readers.
alt.books.anne-rice	The Vampire Thermostat.
alt.books.deryni	Katherine Kurtz's books, especially the Deryni series.
alt.books.isaac-asimov	Fans of the late sci-fi/science author Isaac Asimov.
alt.books.reviews	If you want to know how it turns out, read it!

News Group	Description
alt.books.technical	Discussion of technical books.
alt.brother-jed	The born-again minister touring U.S. campuses.
alt.buddha.short.fat.guy	Religion. And not religion. Both. Neither.
alt.business.multi-level	Multi-level (network) marketing businesses.
alt.cad	Computer-aided design.
alt.cad.autocad	CAD as practiced by customers of Autodesk.
alt.california	The state and the state of mind.
alt.callahans	Callahan's bar for puns and fellowship.
alt.cascade	Art or litter, you decide.
alt.cd-rom	Discussions of optical storage media.
alt.censorship	Discussion about restricting speech/press.
alt.cereal	Breakfast cereals and their (m)ilk.
alt.child-support	Raising children in a split family.
alt.chinchilla	The nature of chinchilla farming in America today.
alt.chinese.text	Postings in Chinese; Chinese language software.
alt.chinese.text.big5	Posting in Chinese[BIG 5].
alt.clearing.technology	Renegades from the Church of Scientology.
alt.co-ops	Discussion about cooperatives.

(continues)

The Internet Resource Quick Reference

News Group	Description
alt.cobol	Relationship between programming and stone axes.
alt.collecting.autographs	WOW! You got Pete Rose's? What about Kibo's?
alt.college.college-bowl	Discussions of the college bowl competition.
alt.college.food	Dining halls, cafeterias, mystery meat, and more.
alt.comedy.british	Discussion of British comedy in a variety of media.
alt.comedy.firesgn-thtre	Firesign Theatre in all its flaming glory.
alt.comics.batman	Marketing mania.
alt.comics.lnh	Interactive net.madness in the superhero genre.
alt.comics.superman	No one knows it is also alt.clark.kent.
alt.commercial-hit-radio.must.die	Video killed the radio star.
alt.comp.acad-freedom.news	Academic freedom issues related to computers. (Moderated)
alt.comp.acad-freedom.talk	Academic freedom issues related to computers.
alt.comp.databases.xbase.clipper	The Clipper database language.
alt.comp.fsp	A file transport protocol.
alt.comp.hardware.homebuilt	Designing devious devices in the den.
alt.computer.consultants	Geeks on patrol.
alt.config	Alternative subnet discussions and connectivity.

News Group	Description
alt.consciousness	Discussions on the study of the human consciousness.
alt.conspiracy	Be paranoid—they're out to get you.
alt.conspiracy.jfk	The Kennedy assassination.
alt.cows.moo.moo.moo	Like cows would cluck or something.
alt.cult-movies	Movies with a cult following.
alt.cult-movies.rocky-horror	Virgin! Virgin! Virgin! Virgin!
alt.culture.alaska	Is this where the ice weasels come from?
alt.culture.argentina	Don't cry for me.
alt.culture.hawaii	Ua Mau Ke Ea O Ka 'Aina I Ka Pono.
alt.culture.indonesia	Indonesian culture, news, etc.
alt.culture.internet	The culture(s) of the Internet.
alt.culture.karnataka	Culture and language of the Indian state of Karnataka.
alt.culture.kerala	People of Keralite origin and the Malayalam language.
alt.culture.ny-upstate	New York State, above Westchester.
alt.culture.oregon	Discussion about the state of Oregon.
alt.culture.tuva	Topics related to the Republic of Tuva, South Siberia.
alt.culture.us.asian-indian	Asian Indians in the U.S. and Canada.

(continues)

News Group	Description
alt.culture.us.southwest	Basking in the sun of the U.S.'s lower left.
alt.culture.usenet	A self-referential oxymoron.
alt.current-events.bosnia	The strife of Bosnia-Herzegovina.
alt.cyberpunk	High-tech low-life.
alt.cyberpunk.chatsubo	Literary virtual reality in a cyberpunk hangout.
alt.cyberpunk.movement	Topics related to the cyberpunk movement.
alt.cyberpunk.tech	Cyberspace and cyberpunk technology.
alt.cyberspace	Cyberspace and how it should work.
alt.dads-rights	Rights of fathers trying to win custody in court.
alt.dcom.telecom	Discussion of telecommunications technology.
alt.dear.whitehouse	When Hints from Heloise aren't enough.
alt.decathena	Digital's DECathena product. (Moderated)
alt.desert-storm	Some wars never end.
alt.destroy.the.earth	Please leave the light on when you leave.
alt.dev.null	The ultimate in moderated news groups. (Moderated)
alt.devilbunnies	Probably better left undescribed.
alt.discordia	All hail Eris, etc.
alt.discrimination	Quotas, affirmative action, bigotry, persecution.

News Group	Description
alt.divination	Divination techniques (e.g., I Ching, Tarot, runes).
alt.dragons-inn	Breathing fire tends to make one very thirsty.
alt.dreams	What do they mean?
alt.dreams.lucid	What do they *really* mean?
alt.drugs	Recreational pharmaceuticals and related flames.
alt.drugs.caffeine	All about the world's most-used stimulant drug.
alt.drwho.creative	Writing about long scarfs and time machines.
alt.education.ib	The International Baccalaureate Diploma Program.
alt.education.ib.tok	International Baccalaureates in Theory of Knowledge.
alt.elvis.king	A fat, dead king, but king nonetheless.
alt.engr.explosives	Building backyard bombs.
alt.ensign.wesley.die.die.die	We just can't get enough of him.
alt.evil	Tales from the dark side.
alt.exotic-music	Exotic music discussions.
alt.fan.bill-gates	Fans of the original micro-softie.
alt.fan.dall-agata	Michele Dall'Agata, famous physicist from Fermi Lab.
alt.fan.dan-quayle	For discussion of the former vice president.
alt.fan.dave_barry	Electronic fan club for humorist Dave Barry.

(continues)

News Group	Description
alt.fan.devo	Funny hats do not a band make.
alt.fan.disney.afternoon	Disney afternoon characters and shows.
alt.fan.douglas-adams	Author of *The Meaning of Liff* and other fine works.
alt.fan.dune	Herbert's drinking buddies.
alt.fan.eddings	The works of writer David Eddings.
alt.fan.frank-zappa	Is that a Sears poncho?
alt.fan.furry	Fans of funny animals, a la Steve Gallacci's book.
alt.fan.g-gordon-liddy	Y'know, I saw him and Rush holding hands in a bar once.
alt.fan.goons	Careful Neddy, it's that dastardly Moriarty again.
alt.fan.greaseman	Fans of Doug Tracht, the DJ.
alt.fan.hofstadter	Douglas Hofstadter and Godel, Escher, Bach.
alt.fan.holmes	Elementary, my dear Watson. Like he ever said that.
alt.fan.howard-stern	Fans of the abrasive radio and TV personality.
alt.fan.jai-maharaj	A contributor to alt.astrology and soc.culture.indian.
alt.fan.james-bond	On his Majesty's Secret Service (and secret linen too).
alt.fan.jen-coolest	Gosh, isn't she just wonderful?
alt.fan.jimmy-buffett	A white sports coat and a pink crustacean.
alt.fan.karla-homolka	Discussion of the Karla Homolka case.

News Group	Description
alt.fan.lemurs	Little critters with *big* eyes.
alt.fan.letterman	One of the top 10 reasons to get the alt groups.
alt.fan.lightbulbs	A hardware problem.
alt.fan.madonna	The Material Girl.
alt.fan.mike-jittlov	Electronic fan club for animator Mike Jittlov.
alt.fan.monty-python	Electronic fan club for those wacky Brits.
alt.fan.oingo-boingo	Have you ever played Ping-Pong in Pago Pago?
alt.fan.pern	Anne McCaffery's sci-fi oeuvre.
alt.fan.piers-anthony	For fans of the sci-fi author Piers Anthony.
alt.fan.pratchett	For fans of Terry Pratchett, sci-fi humor writer.
alt.fan.ronald-reagan	Jellybeans and all.
alt.fan.rush-limbaugh	Derogation of others for fun and profit.
alt.fan.spinal-tap	Down on the sex farm.
alt.fan.tolkien	Mortal Men doomed to die.
alt.fan.tom-robbins	31 flavors for readers.
alt.fan.u2	The Irish rock band U2.
alt.fan.warlord	The War Lord of the West Preservation Fan Club.
alt.fan.wodehouse	Discussion of the works of humor author P.G. Wodehouse.
alt.fan.woody-allen	The diminutive neurotic.

(continues)

News Group	Description
alt.fandom.cons	Announcements of conventions (sci-fi and others).
alt.fashion	All facets of the fashion industry discussed.
alt.feminism	Like soc.feminism, only different.
alt.fishing	Fishing as a hobby and sport.
alt.flame	Alternative, literate, pithy, succinct screaming.
alt.flame.net-cops	Our riot gear is better than yours.
alt.flame.roommate	Putting the pig on a spit.
alt.folklore.college	Collegiate humor.
alt.folklore.computers	Stories and anecdotes about computers (some true!).
alt.folklore.ghost-stories	Boo!
alt.folklore.herbs	Discussion of all aspects of herbs and their uses.
alt.folklore.science	The folklore of science, not the science of folklore.
alt.folklore.urban	Urban legends, a la Jan Harold Brunvand.
alt.food.cocacola	And Royal Crown, Pepsi, Dr Pepper, NEHI, etc.
alt.food.fat-free	Quest for thinness.
alt.food.mcdonalds	Carl Sagan's favorite burger place.
alt.fun.with.tob	An ego on parade.
alt.games.frp.dnd-util	Discussion and creation of utility programs for AD&D.
alt.games.frp.live-action	Discussion of all forms of live-action gaming.

News Group	Description
alt.games.gb	The Galactic Bloodshed conquest game.
alt.games.lynx	The Atari Lynx.
alt.games.mk	Struggling in Mortal Kombat!
alt.games.omega	The computer game Omega.
alt.games.sf2	The video game Street Fighter 2.
alt.games.torg	Gateway for TORG mailing list.
alt.games.vga-planets	Discussion of Tim Wisseman's VGA Planets.
alt.games.xpilot	Discussion on all aspects of the X11 game Xpilot.
alt.gathering.rainbow	For discussing the annual Rainbow Gathering.
alt.geek	To fulfill an observed need.
alt.good.morning	Would you like coffee with that?
alt.good.news	A place for some news that's good news.
alt.gopher	Discussion of the gopher information service.
alt.gothic	The gothic movement: things mournful and dark.
alt.gourmand	Recipes and cooking info. (Moderated)
alt.grad-student.tenured	Most prison terms are finished sooner.
alt.grad.skool.sux	Doctor, it hurts when I study this.
alt.graphics.pixutils	Discussion of pixmap utilities.
alt.great-lakes	Discussions of the Great Lakes and adjacent places.

(continues)

News Group	Description
alt.guitar	You axed for it, you got it.
alt.guitar.bass	Bass guitars.
alt.guitar.tab	Discussions about guitar tablature music.
alt.hackers	Descriptions of projects currently under development. (Moderated)
alt.hemp	It's about knot-tying with rope. Knot!
alt.hindu	The Hindu religion. (Moderated)
alt.history.living	A forum for discussing the hobby of living history.
alt.history.what-if	What would the net have been like without this group?
alt.homosexual	Same as alt.sex.homosexual.
alt.horror	The horror genre.
alt.horror.cthulhu	Campus Crusade for Cthulhu, Ctulhu, Ctulu, and the rest.
alt.horror.werewolves	They were wolves, now they're something to be wary of.
alt.hotrod	High-speed automobiles. (Moderated)
alt.humor.best-of-usenet	What the moderator thinks is funniest. (Moderated)
alt.humor.best-of-usenet.d	Why everyone else doesn't think it's funny.
alt.hypertext	Discussion of hypertext—uses, transport, etc.
alt.hypnosis	When you awaken, you will forget about this news group.

News Group	Description
alt.illuminati	See alt.cabal. Fnord.
alt.image.medical	Medical image exchange discussions.
alt.india.progressive	Progressive politics in the Indian subcontinent. (Moderated)
alt.individualism	Philosophies where individual rights are paramount.
alt.internet.access.wanted	Oh, OK, how about just an MX record for now?
alt.internet.services	Not available in the UUCP world, even via e-mail.
alt.irc	Internet Relay Chat material.
alt.ketchup	*Whak Whak...shake...Whak* Damn, all over my tie.
alt.kids-talk	A place for the precollege set on the net.
alt.lang.asm	Assembly languages of various flavors.
alt.lang.basic	The Language That Would Not Die.
alt.law-enforcement	No, ossifer, there's nothing illegal going on in alt.
alt.lemmings	Rodents with a death wish.
alt.life.sucks	And then you shrivel up.
alt.locksmithing	You locked your keys in *where?*
alt.lucid-emacs.bug	Bug reports about Lucid Emacs.
alt.lucid-emacs.help	Q & A and general discussion of Lucid Emacs.
alt.magic	For discussion about stage magic.

(continues)

News Group	Description
alt.magick	For discussion about supernatural arts.
alt.mcdonalds	Can I get fries with that?
alt.med.cfs	Chronic fatigue syndrome information.
alt.meditation	General discussion of meditation.
alt.meditation.transcendental	Contemplation of states beyond the teeth.
alt.memetics	The evolution of ideas in societies.
alt.messianic	Messianic traditions.
alt.military.cadet	Preparing for the coming apocalypse.
alt.mindcontrol	NothREADing inTHISteresting goiGROUPng on here.
alt.missing-kids	Locating missing children.
alt.msdos.programmer	For the serious MS-DOS programmer (no for sale ads).
alt.mud	Same as rec.games.mud.
alt.music.a-cappella	Voice only, no /dev/sound.
alt.music.alternative	For groups having two or less platinum-selling albums.
alt.music.canada	Oh, Canada, eh?
alt.music.enya	Gaelic set to spacey music.
alt.music.filk	Sci-fi/fantasy-related folk music.
alt.music.hardcore	Could be porno set to music.
alt.music.jewish	Jewish music.
alt.music.marillion	A progressive band. *The Silmarillion* is a book.

News Group	Description
alt.music.prince	Prince.
alt.music.progressive	Yes, Marillion, Asia, King Crimson, etc.
alt.music.queen	He's dead, Jim.
alt.music.rush	For Rushheads.
alt.music.ska	Discussions of ska (skank) music, bands, and the like.
alt.music.tmbg	They Might Be Giants.
alt.music.u2	Another group for the band U2. See also alt.fan.u2.
alt.music.world	Discussion of music from around the world.
alt.mythology	Zeus rules.
alt.native	People indigenous to an area before modern colonization.
alt.necromicon	Yet another sign of the coming apocalypse.
alt.netgames.bolo	A multiplayer tank game for the Macintosh.
alt.news-media	Don't believe the hype.
alt.news.macedonia	News concerning Macedonia in the Balkan Region.
alt.nick.sucks	Probably.
alt.non.sequitur	Richard Nixon.
alt.online-service	Large commercial on-line services and the Internet.
alt.os.multics	30 years old and going strong.
alt.out-of-body	Out-of-body experiences.

(continues)

News Group	Description
alt.pagan	Discussions about paganism and religion.
alt.pantyhose	Stockings are sexier.
alt.paranet.abduct	They replaced Jim-Bob with a look-alike!
alt.paranet.paranormal	If it exists, how can supernatural be beyond natural?
alt.paranet.science	Maybe if we dissect the psychic....
alt.paranet.skeptic	I don't believe they turned you into a newt.
alt.paranet.ufo	Heck, I guess naming it *UFO* identifies it.
alt.paranormal	Phenomena that are not scientifically explicable.
alt.parents-teens	Parent-teenager relationships.
alt.party	Parties, celebration, and general debauchery.
alt.peeves	Discussion of peeves and related info.
alt.personals	Do you really want to meet someone this way?
alt.personals.ads	Geek seeks Dweeb. Object: low-level interfacing.
alt.personals.bondage	Are you tied up this evening?
alt.personals.misc	Dweeb seeks Geek. Object: low-level interfacing.
alt.personals.poly	Hi there, do you multiprocess?
alt.philosophy.objectivism	A product of the Ayn Rand Corporation.

News Group	Description
alt.pixar.typestry	Pixar's Typestry type-styling software package.
alt.politics.british	Politics and a Queen, too.
alt.politics.clinton	Discussing Clinton.
alt.politics.correct	A Neil Bush fan club.
alt.politics.economics	War==Poverty, and other discussions.
alt.politics.greens	Green party politics and activities worldwide.
alt.politics.homosexuality	Homosexual topics.
alt.politics.libertarian	The libertarian ideology.
alt.politics.org.batf	Politics of the U.S. Bureau of Alcohol, Tobacco, and Firearms.
alt.politics.org.cia	Politics of the U.S. Central Intelligence Agency.
alt.politics.org.misc	Political organizations.
alt.politics.org.nsa	Politics of the U.S. National Security Agency.
alt.politics.perot	Discussion of the non-candidate.
alt.politics.radical-left	Who remains after the radicals left?
alt.politics.reform	Political reform.
alt.politics.sex	Not a good idea to mix them, sez Marilyn and Profumo.
alt.politics.usa.constitution	U.S. Constitutional politics.
alt.politics.usa.misc	Miscellaneous U.S. politics.
alt.politics.usa.republican	Discussions of the U.S. Republican Party.

(continues)

News Group	Description
alt.polyamory	For those who maintain multiple love relationships.
alt.postmodern	Postmodernism, semiotics, deconstruction, and the like.
alt.president.clinton	Will the CIA undermine his efforts?
alt.prisons	Can I get an alt.* feed in the slammer?
alt.privacy	Privacy issues in cyberspace.
alt.privacy.anon-server	Technical and policy matters of anonymous contact servers.
alt.prose	Postings of original writings, fictional and otherwise.
alt.psychoactives	Better living through chemistry.
alt.psychology.personality	Personality taxonomy, such as Myers-Briggs.
alt.pub.dragons-inn	Fantasy virtual reality pub similar to alt.callahans.
alt.punk	Burning them keeps insects away.
alt.ql.creative	The *Quantum Leap* TV show.
alt.quotations	Quotations, quips, .sig lines, witticisms, et. al.
alt.radio.networks.npr	Discussion of anything related to U.S. National Public Radio: shows, stories, personalities.
alt.radio.pirate	Hide the gear, here comes the magic station wagons.
alt.radio.scanner	Discussion of scanning radio receivers.
alt.rap	For fans of rap music.

News Group	Description
alt.rave	Techno-culture: music, dancing, drugs, dancing.
alt.recovery	For people in recovery programs (such as AA, ACA, GA).
alt.recovery.codependency	Recovering from the disease of codependency.
alt.religion.emacs	Emacs. Umacs. We all macs.
alt.religion.kibology	He's Fred, Jim.
alt.religion.monica	Discussion about net-venus Monica and her works.
alt.religion.scientology	He's dead, Jim.
alt.revisionism	It can't be that way 'cause here's the facts.
alt.revolution.counter	Discussions of counterrevolutionary issues.
alt.rock-n-roll	Counterpart to alt.sex and alt.drugs.
alt.rock-n-roll.acdc	Dirty deeds done dirt cheap.
alt.rock-n-roll.classic	Classic rock, both the music and its marketing.
alt.rock-n-roll.hard	Music where stance is everything.
alt.rock-n-roll.metal	For the headbangers on the net.
alt.rock-n-roll.metal.gnr	For Guns 'n' Roses fans.
alt.rock-n-roll.metal.heavy	Non-sissyboy metal bands.
alt.rock-n-roll.metal.ironmaiden	Sonic torture methods.
alt.rock-n-roll.metal.metallica	Sort of like Formica with more hair.

(continues)

News Group	Description
alt.rock-n-roll.metal.progressive	Slayer teams up with Tom Cora.
alt.rock-n-roll.oldies	Discussion of rock and roll music from 1950-1970.
alt.rock-n-roll.stones	Gathering plenty of moss by now.
alt.romance	Discussion about the romantic side of love.
alt.romance.chat	Talk about no sex.
alt.rush-limbaugh	Fans of the conservative activist radio announcer.
alt.satanism	Not such a bad dude once you get to know him.
alt.satellite.tv.europe	All about European satellite TV.
alt.save.the.earth	Environmentalist causes.
alt.sb.programmer	Programming the Soundblaster PC sound card.
alt.sci.physics.acoustics	Sound advice.
alt.sci.physics.new-theories	Scientific theories you won't find in journals.
alt.sci.planetary	Studies in planetary science.
alt.sci.sociology	People are really interesting when you watch them.
alt.security	Security issues on computer systems.
alt.security.index	Pointers to good stuff in alt.security. (Moderated)
alt.security.pgp	The Pretty Good Privacy package.
alt.sega.genesis	Another addiction.

News Group	Description
alt.self-improve	Self-improvement in less than 14 characters.
alt.sewing	A group that is not as it seams.
alt.sex	Postings of a prurient nature.
alt.sex.bestiality	Happiness is a warm puppy.
alt.sex.bestiality.barney	For people with big purple newt fetishes.
alt.sex.bondage	Tie me, whip me, make me read the net!
alt.sex.exhibitionism	So you want to be a star.
alt.sex.fetish.feet	Kiss them! Now!
alt.sex.fetish.orientals	The mysteries of Asia are a potent lure.
alt.sex.masturbation	Where one's SO is oneself.
alt.sex.motss	Jesse Helms would not subscribe to this group.
alt.sex.movies	Discussing the ins and outs of certain movies.
alt.sex.pictures	Gigabytes of copyright violations.
alt.sex.spanking	Whose been lighting the Grail light again?
alt.sex.stories	For those who need it *NOW*.
alt.sex.stories.d	For those who talk about needing it *NOW*.
alt.sex.voyeurism	You do it, I'll just sit here and watch.
alt.sex.wanted	Requests for erotica, either literary or in the flesh.
alt.sex.watersports	Fun in the shower.

(continues)

News Group	Description
alt.sex.wizards	Questions for only true sex wizards.
alt.sexual.abuse.recovery	Helping others deal with traumatic experiences.
alt.shenanigans	Practical jokes, pranks, randomness, etc.
alt.showbiz.gossip	A misguided attempt to centralize gossip.
alt.shut.the.hell.up.geek	Group for USENET motto.
alt.skate-board	Discussion of all aspects of skateboarding.
alt.skinheads	The skinhead culture/anticulture.
alt.slack	Posting relating to the Church of the Subgenius.
alt.slick.willy.tax.tax.tax	Not just for rich people anymore.
alt.snail-mail	Mail sent on paper. Some people still do that.
alt.society.anarchy	Societies without rulers.
alt.society.ati	The Activist Times Digest. (Moderated)
alt.society.civil-liberties	Individual rights.
alt.society.civil-liberty	Same as alt.society.civil-liberties.
alt.society.conservatism	Social, cultural, and political conservatism.
alt.society.generation-x	Discussion of lifestyles of those born 1960-early-1970s.
alt.society.resistance	Resistance against governments.
alt.sources	Alternative source code, unmoderated. Caveat Emptor.

News Group	Description
alt.sources.amiga	Source code for the Amiga.
alt.sources.d	Discussion of posted sources.
alt.sources.index	Pointers to source code in alt.sources.*. (Moderated)
alt.sources.wanted	Requests for source code.
alt.spam	What is that stuff that doth jiggle in the breeze?
alt.spleen	Venting as a biological function.
alt.sport.bowling	In the gutter again.
alt.sport.darts	Look what you've done to the wall!
alt.sport.foosball	Table soccer and dizzy little men.
alt.sport.lasertag	Indoor splatball with infrared lasers.
alt.sport.officiating	Discussion of problems related to officiating athletic contests.
alt.sport.pool	Knock your balls into your pockets for fun.
alt.sports.baseball.atlanta-braves	Atlanta Braves baseball talk.
alt.sports.baseball.balt-orioles	Baltimore Orioles baseball talk.
alt.sports.baseball.chicago-cubs	Chicago Cubs baseball talk.
alt.sports.baseball.cinci-reds	Cincinnati Reds baseball talk.
alt.sports.baseball.col-rockies	Colorado Rockies baseball talk.
alt.sports.baseball.houston-astro	Houston Astros baseball talk.
alt.sports.baseball.la-dodgers	Los Angeles Dodgers baseball talk.

(continues)

News Group	Description
alt.sports.baseball.mke-brewers	Milwaukee Brewers baseball talk.
alt.sports.baseball.mn-twins	Minnesota Twins baseball talk.
alt.sports.baseball.montreal-expos	Montreal Expos baseball talk.
alt.sports.baseball.ny-mets	New York Mets baseball talk.
alt.sports.baseball.phila-phillies	Philadelphia Phillies baseball talk.
alt.sports.baseball.pitt-pirates	Pittsburgh Pirates baseball talk.
alt.sports.baseball.sf-giants	San Francisco Giants baseball talk.
alt.sports.baseball.stl-cardinals	St. Louis Cardinals baseball talk.
alt.sports.football.mn-vikings	Minnesota Vikings football talk.
alt.sports.football.pro.washredskins	Washington Redskins football talk.
alt.stagecraft	Technical theatre issues.
alt.startrek.creative	Stories and parodies related to *Star Trek*.
alt.stupidity	Discussion about stupid news groups.
alt.suicide.holiday	Talk of why suicides increase at holidays.
alt.supermodels	Discussing famous and beautiful models.
alt.support	Dealing with emotional situations and experiences.
alt.support.abuse-partners	Partners of people who were abused.
alt.support.big-folks	Sizeism can be as awful as sexism or racism.

News Group	Description
alt.support.cancer	Emotional aid for people with cancer.
alt.support.diet	Seeking enlightenment through weight loss.
alt.support.mult-sclerosis	Discussion about living with multiple sclerosis.
alt.support.step-parents	Difficulties of being a stepparent.
alt.surfing	Riding the ocean waves.
alt.sustainable.agriculture	Such as the Mekong delta before Agent Orange.
alt.swedish.chef.bork.bork.bork.	The beginning of the end.
alt.sys.amiga.demos	Code and talk to show off the Amiga.
alt.sys.amiga.uucp	AmigaUUCP.
alt.sys.intergraph	Support for Intergraph machines.
alt.sys.pc-clone.gateway2000	A PC clone vendor.
alt.sys.sun	Technical discussion of Sun Microsystems products.
alt.tasteless	Truly disgusting.
alt.tasteless.jokes	Sometimes insulting rather than disgusting or humorous.
alt.test	Alternative subnetwork testing.
alt.test.test	More from the people who brought you "BBS systems."
alt.thrash	Thrashlife.
alt.toolkits.xview	The X Window XView toolkit.
alt.toys.hi-tech	Optimus Prime is my hero.

(continues)

News Group	Description
alt.toys.lego	Snap 'em together.
alt.toys.transformers	From robots to vehicles and back again.
alt.transgendered	Boys will be girls, and vice versa.
alt.tv.animaniacs	Steven Spielberg's Animaniacs!
alt.tv.babylon-5	Casablanca in space.
alt.tv.barney	He's everywhere. Now appearing in several alt groups.
alt.tv.beakmans-world	Some sort of science and comedy show.
alt.tv.beavis-n-butthead	Uh huh huh huh uh uh huh uh huh.
alt.tv.bh90210	Fans of *Beverly Hills 90210* TV show.
alt.tv.dinosaurs.barney.die.die.die	Squish the saccharine newt.
alt.tv.la-law	For the folks out in la-law land.
alt.tv.liquid-tv	A BBC/MTV animation showcase program.
alt.tv.mash	Nothing like a good comedy about war and dying.
alt.tv.melrose-place	Cat fights and sleaziness, Wednesdays on FOX.
alt.tv.mst3k	Hey, you robots! Down in front!
alt.tv.muppets	Miss Piggy on the tube.
alt.tv.mwc	*Married... With Children.*
alt.tv.northern-exp	For the TV show with moss growing on it.
alt.tv.prisoner	*The Prisoner* television series from years ago.

News Group	**Description**
alt.tv.red-dwarf	The British sci-fi/comedy show.
alt.tv.ren-n-stimpy	Some change from *Lassie*, eh?
alt.tv.rockford-files	But he won't do windows.
alt.tv.seinfeld	A funny guy.
alt.tv.simpsons	Don't have a cow, man!
alt.tv.tiny-toon	Discussion about the *Tiny Toon Adventures* show.
alt.tv.tiny-toon.fandom	Apparently one fan group could not bind them all.
alt.tv.twin-peaks	Discussion about the popular (and unusual) TV show.
alt.usage.english	English grammar, word usage, and related topics.
alt.usenet.offline-reader	Getting your fix off-line.
alt.uu.future	Does Usenet University have a viable future?
alt.vampyres	Discussion of vampires and related writings, films, etc.
alt.video.laserdisc	LD players and selections available for them.
alt.visa.us	Discussion and information on visas pertaining to U.S.
alt.war	Not just collateral damage.
alt.war.civil.usa	Discussion of the U.S. Civil War (1861-1865).
alt.war.vietnam	Discussion of all aspects of the Vietnam War.
alt.wedding	'Til death or our lawyers do us part.

(continues)

News Group	Description
alt.whine	Why me?
alt.whistleblowing	Whistleblowing on fraud, abuse, and other corruption.
alt.winsock	Windows Sockets.
alt.wired	*Wired* magazine.
alt.wolves	Discussing wolves and wolf-mix dogs.
alt.zima	Not to be confused with zuma.
alt.zines	Small magazines, mostly non-commercial.
alt.znet.aeo	*Atari Explorer Online* magazine. (Moderated)
alt.znet.pc	Z*NET International ASCII magazines (Weekly). (Moderated)
bionet.agroforestry	Discussion of agroforestry.
bionet.announce	Announcements of widespread interest to biologists. (Moderated)
bionet.biology.computational	Computer and mathematical applications. (Moderated)
bionet.biology.n2-fixation	Research issues on biological nitrogen fixation.
bionet.biology.tropical	Discussions about tropical biology.
bionet.cellbiol	Discussions about cell biology.
bionet.chlamydomonas	Discussions about the green alga Chlamydomonas.
bionet.drosophila	Discussions about the biology of fruit flies.
bionet.general	General BIOSCI discussion.

News Group	Description
bionet.genome.arabidopsis	Information about the Arabidopsis project.
bionet.genome.chrom22	Discussion of Chromosome 22.
bionet.genome.chromosomes	Mapping and sequencing of eucaryote chromosomes.
bionet.immunology	Discussions about research in immunology.
bionet.info-theory	Discussions about biological information theory.
bionet.jobs	Scientific job opportunities.
bionet.journals.contents	Contents of biology journal publications. (Moderated)
bionet.journals.note	Advice on dealing with journals in biology.
bionet.metabolic-reg	Kinetics and thermodynamics at the cellular level.
bionet.molbio.ageing	Discussions of cellular and organismal ageing.
bionet.molbio.bio-matrix	Computer applications to biological databases.
bionet.molbio.embldatabank	Information about the EMBL nucleic acid database.
bionet.molbio.evolution	How genes and proteins have evolved.
bionet.molbio.gdb	Messages to and from the GDB database staff.
bionet.molbio.genbank	Info about the GenBank nucleic acid database.
bionet.molbio.genbank.updates	Hot off the presses! (Moderated)

(continues)

News Group	Description
bionet.molbio.gene-linkage	Discussions about genetic linkage analysis.
bionet.molbio.genome-program	Discussion of Human Genome Project issues.
bionet.molbio.hiv	Discussions about the molecular biology of HIV.
bionet.molbio.methds-reagnts	Requests for information and lab reagents.
bionet.molbio.proteins	Research on proteins and protein databases.
bionet.molbio.rapd	Research on Randomly Amplified Polymorphic DNA.
bionet.molbio.yeast	The molecular biology and genetics of yeast.
bionet.mycology	Discussions about filamentous fungi.
bionet.n2-fixation	Research issues on biological nitrogen fixation.
bionet.neuroscience	Research issues in the neuro sciences.
bionet.photosynthesis	Discussions about research on photosynthesis.
bionet.plants	Discussion about all aspects of plant biology.
bionet.population-bio	Technical discussions about population biology.
bionet.sci-resources	Information about funding agencies and so on. (Moderated)
bionet.software	Information about software for biology.
bionet.software.acedb	Discussions by users of genome DBs using ACEDB.

News Group	Description
bionet.software.gcg	Discussions about using the ACEDB software.
bionet.software.sources	Software source relating to biology. (Moderated)
bionet.users.addresses	Who's who in biology.
bionet.virology	Discussions about research in virology.
bionet.women-in-bio	Discussions about women in biology.
bionet.xtallography	Discussions about protein crystallography.
bit.admin	bit.* news group discussions.
bit.general	Discussions relating to BITNET/USENET.
bit.lang.neder-l	Dutch language and literature list. (Moderated)
bit.listserv.3com-l	3Com products discussion list.
bit.listserv.9370-l	IBM 9370 and VM/IS specific topics list.
bit.listserv.ada-law	ADA law discussions.
bit.listserv.advanc-l	Geac advanced integrated library system users.
bit.listserv.advise-l	User services list.
bit.listserv.aix-l	IBM AIX discussion list.
bit.listserv.allmusic	Discussions on all forms of music.
bit.listserv.appc-l	APPC discussion list.
bit.listserv.apple2-l	Apple II list.
bit.listserv.applicat	Applications under BITNET.

(continues)

News Group	Description
bit.listserv.arie-l	RLG Ariel document transmission group.
bit.listserv.ashe-l	Higher education policy and research.
bit.listserv.asm370	IBM 370 assembly programming discussions.
bit.listserv.autism	Autism and developmental disabilities list.
bit.listserv.axslib-l	Library access for people with disabilities.
bit.listserv.banyan-l	Banyan Vines network software discussions.
bit.listserv.big-lan	Campus-size LAN discussion group. (Moderated)
bit.listserv.billing	Chargeback of computer resources.
bit.listserv.biosph-l	Biosphere, ecology discussion list.
bit.listserv.bitnews	BITNET news.
bit.listserv.blindnws	Blindness issues and discussions. (Moderated)
bit.listserv.buslib-l	Business libraries list.
bit.listserv.c+health	Computers and health discussion list.
bit.listserv.c18-l	18th century interdisciplinary discussion.
bit.listserv.c370-l	C/370 discussion list.
bit.listserv.candle-l	Candle products discussion list.
bit.listserv.catala	Catalan discussion list.
bit.listserv.catholic	Free Catholics mailing list.

News Group	Description
bit.listserv.cdromlan	CD-ROM on local area networks.
bit.listserv.cfs.newsletter	Chronic fatigue syndrome newsletter. (Moderated)
bit.listserv.christia	Practical Christian life. (Moderated)
bit.listserv.cics-l	CICS discussion list.
bit.listserv.cinema-l	Discussions on all forms of cinema.
bit.listserv.circplus	Circulation reserve and related library issues.
bit.listserv.cmspip-l	VM/SP CMS pipelines discussion list.
bit.listserv.csg-l	Control system group network.
bit.listserv.cumrec-l	CUMREC-L administrative computer use. (Moderated)
bit.listserv.cw-email	Campus-wide e-mail discussion list.
bit.listserv.cwis-l	Campus-wide information systems.
bit.listserv.cyber-l	CDC computer discussion.
bit.listserv.dasig	Database administration.
bit.listserv.db2-l	DB2 database discussion list.
bit.listserv.dbase-l	Discussion on the use of the dBASE IV.
bit.listserv.deaf-l	Deaf list.
bit.listserv.decnews	Digital Equipment Corporation news list.
bit.listserv.dectei-l	DECUS education software library discussions.

(continues)

News Group	Description
bit.listserv.devel-l	Technology transfer in international development.
bit.listserv.disarm-l	Disarmament discussion list.
bit.listserv.domain-l	Domains discussion group.
bit.listserv.dsshe-l	Disabled student services in higher education.
bit.listserv.earntech	EARN technical group.
bit.listserv.edi-l	Electronic data interchange issues.
bit.listserv.edpolyan	Professionals and students discuss education.
bit.listserv.edtech	EDTECH—educational technology. (Moderated)
bit.listserv.edusig-l	EDUSIG discussions.
bit.listserv.emusic-l	Electronic music discussion list.
bit.listserv.endnote	Bibsoft endnote discussions.
bit.listserv.envbeh-l	Forum on environment and human behavior.
bit.listserv.erl-l	Educational research list.
bit.listserv.ethics-l	Discussion of ethics in computing.
bit.listserv.ethology	Ethology list.
bit.listserv.euearn-l	Computers in Eastern Europe.
bit.listserv.film-l	Film making and reviews list.
bit.listserv.fnord-l	New ways of thinking list.
bit.listserv.frac-l	Fractal discussion list.
bit.listserv.free-l	Fathers' rights and equality discussion list.

News Group	Description
bit.listserv.games-l	Computer games list.
bit.listserv.gaynet	GayNet discussion list. (Moderated)
bit.listserv.gddm-l	The GDDM discussion list.
bit.listserv.geodesic	List for the discussion of Buckminster Fuller.
bit.listserv.gguide	BITNIC GGUIDE list.
bit.listserv.govdoc-l	Discussion of government document issues.
bit.listserv.gutnberg	GUTNBERG discussion list.
bit.listserv.hellas	The Hellenic discussion list. (Moderated)
bit.listserv.help-net	Help on BITNET and the Internet.
bit.listserv.hindu-d	Hindu digest. (Moderated)
bit.listserv.history	History list.
bit.listserv.hp3000-l	HP-3000 computer systems discussion list.
bit.listserv.hytel-l	hytelnet discussions. (Moderated)
bit.listserv.i-amiga	Info-Amiga list.
bit.listserv.ibm-hesc	IBM higher education consortium.
bit.listserv.ibm-main	IBM mainframe discussion list.
bit.listserv.ibm-nets	BITNIC IBM-NETS list.
bit.listserv.ibm7171	Protocol converter list.
bit.listserv.ibmtcp-l	IBM TCP/IP list.
bit.listserv.india-d	India interest group. (Moderated)

(continues)

News Group	Description
bit.listserv.ingrafx	Information graphics.
bit.listserv.innopac	Innovative interfaces on-line public access.
bit.listserv.ioob-l	Industrial psychology.
bit.listserv.ipct-l	Interpersonal computing and technology list. (Moderated)
bit.listserv.isn	ISN data switch technical discussion group.
bit.listserv.jes2-l	JES2 discussion group.
bit.listserv.jnet-l	BITNIC JNET-L list.
bit.listserv.l-hcap	Handicap list. (Moderated)
bit.listserv.l-vmctr	VMCENTER components discussion list.
bit.listserv.lawsch-l	Law school discussion list.
bit.listserv.liaison	BITNIC LIAISON.
bit.listserv.libref-l	Library reference issues. (Moderated)
bit.listserv.libres	Library and information science research. (Moderated)
bit.listserv.license	Software licensing list.
bit.listserv.linkfail	Link failure announcements.
bit.listserv.literary	Discussions about literature.
bit.listserv.lstsrv-l	Forum on LISTSERV.
bit.listserv.mail-l	BITNIC MAIL-L list.
bit.listserv.mailbook	MAIL/MAILBOOK subscription list.
bit.listserv.mba-l	MBA student curriculum discussion.

News Group	Description
bit.listserv.mbu-l	Megabyte University—computers and writing.
bit.listserv.mdphd-l	Dual degree programs discussion list.
bit.listserv.medforum	Medical student discussions. (Moderated)
bit.listserv.medlib-l	Medical libraries discussion list.
bit.listserv.mednews	Health Info-Com network newsletter. (Moderated)
bit.listserv.mideur-l	Middle Europe discussion list.
bit.listserv.mla-l	Music library association.
bit.listserv.netnws-l	NETNWS-L netnews list.
bit.listserv.nettrain	Network trainers list.
bit.listserv.new-list	NEW-LIST—new list announcements. (Moderated)
bit.listserv.next-l	NeXT computer list.
bit.listserv.nodmgt-l	Node management.
bit.listserv.notabene	Nota Bene list.
bit.listserv.notis-l	NOTIS/DOBIS discussion group list.
bit.listserv.novell	Novell LAN interest group.
bit.listserv.omrscan	OMR scanner discussion.
bit.listserv.os2-l	OS/2 discussion.
bit.listserv.ozone	OZONE discussion list.
bit.listserv.pacs-l	Public-Access computer system forum. (Moderated)

(continues)

News Group	Description
bit.listserv.page-l	IBM 3812/3820 tips and problems discussion list.
bit.listserv.pagemakr	PageMaker for desktop publishers.
bit.listserv.physhare	K-12 physics list.
bit.listserv.pmdf-l	PMDF distribution list.
bit.listserv.politics	Forum for the discussion of politics.
bit.listserv.postcard	Postcard collectors discussion group.
bit.listserv.power-l	POWER-L IBM RS/6000 POWER family.
bit.listserv.powerh-l	PowerHouse discussion list.
bit.listserv.psycgrad	Psychology grad student discussions.
bit.listserv.qualrs-l	Qualitative research of the human sciences.
bit.listserv.relusr-l	Relay users forum.
bit.listserv.rra-l	Romance readers anonymous. (Moderated)
bit.listserv.rscs-l	VM/RSCS mailing list.
bit.listserv.rscsmods	The RSCS modifications list.
bit.listserv.s-comput	SuperComputers list.
bit.listserv.script-l	IBM vs. Waterloo SCRIPT discussion group.
bit.listserv.scuba-l	Scuba diving discussion list.
bit.listserv.seasia-l	Southeast Asia discussion list.
bit.listserv.seds-l	Interchapter SEDS communications.

News Group	Description
bit.listserv.sfs-l	VM shared file system discussion list.
bit.listserv.sganet	Student government global mail network.
bit.listserv.simula	The SIMULA language list.
bit.listserv.slart-l	SLA research and teaching.
bit.listserv.slovak-l	Slovak discussion list.
bit.listserv.snamgt-l	SNA network management discussion.
bit.listserv.sos-data	Social science data list.
bit.listserv.spires-l	SPIRES conference list.
bit.listserv.sportpsy	Exercise and sports psychology.
bit.listserv.sqlinfo	Forum for SQL/DS and related topics.
bit.listserv.tech-l	BITNIC TECH-L list.
bit.listserv.techwr-l	Technical writing list.
bit.listserv.tecmat-l	Technology in secondary math.
bit.listserv.test	Test news group.
bit.listserv.tex-l	The TeXnical topics list.
bit.listserv.tn3270-l	tn3270 protocol discussion list.
bit.listserv.toolb-l	Asymetrix toolbook list.
bit.listserv.trans-l	BITNIC TRANS-L list.
bit.listserv.travel-l	Tourism discussions.
bit.listserv.tsorexx	REXX for TSO list.
bit.listserv.ucp-l	University computing project mailing list.

(continues)

News Group	Description
bit.listserv.ug-l	Usage guidelines.
bit.listserv.uigis-l	User interface for geographical info systems.
bit.listserv.urep-l	UREP-L mailing list.
bit.listserv.usrdir-l	User directory list.
bit.listserv.uus-l	Unitarian-Universalist list.
bit.listserv.valert-l	Virus Alert list. (Moderated)
bit.listserv.vfort-l	VS-FORTRAN discussion list.
bit.listserv.vm-util	VM utilities discussion list.
bit.listserv.vmesa-l	VM/ESA mailing list.
bit.listserv.vmslsv-l	VAX/VMS LISTSERV discussion list.
bit.listserv.vmxa-l	VM/XA discussion list.
bit.listserv.vnews-l	VNEWS discussion list.
bit.listserv.vpiej-l	Electronic publishing discussion list.
bit.listserv.win3-l	Microsoft Windows Version 3 forum.
bit.listserv.words-l	English language discussion group.
bit.listserv.wpcorp-l	WordPerfect Corporation products discussions.
bit.listserv.wpwin-l	WordPerfect for Windows.
bit.listserv.wx-talk	Weather issues discussions.
bit.listserv.x400-l	x.400 protocol list.
bit.listserv.xcult-l	International intercultural newsletter.

News Group	Description
bit.listserv.xedit-l	VM system editor list.
bit.listserv.xerox-l	The Xerox discussion list.
bit.listserv.xmailer	Crosswell mailer.
bit.listserv.xtropy-l	Extopian list.
bit.mailserv.word-mac	Word processing on the Macintosh.
bit.mailserv.word-pc	Word processing on the IBM PC.
bit.org.peace-corps	International volunteers discussion group.
bit.software.international	International software list. (Moderated)
biz.americast	AmeriCast announcements.
biz.americast.samples	Samples of AmeriCast. (Moderated)
biz.books.technical	Technical bookstore and publisher advertising and info.
biz.clarinet	Announcements about ClariNet.
biz.clarinet.sample	Samples of ClariNet news groups for the outside world.
biz.comp.hardware	Generic commercial hardware postings.
biz.comp.services	Generic commercial service postings.
biz.comp.software	Generic commercial software postings.
biz.comp.telebit	Support of the Telebit modem.
biz.comp.telebit.netblazer	The Telebit Netblazer.
biz.config	Biz Usenet configuration and administration.

(continues)

News Group	Description
biz.dec	DEC equipment and software.
biz.dec.decathena	DECathena discussions.
biz.dec.decnews	The DECNews newsletter. (Moderated)
biz.dec.ip	IP networking on DEC machines.
biz.dec.workstations	DEC workstation discussions and info.
biz.digex.announce	Announcements from Digex. (Moderated)
biz.jobs.offered	Position announcements.
biz.misc	Miscellaneous postings of a commercial nature.
biz.next.newprod	New product announcements for the NeXT.
biz.oreilly.announce	New product announcements from O'Reilly and Associates. (Moderated)
biz.pagesat	For discussion of the Pagesat Satellite Usenet Newsfeed.
biz.sco.announce	SCO and related product announcements. (Moderated)
biz.sco.binaries	Binary packages for SCO Xenix, UNIX, or ODT. (Moderated)
biz.sco.general	Q & A, discussions, and comments on SCO products.
biz.sco.magazine	To discuss SCO Magazine and its contents.
biz.sco.opendesktop	ODT environment and applications tech info, Q & A.
biz.sco.sources	Source code ported to an SCO operating environment. (Moderated)

News Group	Description
biz.sco.wserver	SCO widget server questions, answers, and discussion.
biz.stolen	Postings about stolen merchandise.
biz.tadpole.sparcbook	Discussions on the Sparcbook portable computer.
biz.test	Biz news group test messages.
biz.univel.misc	Discussions and comments on Univel products.
biz.zeos.announce	Zeos product announcements. (Moderated)
biz.zeos.general	Zeos technical support and general information.
clari.biz.commodity	Commodity news and price reports. (Moderated)
clari.biz.courts	Lawsuits and business-related legal matters. (Moderated)
clari.biz.economy	Economic news and indicators. (Moderated)
clari.biz.economy.world	Economy stories for non-U.S. countries. (Moderated)
clari.biz.features	Business feature stories. (Moderated)
clari.biz.finance	Finance, currency, corporate finance. (Moderated)
clari.biz.finance.earnings	Earnings and dividend reports. (Moderated)
clari.biz.finance.personal	Personal investing and finance. (Moderated)
clari.biz.finance.services	Banks and financial industries. (Moderated)

(continues)

News Group	Description
clari.biz.invest	News for investors. (Moderated)
clari.biz.labor	Strikes, unions, and labor relations. (Moderated)
clari.biz.market	General stock market news. (Moderated)
clari.biz.market.amex	American Stock Exchange reports and news. (Moderated)
clari.biz.market.dow	Dow Jones NYSE reports. (Moderated)
clari.biz.market.ny	NYSE reports. (Moderated)
clari.biz.market.otc	NASDAQ reports. (Moderated)
clari.biz.market.report	General market reports, S & P, etc. (Moderated)
clari.biz.mergers	Mergers and acquisitions. (Moderated)
clari.biz.misc	Other business news. (Moderated)
clari.biz.products	Important new products and services. (Moderated)
clari.biz.top	Top business news. (Moderated)
clari.biz.urgent	Breaking business news. (Moderated)
clari.canada.biz	Canadian business summaries. (Moderated)
clari.canada.briefs	Regular updates of Canadian news in brief. (Moderated)
clari.canada.briefs.ont	News briefs for Ontario and Toronto. (Moderated)
clari.canada.briefs.west	News briefs for Alberta, the Prairies, and B.C. (Moderated)

News Group	Description
clari.canada.features	Almanac, Ottawa Special, Arts. (Moderated)
clari.canada.general	Short items on Canadian news stories. (Moderated)
clari.canada.gov	Government-related news (all levels). (Moderated)
clari.canada.law	Crimes, the courts, and the law. (Moderated)
clari.canada.newscast	Regular newscast for Canadians. (Moderated)
clari.canada.politics	Political and election items. (Moderated)
clari.canada.trouble	Mishaps, accidents, and serious problems. (Moderated)
clari.feature.dave_barry	Columns of humorist Dave Barry. (Moderated)
clari.feature.mike_royko	Chicago opinion columnist Mike Royko. (Moderated)
clari.feature.miss_manners	Judith Martin's humorous etiquette advice. (Moderated)
clari.local.alberta.briefs	Local news briefs. (Moderated)
clari.local.arizona	Local news. (Moderated)
clari.local.arizona.briefs	Local news briefs. (Moderated)
clari.local.bc.briefs	Local news briefs. (Moderated)
clari.local.california	Local news. (Moderated)
clari.local.california.briefs	Local news briefs. (Moderated)
clari.local.chicago	Local news. (Moderated)
clari.local.chicago.briefs	Local news briefs. (Moderated)

(continues)

News Group	Description
clari.local.florida	Local news. (Moderated)
clari.local.florida.briefs	Local news briefs. (Moderated)
clari.local.georgia	Local news. (Moderated)
clari.local.georgia.briefs	Local news briefs. (Moderated)
clari.local.headlines	Various local headline summaries. (Moderated)
clari.local.illinois	Local news. (Moderated)
clari.local.illinois.briefs	Local news briefs. (Moderated)
clari.local.indiana	Local news. (Moderated)
clari.local.indiana.briefs	Local news briefs. (Moderated)
clari.local.iowa	Local news. (Moderated)
clari.local.iowa.briefs	Local news briefs. (Moderated)
clari.local.los_angeles	Local news. (Moderated)
clari.local.los_angeles.briefs	Local news briefs. (Moderated)
clari.local.louisiana	Local news. (Moderated)
clari.local.manitoba.briefs	Local news briefs. (Moderated)
clari.local.maritimes.briefs	Local news briefs. (Moderated)
clari.local.maryland	Local news. (Moderated)
clari.local.maryland.briefs	Local news briefs. (Moderated)
clari.local.massachusetts	Local news. (Moderated)
clari.local.massachusetts.briefs	Local news briefs. (Moderated)
clari.local.michigan	Local news. (Moderated)
clari.local.michigan.briefs	Local news briefs. (Moderated)
clari.local.minnesota	Local news. (Moderated)

News Group	Description
clari.local.minnesota.briefs	Local news briefs. (Moderated)
clari.local.missouri	Local news. (Moderated)
clari.local.missouri.briefs	Local news briefs. (Moderated)
clari.local.nebraska	Local news. (Moderated)
clari.local.nebraska.briefs	Local news briefs. (Moderated)
clari.local.nevada	Local news. (Moderated)
clari.local.nevada.briefs	Local news briefs. (Moderated)
clari.local.new_england	Local news. (Moderated)
clari.local.new_hampshire	Local news. (Moderated)
clari.local.new_jersey	Local news. (Moderated)
clari.local.new_jersey.briefs	Local news briefs. (Moderated)
clari.local.new_york	Local news. (Moderated)
clari.local.new_york.briefs	Local news briefs. (Moderated)
clari.local.nyc	Local news (New York City). (Moderated)
clari.local.nyc.briefs	Local news briefs. (Moderated)
clari.local.ohio	Local news. (Moderated)
clari.local.ohio.briefs	Local news briefs. (Moderated)
clari.local.ontario.briefs	Local news briefs. (Moderated)
clari.local.oregon	Local news. (Moderated)
clari.local.oregon.briefs	Local news briefs. (Moderated)
clari.local.pennsylvania	Local news. (Moderated)
clari.local.pennsylvania.briefs	Local news briefs. (Moderated)
clari.local.saskatchewan.briefs	Local news briefs. (Moderated)

(continues)

News Group	Description
clari.local.sfbay	Stories datelined San Francisco Bay Area. (Moderated)
clari.local.texas	Local news. (Moderated)
clari.local.texas.briefs	Local news briefs. (Moderated)
clari.local.utah	Local news. (Moderated)
clari.local.utah.briefs	Local news briefs. (Moderated)
clari.local.virginia+dc	Local news. (Moderated)
clari.local.virginia+dc.briefs	Local news briefs. (Moderated)
clari.local.washington	Local news. (Moderated)
clari.local.washington.briefs	Local news briefs. (Moderated)
clari.local.wisconsin	Local news. (Moderated)
clari.local.wisconsin.briefs	Local news briefs. (Moderated)
clari.matrix_news	Monthly journal on the Internet. (Moderated)
clari.nb.apple	Newsbytes Apple/Macintosh news. (Moderated)
clari.nb.business	Newsbytes business and industry news. (Moderated)
clari.nb.general	Newsbytes general computer news. (Moderated)
clari.nb.govt	Newsbytes legal and government computer news. (Moderated)
clari.nb.ibm	Newsbytes IBM PC World coverage. (Moderated)
clari.nb.review	Newsbytes new product reviews. (Moderated)
clari.nb.telecom	Newsbytes telecom and on-line industry news. (Moderated)

News Group	Description
clari.nb.top	Newsbytes top stories (cross-posted). (Moderated)
clari.nb.trends	Newsbytes new developments and trends. (Moderated)
clari.nb.unix	Newsbytes UNIX news. (Moderated)
clari.net.admin	Announcements for news administration at ClariNet sites. (Moderated)
clari.net.announce	Announcements for all ClariNet readers. (Moderated)
clari.net.newusers	On-line information about ClariNet. (Moderated)
clari.net.products	New ClariNet products. (Moderated)
clari.net.talk	Discussion of ClariNet—only unmoderated group.
clari.news.almanac	Daily almanac—quotes, "this date in history," etc. (Moderated)
clari.news.arts	Stage, drama, and other fine arts. (Moderated)
clari.news.aviation	Aviation industry and mishaps. (Moderated)
clari.news.books	Books and publishing. (Moderated)
clari.news.briefs	Regular news summaries. (Moderated)
clari.news.bulletin	Major breaking stories of the week. (Moderated)
clari.news.canada	News related to Canada. (Moderated)

(continues)

News Group	Description
clari.news.cast	Regular U.S. news summary. (Moderated)
clari.news.children	Stories related to children and parenting. (Moderated)
clari.news.consumer	Consumer news, car reviews, etc. (Moderated)
clari.news.demonstration	Demonstrations around the world. (Moderated)
clari.news.disaster	Major problems, accidents, and natural disasters. (Moderated)
clari.news.economy	General economic news. (Moderated)
clari.news.election	News regarding both U.S. and international elections. (Moderated)
clari.news.entertain	Entertainment industry news and features. (Moderated)
clari.news.europe	News related to Europe. (Moderated)
clari.news.features	Unclassified feature stories. (Moderated)
clari.news.fighting	Clashes around the world. (Moderated)
clari.news.flash	Ultra-important, once-a-year news flashes. (Moderated)
clari.news.goodnews	Stories of success and survival. (Moderated)
clari.news.gov	General government-related stories. (Moderated)
clari.news.gov.agency	Government agencies, FBI, etc. (Moderated)
clari.news.gov.budget	Budgets at all levels. (Moderated)

News Group	Description
clari.news.gov.corrupt	Government corruption, kickbacks, etc. (Moderated)
clari.news.gov.international	International government-related stories. (Moderated)
clari.news.gov.officials	Government officials and their problems. (Moderated)
clari.news.gov.state	State government stories of national importance. (Moderated)
clari.news.gov.taxes	Tax laws, trials, etc. (Moderated)
clari.news.gov.usa	U.S. federal government news. (High volume, moderated)
clari.news.group	Special interest groups not covered in their own group. (Moderated)
clari.news.group.blacks	News of interest to black people. (Moderated)
clari.news.group.gays	Homosexuality and gay rights. (Moderated)
clari.news.group.jews	Jews and Jewish interests. (Moderated)
clari.news.group.women	Women's issues and abortion. (Moderated)
clari.news.headlines	Hourly list of the top U.S./world headlines. (Moderated)
clari.news.hot.east_europe	News from Eastern Europe. (Moderated)
clari.news.hot.somalia	News from Somalia. (Moderated)
clari.news.hot.ussr	News from the Soviet Union. (Moderated)

(continues)

News Group	Description
clari.news.interest	Human interest stories. (Moderated)
clari.news.interest.animals	Animals in the news. (Moderated)
clari.news.interest.history	Human interest stories and history in the making. (Moderated)
clari.news.interest.people	Famous people in the news. (Moderated)
clari.news.interest.people.column	Daily *People* column—tidbits on celebrities. (Moderated)
clari.news.interest.quirks	Unusual or funny news stories. (Moderated)
clari.news.issues	Stories on major issues not covered in their own group. (Moderated)
clari.news.issues.civil_rights	Freedom, racism, civil rights issues. (Moderated)
clari.news.issues.conflict	Conflict between groups around the world. (Moderated)
clari.news.issues.family	Family, child abuse, etc. (Moderated)
clari.news.labor	Unions, strikes. (Moderated)
clari.news.labor.strike	Strikes. (Moderated)
clari.news.law	General group for law-related issues. (Moderated)
clari.news.law.civil	Civil trials and litigation. (Moderated)
clari.news.law.crime	Major crimes. (Moderated)
clari.news.law.crime.sex	Sex crimes and trials. (Moderated)

News Group	Description
clari.news.law.crime.trial	Trials for criminal actions. (Moderated)
clari.news.law.crime.violent	Violent crime and criminals. (Moderated)
clari.news.law.drugs	Drug-related crimes and drug stories. (Moderated)
clari.news.law.investigation	Investigation of crimes. (Moderated)
clari.news.law.police	Police and law enforcement. (Moderated)
clari.news.law.prison	Prisons, prisoners, and escapes. (Moderated)
clari.news.law.profession	Lawyers, judges, etc. (Moderated)
clari.news.law.supreme	U.S. Supreme court rulings and news. (Moderated)
clari.news.lifestyle	Fashion, leisure, etc. (Moderated)
clari.news.military	Military equipment, people, and issues. (Moderated)
clari.news.movies	Reviews, news, and stories on movie stars. (Moderated)
clari.news.music	Reviews and issues concerning music and musicians. (Moderated)
clari.news.politics	Politicians and politics. (Moderated)
clari.news.politics.people	Politicians and political personalities. (Moderated)
clari.news.religion	Religion, religious leaders, televangelists. (Moderated)
clari.news.sex	Sexual issues, sex-related political stories. (Moderated)

(continues)

News Group	Description
clari.news.terrorism	Terrorist actions and related news around the world. (Moderated)
clari.news.top	Top U.S. news stories. (Moderated)
clari.news.top.world	Top international news stories. (Moderated)
clari.news.trends	Surveys and trends. (Moderated)
clari.news.trouble	Less major accidents, problems, and mishaps. (Moderated)
clari.news.tv	TV news, reviews, and stars. (Moderated)
clari.news.urgent	Major breaking stories of the day. (Moderated)
clari.news.weather	Weather and temperature reports. (Moderated)
clari.sfbay.briefs	Twice-daily news roundups for San Francisco Bay Area. (Moderated)
clari.sfbay.entertain	Reviews and entertainment news for San Francisco Bay Area. (Moderated)
clari.sfbay.fire	Stories from fire departments of the San Francisco Bay Area. (Moderated)
clari.sfbay.general	Main stories for San Francisco Bay Area. (Moderated)
clari.sfbay.misc	Shorter general items for San Francisco Bay Area. (Moderated)
clari.sfbay.police	Stories from police departments of the San Francisco Bay Area. (Moderated)
clari.sfbay.roads	Reports from Caltrans and the CHP. (Moderated)

News Group	Description
clari.sfbay.short	Very short items for San Francisco Bay Area. (Moderated)
clari.sfbay.weather	San Francisco Bay and California weather reports. (Moderated)
clari.sports.baseball	Baseball scores, stories, stats. (Moderated)
clari.sports.baseball.games	Baseball games and box scores. (Moderated)
clari.sports.basketball	Basketball coverage. (Moderated)
clari.sports.basketball.college	College basketball coverage. (Moderated)
clari.sports.features	Sports feature stories. (Moderated)
clari.sports.football	Pro football coverage. (Moderated)
clari.sports.football.college	College football coverage. (Moderated)
clari.sports.football.games	Coverage of individual pro games. (Moderated)
clari.sports.hockey	NHL coverage. (Moderated)
clari.sports.misc	Other sports, plus general sports news. (Moderated)
clari.sports.motor	Racing, motor sports. (Moderated)
clari.sports.olympic	The Olympic Games. (Moderated)
clari.sports.tennis	Tennis news and scores. (Moderated)
clari.sports.top	Top sports news. (Moderated)
clari.tw.aerospace	Aerospace industry and companies. (Moderated)

(continues)

News Group	Description
clari.tw.computers	Computer industry, applications, and developments. (Moderated)
clari.tw.defense	Defense industry issues. (Moderated)
clari.tw.education	Stories involving universities and colleges. (Moderated)
clari.tw.electronics	Electronics makers and sellers. (Moderated)
clari.tw.environment	Environmental news, hazardous waste, forests. (Moderated)
clari.tw.health	Disease, medicine, health care, sick celebrities. (Moderated)
clari.tw.health.aids	AIDS stories, research, political issues. (Moderated)
clari.tw.misc	General technical industry stories. (Moderated)
clari.tw.nuclear	Nuclear power and waste. (Moderated)
clari.tw.science	General science stories. (Moderated)
clari.tw.space	NASA, astronomy, space flight. (Moderated)
clari.tw.stocks	Regular reports on computer and technology stock prices. (Moderated)
clari.tw.telecom	Phones, satellites, media, and general Telecom. (Moderated)
comp.admin.policy	Discussions of site administration policies.
comp.ai	Artificial intelligence discussions.
comp.ai.fuzzy	Fuzzy set theory, aka fuzzy logic.
comp.ai.genetic	Genetic algorithms in computing.

News Group	Description
comp.ai.jair.announce	Announcements and abstracts of the *Journal of AI Research*. (Moderated)
comp.ai.jair.papers	Papers published by the *Journal of AI Research*. (Moderated)
comp.ai.nat-lang	Natural language processing by computers.
comp.ai.neural-nets	All aspects of neural networks.
comp.ai.nlang-know-rep	Natural language and knowledge representation. (Moderated)
comp.ai.philosophy	Philosophical aspects of artificial intelligence.
comp.ai.shells	Artificial intelligence applied to shells.
comp.answers	Repository for periodic USENET articles. (Moderated)
comp.apps.spreadsheets	Spreadsheets on various platforms.
comp.arch	Computer architecture.
comp.arch.bus.vmebus	Hardware and software for VMEbus systems.
comp.arch.storage	Storage system issues, both hardware and software.
comp.archives	Descriptions of public access archives. (Moderated)
comp.archives.admin	Issues relating to computer archive administration.
comp.archives.msdos.	Announcements about MS-DOS announce archives. (Moderated)
comp.archives.msdos.d	Discussion of materials available in MS-DOS archives.

(continues)

News Group	Description
comp.bbs.misc	All aspects of computer bulletin board systems.
comp.bbs.waffle	The Waffle BBS and USENET system on all platforms.
comp.benchmarks	Discussion of benchmarking techniques and results.
comp.binaries.acorn	Binary-only postings for Acorn machines. (Moderated)
comp.binaries.amiga	Encoded public domain programs in binary. (Moderated)
comp.binaries.apple2	Binary-only postings for the Apple II computer.
comp.binaries.atari.st	Binary-only postings for the Atari ST. (Moderated)
comp.binaries.cbm	For the transfer of 8-bit Commodore binaries. (Moderated)
comp.binaries.ibm.pc	Binary-only postings for IBM PC/MS-DOS. (Moderated)
comp.binaries.ibm.pc.d	Discussions about IBM PC binary postings.
comp.binaries.ibm.pc.wanted	Requests for IBM PC and compatible programs.
comp.binaries.mac	Encoded Macintosh programs in binary. (Moderated)
comp.binaries.ms-windows	Binary programs for Microsoft Windows. (Moderated)
comp.binaries.os2	Binaries for use under the OS/2 ABI. (Moderated)
comp.bugs.2bsd	Reports of UNIX version 2BSD related bugs.
comp.bugs.4bsd	Reports of UNIX version 4BSD related bugs.

News Group	Description
comp.bugs.4bsd.ucb-fixes	Bug reports/fixes for BSD UNIX. (Moderated)
comp.bugs.misc	General UNIX bug reports and fixes (including V7, UUCP).
comp.bugs.sys5	Reports of USG (System III, V, etc.) bugs.
comp.cad.cadence	Users of Cadence Design Systems products.
comp.cad.compass	Compass Design Automation EDA tools.
comp.cad.pro-engineer	Parametric Technology's Pro/Engineer design package.
comp.cad.synthesis	Research and production in the field of logic synthesis.
comp.client-server	Topics relating to client/server technology.
comp.cog-eng	Cognitive engineering.
comp.compilers	Compiler construction, theory, etc. (Moderated)
comp.compression	Data compression algorithms and theory.
comp.compression.research	Discussions about data compression research.
comp.databases	Database and data management issues and theory.
comp.databases.informix	Informix database management software discussions.
comp.databases.ingres	Issues relating to INGRES products.
comp.databases.ms-access	MS Windows' relational database system, Access.

(continues)

News Group	Description
comp.databases.object	Object-oriented paradigms in database systems.
comp.databases.oracle	The SQL database products of the Oracle Corporation.
comp.databases.pick	Pick-like, postrelational database systems.
comp.databases.rdb	The relational database engine RDB from DEC.
comp.databases.sybase	Implementations of the SQL server.
comp.databases.theory	Discussing advances in database technology.
comp.databases.xbase.fox	Fox Software's xBase system and compatibles.
comp.databases.xbase.misc	Discussion of xBase (dBASE-like) products.
comp.dcom.cell-relay	Forum for discussion of Cell Relay-based products.
comp.dcom.fax	Fax hardware, software, and protocols.
comp.dcom.isdn	The Integrated Services Digital Network (ISDN).
comp.dcom.lans.ethernet	Discussions of the EtherNet/IEEE 802.3 protocols.
comp.dcom.lans.fddi	Discussions of the FDDI protocol suite.
comp.dcom.lans.misc	Local area network hardware and software.
comp.dcom.lans.token-ring	Installing and using token ring networks.
comp.dcom.modems	Data communications hardware and software.

News Group	Description
comp.dcom.servers	Selecting and operating data communications servers.
comp.dcom.sys.cisco	Info on Cisco routers and bridges.
comp.dcom.sys.wellfleet	Wellfleet bridge and router systems hardware and software.
comp.dcom.telecom	Telecommunications digest. (Moderated)
comp.doc	Archived public-domain documentation. (Moderated)
comp.doc.techreports	Lists of technical reports. (Moderated)
comp.dsp	Digital Signal Processing using computers.
comp.edu	Computer science education.
comp.emacs	Emacs editors of different flavors.
comp.fonts	Typefonts—design, conversion, use, etc.
comp.graphics	Computer graphics, art, animation, image processing.
comp.graphics.algorithms	Algorithms used in producing computer graphics.
comp.graphics.animation	Technical aspects of computer animation.
comp.graphics.avs	The Application Visualization System.
comp.graphics.data-explorer	IBM's Visualization Data Explorer, aka DX.
comp.graphics.explorer	The Explorer Modular Visualisation Environment (MVE).
comp.graphics.gnuplot	The GNUPLOT interactive function plotter.

(continues)

News Group	Description
comp.graphics.opengl	The OpenGL 3-D application programming interface.
comp.graphics.research	Highly technical computer graphics discussion. (Moderated)
comp.graphics.visualization	Info on scientific visualization.
comp.groupware	Software and hardware for shared interactive environments.
comp.human-factors	Issues related to human-computer interaction (HCI).
comp.infosystems	Any discussion about information systems.
comp.infosystems.gis	All aspects of Geographic Information Systems.
comp.infosystems.gopher	Discussion of the Gopher information service.
comp.infosystems.wais	The Z39.50-based WAIS full-text search system.
comp.infosystems.www	The World Wide Web information system.
comp.internet.library	Discussing electronic libraries. (Moderated)
comp.ivideodisc	Interactive videodiscs—uses, potential, etc.
comp.lang.ada	Discussion about Ada.
comp.lang.apl	Discussion about APL.
comp.lang.c	Discussion about C.
comp.lang.c++	The object-oriented C++ language.
comp.lang.clos	Common Lisp Object System discussions.

News Group	Description
comp.lang.dylan	For discussion of the Dylan language.
comp.lang.eiffel	The object-oriented Eiffel language.
comp.lang.forth	Discussion about Forth.
comp.lang.fortran	Discussion about FORTRAN.
comp.lang.functional	Discussion about functional languages.
comp.lang.hermes	The Hermes language for distributed applications.
comp.lang.idl-pvwave	IDL and PV-Wave language discussions.
comp.lang.lisp	Discussion about LISP.
comp.lang.lisp.mcl	Discussing Apple's Macintosh Common Lisp.
comp.lang.logo	The Logo teaching and learning language.
comp.lang.misc	Different computer languages not specifically listed.
comp.lang.ml	ML languages including Standard ML, CAML, Lazy ML, etc. (Moderated)
comp.lang.modula2	Discussion about Modula-2.
comp.lang.modula3	Discussion about the Modula-3 language.
comp.lang.oberon	The Oberon language and system.
comp.lang.objective-c	The Objective-C language and environment.
comp.lang.pascal	Discussion about Pascal.

(continues)

News Group	Description
comp.lang.perl	Discussion of Larry Wall's Perl system.
comp.lang.pop	Pop11 and the Plug user group.
comp.lang.postscript	The PostScript page description language.
comp.lang.prolog	Discussion about PROLOG.
comp.lang.sather	The object-oriented computer language Sather.
comp.lang.scheme	The Scheme programming language.
comp.lang.sigplan	Info and announcements from ACM SIGPLAN. (Moderated)
comp.lang.smalltalk	Discussion about Smalltalk 80.
comp.lang.tcl	The Tcl programming language and related tools.
comp.lang.verilog	Discussing Verilog and PLI.
comp.lang.vhdl	VHSIC Hardware Description Language, IEEE 1076/87.
comp.laser-printers	Laser printers, hardware, and software. (Moderated)
comp.lsi	Large-scale integrated circuits.
comp.lsi.testing	Testing of electronic circuits.
comp.mail.elm	Discussion and fixes for the ELM mail system.
comp.mail.headers	Gatewayed from the Internet header-people list.
comp.mail.maps	Various maps, including UUCP maps. (Moderated)
comp.mail.mh	The UCI version of the Rand Message Handling system.

News Group	Description
comp.mail.mime	Multipurpose Internet Mail Extensions of RFC 1341.
comp.mail.misc	General discussions about computer mail.
comp.mail.mush	The Mail User's Shell (MUSH).
comp.mail.sendmail	Configuring and using the BSD sendmail agent.
comp.mail.uucp	Mail in the UUCP network environment.
comp.misc	General topics about computers not covered elsewhere.
comp.multimedia	Interactive multimedia technologies of all kinds.
comp.newprod	Announcements of new products of interest. (Moderated)
comp.object	Object-oriented programming and languages.
comp.object.logic	Integrating object-oriented and logic programming.
comp.org.acm	Topics about the Association for Computing Machinery.
comp.org.decus	Digital Equipment Computer Users' Society news group.
comp.org.eff.news	News from the Electronic Frontier Foundation. (Moderated)
comp.org.eff.talk	Discussion of EFF goals, strategies, etc.
comp.org.fidonet	FidoNews digest, official news of FidoNet Assoc. (Moderated)
comp.org.ieee	Issues and announcements about the IEEE and its members.

(continues)

News Group	Description
comp.org.issnnet	The International Student Society for Neural Networks.
comp.org.sug	Talk about/for the The Sun User's Group.
comp.org.usenix	USENIX Association events and announcements.
comp.org.usenix.roomshare	Finding lodging during USENIX conferences.
comp.os.386bsd.announce	Announcements relating to the 386bsd operating system. (Moderated)
comp.os.386bsd.apps	Applications that run under 386bsd.
comp.os.386bsd.bugs	Bugs and fixes for the 386bsd OS and its clients.
comp.os.386bsd.development	Working on 386bsd internals.
comp.os.386bsd.misc	General aspects of 386bsd not covered by other groups.
comp.os.386bsd.questions	General questions about 386bsd.
comp.os.coherent	Discussion and support of the Coherent operating system.
comp.os.cpm	Discussion about the CP/M operating system.
comp.os.geos	The GEOS operating system by GeoWorks for PC clones.
comp.os.linux.admin	Installing and administering LINUX systems.
comp.os.linux.announce	Announcements important to the LINUX community. (Moderated)
comp.os.linux.development	Ongoing work on the LINUX operating system.

News Group	Description
comp.os.linux.help	Questions and advice about LINUX.
comp.os.linux.misc	LINUX-specific topics not covered by other groups.
comp.os.lynx	Discussion of LynxOS and Lynx Real-Time Systems.
comp.os.mach	The MACH OS from CMU and other places.
comp.os.minix	Discussion of Tanenbaum's MINIX system.
comp.os.misc	General OS-oriented discussion not carried elsewhere.
comp.os.ms-windows.advocacy	Speculation and debate about Microsoft Windows.
comp.os.ms-windows.announce	Announcements relating to Windows. (Moderated)
comp.os.ms-windows.apps	Applications in the Windows environment.
comp.os.ms-windows.misc	General discussions about Windows issues.
comp.os.ms-windows.nt.misc	General discussion about Windows NT.
comp.os.ms-windows.nt.setup	Configuring Windows NT systems.
comp.os.ms-windows.programmer.misc	Programming Microsoft Windows.
comp.os.ms-windows.programmer.tools	Development tools in Windows.
comp.os.ms-windows.programmer.win32	32-bit Windows programming interfaces.
comp.os.ms-windows.setup	Installing and configuring Microsoft Windows.

(continues)

News Group	Description
comp.os.msdos.apps	Discussion of applications that run under MS-DOS.
comp.os.msdos.desqview	QuarterDeck's DESQview and related products.
comp.os.msdos.mail-news	Administering mail and network news systems under MS-DOS.
comp.os.msdos.misc	Miscellaneous topics about MS-DOS machines.
comp.os.msdos.pcgeos	GeoWorks PC/GEOS and PC/GEOS-based packages.
comp.os.msdos.programmer	Programming MS-DOS machines.
comp.os.msdos.programmer.turbovision	Borland's text application libraries.
comp.os.os2.advocacy	Supporting and flaming OS/2.
comp.os.os2.announce	Notable news and announcements related to OS/2. (Moderated)
comp.os.os2.apps	Discussions of applications under OS/2.
comp.os.os2.beta	All aspects of beta releases of OS/2 systems software.
comp.os.os2.bugs	OS/2 system bug reports, fixes, and workarounds.
comp.os.os2.misc	Miscellaneous topics about the OS/2 system.
comp.os.os2.multimedia	Multimedia on OS/2 systems.
comp.os.os2.networking	Networking in OS/2 environments.
comp.os.os2.programmer.misc	Programming OS/2 machines.

News Group	Description
comp.os.os2.programmer.porting	Porting software to OS/2 machines.
comp.os.os2.setup	Installing and configuring OS/2 systems.
comp.os.os2.ver1x	All aspects of OS/2 versions 1.0 through 1.3.
comp.os.os9	Discussions about the OS9 operating system.
comp.os.qnx	Using and developing under the QNX operating system.
comp.os.research	Operating systems and related areas. (Moderated)
comp.os.vms	DEC's VAX-* line of computers and VMS.
comp.os.vxworks	The VxWorks real-time operating system.
comp.os.xinu	The XINU operating system from Purdue (D. Comer).
comp.parallel	Massively parallel hardware/software. (Moderated)
comp.parallel.pvm	The PVM system of multi-computer parallelization.
comp.patents	Discussing patents of computer technology. (Moderated)
comp.periphs	Peripheral devices.
comp.periphs.scsi	Discussion of SCSI-based peripheral devices.
comp.programming	Programming issues that transcend languages and OSs.
comp.programming.literate	Literate programs and programming tools.

(continues)

News Group	Description
comp.protocols.appletalk	Applebus hardware and software.
comp.protocols.dicom	Digital Imaging and Communications in Medicine.
comp.protocols.ibm	Networking with IBM mainframes.
comp.protocols.iso	The ISO protocol stack.
comp.protocols.kerberos	The Kerberos authentication server.
comp.protocols.kermit	Info about the Kermit package. (Moderated)
comp.protocols.misc	Various forms and types of protocols.
comp.protocols.nfs	Discussion about the Network File System protocol.
comp.protocols.ppp	Discussion of the Internet Point-to-Point Protocol.
comp.protocols.tcp-ip	TCP and IP network protocols.
comp.protocols.tcp-ip.ibmpc	TCP/IP for IBM(-like) personal computers.
comp.publish.cdrom.hardware	Hardware used in publishing with CD-ROM.
comp.publish.cdrom.multimedia	Software for multimedia authoring and publishing.
comp.publish.cdrom.software	Software used in publishing with CD-ROM.
comp.realtime	Issues related to real-time computing.
comp.research.japan	The nature of research in Japan. (Moderated)
comp.risks	Risks to the public from computers and users. (Moderated)

News Group	Description
comp.robotics	All aspects of robots and their applications.
comp.security.misc	Security issues of computers and networks.
comp.security.unix	Discussion of UNIX security.
comp.simulation	Simulation methods, problems, uses. (Moderated)
comp.society	The impact of technology on society. (Moderated)
comp.society.cu-digest	The Computer Underground Digest. (Moderated)
comp.society.development	Computer technology in developing countries.
comp.society.folklore	Computer folklore and culture, past and present. (Moderated)
comp.society.futures	Events in technology affecting future computing.
comp.society.privacy	Effects of technology on privacy. (Moderated)
comp.soft-sys.khoros	The Khoros X11 visualization system.
comp.soft-sys.matlab	The MathWorks calculation and visualization package.
comp.soft-sys.sas	The SAS statistics package.
comp.soft-sys.shazam	The SHAZAM econometrics computer program.
comp.soft-sys.spss	The SPSS statistics package.
comp.soft-sys.wavefront	Wavefront software products, problems, etc.
comp.software-eng	Software engineering and related topics.

(continues)

News Group	Description
comp.software.licensing	Software licensing technology.
comp.software.testing	All aspects of testing computer systems.
comp.sources.3b1	Source code-only postings for the AT&T 3b1. (Moderated)
comp.sources.acorn	Source code-only postings for the Acorn. (Moderated)
comp.sources.amiga	Source code-only postings for the Amiga. (Moderated)
comp.sources.apple2	Source code and discussion for the Apple2. (Moderated)
comp.sources.atari.st	Source code-only postings for the Atari ST. (Moderated)
comp.sources.bugs	Bug reports, fixes, discussion for posted sources.
comp.sources.d	For any discussion of source postings.
comp.sources.games	Postings of recreational software. (Moderated)
comp.sources.games.bugs	Bug reports and fixes for posted game software.
comp.sources.hp48	Programs for the HP48 and HP28 calculators. (Moderated)
comp.sources.mac	Software for the Apple Macintosh. (Moderated)
comp.sources.misc	Posting of software. (Moderated)
comp.sources.postscript	Source code for programs written in PostScript. (Moderated)
comp.sources.reviewed	Source code evaluated by peer review. (Moderated)

News Group	Description
comp.sources.sun	Software for Sun workstations. (Moderated)
comp.sources.testers	Finding people to test software.
comp.sources.unix	Postings of complete, UNIX-oriented sources. (Moderated)
comp.sources.wanted	Requests for software and fixes.
comp.sources.x	Software for the X Window system. (Moderated)
comp.specification	Languages and methodologies for formal specification.
comp.specification.z	Discussion about the formal specification notation Z.
comp.speech	Research and applications in speech science and technology.
comp.std.c	Discussion about C language standards.
comp.std.c++	Discussion about C++ language, library, standards.
comp.std.internat	Discussion about international standards.
comp.std.misc	Discussion about various standards.
comp.std.mumps	Discussion for the X11.1 Committee on Mumps. (Moderated)
comp.std.unix	Discussion for the P1003 Committee on UNIX. (Moderated)
comp.std.wireless	Examining standards for wireless network technology. (Moderated)

(continues)

News Group	Description
comp.sw.components	Software components and related technology.
comp.sys.3b1	Discussion and support of AT&T 7300/3B1/UnixPC.
comp.sys.acorn	Discussion on Acorn and ARM-based computers.
comp.sys.acorn.advocacy	Why Acorn computers and programs are better.
comp.sys.acorn.announce	Announcements for Acorn and ARM users. (Moderated)
comp.sys.acorn.tech	Software and hardware aspects of Acorn and ARM products.
comp.sys.alliant	Info and discussion about Alliant computers.
comp.sys.amiga.advocacy	Why an Amiga is better than XYZ.
comp.sys.amiga.announce	Announcements about the Amiga. (Moderated)
comp.sys.amiga.applications	Miscellaneous applications.
comp.sys.amiga.audio	Music, MIDI, speech synthesis, other sounds.
comp.sys.amiga.datacomm	Methods of getting bytes in and out.
comp.sys.amiga.emulations	Various hardware and software emulators.
comp.sys.amiga.games	Discussion of games for the Commodore Amiga.
comp.sys.amiga.graphics	Charts, graphs, pictures, etc.
comp.sys.amiga.hardware	Amiga computer hardware, Q & A, reviews, etc.
comp.sys.amiga.introduction	Group for newcomers to Amigas.

News Group	Description
comp.sys.amiga.marketplace	Where to find it, prices, etc.
comp.sys.amiga.misc	Discussions not falling in another Amiga group.
comp.sys.amiga.multimedia	Animations, video, and multimedia.
comp.sys.amiga.programmer	Developers and hobbyists discuss code.
comp.sys.amiga.reviews	Reviews of Amiga software, hardware. (Moderated)
comp.sys.apollo	Apollo computer systems.
comp.sys.apple2	Discussion about Apple II micros.
comp.sys.apple2.comm	Apple II data communications.
comp.sys.apple2.gno	The AppleIIgs GNO multitasking environment.
comp.sys.apple2.marketplace	Buying, selling and trading Apple II equipment.
comp.sys.apple2.programmer	Programming on the Apple II.
comp.sys.apple2.usergroups	All about Apple II user groups.
comp.sys.atari.8bit	Discussion about 8-bit Atari micros.
comp.sys.atari.advocacy	Attacking and defending Atari computers.
comp.sys.atari.st	Discussion about 16-bit Atari micros.
comp.sys.atari.st.tech	Technical discussions of Atari ST hard/software.
comp.sys.att	Discussions about AT&T microcomputers.
comp.sys.cbm	Discussion about Commodore micros.

(continues)

News Group	Description
comp.sys.concurrent	The Concurrent/Masscomp line of computers. (Moderated)
comp.sys.convex	Convex computer systems hardware and software.
comp.sys.dec	Discussions about DEC computer systems.
comp.sys.dec.micro	DEC Micros (Rainbow, Professional 350/380).
comp.sys.encore	Encore's MultiMax computers.
comp.sys.harris	Harris computer systems, especially real-time systems.
comp.sys.hp	Discussion about Hewlett-Packard equipment.
comp.sys.hp.apps	Discussion of software and apps on all HP platforms.
comp.sys.hp.hardware	Discussion of Hewlett-Packard system hardware.
comp.sys.hp.hpux	Issues pertaining to HP-UX and 9000 series computers.
comp.sys.hp.misc	Issues not covered in any other comp.sys.hp.* group.
comp.sys.hp.mpe	Issues pertaining to MPE and 3000 series computers.
comp.sys.hp48	Hewlett-Packard's HP48 and HP28 calculators.
comp.sys.ibm.pc.demos	Demonstration programs that showcase programmer skill.
comp.sys.ibm.pc.digest	The IBM PC, PC-XT, and PC-AT. (Moderated)
comp.sys.ibm.pc.games.action	Arcade-style games on PCs.

News Group	Description
comp.sys.ibm.pc.games.adventure	Adventure (non-rpg) games on PCs.
comp.sys.ibm.pc.games.announce	Announcements for all PC gamers. (Moderated)
comp.sys.ibm.pc.games.flight-sim	Flight simulators on PCs.
comp.sys.ibm.pc.games.misc	Games not covered by other PC groups.
comp.sys.ibm.pc.games.rpg	Role-playing games on the PC.
comp.sys.ibm.pc.games.strategic	Strategy/planning games on PCs.
comp.sys.ibm.pc.hardware	XT/AT/EISA hardware, any vendor.
comp.sys.ibm.pc.hardware.cd-rom	CD-ROM drives and interfaces for the PC.
comp.sys.ibm.pc.hardware.chips	Processor, cache, memory chips, etc.
comp.sys.ibm.pc.hardware.comm	Modems and communication cards for the PC.
comp.sys.ibm.pc.hardware.misc	Miscellaneous PC hardware topics.
comp.sys.ibm.pc.hardware.networking	Network hardware and equipment for the PC.
comp.sys.ibm.pc.hardware.storage	Hard drives and other PC storage devices.
comp.sys.ibm.pc.hardware.systems	Whole IBM PC computer and clone systems.
comp.sys.ibm.pc.hardware.video	Video cards and monitors for the PC.
comp.sys.ibm.pc.misc	Discussion about IBM personal computers.

(continues)

News Group	Description
comp.sys.ibm.pc.rt	Topics related to IBM's RT computer.
comp.sys.ibm.pc.soundcard	Hardware and software aspects of PC sound cards.
comp.sys.ibm.ps2.hardware	Microchannel hardware, any vendor.
comp.sys.intel	Discussions about Intel systems and parts.
comp.sys.isis	The ISIS distributed system from Cornell.
comp.sys.laptops	Laptop (portable) computers.
comp.sys.m6809	Discussion about 6809s.
comp.sys.m68k	Discussion about 68k's.
comp.sys.m68k.pc	Discussion about 68k-based PCs. (Moderated)
comp.sys.m88k	Discussion about 88k-based computers.
comp.sys.mac.advocacy	The Macintosh computer family compared to others.
comp.sys.mac.announce	Important notices for Macintosh users. (Moderated)
comp.sys.mac.apps	Discussions of Macintosh applications.
comp.sys.mac.comm	Discussion of Macintosh communications.
comp.sys.mac.databases	Database systems for the Apple Macintosh.
comp.sys.mac.digest	Apple Macintosh: info and uses, but no programs. (Moderated)
comp.sys.mac.games	Discussions of games on the Macintosh.

News Group	Description
comp.sys.mac.hardware	Macintosh hardware issues and discussions.
comp.sys.mac.hypercard	The Macintosh HyperCard: info and uses.
comp.sys.mac.misc	General discussions about the Apple Macintosh.
comp.sys.mac.oop.macapp3	Version 3 of the MacApp object-oriented system.
comp.sys.mac.oop.misc	Object-oriented programming issues on the Mac.
comp.sys.mac.oop.tcl	Symantec's THINK Class Library for object programming.
comp.sys.mac.portables	Discussion particular to laptop Macintoshes.
comp.sys.mac.programmer	Discussion by people programming the Apple Macintosh.
comp.sys.mac.scitech	Using the Macintosh in scientific and technological work.
comp.sys.mac.system	Discussions of Macintosh system software.
comp.sys.mac.wanted	Postings of "I want XYZ for my Mac."
comp.sys.mentor	Mentor Graphics products and the Silicon Compiler System.
comp.sys.mips	Systems based on MIPS chips.
comp.sys.misc	Discussion about computers of all kinds.
comp.sys.ncr	Discussion about NCR computers.
comp.sys.newton.announce	Newton information posts. (Moderated)

(continues)

News Group	Description
comp.sys.newton.misc	Miscellaneous discussion about Newton systems.
comp.sys.newton.programmer	Discussion of Newton software development.
comp.sys.next.advocacy	The NeXT religion.
comp.sys.next.announce	Announcements related to the NeXT computer system. (Moderated)
comp.sys.next.bugs	Discussion and solutions for known NeXT bugs.
comp.sys.next.hardware	Discussing the physical aspects of NeXT computers.
comp.sys.next.marketplace	NeXT hardware, software, and jobs.
comp.sys.next.misc	General discussion about the NeXT computer system.
comp.sys.next.programmer	NeXT-related programming issues.
comp.sys.next.software	Function, use, and availability of NeXT programs.
comp.sys.next.sysadmin	Discussions related to NeXT system administration.
comp.sys.novell	Discussion of Novell NetWare products.
comp.sys.nsc.32k	National Semiconductor 32000 series chips.
comp.sys.palmtops	Super-powered calculators in the palm of your hand.
comp.sys.pen	Interacting with computers through pen gestures.
comp.sys.powerpc	General PowerPC discussion.

News Group	Description
comp.sys.prime	Prime Computer products.
comp.sys.proteon	Proteon gateway products.
comp.sys.psion	Discussion about PSION personal computers and organizers.
comp.sys.pyramid	Pyramid 90x computers.
comp.sys.ridge	Ridge 32 computers and ROS.
comp.sys.sequent	Sequent systems (Balance and Symmetry).
comp.sys.sgi.admin	System administration on Silicon Graphics's Irises.
comp.sys.sgi.announce	Announcements for the SGI community. (Moderated)
comp.sys.sgi.apps	Applications that run on the Iris.
comp.sys.sgi.bugs	Bugs found in the IRIX operating system.
comp.sys.sgi.graphics	Graphics packages and issues on SGI machines.
comp.sys.sgi.hardware	Base systems and peripherals for Iris computers.
comp.sys.sgi.misc	General discussion about Silicon Graphics's machines.
comp.sys.stratus	Stratus products, including System/88, CPS-32, VOS, and FTX.
comp.sys.sun.admin	Sun system administration issues and questions.
comp.sys.sun.announce	Sun announcements and Sunergy mailings. (Moderated)
comp.sys.sun.apps	Software applications for Sun computer systems.

(continues)

News Group	Description
comp.sys.sun.hardware	Sun Microsystems hardware.
comp.sys.sun.misc	Miscellaneous discussions about Sun products.
comp.sys.sun.wanted	People looking for Sun products and support.
comp.sys.tahoe	CCI 6/32, Harris HCX/7, and Sperry 7000 computers.
comp.sys.tandy	Discussion about Tandy computers: new and old.
comp.sys.ti	Discussion about Texas Instruments.
comp.sys.transputer	The Transputer computer and OCCAM language.
comp.sys.unisys	Sperry, Burroughs, Convergent, and Unisys systems.
comp.sys.xerox	Xerox 1100 workstations and protocols.
comp.sys.zenith.z100	The Zenith Z-100 (Heath H-100) family of computers.
comp.terminals	All sorts of terminals.
comp.text	Text processing issues and methods.
comp.text.desktop	Technology and techniques of desktop publishing.
comp.text.frame	Desktop publishing with FrameMaker.
comp.text.interleaf	Applications and use of Interleaf software.
comp.text.sgml	ISO 8879 SGML, structured documents, markup languages.

News Group	Description
comp.text.tex	Discussion about the TeX and LaTeX systems and macros.
comp.theory.info-retrieval	Information Retrieval topics. (Moderated)
comp.unix.admin	Administering a UNIX-based system.
comp.unix.aix	IBM's version of UNIX.
comp.unix.amiga	Minix, SYSV4, and other *nix on an Amiga.
comp.unix.aux	The version of UNIX for Apple Macintosh II computers.
comp.unix.bsd	Discussion of Berkeley Software Distribution UNIX.
comp.unix.dos-under-unix	MS-DOS running under UNIX by whatever means.
comp.unix.internals	Discussions on hacking UNIX internals.
comp.unix.large	UNIX on mainframes and in large networks.
comp.unix.misc	Various topics that don't fit other groups.
comp.unix.osf.misc	Various aspects of Open Software Foundation products.
comp.unix.osf.osf1	The Open Software Foundation's OSF/1.
comp.unix.pc-clone.16bit	UNIX on 286 architectures.
comp.unix.pc-clone.32bit	UNIX on 386 and 486 architectures.
comp.unix.programmer	Q & A for people programming under UNIX.

(continues)

News Group	Description
comp.unix.questions	UNIX neophytes group.
comp.unix.shell	Using and programming the UNIX shell.
comp.unix.sys3	System III UNIX discussions.
comp.unix.sys5.misc	Versions of System V that predate Release 3.
comp.unix.sys5.r3	Discussing System V Release 3.
comp.unix.sys5.r4	Discussing System V Release 4.
comp.unix.ultrix	Discussions about DEC's Ultrix.
comp.unix.unixware	Discussion about Novell's UnixWare products.
comp.unix.user-friendly	Discussion of UNIX user-friendliness.
comp.unix.wizards	Questions for only true UNIX wizards.
comp.unix.xenix.misc	General discussions regarding XENIX (except SCO).
comp.unix.xenix.sco	XENIX versions from the Santa Cruz Operation.
comp.virus	Computer viruses and security. (Moderated)
comp.windows.garnet	The Garnet user interface development environment.
comp.windows.interviews	The InterViews object-oriented windowing system.
comp.windows.misc	Various issues about windowing systems.
comp.windows.news	Sun Microsystems' NeWS window system.

News Group	Description
comp.windows.open-look	Discussion about the Open Look GUI.
comp.windows.suit	The SUIT user-interface toolkit.
comp.windows.x	Discussion about the X Window System.
comp.windows.x.apps	Getting and using, not programming, applications for X.
comp.windows.x.i386unix	The XFree86 window system and others.
comp.windows.x.intrinsics	Discussion of the X toolkit.
comp.windows.x.pex	The PHIGS extension of the X Window system.
gnu.announce	Status and announcements from the project. (Moderated)
gnu.bash.bug	Bourne Again SHell bug reports and suggested fixes. (Moderated)
gnu.chess	Announcements about the GNU Chess program.
gnu.emacs.announce	Announcements about GNU Emacs. (Moderated)
gnu.emacs.bug	GNU Emacs bug reports and suggested fixes. (Moderated)
gnu.emacs.gnews	News reading under GNU Emacs using Weemba's Gnews.
gnu.emacs.gnus	News reading under GNU Emacs using GNUS (in English).
gnu.emacs.help	User queries and answers.
gnu.emacs.sources	Only (*please!*) C and Lisp source code for GNU Emacs.
gnu.emacs.vm.bug	Bug reports on the Emacs VM mail package.

(continues)

News Group	Description
gnu.emacs.vm.info	Information about the Emacs VM mail package.
gnu.emacs.vms	VMS port of GNU Emacs.
gnu.epoch.misc	The Epoch X11 extensions to Emacs.
gnu.g++.announce	Announcements about the GNU C++ Compiler. (Moderated)
gnu.g++.bug	g++ bug reports and suggested fixes. (Moderated)
gnu.g++.help	GNU C++ compiler (g++) user queries and answers.
gnu.g++.lib.bug	g++ library bug reports/ suggested fixes. (Moderated)
gnu.gcc.announce	Announcements about the GNU C Compiler. (Moderated)
gnu.gcc.bug	GNU C Compiler bug reports/ suggested fixes. (Moderated)
gnu.gcc.help	GNU C Compiler (gcc) user queries and answers.
gnu.gdb.bug	gcc/g++ DeBugger bugs and suggested fixes. (Moderated)
gnu.ghostscript.bug	GNU Ghostscript interpreter bugs. (Moderated)
gnu.gnusenet.config	GNU's Not Usenet administration and configuration.
gnu.gnusenet.test	GNU's Not Usenet alternative hierarchy testing.
gnu.groff.bug	Bugs in the GNU roff programs. (Moderated)
gnu.misc.discuss	Serious discussion about GNU and freed software.

News Group	Description
gnu.smalltalk.bug	Bugs in GNU Smalltalk. (Moderated)
gnu.utils.bug	GNU utilities bugs (e.g., make, gawk, ls). (Moderated)
hepnet.admin	Discussions among hepnet.* netnews administrators.
hepnet.announce	Announcement of general interest.
hepnet.conferences	Discussions of conference and workshops.
hepnet.freehep	Discussions about the freehep archives.
hepnet.general	Discussions of general interest.
hepnet.hepix	Discussions on the use of UNIX.
hepnet.heplib	Discussions about HEPLIB.
hepnet.jobs	Job announcements and discussions.
hepnet.lang.c++	Discussions of the use of C++.
hepnet.test	Test postings.
hepnet.videoconf	Discussions on the use of videoconferencing.
ieee.announce	General announcements for IEEE community.
ieee.config	Postings about managing the ieee.* groups.
ieee.general	IEEE—general discussion.
ieee.pcnfs	Discussion and tips on PC-NFS.
ieee.rab.announce	Regional Activities Board—announcements.

(continues)

News Group	Description
ieee.rab.general	Regional Activities Board—general discussion.
ieee.region1	Region 1 announcements.
ieee.tab.announce	Technical Activities Board—announcements.
ieee.tab.general	Technical Activities Board—general discussion.
ieee.tcos	The Technical Committee on Operating Systems. (Moderated)
ieee.usab.announce	USAB—announcements.
ieee.usab.general	USAB—general discussion.
(inet) comp.ai.edu	Applications of artificial intelligence to education.
(inet) comp.ai.vision	Artificial intelligence vision research. (Moderated)
(inet) comp.dcom.lans.hyperchannel	Hyperchannel networks within an IP network.
(inet) comp.editors	Topics related to computerized text editing.
(inet) comp.edu.composition	Writing instruction in computer-based classrooms.
(inet) comp.lang.asm370	Programming in IBM System/370 assembly language.
(inet) comp.lang.clu	The CLU language and related topics.
(inet) comp.lang.forth.mac	The CSI MacForth programming environment.
(inet) comp.lang.icon	Topics related to the ICON programming language.
(inet) comp.lang.idl	IDL- (Interface Description Language) related topics.

News Group	Description
(inet) comp.lang.lisp.franz	The Franz Lisp programming language.
(inet) comp.lang.lisp.x	The XLISP language system.
(inet) comp.lang.rexx	The REXX command language.
(inet) comp.lang.scheme.c	The Scheme language environment.
(inet) comp.lang.visual	Visual programming languages.
(inet) comp.lsi.cad	Electrical computer-aided design.
(inet) comp.mail.multi-media	Multimedia mail.
(inet) comp.music	Applications of computers in music research.
(inet) comp.networks.noctools.announce	Info and announcements about NOC tools. (Moderated)
(inet) comp.networks.noctools.bugs	Bug reports and fixes for NOC tools.
(inet) comp.networks.noctools.d	Discussion about NOC tools.
(inet) comp.networks.noctools.submissions	New NOC tools submissions.
(inet) comp.networks.noctools.tools	Descriptions of available NOC tools. (Moderated)
(inet) comp.networks.noctools.wanted	Requests for NOC software.
(inet) comp.org.isoc.interest	Discussion about the Internet Society.
(inet) comp.os.aos	Topics related to Data General's AOS/VS.
(inet) comp.os.cpm.amethyst	Discussion of Amethyst, CP/M-80 software package.

(continues)

News Group	Description
(inet) comp.os.msdos.4dos	The 4DOS command processor for MS-DOS.
(inet) comp.os.rsts	Topics related to the PDP-11 RSTS/E operating system.
(inet) comp.os.v	The V distributed operating system from Stanford.
(inet) comp.periphs.printers	Information on printers.
(inet) comp.protocols.iso.dev-environ	The ISO Development Environment.
(inet) comp.protocols.iso.x400	X400 mail protocol discussions.
(inet) comp.protocols.iso.x400.gateway	X400 mail gateway discussions. (Moderated)
(inet) comp.protocols.pcnet	Topics related to PCNET (a personal computer network).
(inet) comp.protocols.snmp	The Simple Network Management Protocol.
(inet) comp.protocols.tcp-ip.domains	Topics related to Domain Style names.
(inet) comp.protocols.time.ntp	The network time protocol.
(inet) comp.security.announce	Announcements from the CERT about security. (Moderated)
(inet) comp.soft-sys.andrew	The Andrew system from CMU.
(inet) comp.soft-sys.nextstep	The NeXTstep computing environment.
(inet) comp.std.announce	Announcements about standards activities. (Moderated)
(inet) comp.sys.cdc	Control Data Corporation computers (e.g., Cybers).

News Group	Description
(inet) comp.sys.handhelds	Hand-held computers and programmable calculators.
(inet) comp.sys.intel.ipsc310	Anything related to the Intel 310.
(inet) comp.sys.northstar	Northstar microcomputer users.
(inet) comp.sys.super	Supercomputers.
(inet) comp.sys.ti.explorer	The Texas Instruments Explorer.
(inet) comp.sys.zenith	Heath terminals and related Zenith products.
(inet) comp.terminals.bitgraph	The BB&N BitGraph Terminal.
(inet) comp.terminals.tty5620	AT&T Dot-mapped display terminals (5620 and BLIT).
(inet) comp.theory	Theoretical computer science.
(inet) comp.theory.cell-automata	Discussion of all aspects of cellular automata.
(inet) comp.theory.dynamic-sys	Ergodic theory and dynamical systems.
(inet) comp.theory.self-org-sys	Topics related to self-organization.
(inet) comp.unix.cray	Cray computers and their operating systems.
(inet) comp.unix.solaris	Discussions about the Solaris operating system.
(inet) comp.windows.x.announce	X Consortium announcements. (Moderated)
(inet) comp.windows.x.motif	The Motif GUI for the X Window system.
(inet) ddn.mgt-bulletin	The DDN management bulletin from nic.ddn.mil. (Moderated)

(continues)

News Group	Description
(inet) ddn.newsletter	The DDN newsletter from nic.ddn.mil. (Moderated)
(inet) news.software.nntp	The Network News Transfer Protocol.
(inet) rec.games.vectrex	The Vectrex game system.
(inet) rec.mag.fsfnet	A science-fiction "fanzine." (Moderated)
(inet) sci.bio.technology	Any topic relating to biotechnology.
(inet) sci.math.num-analysis	Numerical analysis.
(inet) sci.philosophy.meta	Discussions within the scope of "metaphilosophy."
(inet) soc.culture.esperanto	The neutral international language Esperanto.
info.admin	Administrative messages regarding info* groups (usenet@ux1.cso.uiuc.edu). (Moderated)
info.big-internet	Issues facing a huge Internet (big-internet@munnari.oz.au). (Moderated)
info.bind	The Berkeley BIND server (bind@arpa.berkeley.edu). (Moderated)
info.brl-cad	BRL's Solid Modeling CAD system (cad@brl.mil). (Moderated)
info.bytecounters	NSstat network analysis program (bytecounters@venera.isi.edu). (Moderated)
info.convex	Convex Corp machines (info-convex@pemrac.space.swri.edu). (Moderated)

News Group	Description
info.firearms	Non-political firearms discussions (firearms@cs.cmu.edu). (Moderated)
info.firearms.politics	Political firearms discussions (firearms-politics@cs.cmu.edu). (Moderated)
info.gated	Cornell's GATED program (gated-people@devvax.tn.cornell.edu). (Moderated)
info.grass.programmer	GRASS geographic information system programmer issues (grassp-list @moon.cecer.army.mil). (Moderated)
info.grass.user	GRASS geographic information system user issues (grassu-list@moon.cecer.army.mil). (Moderated)
info.ietf	Internet Engineering Task Force (IETF) discussions (ietf@venera.isi.edu). (Moderated)
info.ietf.hosts	IETF host requirements discussions (ietf-hosts@nnsc.nsf.net). (Moderated)
info.ietf.isoc	Internet Society discussions (isoc-interest@relay.sgi.com). (Moderated)
info.ietf.njm	Jo-MAAN—the Joint Monitoring Access between Adjacent Networks IETF working group (njm@merit.edu). (Moderated)
info.ietf.smtp	IETF SMTP extension discussions (ietf-smtp@dimacs.rutgers.edu). (Moderated)

(continues)

News Group	Description
info.isode	The ISO Development Environment package (isode@nic.ddn.mil). (Moderated)
info.jethro-tull	Discussions about Jethro Tull's music (jtull@remus.rutgers.edu). (Moderated)
info.labmgr	Computer lab managers list (labmgr@ukcc.uky.edu). (Moderated)
info.mach	The Mach operating system (info-mach@cs.cmu.edu). (Moderated)
info.mh.workers	MH development discussions (mh-workers@ics.uci.edu). (Moderated)
info.nets	Inter-network connectivity (infonets@think.com).
info.nsf.grants	NSF grant notes (grants@note.nsf.gov). (Moderated)
info.nsfnet.cert	Computer Emergency Response Team announcements (nsfnet-cert@merit.edu). (Moderated)
info.nsfnet.status	NSFNET status reports. (Moderated)
info.nupop	Northwestern University's POP for PCs (nupop@casbah.acns.nwu.edu). (Moderated)
info.nysersnmp	The SNMP software distributed by PSI (nysersnmp@nisc.nyser.net). (Moderated)
info.osf	OSF Electronic Bulletin mailings (roma@uiuc.edu). (Moderated)

News Group	Description
info.pem-dev	IETF privacy enhanced mail discussions (pem-dev@tis.com). (Moderated)
info.ph	Qi, ph, sendmail/phquery discussions (info-ph@uxc.cso.uiuc.edu). (Moderated)
info.rfc	Announcements of newly released RFCs (rfc-request@nic.ddn.mil). (Moderated)
info.slug	Care and feeding of Symbolics Lisp machines (slug@iu.ai.sri.com). (Moderated)
info.snmp	SNMP—Simple Gateway/Network Monitoring Protocol (snmp@nisc.nyser.net). (Moderated)
info.solbourne	Discussions and info about Solbourne computers (info-solbourne@acsu.buffalo.edu). (Moderated)
info.sun-managers	Sun-managers digest (sun-managers@rice.edu). (Moderated)
info.sun-nets	Sun-nets (nee Sun Spots) digest (sun-nets@umiacs.umd.edu). (Moderated)
info.theorynt	Theory list (theorynt@vm1.nodak.edu). (Moderated)
info.unix-sw	Software available for anonymous ftp (unix-sw-request@wsmr-simtel20.army.mil). (Moderated)
info.wisenet	Women in Science and Engineering NETwork (wisenet@uicvm.uic.edu). (Moderated)

(continues)

News Group	Description
k12.ed.art	Arts and crafts curricula in K-12 education.
k12.ed.business	Business education curricula in grades K-12.
k12.ed.comp.literacy	Teaching computer literacy in grades K-12.
k12.ed.health-pe	Health and physical education curricula in grades K-12.
k12.ed.life-skills	Home economics, career education, and school counseling.
k12.ed.math	Mathematics curriculum in K-12 education.
k12.ed.music	Music and performing arts curriculum in K-12 education.
k12.ed.science	Science curriculum in K-12 education.
k12.ed.soc-studies	Social studies and history curriculum in K-12 education.
k12.ed.special	Educating students with handicaps and/or special needs.
k12.ed.tag	K-12 education for gifted and talented students.
k12.ed.tech	Industrial arts and vocational education in grades K-12.
k12.library	Implementing info technologies in school libraries.
k12.lang.art	The art of teaching language skills in grades K-12.
k12.lang.deutsch-eng	Bilingual German/English practice with native speakers.

News Group	Description
k12.lang.esp-eng	Bilingual Spanish/English practice with native speakers.
k12.lang.francais	French practice with native speakers.
k12.lang.russian	Bilingual Russian/English practice with native speakers.
k12.sys.projects	Discussion of potential projects.
k12.sys.channel0	Current projects.
k12.sys.channel1	Current projects.
k12.sys.channel2	Current projects.
k12.sys.channel3	Current projects.
k12.sys.channel4	Current projects.
k12.sys.channel5	Current projects.
k12.sys.channel6	Current projects.
k12.sys.channel7	Current projects.
k12.sys.channel8	Current projects.
k12.sys.channel9	Current projects.
k12.sys.channel10	Current projects.
k12.sys.channel11	Current projects.
k12.sys.channel12	Current projects.
k12.chat.elementary	Casual conversation for elementary students, grades K-5.
k12.chat.junior	Casual conversation for students in grades 6-8.
k12.chat.senior	Casual conversation for high school students.

(continues)

News Group	Description
k12.chat.teacher	Casual conversation for teachers of grades K-12.
misc.activism.progressive	Information for Progressive activists. (Moderated)
misc.answers	Repository for periodic USENET articles. (Moderated)
misc.books.technical	Discussion of books about technical topics.
misc.consumers	Consumer interests, product reviews, etc.
misc.consumers.house	Discussion about owning and maintaining a house.
misc.education	Discussion of the educational system.
misc.education.language.english	Teaching English to speakers of other languages.
misc.emerg-services	Forum for paramedics and other first responders.
misc.entrepreneurs	Discussion on operating a business.
misc.fitness	Physical fitness, exercise, etc.
misc.forsale	Short, tasteful postings about items for sale.
misc.forsale.computers.d	Discussion of misc.forsale.computers.*.
misc.forsale.computers.mac	Apple Macintosh-related computer items.
misc.forsale.computers.other	Selling miscellaneous computer stuff.
misc.forsale.computers.pc-clone	IBM PC-related computer items.

News Group	Description
misc.forsale.computers.workstation	Workstation-related computer items.
misc.handicap	Items of interest for/about the handicapped. (Moderated)
misc.headlines	Current interest: drug testing, terrorism, etc.
misc.health.alternative	Alternative, complementary, and holistic health care.
misc.health.diabetes	Discussion of diabetes management in day-to-day life.
misc.int-property	Discussion of intellectual property rights.
misc.invest	Investments and the handling of money.
misc.invest.canada	Investing in Canadian financial markets.
misc.invest.real-estate	Property investments.
misc.invest.technical	Analyzing market trends with technical methods.
misc.jobs.contract	Discussions about contract labor.
misc.jobs.misc	Discussion about employment, workplaces, careers.
misc.jobs.offered	Announcements of positions available.
misc.jobs.offered.entry	Job listings only for entry-level positions.
misc.jobs.resumes	Postings of resumes and "situation-wanted" articles.
misc.kids	Children, their behavior and activities.

(continues)

News Group	Description
misc.kids.computer	The use of computers by children.
misc.legal	Legalities and the ethics of law.
misc.legal.computing	Discussing the legal climate of the computing world.
misc.legal.moderated	All aspects of law. (Moderated)
misc.misc	Various discussions not fitting in any other group.
misc.news.east-europe.rferl	Radio Free Europe/Radio Liberty Daily Report. (Moderated)
misc.news.southasia	News from Bangladesh, India, Nepal, etc. (Moderated)
misc.rural	Devoted to issues concerning rural living.
misc.taxes	Tax laws and advice.
misc.test	For testing of network software. Very boring.
misc.wanted	Requests for things that are needed (*not* software).
misc.writing	Discussion of writing in all its forms.
news.admin.misc	General topics of network news administration.
news.admin.policy	Policy issues of USENET.
news.admin.technical	Technical aspects of maintaining network news. (Moderated)
news.announce.conferences	Calls for papers and conference announcements. (Moderated)
news.announce.important	General announcements of interest to all. (Moderated)

News Group	Description
news.announce.newgroups	Calls for news groups and announcements of same. (Moderated)
news.announce.newusers	Explanatory postings for new users. (Moderated)
news.answers	Repository for periodic USENET articles. (Moderated)
news.config	Postings of system down times and interruptions.
news.future	The future technology of network news systems.
news.groups	Discussions and lists of news groups.
news.lists	News-related statistics and lists. (Moderated)
news.lists.ps-maps	Maps relating to USENET traffic flows. (Moderated)
news.misc	Discussions of USENET itself.
news.newsites	Postings of new site announcements.
news.newusers.questions	Q & A for users new to the USENET.
news.software.anu-news	VMS B-news software from Australian National University.
news.software.b	Discussion about B-news-compatible software.
news.software.nn	Discussion about the "nn" news reader package.
news.software.notes	Notesfile software from the University of Illinois.
news.software.readers	Discussion of software used to read network news.

(continues)

News Group	Description
rec.answers	Repository for periodic USENET articles. (Moderated)
rec.antiques	Discussing antiques and vintage items.
rec.aquaria	Keeping fish and aquaria as a hobby.
rec.arts.animation	Discussion of various kinds of animation.
rec.arts.anime	Japanese animation fan discussion.
rec.arts.anime.info	Announcements about Japanese animation. (Moderated)
rec.arts.anime.marketplace	Things for sale in the Japanese animation world.
rec.arts.anime.stories	All about Japanese comic fanzines. (Moderated)
rec.arts.bodyart	Tattoos and body decoration discussions.
rec.arts.bonsai	Dwarfish trees and shrubbery.
rec.arts.books	Books of all genres, and the publishing industry.
rec.arts.books.tolkien	The works of J.R.R. Tolkien.
rec.arts.cinema	Discussion of the art of cinema. (Moderated)
rec.arts.comics.info	Reviews, convention information, and other comics news. (Moderated)
rec.arts.comics.marketplace	The exchange of comics and comic-related items.
rec.arts.comics.misc	Comic books, graphic novels, sequential art.

News Group	Description
rec.arts.comics.strips	Discussion of short-form comics.
rec.arts.comics.xbooks	The Mutant Universe of Marvel Comics.
rec.arts.dance	Any aspects of dance not covered in another news group.
rec.arts.disney	Discussion of any Disney-related subjects.
rec.arts.drwho	Discussion about Dr. Who.
rec.arts.erotica	Erotic fiction and verse. (Moderated)
rec.arts.fine	Fine arts and artists.
rec.arts.int-fiction	Discussions about interactive fiction.
rec.arts.manga	All aspects of the Japanese storytelling art form.
rec.arts.marching.drumcorps	Drum and bugle corps.
rec.arts.marching.misc	Marching-related performance activities.
rec.arts.misc	Discussions about the arts not in other groups.
rec.arts.movies	Discussions of movies and movie making.
rec.arts.movies.reviews	Reviews of movies. (Moderated)
rec.arts.poems	For the posting of poems.
rec.arts.prose	Short works of prose fiction and follow-up discussion.
rec.arts.sf.announce	Major announcements of the sci-fi world. (Moderated)
rec.arts.sf.fandom	Discussions of sci-fi fan activities.

(continues)

News Group	Description
rec.arts.sf.marketplace	Personal for-sale notices of sci-fi materials.
rec.arts.sf.misc	Science-fiction lovers' news group.
rec.arts.sf.movies	Discussing sci-fi motion pictures.
rec.arts.sf.reviews	Reviews of science fiction/fantasy/horror works. (Moderated)
rec.arts.sf.science	Real and speculative aspects of sci-fi science.
rec.arts.sf.starwars	Discussion of the *Star Wars* universe.
rec.arts.sf.tv	Discussing general television science fiction.
rec.arts.sf.written	Discussion of written science fiction and fantasy.
rec.arts.startrek.current	New *Star Trek* shows, movies, and books.
rec.arts.startrek.fandom	*Star Trek* conventions and memorabilia.
rec.arts.startrek.info	Information about the universe of *Star Trek*. (Moderated)
rec.arts.startrek.misc	General discussions of *Star Trek*.
rec.arts.startrek.reviews	Reviews of *Star Trek* books, episodes, films, etc. (Moderated)
rec.arts.startrek.tech	*Star Trek*'s depiction of future technologies.
rec.arts.theatre	Discussion of all aspects of stage work and theatre.
rec.arts.tv	The boob tube, its history, and past and current shows.

News Group	Description
rec.arts.tv.soaps	Postings about soap operas.
rec.arts.tv.uk	Discussions of telly shows from the U.K.
rec.arts.wobegon	*A Prairie Home Companion* radio show discussion.
rec.audio	High-fidelity audio.
rec.audio.car	Discussions of automobile audio systems.
rec.audio.high-end	High-end audio systems. (Moderated)
rec.audio.pro	Professional audio recording and studio engineering.
rec.autos	Automobiles, automotive products, and laws.
rec.autos.antique	Discussing all aspects of automobiles over 25 years old.
rec.autos.driving	Driving automobiles.
rec.autos.rod-n-custom	High-performance automobiles.
rec.autos.sport	Discussion of organized, legal auto competitions.
rec.autos.tech	Technical aspects of automobiles and so on.
rec.autos.vw	Issues pertaining to Volkswagen products.
rec.aviation.announce	Events of interest to the aviation community. (Moderated)
rec.aviation.answers	Frequently asked questions about aviation. (Moderated)
rec.aviation.homebuilt	Selecting, designing, building, and restoring aircraft.

(continues)

News Group	Description
rec.aviation.ifr	Flying under Instrument Flight Rules.
rec.aviation.military	Military aircraft of the past, present, and future.
rec.aviation.misc	Miscellaneous topics in aviation.
rec.aviation.owning	Information on owning airplanes.
rec.aviation.piloting	General discussion for aviators.
rec.aviation.products	Reviews and discussion of products useful to pilots.
rec.aviation.simulators	Flight simulation on all levels.
rec.aviation.soaring	All aspects of sailplanes and hang-gliders.
rec.aviation.stories	Anecdotes of flight experiences. (Moderated)
rec.aviation.student	Learning to fly.
rec.backcountry	Activities in the great outdoors.
rec.bicycles.marketplace	Buying, selling, and reviewing items for cycling.
rec.bicycles.misc	General discussion of bicycling.
rec.bicycles.racing	Bicycle racing techniques, rules, and results.
rec.bicycles.rides	Discussions of tours and training or commuting routes.
rec.bicycles.soc	Societal issues of bicycling.
rec.bicycles.tech	Cycling product design, construction, maintenance, etc.
rec.birds	Hobbyists interested in bird watching.

News Group	Description
rec.boats	Hobbyists interested in boating.
rec.boats.paddle	Talk about any boats with oars, paddles, etc.
rec.climbing	Climbing techniques, competition announcements, etc.
rec.collecting	Discussion among collectors of many things.
rec.collecting.cards	Collecting all sorts of sport and non-sport cards.
rec.crafts.brewing	The art of making beers and meads.
rec.crafts.metalworking	All aspects of working with metal.
rec.crafts.misc	Handiwork arts not covered elsewhere.
rec.crafts.quilting	All about quilts and other quilted items.
rec.crafts.textiles	Sewing, weaving, knitting, and other fiber arts.
rec.crafts.winemaking	The tasteful art of making wine.
rec.equestrian	Discussion of things equestrian.
rec.folk-dancing	Folk dances, dancers, and dancing.
rec.food.cooking	Food, cooking, cookbooks, and recipes.
rec.food.drink	Wines and spirits.
rec.food.historic	The history of food-making arts.
rec.food.recipes	Recipes for interesting food and drink. (Moderated)
rec.food.restaurants	Discussion of dining out.

(continues)

News Group	Description
rec.food.sourdough	Making and baking with sourdough.
rec.food.veg	Vegetarians.
rec.gambling	Articles on games of chance and betting.
rec.games.abstract	Perfect information, pure strategy games.
rec.games.backgammon	Discussion of the game of backgammon.
rec.games.board	Discussion and hints on board games.
rec.games.board.ce	The Cosmic Encounter board game.
rec.games.bridge	Hobbyists interested in bridge.
rec.games.chess	Chess and computer chess.
rec.games.chinese-chess	Discussion of the game of Chinese chess, Xiangqi.
rec.games.corewar	The Core War computer challenge.
rec.games.design	Discussion of game-design-related issues.
rec.games.diplomacy	The conquest game Diplomacy.
rec.games.empire	Discussion and hints about Empire.
rec.games.frp.advocacy	Flames and rebuttals about various role-playing systems.
rec.games.frp.announce	Announcements of happenings in the role-playing world. (Moderated)
rec.games.frp.archives	Archivable fantasy stories and other projects. (Moderated)

News Group	Description
rec.games.frp.cyber	Discussions of cyberpunk-related role-playing games.
rec.games.frp.dnd	Fantasy role-playing with TSR's Dungeons and Dragons.
rec.games.frp.marketplace	Role-playing game materials wanted and for sale.
rec.games.frp.misc	General discussions of role-playing games.
rec.games.go	Discussion about Go.
rec.games.hack	Discussion, hints, etc., about the Hack game.
rec.games.int-fiction	All aspects of interactive fiction games.
rec.games.mecha	Giant robot games.
rec.games.miniatures	Tabletop war-gaming.
rec.games.misc	Games and computer games.
rec.games.moria	Comments, hints, and info about the Moria game.
rec.games.mud.admin	Administrative issues of multiuser dungeons.
rec.games.mud.announce	Informational articles about multiuser dungeons. (Moderated)
rec.games.mud.diku	All about DikuMuds.
rec.games.mud.lp	Discussions of the LPMUD computer role-playing game.
rec.games.mud.misc	Various aspects of multiuser computer games.
rec.games.mud.tiny	Discussion about Tiny muds, like MUSH, MUSE, and MOO.

(continues)

News Group	Description
rec.games.netrek	Discussion of the X Window system game Netrek (XtrekII).
rec.games.pbm	Discussion about Play by Mail games.
rec.games.pinball	Discussing pinball-related issues.
rec.games.programmer	Discussion of adventure-game programming.
rec.games.rogue	Discussion and hints about Rogue.
rec.games.roguelike.angband	The computer game Angband.
rec.games.roguelike.announce	Major info about rogue-styled games. (Moderated)
rec.games.roguelike.misc	Rogue-style dungeon games without other groups.
rec.games.trivia	Discussion about trivia.
rec.games.video.arcade	Discussions about coin-operated video games.
rec.games.video.classic	Older home video entertainment systems.
rec.games.video.marketplace	Home video game stuff for sale or trade.
rec.games.video.misc	General discussion about home video games.
rec.games.video.nintendo	All Nintendo video game systems and software.
rec.games.video.sega	All Sega video game systems and software.
rec.games.xtank.play	Strategy and tactics for the distributed game Xtank.
rec.games.xtank.programmer	Coding the Xtank game and its robots.

News Group	Description
rec.gardens	Gardening, methods and results.
rec.guns	Discussions about firearms. (Moderated)
rec.heraldry	Discussion of coats of arms.
rec.humor	Jokes and the like. May be somewhat offensive.
rec.humor.d	Discussions on the content of rec.humor articles.
rec.humor.funny	Jokes that are funny (in the moderator's opinion). (Moderated)
rec.humor.oracle	Sagacious advice from the USENET Oracle. (Moderated)
rec.humor.oracle.d	Comments about the USENET Oracle's comments.
rec.hunting	Discussions about hunting. (Moderated)
rec.juggling	Juggling techniques, equipment, and events.
rec.kites	Talk about kites and kiting.
rec.mag	Magazine summaries, tables of contents, etc.
rec.martial-arts	Discussion of the various martial art forms.
rec.misc	General topics about recreational/participant sports.
rec.models.railroad	Model railroads of all scales.
rec.models.rc	Radio-controlled models for hobbyists.
rec.models.rockets	Model rockets for hobbyists.

(continues)

News Group	Description
rec.models.scale	Construction of models.
rec.motorcycles	Motorcycles and related products and laws.
rec.motorcycles.dirt	Riding motorcycles and ATVs off-road.
rec.motorcycles.harley	All aspects of Harley-Davidson motorcycles.
rec.motorcycles.racing	Discussion of all aspects of racing motorcycles.
rec.music.a-cappella	Vocal music without instrumental accompaniment.
rec.music.afro-latin	Music with Afro-Latin, African, and Latin influences.
rec.music.beatles	Postings about the Fab Four and their music.
rec.music.bluenote	Discussion of jazz, blues, and related types of music.
rec.music.cd	CDs—availability and other discussions.
rec.music.celtic	Traditional and modern music with a Celtic flavor.
rec.music.christian	Christian music, both contemporary and traditional.
rec.music.classical	Discussion about classical music.
rec.music.classical.guitar	Classical music performed on guitar.
rec.music.classical.performing	Performing classical (including early) music.
rec.music.compose	Creating musical and lyrical works.
rec.music.country.western	C & W music, performers, performances, etc.

News Group	Description
rec.music.dementia	Discussion of comedy and novelty music.
rec.music.dylan	Discussion of Bob's works and music.
rec.music.early	Discussion of preclassical European music.
rec.music.folk	Folks discussing folk music of various sorts.
rec.music.funky	Funk, rap, hip-hop, house, soul, R & B, and related topics.
rec.music.gaffa	Discussion of Kate Bush and other alternative music. (Moderated)
rec.music.gdead	A group for (Grateful) Deadheads.
rec.music.indian.classical	Hindustani and Carnatic Indian classical music.
rec.music.indian.misc	Discussing Indian music in general.
rec.music.industrial	Discussion of all industrial-related music styles.
rec.music.info	News and announcements on musical topics. (Moderated)
rec.music.makers	For performers and their discussions.
rec.music.makers.bass	Upright bass and bass guitar techniques and equipment.
rec.music.makers.guitar	Electric and acoustic guitar techniques and equipment.
rec.music.makers.guitar.acoustic	Discussion of acoustic guitar playing.
rec.music.makers.guitar.tablature	Guitar tablature/chords.

(continues)

News Group	Description
rec.music.makers.marketplace	Buying and selling used music-making equipment.
rec.music.makers.percussion	Drum and other percussion techniques and equipment.
rec.music.makers.synth	Synthesizers and computer music.
rec.music.marketplace	Records, tapes, and CDs: wanted, for sale, etc.
rec.music.misc	Music lovers' group.
rec.music.newage	"New Age" music discussions.
rec.music.phish	Discussing the musical group Phish.
rec.music.reggae	Roots, Rockers, Dancehall Reggae.
rec.music.reviews	Reviews of music of all genres and mediums. (Moderated)
rec.music.video	Discussion of music videos and music video software.
rec.nude	Hobbyists interested in naturist/nudist activities.
rec.org.mensa	Talking with members of the high IQ society Mensa.
rec.org.sca	Society for Creative Anachronism.
rec.outdoors.fishing	All aspects of sport and commercial fishing.
rec.parks.theme	Entertainment theme parks.
rec.pets	Pets, pet care, and household animals in general.
rec.pets.birds	The culture and care of indoor birds.

News Group	Description
rec.pets.cats	Discussion about domestic cats.
rec.pets.dogs	Any and all subjects relating to dogs as pets.
rec.pets.herp	Reptiles, amphibians, and other exotic vivarium pets.
rec.photo	Hobbyists interested in photography.
rec.puzzles	Puzzles, problems, and quizzes.
rec.puzzles.crosswords	Making and playing gridded word puzzles.
rec.pyrotechnics	Fireworks, rocketry, safety, and other topics.
rec.radio.amateur.antenna	Antennas: theory, techniques, and construction.
rec.radio.amateur.digital.misc	Packet radio and other digital radio modes.
rec.radio.amateur.equipment	All about production amateur radio hardware.
rec.radio.amateur.homebrew	Amateur radio construction and experimentation.
rec.radio.amateur.misc	Amateur radio practices, contests, events, rules, etc.
rec.radio.amateur.policy	Radio use and regulation policy.
rec.radio.amateur.space	Amateur radio transmissions through space.
rec.radio.broadcasting	Local area broadcast radio. (Moderated)
rec.radio.cb	Citizens band radio.
rec.radio.info	Informational postings related to radio. (Moderated)

(continues)

News Group	Description
rec.radio.noncomm	Topics relating to non-commercial radio.
rec.radio.scanner	"Utility" broadcasting traffic above 30 MHz.
rec.radio.shortwave	Shortwave radio enthusiasts.
rec.radio.swap	Offers to trade and swap radio equipment.
rec.railroad	For fans of real trains, ferroequinologists.
rec.roller-coaster	Roller coasters and other amusement park rides.
rec.running	Running for enjoyment, sport, exercise, etc.
rec.scouting	Scouting youth organizations worldwide.
rec.scuba	Hobbyists interested in SCUBA diving.
rec.skate	Ice skating and roller skating.
rec.skiing	Hobbyists interested in snow skiing.
rec.skydiving	Hobbyists interested in skydiving.
rec.sport.baseball	Discussion about baseball.
rec.sport.baseball.college	Baseball on the collegiate level.
rec.sport.baseball.fantasy	Rotisserie (fantasy) baseball play.
rec.sport.basketball.college	Hoops on the collegiate level.
rec.sport.basketball.misc	Discussion about basketball.
rec.sport.basketball.pro	Talk of professional basketball.
rec.sport.cricket	Discussion about the sport of cricket.

News Group	Description
rec.sport.cricket.scores	Scores from cricket matches around the globe. (Moderated)
rec.sport.disc	Discussion of flying-disc-based sports.
rec.sport.fencing	All aspects of swordplay.
rec.sport.football.australian	Discussion of Australian (rules) football.
rec.sport.football.canadian	All about Canadian rules football.
rec.sport.football.college	U.S.-style college football.
rec.sport.football.fantasy	Rotisserie (fantasy) football play.
rec.sport.football.misc	Discussion about U.S.-style football.
rec.sport.football.pro	U.S.-style professional football.
rec.sport.golf	Discussion about all aspects of golfing.
rec.sport.hockey	Discussion about ice hockey.
rec.sport.hockey.field	Discussion of the sport of field hockey.
rec.sport.misc	Spectator sports.
rec.sport.olympics	All aspects of the Olympic Games.
rec.sport.paintball	Discussing all aspects of the survival game Paintball.
rec.sport.pro-wrestling	Discussion about professional wrestling.
rec.sport.rowing	Crew for competition or fitness.
rec.sport.rugby	Discussion about the game of rugby.

(continues)

News Group	Description
rec.sport.soccer	Discussion about soccer (Association Football).
rec.sport.swimming	Training for and competing in swimming events.
rec.sport.table-tennis	Things related to table tennis (aka Ping-Pong).
rec.sport.tennis	Things related to the sport of tennis.
rec.sport.triathlon	Discussing all aspects of multievent sports.
rec.sport.volleyball	Discussion about volleyball.
rec.sport.waterski	Waterskiing and other boat-towed activities.
rec.travel	Traveling all over the world.
rec.travel.air	Airline travel around the world.
rec.travel.marketplace	Tickets and accommodations wanted and for sale.
rec.video	Video and video components.
rec.video.cable-tv	Technical and regulatory issues of cable television.
rec.video.production	Making professional-quality video productions.
rec.video.releases	Prerecorded video releases on laserdisc and videotape.
rec.video.satellite	Getting shows via satellite.
rec.windsurfing	Riding the waves as a hobby.
rec.woodworking	Hobbyists interested in woodworking.
relcom.ads	Non-commercial ads. (Moderated)

News Group	Description
relcom.archives	Messages about new items on archive sites.
relcom.archives.d	Discussions on file servers, archives.
relcom.bbs	BBS news.
relcom.bbs.list	Lists of Russian-language BBSs. (Moderated)
relcom.commerce.audio-video	Audio and video equipment.
relcom.commerce.chemical	Chemical production.
relcom.commerce.computers	Computer hardware.
relcom.commerce.construction	Construction materials and equipment.
relcom.commerce.consume	Cosmetics, perfumes, dresses, shoes.
relcom.commerce.energy	Gas, coal, oil, fuel, generators, etc.
relcom.commerce.estate	Real estate.
relcom.commerce.food	Food and drinks (including alcoholic).
relcom.commerce.food.drinks	Spirits and soft drinks.
relcom.commerce.food.sweet	Sweets and sugar.
relcom.commerce.household	All for house—furniture, freezers, ovens, etc.
relcom.commerce.infoserv	Information services.
relcom.commerce.jobs	Jobs offered/wanted.
relcom.commerce.machinery	Machinery, plant equipment.
relcom.commerce.medicine	Medical services, equipment, drugs.

(continues)

News Group	Description
relcom.commerce.metals	Metals and metal products.
relcom.commerce.money	Credits, deposits, currency.
relcom.commerce.orgtech	Office equipment.
relcom.commerce.other	Miscellanea.
relcom.commerce.software	Software.
relcom.commerce.stocks	Stocks and bonds.
relcom.commerce.talk	Discussions about commercial groups.
relcom.commerce.tobacco	Cigarettes and tobacco.
relcom.commerce.tour	Tourism, leisure, and entertainment opportunities.
relcom.commerce.transport	Vehicles and spare parts.
relcom.comp.animation	Discussions on computer animation programs. (Moderated)
relcom.comp.binaries	Binary codes of computer programs. (Moderated)
relcom.comp.dbms.foxpro	FoxPro database development system.
relcom.comp.demo	Demo versions of various software. (Moderated)
relcom.comp.demo.d	Discussions on demonstration programs.
relcom.comp.lang.pascal	Using Pascal programming language.
relcom.comp.os.os2	FidoNet area, OS/2 operational system.
relcom.comp.os.vms	VMS operational system.

News Group	Description
relcom.comp.os.windows	FidoNet area, MS-Windows operational system.
relcom.comp.os.windows.prog	FidoNet area, programming under MS-Windows.
relcom.comp.sources.d	Discussions on sources.
relcom.comp.sources.misc	Software sources. (Moderated)
relcom.currency	Money matters in the ex-USSR.
relcom.exnet	Discussions on ExNet electronic exchange.
relcom.exnet.quote	ExNet quotes.
relcom.expo	Exhibitions and fairs announcements and reviews. (Moderated)
relcom.fido.flirt	FidoNet, just talking of love.
relcom.fido.ru.hacker	FidoNet, hackers and crackers (legal!).
relcom.fido.ru.modem	Internetwork discussion on modems.
relcom.fido.ru.networks	Internetwork discussion of global nets.
relcom.fido.ru.strack	FidoNet, digitized sound.
relcom.fido.ru.unix	Internetwork challenge to OS UNIX.
relcom.fido.su.books	FidoNet, for book readers and lovers.
relcom.fido.su.c-c++	FidoNet, C and C++ languages.
relcom.fido.su.dbms	FidoNet, database management systems.
relcom.fido.su.general	FidoNet, about everything and nothing.

(continues)

News Group	Description
relcom.fido.su.hardw	FidoNet, computer hardware.
relcom.fido.su.magic	FidoNet, magic and occult sciences.
relcom.fido.su.softw	FidoNet, software in general.
relcom.fido.su.tolkien	FidoNet, creations of J.R.R Tolkien.
relcom.fido.su.virus	FidoNet, viruses and vaccines.
relcom.humor	Ha-ha-ha. Jokes, you know them, funny.
relcom.infomarket.quote	Ex-USSR exchanges' quotes /ASMP/. (Moderated)
relcom.infomarket.talk	Discussion on market development /ASMP/. (Moderated)
relcom.jusinf	Information on laws by "Justicinform." (Moderated)
relcom.kids	About kids.
relcom.lan	Internetwork discussion on local area networks.
relcom.maps	Relcom maps.
relcom.msdos	MS-DOS software.
relcom.music	Music lovers.
relcom.netnews	Announcements and articles important for all netters.
relcom.netnews.big	General BIG articles.
relcom.newusers	Q & A of new Relcom users.
relcom.penpals	To find friends, colleagues, etc.
relcom.politics	Political discussions.

News Group	Description
relcom.postmasters	For RELCOM postmasters, official. (Moderated)
relcom.postmasters.d	Discussion of postmaster's troubles and bright ideas.
relcom.relarn.general	Scientific academical subnet RELARN: general issues. (Moderated)
relcom.renews	Net magazine RENEWS. (Moderated)
relcom.spbnews	Political and economic news digest by SPB-News Agency. (Moderated)
relcom.talk	Unfettered talk.
relcom.tcpip	TCP/IP protocols and their implementation.
relcom.terms	Discussion of various terms and terminology.
relcom.test	Wow, does it really work?
relcom.wtc	Commercial proposals of World Trade Centers.
relcom.x	X Window discussion.
sci.aeronautics	The science of aeronautics and related technology. (Moderated)
sci.aeronautics.airliners	Airliner technology. (Moderated)
sci.answers	Repository for periodic USENET articles. (Moderated)
sci.anthropology	All aspects of studying humankind.
sci.aquaria	Only scientifically oriented postings about aquaria.
sci.archaeology	Studying antiquities of the world.

(continues)

News Group	Description
sci.astro	Astronomy discussions and information.
sci.astro.fits	Issues related to the Flexible Image Transport System.
sci.astro.hubble	Processing Hubble Space Telescope data. (Moderated)
sci.astro.planetarium	Discussion of planetariums.
sci.bio	Biology and related sciences.
sci.bio.ecology	Ecological research.
sci.chem	Chemistry and related sciences.
sci.chem.organomet	Organometallic chemistry.
sci.classics	Studying classical history, languages, art, and more.
sci.cognitive	Perception, memory, judgment, and reasoning.
sci.comp-aided	The use of computers as tools in scientific research.
sci.cryonics	Theory and practice of biostasis, suspended animation.
sci.crypt	Different methods of data en/decryption.
sci.data.formats	Modelling, storage, and retrieval of scientific data.
sci.econ	The science of economics.
sci.econ.research	Research in all fields of economics. (Moderated)
sci.edu	The science of education.
sci.electronics	Circuits, theory, electrons, and discussions.

News Group	Description
sci.energy	Discussions about energy, science, and technology.
sci.energy.hydrogen	All about hydrogen as an alternative fuel.
sci.engr	Technical discussions about engineering tasks.
sci.engr.advanced-tv	HDTV/DATV standards, formats, equipment, practices.
sci.engr.biomed	Discussing the field of biomedical engineering.
sci.engr.chem	All aspects of chemical engineering.
sci.engr.civil	Topics related to civil engineering.
sci.engr.control	The engineering of control systems.
sci.engr.manufacturing	Manufacturing technology.
sci.engr.mech	The field of mechanical engineering.
sci.environment	Discussions about the environment and ecology.
sci.fractals	Objects of non-integral dimension and other chaos.
sci.geo.fluids	Discussion of geophysical fluid dynamics.
sci.geo.geology	Discussion of solid earth sciences.
sci.geo.meteorology	Discussion of meteorology and related topics.
sci.image.processing	Scientific image processing and analysis.

(continues)

News Group	Description
sci.lang	Natural languages, communication, etc.
sci.lang.japan	The Japanese language, both spoken and written.
sci.life-extension	Slowing, stopping, or reversing the aging process.
sci.logic	Logic—math, philosophy, and computational aspects.
sci.materials	All aspects of materials engineering.
sci.math	Mathematical discussions and pursuits.
sci.math.research	Discussion of current mathematical research. (Moderated)
sci.math.symbolic	Symbolic algebra discussion.
sci.med	Medicine and its related products and regulations.
sci.med.aids	AIDS: treatment, pathology/biology of HIV, prevention. (Moderated)
sci.med.dentistry	Dentally related topics; all about teeth.
sci.med.nutrition	Physiological impacts of diet.
sci.med.occupational	Preventing, detecting, and treating occupational injuries.
sci.med.pharmacy	The teaching and practice of pharmacy.
sci.med.physics	Issues of physics in medical testing/care.
sci.med.telemedicine	Clinical consulting through computer networks.

News Group	Description
sci.military	Discussion about science and the military. (Moderated)
sci.misc	Short-lived discussions on subjects in the sciences.
sci.nanotech	Self-reproducing molecular-scale machines. (Moderated)
sci.nonlinear	Chaotic systems and other nonlinear scientific study.
sci.op-research	Research, teaching, and application of operations research.
sci.optics	Discussion relating to the science of optics.
sci.philosophy.tech	Technical philosophy: math, science, logic, etc.
sci.physics	Physical laws, properties, etc.
sci.physics.accelerators	Particle accelerators and the physics of beams.
sci.physics.fusion	Info on fusion, especially "cold" fusion.
sci.physics.research	Current physics research. (Moderated)
sci.polymers	All aspects of polymer science.
sci.psychology	Topics related to psychology.
sci.psychology.digest	PSYCOLOQUY: Refereed Psychology Journal and Newsletter. (Moderated)
sci.research	Research methods, funding, ethics, and whatever.
sci.research.careers	Issues relevant to careers in scientific research.

(continues)

News Group	Description
sci.skeptic	Skeptics discussing pseudoscience.
sci.space	Space, space programs, space-related research, etc.
sci.space.news	Announcements of space-related news items. (Moderated)
sci.space.shuttle	The space shuttle and the STS program.
sci.stat.consult	Statistical consulting.
sci.stat.edu	Statistics education.
sci.stat.math	Statistics from a strictly mathematical viewpoint.
sci.systems	The theory and application of systems science.
sci.techniques.xtallography	The field of crystallography.
sci.virtual-worlds	Virtual Reality—technology and culture. (Moderated)
sci.virtual-worlds.apps	Current and future uses of virtual-worlds technology. (Moderated)
soc.answers	Repository for periodic USENET articles. (Moderated)
soc.bi	Discussions of bisexuality.
soc.college	College, college activities, campus life, etc.
soc.college.grad	General issues related to graduate schools.
soc.college.gradinfo	Information about graduate schools.
soc.college.org.aiesec	The Int'l Assoc. of Business and Commerce Students.

News Group	Description
soc.college.teaching-asst	Issues affecting collegiate teaching assistants.
soc.couples	Discussions for couples (cf. soc.singles).
soc.couples.intercultural	Intercultural and interracial relationships.
soc.culture.afghanistan	Discussion of the Afghan society.
soc.culture.african	Discussions about Africa and things African.
soc.culture.african.american	Discussions about Afro-American issues.
soc.culture.arabic	Technological and cultural issues, not politics.
soc.culture.argentina	All about life in Argentina.
soc.culture.asean	Countries of the Association of SE Asian Nations.
soc.culture.asian.american	Issues and discussion about Asian-Americans.
soc.culture.australian	Australian culture and society.
soc.culture.austria	Austria and its people.
soc.culture.baltics	People of the Baltic states.
soc.culture.bangladesh	Issues and discussion about Bangladesh.
soc.culture.bosna-herzgvna	The independent state of Bosnia and Herzegovina.
soc.culture.brazil	Talking about the people and country of Brazil.
soc.culture.british	Issues about Britain and those of British descent.
soc.culture.bulgaria	Discussing Bulgarian society.

(continues)

News Group	Description
soc.culture.canada	Discussions of Canada and its people.
soc.culture.caribbean	Life in the Caribbean.
soc.culture.celtic	Irish, Scottish, Breton, Cornish, Manx, and Welsh.
soc.culture.chile	All about Chile and its people.
soc.culture.china	About China and Chinese culture.
soc.culture.croatia	The lives of people of Croatia.
soc.culture.czecho-slovak	Bohemian, Slovak, Moravian, and Silesian life.
soc.culture.europe	Discussing all aspects of all-European society.
soc.culture.filipino	Group about the Filipino culture.
soc.culture.french	French culture, history, and related discussions.
soc.culture.german	Discussions about German culture and history.
soc.culture.greek	Group about Greeks.
soc.culture.hongkong	Discussions pertaining to Hong Kong.
soc.culture.indian	Group for discussion about India and things Indian.
soc.culture.indian.telugu	The culture of the Telugu people of India.
soc.culture.indonesia	All about the Indonesian nation.
soc.culture.iranian	Discussions about Iran and things Iranian/Persian.
soc.culture.israel	Israel and Israelis.

News Group	Description
soc.culture.italian	The Italian people and their culture.
soc.culture.japan	Everything Japanese, except the Japanese language.
soc.culture.jewish	Jewish culture and religion (cf. talk.politics.mideast).
soc.culture.korean	Discussions about Korea and things Korean.
soc.culture.laos	Cultural and social aspects of Laos.
soc.culture.latin-america	Topics about Latin America.
soc.culture.lebanon	Discussion about things Lebanese.
soc.culture.maghreb	North African society and culture.
soc.culture.magyar	The Hungarian people and their culture.
soc.culture.malaysia	All about Malaysian society.
soc.culture.mexican	Discussion of Mexico's society.
soc.culture.misc	Group for discussion about other cultures.
soc.culture.native	Aboriginal people around the world.
soc.culture.nepal	Discussion of people and things in and from Nepal.
soc.culture.netherlands	People from the Netherlands and Belgium.
soc.culture.new-zealand	Discussion of topics related to New Zealand.
soc.culture.nordic	Discussion about culture up north.

(continues)

News Group	Description
soc.culture.pakistan	Topics of discussion about Pakistan.
soc.culture.palestine	Palestinian people, culture, and politics.
soc.culture.peru	All about the people of Peru.
soc.culture.polish	Polish culture, Polish past, and Polish politics.
soc.culture.portuguese	Discussion of the people of Portugal.
soc.culture.romanian	Discussion of Romanian and Moldavian people.
soc.culture.scientists	Cultural issues about scientists and scientific projects.
soc.culture.singapore	The past, present, and future of Singapore.
soc.culture.soviet	Topics relating to Russian or Soviet culture.
soc.culture.spain	Discussion of culture on the Iberian peninsula.
soc.culture.sri-lanka	Things and people from Sri Lanka.
soc.culture.taiwan	Discussion about things Taiwanese.
soc.culture.tamil	Tamil language, history, and culture.
soc.culture.thai	Thai people and their culture.
soc.culture.turkish	Discussion about things Turkish.
soc.culture.ukrainian	The lives and times of the Ukrainian people.
soc.culture.uruguay	Discussions of Uruguay for those at home and abroad.

News Group	Description
soc.culture.usa	The culture of the United States of America.
soc.culture.venezuela	Discussion of topics related to Venezuela.
soc.culture.vietnamese	Issues and discussions of Vietnamese culture.
soc.culture.yugoslavia	Discussions of Yugoslavia and its people.
soc.feminism	Discussion of feminism and feminist issues. (Moderated)
soc.history	Discussions of things historical.
soc.libraries.talk	Discussing all aspects of libraries.
soc.men	Issues related to men, their problems, and relationships.
soc.misc	Socially oriented topics not in other groups.
soc.motss	Issues pertaining to homosexuality.
soc.net-people	Announcements, requests, etc., about people on the net.
soc.penpals	In search of net.friendships.
soc.politics	Political problems, systems, solutions. (Moderated)
soc.politics.arms-d	Arms discussion digest. (Moderated)
soc.religion.bahai	Discussion of the Baha'i faith. (Moderated)
soc.religion.christian	Christianity and related topics. (Moderated)
soc.religion.christian.bible-study	Examining the Holy Bible. (Moderated)

(continues)

News Group	Description
soc.religion.eastern	Discussions of Eastern religions. (Moderated)
soc.religion.islam	Discussions of the Islamic faith. (Moderated)
soc.religion.quaker	The Religious Society of Friends.
soc.religion.shamanism	Discussion of the full range of shamanic experience. (Moderated)
soc.rights.human	Human rights and activism (e.g., Amnesty International).
soc.roots	Discussing genealogy and genealogical matters.
soc.singles	News group for single people, their activities, etc.
soc.veterans	Social issues relating to military veterans.
soc.women	Issues related to women, their problems, and relationships.
talk.abortion	All sorts of discussions and arguments on abortion.
talk.answers	Repository for periodic USENET articles. (Moderated)
talk.bizarre	The unusual, bizarre, curious, and often stupid.
talk.environment	Discussing the state of the environment and what to do.
talk.origins	Evolution versus creationism (sometimes hot!).
talk.philosophy.misc	Philosophical musings on all topics.
talk.politics.animals	The use and/or abuse of animals.

News Group	Description
talk.politics.china	Discussion of political issues related to China.
talk.politics.crypto	The relation between cryptography and government.
talk.politics.drugs	The politics of drug issues.
talk.politics.guns	The politics of firearm ownership and (mis)use.
talk.politics.medicine	The politics and ethics involved with health care.
talk.politics.mideast	Discussion and debate over Middle Eastern events.
talk.politics.misc	Political discussions and ravings of all kinds.
talk.politics.soviet	Discussion of Soviet politics, domestic and foreign.
talk.politics.space	Non-technical issues affecting space exploration.
talk.politics.theory	Theory of politics and political systems.
talk.politics.tibet	The politics of Tibet and the Tibetan people.
talk.rape	Discussions on stopping rape; not to be cross-posted.
talk.religion.misc	Religious, ethical, and moral implications.
talk.religion.newage	Esoteric and minority religions and philosophies.
talk.rumors	For the posting of rumors.
u3b.config	3B distribution configuration.
u3b.misc	3B miscellaneous discussions.

(continues)

News Group	Description
u3b.sources	Sources for AT&T 3B systems.
u3b.tech	3B technical discussions.
u3b.test	3B distribution testing.
vmsnet.admin	Administration of the VMSnet news groups.
vmsnet.alpha	Discussion about Alpha AXP architecture, systems, porting, etc.
vmsnet.announce	General announcements of interest to all. (Moderated)
vmsnet.announce.newusers	Orientation info for new users. (Moderated)
vmsnet.databases.rdb	DEC's Rdb relational DBMS and related topics.
vmsnet.decus.journal	The DECUServe Journal. (Moderated)
vmsnet.decus.lugs	Discussion of DECUS Local User Groups and related issues.
vmsnet.employment	Jobs sought/offered, workplace- and employment-related issues.
vmsnet.infosystems.gopher	Gopher software for VMS, gatewayed to VMSGopher-L.
vmsnet.infosystems.misc	Miscellaneous infosystem software for VMS (e.g., WAIS, WWW).
vmsnet.internals	VMS internals, MACRO-32, Bliss, etc., gatewayed to MACRO32 list.
vmsnet.mail.misc	Other electronic mail software.
vmsnet.mail.mx	MX e-mail system, gatewayed to the MX mailing list.

News Group	Description
vmsnet.mail.pmdf	PMDF e-mail system, gatewayed to the ipmdf mailing list.
vmsnet.misc	General VMS topics not covered elsewhere.
vmsnet.networks.desktop.misc	Other desktop integration software.
vmsnet.networks.desktop.pathworks	DEC Pathworks desktop integration software.
vmsnet.networks.management.decmcc	DECmcc and related software.
vmsnet.networks.management.misc	Other network management solutions.
vmsnet.networks.misc	General networking topics not covered elsewhere.
vmsnet.networks.tcp-ip.cmu-tek	CMU-TEK TCP/IP package, gatewayed to cmu-tek-tcp+@andrew.cmu.edu.
vmsnet.networks.tcp-ip.misc	Other TCP/IP solutions for VMS.
vmsnet.networks.tcp-ip.multinet	TGV's Multinet TCP/IP, gatewayed to info-multinet.
vmsnet.networks.tcp-ip.tcpware	Discussion of Process Software's TCPWARE TCP/IP software.
vmsnet.networks.tcp-ip.ucx	DEC's VMS/Ultrix Connection (or TCP/IP services for VMS) product.
vmsnet.networks.tcp-ip.wintcp	The Wollongong Group's WIN-TCP TCP/IP software.
vmsnet.pdp-11	PDP-11 hardware and software, gatewayed to info-pdp11.
vmsnet.sources	Source code postings only. (Moderated)
vmsnet.sources.d	Discussion about or requests for sources.

(continues)

News Group	Description
vmsnet.sources.games	Recreational software postings.
vmsnet.sysmgt	VMS system management.
vmsnet.test	Test messages.
vmsnet.tpu	TPU language and applications, gatewayed to info-tpu.
vmsnet.uucp	DECUS UUCP software, gatewayed to vmsnet mailing list.
vmsnet.vms-posix	Discussion about VMS POSIX.

Part II

Publicly Accessible Mailing List

Although USENET may be a wonderful way to exchange information with others on your favorite topics, it certainly isn't the only means available. Also, your service provider may not allow access to the USENET, or at least not all the news groups you may be interested in (the news groups currently generate more than 1.5 gigabytes of data per month). Or you may not have access to news reader software on your machine.

Another popular way to exchange information via the Internet is the mailing list. Internet-based mailing lists work pretty much like their off-line counterparts (except that the possibility of your address being sold to an annoying telemarketer or persistent charity is much lower). Simply put, you sign up for a mailing list by sending an e-mail message to a designated address, and you're put on the list. When you're on the list, you'll receive regular, automatic e-mail messages on your topic.

As usual, a good part of the trick to getting on a mailing list is finding out whether one exists for your topic, and who to send your sign-up message to. That's the information that the Publicly Accessible Mailing List (PAML) provides. The PAML provides information on more than 500 mailing lists.

The format for the PAML is quite straightforward. List entries are in alphabetical order based on topic addressed. Each entry in the list has a field for contact information, and a description of the purpose of the mailing list. Suppose that you want to subscribe to a mailing list that covers Microsoft's Access database product. In the PAML, you would find the following:

```
MS-Access
    Contact: MS-ACCESS-REQUEST@EUNET.CO.AT (Martin Hilger)


    Purpose: An unmoderated list for MS Access topics, including

    Access Basic questions, reviews, rumors, etc.  Open to owners,

    users, prospective users, and the merely curious.


    All requests to be added to or deleted from this list, problems,

    questions, etc., should be sent to

    MS-ACCESS-REQUEST@EUNET.CO.AT.
```

As with USENET news groups, some mailing lists are moderated to ensure that the material disseminated to mailing list members fits with the purpose of the group.

> **Note**
>
> Although the following list has come directly from the Internet, some descriptions have been edited for content and consistency.

12step

Contact: muller@camp.rutgers.edu (Mike Muller)

Purpose: To discuss/share experiences about 12-step programs such as Alcoholics Anonymous, Overeaters Anonymous, Al-Anon, ACA, etc. Questions are answered. Please include a phone number in case of trouble establishing an e-mail path.

30something

Contact: 30something-request@fuggles.acc.virginia.edu (Marc Rouleau)

Purpose: To discuss the TV show by the same name, including actors, episodes, plots, characters, etc.

386users

Contact: 386users-request@udel.edu (William Davidsen Jr.)

Purpose: To discuss 80386-based computers and all hardware and software that is either 386-specific or has special interest concerning the 386.

3d

Contact: jhbercovitz@lbl.gov (John Bercovitz)

Purpose: To discuss 3-D (stereo) photography. General info, hints, experiences, equipment, techniques, and stereo "happenings." Anyone interested is welcome to join.

900#

Contact: bbl7597@ritvax.isc.rit.edu (Bruce B. LeRoy)

Purpose: To discuss issues in running a 900 telephone number business. Membership restricted to 900# information providers.

90210

Contact: 90210-request@ferkel.ucsb.edu (Jim Lick)

Purpose: Discussion of the Fox TV show *Beverly Hills, 90210*.

ABC

Contact: abc-list-request@cwi.nl (Steven Pemberton)

Purpose: To discuss the ABC programming language and its implementations. Information on ABC is available in *The ABC Programmer's Handbook*, Leo Geurts, et al., Prentice Hall 1990; "An Alternative Simple Language and Environment for PCs," Steven Pemberton, *IEEE Software*, Vol. 4, No. 1, January 1987, pp. 56-64; by ftp from mcsun.eu.net in file programming/languages/abc/abc.intro; and by mail-server from info-server@hp4nl.nluug.nl: send two-line message: request programming/languages/abc topic abc.intro.

Accordion

Contact: accordion@marie.stat.uga.edu

Purpose: For individuals with an interest in accordions and accordion music to communicate over the Internet. This is an unmoderated mailing list accessible to everyone with a connected computer. All aspects of acquiring, playing, collecting, repairing, and discography of the accordion are fair topics of conversation. Accordions of all types and designs, including concertinas and button accordions, are discussed. The general philosophy is that we can all learn a great deal if we share what we know with the other members of the e-mail list.

ACTION-ALERT

Contact: action-alert-request@vector.intercon.com (Ron Buckmire) (David Casti)

Purpose: To provide the LGBTF community a resource by which we can respond to attacks on our community that are occurring anywhere.

ACTION-ALERT is moderated and accepts only postings that include a brief summary of the situation requiring the ACTION along with contact information that members of the ACTION-ALERT distribution list can use to take ACTION! Be sure to include fax numbers and e-mail addresses if at all possible. Messages that do not address a specific issue for ACTION will be returned to the sender.

ACTIV-L

Contact: listserv@mizzou1.missouri.edu

Purpose: Concerned with peace, empowerment, justice, and environmental issues. To subscribe, send the message SUB ACTIV-L *yourfullname* to listserv@mizzou1.missouri.edu.

Act-Up

Contact: act-up-request@world.std.com (Lenard Diggins)

Purpose: To discuss the work being done by the various Act-Up chapters worldwide, to announce events, to exchange ideas related to AIDS activism, and, more broadly, to discuss the politics of AIDS and health care.

ADA-Law

Contact: wtm@bunker.afd.olivetti.com

Purpose: Discussion of the Americans with Disabilities Act (ADA) and other disability-related legislation, not only in the United States but other countries as well. To subscribe, send mail to listserv@vm1.nodak.edu with a message body of this form: Subscribe ADA-Law *yourname*, or send mail to wtm@bunker.afd.olivetti.com.

Add-Parents

Contact: `listserv@n7kbt.rain.com`

Purpose: For providing support and information to parents of children with Attention Deficit/Hyperactivity Disorder. To subscribe, send mail to `listserv@n7kbt.rain.com` with a message body of this form: `subscribe add-parents` *yourfullname*.

Adoptees

Contact: `listserv@ucsd.edu`

Purpose: A forum for discussion among adult adoptees of any topic related to adoption. It is not intended to be a general discussion forum for adoption among non-adoptees.

To subscribe, mail to `listserv@ucsd.edu` with `subscribe` *youraccount@yoursubdomain.yourdomain* `adoptees` in the body of the text.

Adoption

Contact: `adoption-request@think.com`

Purpose: To discuss anything and everything connected with adoption.

AFRICA-N

Contact: `frabbani@epas.utoronto.ca` (Faraz Rabbani)

Purpose: A moderated mailing list dedicated to the exchange of news and information on Africa from many sources.

To subscribe, e-mail `listserv@utoronto.bitnet`, and send the following one-line message (the subject header is ignored):

```
SUBSCRIBE AFRICA-N yourfullname
```

Aeronautics

Contact: aeronautics-request@rascal.ics.utexas.edu

Purpose: A news-to-mail feed of the sci.aeronautics news group. A moderated discussion group dealing with atmospheric flight, specifically: aerodynamics, flying qualities, simulation, structures, systems, propulsion, and design human factors.

Subscribers can participate in real time with the main group.

AF

Contact: af-request@crl.dec.com

Purpose: Discussion of AudioFile, a client/server, network-transparent, device-independent audio system.

Agenda-Users

Contact: agenda-users-request@newcastle.ac.uk

Purpose: A new mailing list for users of the Microwriter Agenda hand-held computer.

Agmodels-I

Contact: jp@unl.edu (Jerome Pier)

Purpose: A forum for the discussion of agricultural simulation models of all types. Plant growth, micro-meteorological, soil hydrology, transport, economic, farm systems, and many other models may be discussed. Problems and advantages of computer simulation models for agriculture as well as the role played by models in the future of agriculture may also be discussed. The list is unmoderated. To subscribe, send e-mail to listserv@unl.edu, containing the one-line message sub agmodels-1 *yourname*.

AIDS

Contact: aids-request@cs.ucla.edu (Daniel R. Greening)

Purpose: A distribution list for people who can't read sci.med.aids. This list covers predominantly medical issues of AIDS, with some discussion of political and social issues. Postings to AIDSNEWS and Health InfoCom News mailing lists are also carried.

Unlike info-aids, postings to aids@cs.ucla.edu are *non-confidential*. The average number of postings to aids is about two per day. The average size of articles is very large (statistics, news summaries, etc.). sci.med.aids and aids@cs.ucla.edu are moderated. (See also the info-aids mailing list.)

Aikido-L

Contact: listserv@psuvm.psu.edu (Gerry Santoro)

Purpose: Discussion and information exchange regarding the Japanese martial art Aikido.

Send subscription requests to listserv@psuvm.psu.edu as electronic mail with the following in the body of the mail:

    // JOB SUBSCRIBE AIKIDO-L yourfullname// EOJ

This is based on an IBM LISTSERV.

Airplane-Clubs

Contact: airplane-clubs-request@dg-rtp.dg.com (Matthew Waugh)

Purpose: To discuss all matters relating to the management and operation of groups operating aircraft.

Ajax Amsterdam

Contact: vdpoll@fwi.uva.nl

Purpose: For fans or anyone else who's interested.

Alife

Contact: alife-request@cognet.ucla.edu

Purpose: For communications regarding artificial life, a formative interdisciplinary field involving computer science, the natural sciences, mathematics, medicine, and others. The recent book *Artificial Life*, Christopher Langton, ed., Addison Wesley, 1989, introduces the scope of artificial life as a field of study.

Alife was chartered in February 1990 at the Second Artificial Life Workshop, held in Santa Fe and organized by the Center for Nonlinear Studies at the Los Alamos National Laboratory and the Santa Fe Institute. The list is intended primarily for low-volume, high-content scientific correspondence and as a publicly accessible forum for interested members of the public. Membership as of July 1990 includes over 1,200 addresses on four continents. There is an ftp-accessible archives/repository of past traffic, software, and papers.

The list is maintained by the Artificial Life Research Group, Computer Science Department, Lindley Hall 101, Indiana University, Bloomington, IN 47405. Redistribution of the list is conditional, to minimize any misunderstanding or exaggeration concerning this new area of study.

Allman

Contact: allman-request@world.std.com (Eric Budke)

Purpose: The discussion of the Allman Brothers Band and its derivatives. Some tape trading, tour info, and whatever else happens to pop up.

Alpha-OSF-Managers

Contact: alpha-osf-managers-request@ornl.gov

majordomo@ornl.gov

Purpose: Fast-turnaround troubleshooting tool for managers of DEC Alpha AXP systems running OSF/1.

Alspa

Contact: alspa-users-request@ssyx.ucsc.edu (Brad Allen)

Purpose: Discussion by owners/users of the CP/M machines made by (the now defunct) Alspa Computer, Inc.

Alternates

Contact: alternates-request@ns1.rutgers.edu

Purpose: For people who advocate and/or practice an open sexual lifestyle. Its members are primarily bisexual men and women, and their SOs. Mail.alternates is intended as a forum and support group for adult men and women who espouse their freedom of choice and imagination in human sexual relations, no matter what their orientations. Those who are offended by frank and uninhibited discussions relating to sexual issues should not subscribe.

AltInst

Contact: altinst-request@cs.cmu.edu (Robin Hanson)

Purpose: You are invited to join AltInst, a new e-mail list on Alternative Institutions. AltInst is solely for proposing and critiquing alternative institutions for various walks of life. Alternative ways to run conversations, countries, households, markets, offices, romances, schools, etc., are all fair game.

AltInst is open to folks from any political persuasion, but general political flaming/discussion is forbidden. Skip the theory and just tell us your vision of how something could be different and how that would work. Many of us are truly excited to hear about creative, well-considered suggestions, no matter what the source, but quickly bored by both ideological is-too/is-not flaming and partisan rah-rahs for anything "politically correct" in some camp.

Amazons International

Contact: amazons-request@math.uio.no (Thomas Gramstad)

Purpose: An electronic digest newsletter for and about Amazons (physically and psychologically strong assertive women who are not afraid to break free from traditional ideas about gender roles, femininity, and the female physique) and their friends and lovers. Amazons International is dedicated to the image of the female hero in fiction as it is expressed in art and literature, in the physiques and feats of female athletes, and in sexual values and practices; and provides information, discussion, and a supportive environment for these values and issues. Gender-role traditionalists and others who are opposed to Amazon ideals should not subscribe.

Amend2-Discuss, Amend2-Info

Contact: majordomo@cs.colorado.edu

Purpose: Colorado voted in an amendment to their state constitution that revokes any existing gay/lesbian/bisexual civil rights legislation and prohibits the drafting of any new legislation. The amendment was spearheaded by a right-wing organization named Colorado Family Values (CFV). It is our understanding that they have no intention of stopping their campaign here.

Two mail/news groups have been created in response to this discriminatory amendment.

> Amend2-discuss is for people who are discussing the implications and issues surrounding the passing of amendment 2.
>
> Amend2-info is a moderated mailing list for people interested in information on the implication and issues of amendment 2.

Sending mail to either mailing list has the effect of also posting the message to the corresponding shadow news group. We encourage people to use the mailing list address when disseminating information so that those people who are on the mailing list but who do not have access to news can benefit from the discussion/information.

To subscribe to either list, send mail to majordomo@cs.colorado.edu, where the body of the message is subscribe *listname*.

America

Contact: subscribe@xamiga.linet.org

Purpose: For people interested in how the United States is dealing with foreign trade policies, congressional status, and other inside information about the government that is freely distributable. This list has monthly postings that are generally in large batches, with posts exceeding a few hundred lines. America tends to receive mail only a few times per month and is a moderated group. An unmoderated group is also available.

Send subscription requests to subscribe@xamiga.linet.org, using this format:

> #america *youraccount@yoursubdomain.yourdomain*;

American Hockey League

Contact: ahl-news-request@andrew.cmu.edu

Purpose: For people interested in discussing and following the American Hockey League.

AM/FM

Contact: listserv@orbital.demon.co.uk

Purpose: For the AM/FM Online Edition, a monthly compilation of news stories concerning the U.K. radio industry. To subscribe to the list, write to listserv@orbital.demon.co.uk with subscribe amfm *yourfullname* as the first line in the message body, replacing *yourfullname* with your real name, not your e-mail address.

Amiga CDROM

Contact: cdrom-list-request@ben.com

Purpose: For Amigans who use or are interested in CD-ROM drives and discs. Questions or comments about the list can be sent to ben@ben.com. Questions about CD-ROMs (installation, troubleshooting, and so forth) should be sent to the list.

AMOS

Contact: subscribe@xamiga.linet.org

Purpose: For the AMOS programming language on Amiga computers. Features source, bug reports, and help from users around the world, but mainly European users. Most posts will be in English, but there are no limitations to the language used, since AMOS is very popular in most European countries.

Send subscription requests to subscribe@xamiga.linet.org using this format:

```
#amos youraccount@yoursubdomain.yourdomain;
```

Anneal

Contact: anneal-request@cs.ucla.edu (Daniel R. Greening)

Purpose: Discussion of simulated annealing techniques and analysis, as well as other related issues (stochastic optimization, Boltzmann machines, metricity of NP-complete move spaces, etc.).

Membership is restricted to those doing active research in simulated annealing or related areas. Current membership is international, and about half of the members are published authors. The list itself is unmoderated.

APC-Open

Contact: apc-open-request@uunet.uu.net (Fred Rump)

fred@compu.com

Purpose: To interchange information relevant to SCO Advanced Product Centers. Membership restricted to APC OPEN members or those specifically invited.

apE-Info

Contact: ape-info-request@ferkel.ucsb.edu (Jim Lick)

Purpose: Discussion of the scientific visualization software package apE.

Argentina

Contact: argentina-request@ois.db.toronto.edu (Carlos G. Mendioroz)

Purpose: Mailing list for general discussion and information. By joining, you can learn how to make those patties (*empanadas*) that you miss so much, how to *cebar un buen mate*, and, of course, how to solve Argentina's most outstanding problems. We don't have a regular news service yet, but some members send a briefing every now and then. To join, send name, e-mail, phone number, address, and topics of interest. List contents are primarily in Spanish.

Arlist

Contact: `arlist-request@psych.psy.uq.oz.au` (Bob Dick)

Purpose: Arlist is an open, unmoderated mailing list to provide a forum for discussing action research and its use in a variety of disciplines and situations. As its name implies, action research is often a suitable research paradigm when both action outcomes and research outcomes are required. It is usually (but perhaps not always) cyclic, participative, and qualitative.

Appropriate topics include (but are not limited to)

- Philosophical and methodological issues in action research
- Specific action research methodologies and methods
- The use of action research for evaluation
- Actual case studies of action research
- The use of action research methodologies for thesis research
- Increasing the rigor of action research

To subscribe, send e-mail to `arlist-request@psych.psy.uq.oz.au` with the subject line `arlist subscribe` and the message `subscribe arlist your-name your-email-address`.

AR-News

Contact: Ar-news-request@cygnus.com (Ian Lance Taylor) (Chip Roberson)

Purpose: A public news wire for items relating to animal rights and welfare.

Appropriate postings to AR-News include posting a news item, requesting information on some event, or responding to a request for information. Discussions on AR-News will *not* be allowed, and we ask that any commentary be taken either to AR-Talk or to private e-mail.

Currently, no resources are available for archiving this list.

Ars Magica

Contact: ars-magica-request@soda.berkeley.edu

Purpose: A mailing list for the discussion of White Wolf's Role Playing Game, Ars Magica. Also available as a nightly digest, upon request.

AR-Talk

Contact: ar-talk-request@cygnus.com (Chip Roberson) (Ian Lance Taylor)

Purpose: An unmoderated list for the discussion of animal rights. Peter Singer's book *Animal Liberation* proposes a "New Ethics for our Treatment of Animals," and many activist groups, such as PETA (People for the Ethical Treatment of Animals), regard this as the "Bible of the Animal Rights movement." Consumers and researchers alike are facing new questions concerning the human animals' treatment of the rest of the animal kingdom. The purpose of this list is to provide students, researchers, and activists a forum for discussing issues like the following:

Animal rights	Animal liberation
Consumer product testing	Cruelty-free products
Vivisection/dissection	Medical testing
Animals in laboratories	Research using animals
Hunting/trapping/fishing	Animals in entertainment
Factory farming	Fur
Ecology	Environmental protection
Vegetarianism	Vegan lifestyles
Christian perspectives	Other perspectives

Currently, no resources are available for archiving this list.

Artist-Users

Contact: artist-users-request@uicc.com (Jeff Putsch)

Purpose: Discussion group for users and potential users of the software tools from Cadence Design Systems. This can be used to

- Discuss current problems and their solutions/workarounds
- Discuss usage of the product
- Discuss enhancements and product improvements
- Anything else regarding these products in an analog circuit design environment

All users or potential users of the Cadence Design Systems tools are encouraged to join. (The name is a holdover from pre-comp.cad.cadence days—when the group was specifically for users of Cadence's Analog Artist product.)

This mailing list is bidirectionally gatewayed to the USENET news group comp.cad.cadence.

ATT-PC+

Contact: bill@ssbn.wlk.com

    ...!{att,cs.utexas.edu,sun!daver}!ssbn!bill
(Bill Kennedy)

Purpose: For people interested in the AT&T PC 63xx series of systems. Sublists are maintained for MS-DOS-only and Simul-Task mailings, as well as the full list for items of general interest. Membership must be requested and mail path verification is required before membership is granted.

AUC-TeX

Contact: auc-tex-request@iesd.auc.dk
(Kresten Krab Thorup)

Purpose: Discussion and information exchange about the AUC TeX package, which runs under GNU Emacs.

AUGLBC-L

Contact: listserv@american.edu (Erik G. Paul)

Purpose: The American University Gay, Lesbian, and Bisexual Community is a support group for lesbian, gay, bisexual, transgender, and supportive students. The group is open to all. The group is also connected with the International Lesbian, Gay Youth organization (known as IGLYO).

To subscribe, send a message with one line containing SUB AUGLBC-L *yourfullname* to listserv@american.edu.

AusGBLF

Contact: ausgblf-request@minyos.xx.rmit.oz.au

Purpose: Welcome to AusGBLF, an Australian-based mailing list for gays, bisexuals, lesbians, and friends. The mailing list is maintained from zglc@minyos.xx.rmit.oz.au, an account belonging to RMIT's Gay and Lesbian Collective.

Autox

Contact: autox-request@autox.team.net

autox-request@hoosier.cs.utah.edu

Purpose: Discussion of autocrossing, SCCA Solo events. Also available as a digest. Many of the list's members are SCCA (Sports Car Club of America).

Aviator

Contact: aviator-request@icdwest.teradyne.com
(Jim Hickstein)

Purpose: A mailing list of, by, and for users of Aviator, the flight simulation program from Artificial Horizons, Inc. Aviator runs on Sun workstations with the GX graphics accelerator option. The list is unmoderated at present and is unaffiliated with AHI.

Its charter is simply to facilitate communication among users of Aviator. It is *not* intended to communicate with the *providers* of Aviator. All mail received at the submission address is reflected to all the subscribers of the list.

Ayurveda

Contact: ayurveda-request@netcom.com

Purpose: Ayurveda is the ancient science of life originating in India. This mailing list is used to help people find out more about ayurveda such as lectures, workshops, stores that sell ayurvedic herbs, and so on.

Backstreets

Contact: backstreets-request@virginia.edu (Marc Rouleau)

Purpose: Our purpose is to discuss any and all issues likely to be of interest to people who enjoy Bruce Springsteen's music.

Bagpipes

Contact: pipes-request@sunapee.dartmouth.edu

Purpose: Any topic related to bagpipes, most generally defined as any instrument where air is forced manually from a bellows or bag through drones and/or over reeds. All manner of Scottish, Irish, English, and other instruments are discussed. Anyone with an interest is welcome.

Bahai-Faith

Contact: bahai-faith-request@oneworld.wa.com
(Charles W. Cooper II)

Purpose: A non-threatening forum for discussing and sharing information about the tenets, history, and texts of the Baha'i Faith. This mailing list is gatewayed into the Usenet news group soc.religion.bahai.

Balloon

Contact: balloon-request@lut.ac.uk (Phil Herbert)

Purpose: This is a list for balloonists of any sort, be they hot air or gas, commercial or sport. Currently the number of subscribers is low. Discussion topics include just about anything related to ballooning.

Ballroom

Contact: ballroom-request@athena.mit.edu
(Shahrukh Merchant)

Purpose: Discussion of any aspect of ballroom dancing. For instance, places to dance, announcements of special events (e.g., inter-university competitions), exchange of information about clubs, ballroom dance music, discussion of dances, steps, etc.

Anyone may join; please send *all* of the following information: (1) full name; (2) Internet-compatible e-mail address; (3) affiliation with any ballroom dance organization or group, if any; (4) ZIP or postal code, and country if other than the U.S.; (5) whether you have access to netnews (Yes/No/Don't know/Yes but don't use).

BA-Poker-List

Contact: ba-poker-request@netcom.com (Martin Veneroso)

Purpose: Discussion of poker as it is available to residents of and visitors to the San Francisco Bay Area (broadly defined), in home games as well as in licensed card rooms. Topics include upcoming events, unusual games, strategies, comparisons of various venues, and player "networking."

BA-Sappho

Contact: ba-sappho-request@labrys.mti.sgi.com

Purpose: A Bay Area lesbian mailing list intended for local networking and announcements. BA-Sappho is *not* a discussion group. In order to maintain its effectiveness as a networking tool and ensure that as many women as possible can participate, it is important for the volume to remain low.

bass

Contact: bass-request@gsbcs.uchicago.edu

Purpose: The purpose of this list is to discuss the reproduction and enjoyment of deep bass, primarily in consumer audio. Ownership of a subwoofer is not required; entry is welcome to anyone with an interest in deep bass reproduction.

BBLISA

Contact: bblisa-request@cs.umb.edu

Purpose: Discussion about system administration issues, and announcements concerning Back Bay LISA (Large Installation Systems Administration (Boston MA/New England)) activities, meetings, etc.

BBLISA-Announce

Contact: bblisa-announce-request@cs.umb.edu

Purpose: Announcements list for Back Bay LISA (Large Installation Systems Administration (Boston MA/New England)) activities, meetings, etc.

Bbones

Contact: mail-bbones-request@yorku.ca

Purpose: A list discussing the construction of mail backbones for organizations and campuses. Bbones was created as a follow-up to a discussion of the 1992 spring Inetrop hosted by Einger Stefferud.

Bcdv

Contact: bike-request@bcdv.drexel.edu

Purpose: To discuss issues related to cycling in the Philadelphia greater metropolitan region, and the advocacy work of the Bicycle Coalition of the Delaware Valley, including current efforts to ensure that an appropriate amount of Federal ISTEA and Congestion Mitigation and Air Quality grants are spent on removing barriers to bicycling.

Bears

Contact: bears-request@spdcc.com (Steve Dyer and Brian Gollum)

```
...!{harvard,ima,linus,mirror}!spdcc!bears-request
```

Purpose: A mailing list in digest format for gay and bisexual men who are bears themselves and for those who enjoy the company of bears. The exact definition of a "bear" seems to be a personal one, but it encompasses men who are variously cuddly, furry, perhaps stocky, or bearded. mail.bears is designed to be a forum to bring together folks with similar interests for conversation, friendship, and sharing of experiences. The tone of mail.bears is determined by its members, but people uncomfortable with discussing sexually explicit topics via electronic mail should not subscribe.

Bel Canto

Contact: dewy-fields-request@ifi.uio.no

Purpose: A list open to all discussion regarding the music, lyrics, shows of the group, or the group members' solo projects, or even related artists if appropriate.

BETA

Contact: usergroup-request@mjolner.dk
(Elmer Soerensen Sandvad)

Purpose: A discussion forum for BETA users. BETA is a modern object-oriented programming language with powerful abstraction mechanisms including class, subclass, virtual class, class variable, procedure, subprocedure, virtual procedure, procedure variable, coroutine, subcoroutine, virtual coroutine, coroutine variable, and many more, all unified to the ultimate abstraction mechanism: the pattern. Other features include general block structure, coroutines, concurrency, strong typing, part objects, separate objects, and classless objects.

Between the Lines

Contact: mkwong@scf.nmsu.edu (Myra Wong)

Purpose: To share information and discuss Debbie Gibson and her music.

BiAct-L

Contact: el406010@brownvm.brown.edu (Elaine Brennan)

Purpose: Bisexual activists' discussion list. Directions for posting to the list will be sent to you when you are added to the list.

BiFem-L

Contact: listserv@brownvm.brown.edu (Elaine Brennan)

Purpose: A mailing list for bi women and bi-friendly women. To subscribe, send a message to listserv@brownvm.brown.edu with no subject line and the following message body:

    SUBSCRIBE BIFEM-L *yourfullname*

You will receive an acknowledgment of your message and will later receive a message welcoming you to the list and explaining how to post messages. The list volume is 80-100 messages per day.

Big-DB

Contact: big-db@midway.uchicago.edu (Fareed Asad-Harooni)

Purpose: Discussions pertaining to large databases (generally greater than 1 million records) and large database management systems such as IMS, DB2, and CCA's Model/204. Anyone interested in large database issues is welcome.

Bikecommute

Contact: bikecommute-request@bike2work.eng.sun.com

Purpose: Mainly Silicon Valley folk. The discussion centers around bicycle transportation and the steps necessary for improved bicycling conditions in (sub)urban areas.

We do have several folks from around the area, as well as a few national organizations (the League of American Wheelmen, Bikecentennial, and the Bicycle Federation of America).

Bikepeople

Contact: karplus@ce.ucsc.edu (Kevin Karplus)

Purpose: An area group of bicycle activists, mainly in Santa Cruz County, CA. We discuss bicycle issues: local, state, and national. Public hearings and government meetings are announced and reported on. Messages are occasionally cross-posted with the bikecommute mailing list.

BiNet New Jersey

Contact: bnnj-request@plts.org

Purpose: Local BiNet New Jersey mailing list; mostly announcements.

Biodiv-L

Contact: listserv@bdt.ftpt.ansp.br

Purpose: To discuss technical opportunities, administrative and economic issues, practical limitations, and scientific goals, leading to recommendations for the establishment of a biodiversity network.

Individual contributions are requested, not only as to network capabilities, but also as to existing databases of interest to biodiversity.

For those interested in receiving a summary of all contributions that have been sent to this list, please send the following message to listserv@bdt.ftpt.ansp.br: get biodiv-l readme.first.

To subscribe, send a message containing subscribe biodiv-l *yourfullname, institution* to listserv@bdt.ftpt.ansp.br.

Biomch-L

Contact: listserv@nic.surfnet.nl (Ton van den Bogert)

Purpose: For members of the International, European, American, Canadian, and other Societies of Biomechanics, ISEK (International Society of Electrophysiological Kinesiology), and for all others with an interest in the general field of biomechanics and human or animal movement. For the scope of this list, see, e.g., the *Journal of Biomechanics* (Pergamon Press), the *Journal of Biomechanical Engineering* (ASME), or *Human Movement Science* (North-Holland).

Biomch-L is operated under the Patronage of the International Society of Biomechanics.

Technical help can be obtained by sending the command send biomch-l guide to listserv@hearn or listserv@nic.surfnet.nl, or by contacting one of the list owners.

Subscribe by sending subscribe biomch-l *yourfirstname yourlastname* to listserv@hearn (BITNET) or listserv@nic.surfnet.nl (Internet and others).

Biosym

Contact: dibug-request@comp.bioz.unibas.ch (Reinhard Doelz)

Purpose: For users of Biosym Technologies software. This includes the products InsightII, Discover, Dmol, Homology, Delphi, and Polymer. The list is not run by Biosym.

Birthmother

Contact: nadir@acca.nmsu.edu

Purpose: For any birthmother who has relinquished a child for adoption. To join the mailing list, send mail to nadir@acca.nmsu.edu with your e-mail address and brief information about your situation (e.g., bmom who relinquished *x* years ago, and does/does not have contact, has/has not been reunited).

Bisexu-L

Contact: listserv@brownvm.brown.edu (Bill Sklar)

Purpose: For discussion of issues of bisexuality. Cordial and civilized exchange of relevant ideas, opinions, and experiences between members of all orientations is encouraged—we do not discriminate on the basis of orientation, religion, gender, race, etc.

This list is not intended in the spirit of separatism from any other lists devoted to lesbian, gay, and bisexual issues but as an additional resource for discussion of bisexual concerns in particular. By the same token, the existence of Bisexu-L should not imply in any way that other discussion lists are no longer appropriate forums for discussion of bisexuality.

BITNET users can subscribe by sending the following command to listserv@brownvm: subscribe bisexu-l *yourfullname*, where *yourfullname* is your real name, not your login ID. Internet users can subscribe by sending the above command in the text/body of a message to listserv@brownvm.brown.edu.

BITHRY-L

Contact: listserv@brownvm.brown.edu (Elaine Brennan)

Purpose: For the theoretical discussion of bisexuality and gender issues. It is neither a social group, nor a support group, nor an announcement or news forum. There are many other lists that serve those purposes on the networks. Cross-postings from other groups are strongly discouraged.

To subscribe, send the message SUB BITHRY-L *yourfullname* to listserv@brownvm.brown.edu.

BIVERSITY

Contact: liz@ai.mit.edu

Purpose: For announcement of Boston-area events and organizing (not a discussion-type list).

Blind News Digest

Contact: wtm@bunker.afd.olivetti.com

Purpose: This is a moderated mailing list in digest format that deals with all aspects of the visually impaired/blind. To subscribe, send the message Subscribe BlindNws *yourname* to listserv@vm1.nodak.edu, or send mail to wtm@bunker.afd.olivetti.com.

BLUES-L

Contact: listserv@brownvm.brown.edu

Purpose: For everyone who can't get enough of the blues, there is a mailing list for blues.

To subscribe, send e-mail to listserv@brownvm.brown.edu with the message (no subject) SUBSCRIBE BLUES-L followed by your first and last name.

Also, do not include a .sig as this seems to confuse the mailer. If you have trouble getting through to listserv@brownvm.brown.edu, try listserv@brownvm.bitnet or listserv at brownvm.

There is an option to receive it in digest form if you desire. Once you get acknowledgment from the listserver that you are on the list, send another message to the listserver (not the list!) with the message SET BLUES-L DIG. This should get you on with digest form.

If you send the command help to the listserver, you will get a list of useful commands and pointers to other help documents.

BMW

Contact: bmw-request@balltown.cma.com (Richard Welty)

Purpose: Discussion of cars made by BMW. Both regular and digest forms are available.

BMW Motorcycles

Contact: bmw-request@rider.cactus.org

Purpose: Talk about all years of BMW motorcycles.

Bolton

Contact: ai411@yfn.ysu.edu

Purpose: The purpose of this list is to allow Bolton fans to discuss Michael, his music, and his work.

Bonsai

Contact: listserv@cms.cc.wayne.edu
(Dan@foghorn.pass.wayne.edu)

Purpose: To facilitate discussion of the art and craft of Bonsai and related art forms. Bonsai is the Oriental art (craft?) of miniaturizing trees and plants into forms that mimic nature. Everyone interested, whether novice or professional, is invited to subscribe.

BosNet

Contact: hozo@math.lsa.umich.edu (Hozo Iztok)

Purpose: A moderated mailing list published daily, covering news and discussions mainly about Bosnia and Hercegovina. The service is run by volunteers. Language is English and

Bosnian, whichever the contributor is most comfortable with. It also includes news from the international press and important announcements related to Bosnia and Hercegovina. Readers are encouraged to send original contributions.

Boston Bruins

Contact: bruins-request@cristal.umd.edu (Garry Knox)

Purpose: Discussion of the Boston Bruins of the National Hockey League and their farm teams. To subscribe to the list, please send e-mail to bruins-request@cristal.umd.edu. The list is available in two formats: all messages are forwarded to the recipient immediately, or as a digest, which is sent out daily.

Brasil

Contact: bras-net-request@cs.ucla.edu (B.R. Araujo Neto)

Purpose: Mailing list for general discussion and information. To join, send name, e-mail, phone number, address, and topics of interest. Portuguese is the main language of discussion.

Brass

Contact: brass-request@geomag.gly.fsu.edu (Ted Zateslo)

Purpose: A discussion group for people interested in brass musical performance and related topics, especially small musical ensembles of all kinds.

Brit-Iron

Contact: brit-iron@indiana.edu

cstringe@indiana.edu

Purpose: To provide a friendly forum for riders, owners, and admirers of British motorcycles to share information and experiences. We maintain a list of parts sources and shops that repair these classic machines. All marques are welcome from AJS to Vellocette.

British-Cars

Contact: british-cars-request@autox.team.net (Mark Bradakis)

british-cars-request@hoosier.cs.utah.edu

Purpose: Discussion of owning, repairing, racing, cursing, and loving British cars, predominantly sports cars, some Land Rover and sedan stuff. Also available as a digest.

BTHS-ENews-L

Contact: listserv@cornell.edu

Purpose: For providing an open forum for students, teachers, and alumni of Brooklyn Technical High School. To subscribe, send mail to listserv@cornell.edu with a message body of this form: subscribe BTHS-ENews-L *yourfullname*

Bugs-386bsd

Contact: bugs-386bsd-request@ms.uky.edu

Purpose: For 386bsd bugs, patches, and ports. Requirements to join: interest in actively working on 386bsd to improve the operating system for use by yourself and others.

BX-Talk

Contact: bx-talk-request@qiclab.scn.rain.com
(Darci L. Chapman)

Purpose: For users of Builder Xcessory (BX) to discuss problems (and solutions!) and ideas for using BX.

BX is a graphical user interface builder for Motif applications, sold by ICS. Please note that this list is not associated with ICS (the authors of BX) in any way. This list is unmoderated.

c2man

Contact: listserv@research.canon.oz.au

Purpose: Discussion of Graham Stoney's c2man program. c2man parses comments from C and C++ programs and produces documentation for man pages, info files, and so forth. This list is archived and unmoderated.

Cabot

Contact: cabot-request@sol.crd.ge.com (Richard Welty)

Purpose: Official mailing list of the New York State Institute for Sebastian Cabot Studies.

CA-Firearms

Contact: ca-firearms-request@shell.portal.com (Jeff Chan)

BA-Firearms

Contact: ba-firearms-request@shell.portal.com (Jeff Chan)

Purpose: Announcement and discussion of firearms legislation and related issues.

The ca- list is for California statewide issues; the ba- list is for the San Francisco Bay Area and gets all messages sent to the ca- list. You subscribe to one or the other, generally depending on whether you're in the San Francisco Bay Area.

CA-Liberty

Contact: ca-liberty-request@shell.portal.com (Jeff Chan)

BA-Liberty

Contact: ba-liberty-request@shell.portal.com (Jeff Chan)

Purpose: Announcement of local libertarian meetings, events, activities, etc.

The ca- list is for California statewide issues; the ba- list is for the San Francisco Bay Area and gets all messages sent to the ca- list. You subscribe to one or the other, generally depending on whether you're in the San Francisco Bay Area.

Can-stud-assoc

Contact: can-stud-assoc-request@unixg.ubc.ca

Purpose: A Canada-specific e-mail list to discuss issues of concern to Canadian students, Canadian post-secondary education, and student associations' involvement in it. This is intended as an easy means for Canadian post-secondary student governments and those interested in them to communicate.

Cards

Contact: cards-request@tanstaafl.uchicago.edu
(Keane Arase)

Purpose: For people interested in collection, speculation, and investing in baseball, football, basketball, hockey, and other trading cards and/or memorabilia. Discussion and want/sell lists are welcome. Open to anyone.

Catholic

Contact: listserv@american.edu (Cindy Smith)

    cms@dragon.com

Purpose: A forum for Catholics who want to discuss their discipleship to Jesus Christ in terms of the Catholic approach to Christianity. "Catholic" is loosely defined as anyone embracing the Catholic approach to Christianity, whether Roman Catholic, Anglo-Catholic, or Orthodox. Protestants or non-Christians are invited to listen in on discussions, but full-blown debates between Catholics and Protestants are best carried out in Internet's soc.religion.christian or talk.religion.misc news groups. Discussions on ecumenism are encouraged.

To subscribe, send a one-line message body (not subject) to the subscription address:

    SUBSCRIBE CATHOLIC yourfullname

This list is also bidirectionally forwarded to the news group bit.listserv.catholic.

Catholic-Action

Contact: rfreeman@vpnet.chi.il.us (Richard Freeman)

Purpose: A moderated list concerned with Catholic evangelism, church revitalization, and preservation of Catholic teachings, traditions and values, and the vital effort to decapitate modernist heresy.

Catholic Doctrine

Contact: catholic-request@sarto.gaithersburg.md.us

Purpose: For discussions of orthodox Catholic theology by everyone under the jurisdiction of the Holy Father, John Paul II. Moderated. No attacks on the Catholic Church here, please. There is an archive server (containing Catholic art and magisterial documents) associated with this list. Send mail to the above address to subscribe or to get details about the archive server.

Cavers

Contact: cavers-request@vlsi.bu.edu (John D. Sutter)

Purpose: Information resource and forum for all interested in exploring caves. To join, send a note to the above address, including your geographical location as well as e-mail address; details of caving experience and locations where you've caved; NSS number, if you have one; and any other information that might be useful.

CD-Forum

Contact: cd-request@valis.biocad.com (Valerie)

Purpose: To provide support/discuss/share experiences about gender-related issues: cross-dressing, transvestism, transsexualism, etc. This list is in digest format.

CDPub

Contact: cdpub-info@knex.via.mind.org

Purpose: An electronic mailing list for folks engaged or interested in CD-ROM publishing in general and desktop CD-ROM recorders and publishing systems in particular.

Topics of interest to the list include information on the various desktop publishing systems for premastering using CD-ROM media and tapes (DAT, e.g.), replication services, various standards of interest to publishers (ISO9660, RockRidge, and so forth), retrieval engines, platform independence issues, and so on.

Discussions on all platforms are welcome, be it MS-DOS-based PCs, Apple, UNIX, Amiga, etc. Also of interest will be publishing for platforms such as CD-I, 3DO, et al.

In short, if it relates to CD-ROM publishing, we want to talk about it, exchange information, inform, and be informed.

To subscribe, send the following command to mail-server@knex.via.mind.org:

    SUBSCRIBE CDPub *yourfirstname yourlastname*

Cerebi

Contact: cerebi-request@tomservo.b23b.ingr.com (Christian Walters)

Purpose: About the Cerebus comic book by Dave Sim. Anything relating to Cerebus or Sim is welcome. It's just an echo list, so anything that gets mailed is bounced to everyone.

Cfcp-members

Contact: mlindsey@nyx.cs.du.edu

Purpose: The Confederation of Future Computer Professionals is a group of users on the Internet who are interested in various fields of computers enough to consider them as their future. Members' ages range from 12 years old (accomplished C++ programmer) to 40 years old (engineer that writes X code), and this is because the ages aren't important. We are here to foster education, stimulate communication, to have a place to brag about what wonderful things we're doing, and to feel challenged to work harder.

Chalkhills

Contact: chalkhills-request@presto.ig.com (John M. Relph)

Purpose: A mailing list for the discussion of the music and records of XTC (the band). Chalkhills is moderated and is distributed in a digest format.

The Chaosium Digest

Contact: appel@erzo.berkeley.edu

Purpose: A weekly digest for the discussion of Chaosium's many games, including Call of Cthulhu, Elric!, Elfquest, and Pendragon.

Chem-Eng

Contact: trayms@cc.curtin.edu.au (Dr. Martyn Ray)

Purpose: An electronic newsletter on chemical engineering.

Chem-Talk

Contact: ...!{ames,cbosgd}!pacbell!unicom!manus (Dr. Manus Monroe)

Purpose: As chemists, dialogue and conversation with other scientists are essential to stimulating or provoking new ideas. As teachers and researchers, we can find the demands of our profession extensive, which may lead to a reduction in our ability to keep abreast of new data and changes in theories. Sometimes, conversation helps to clarify articles, illuminate new perceptions of theories, and sustain us through our precarious journey in chemistry. A solution to this problem or concern is the creation of an efficient communication network using this mailing list.

Chessnews

Contact: chessnews-request@tssi.com (Michael Nolan)

Purpose: A repeater for the USENET news group rec.games.chess. This is a bidirectional repeater. Postings originating from USENET are sent to the list, and those originating from the list are sent to rec.games.chess.

Chorus

Contact: chorus-request@psych.toronto.edu

Purpose: Lesbian and gay chorus mailing list, formed November 1991 by John Schrag (jschrag@alias.com) and Brian Jarvis (jarvis@psych.toronto.edu). Membership includes artistic directors, singers, chorus officers, interpreters, support staff, and friends. Topics of discussion include repertoire, arrangements, staging, costuming, management, fund raising, music, events, concerts, and much more.

Christian

Contact: ames!elroy!grian!mailjc-request

mailjc-request@grian.cps.altadena.ca.us

Purpose: To provide a non-hostile environment for discussion among Christians. Non-Christians may join the list and "listen-in," but full-blown debates between Christians and non-Christians are best carried out in talk.religion.misc or soc.religion.christian.

C-IBM-370

Contact: {spsd,zardoz,felix,elroy}!dhw68k!C-ibm-370 request

c-ibm-370-request@dhw68k.cts.com (David Wolfskill)

Purpose: A place to discuss aspects of using the C programming language on s/370-architecture computers—especially under IBM's operating systems for that environment.

Cisco

Contact: cisco-request@spot.colorado.edu (David Wood)

Purpose: For discussion of the network products from Cisco Systems, Inc; primarily the AGS gateway, but also the ASM terminal multiplexor and any other relevant products. Discussions about operation, problems, features, topology, configuration, protocols, routing, loading, serving, etc., are all encouraged. Other topics include vendor relations, new product announcements, availability of fixes and new features, and discussion of new requirements and desirables.

CJI

Contact: listserv@jerusalem1.datasrv.co.il
(Jacob Richman)

Purpose: A one-way list that will automatically send you the monthly updated computer jobs document. The Computer Jobs in Israel (CJI) list will also send you other special documents/announcements regarding finding computer work in Israel.

During the first 2-3 months (startup), please do not send any requests to the list owner regarding "I have this experience, who should I contact?" Eventually this list will be an open, moderated list for everyone to exchange information about computer jobs in Israel.

To subscribe, send mail to
listserv@jerusalem1.datasrv.co.il with the following text:

```
sub cji yourfirstname yourlastname
```

Clarissa

Contact: clarissa-request@tcp.com (Jim Lick)

Purpose: Discussion of the Nickelodeon TV show *Clarissa Explains It All*.

Cleveland Sports

Contact: aj755@cleveland.freenet.edu (Richard Kowicki)

Purpose: Provides a forum for people to discuss their favorite Cleveland sports teams/personalities, and provides news and information about those teams that most out-of-towners couldn't get otherwise.

Teams discussed include the Cleveland Indians, the Cleveland Browns, the Cleveland Cavaliers, and the teams from Ohio State University. Topics of discussion have included local high school teams, local Olympic personalities, other local college teams, and other local professional teams. Anything related to the Cleveland sports scene is fair game here.

CM5-Managers

Contact: listserv@boxer.nas.nasa.gov (machine)

jet@nas.nasa.gov (human) (J. Eric Townsend)

Purpose: Discussion of administrating the Thinking Machines CM5 parallel supercomputer. To subscribe, send a message to listserv@boxer.nas.nasa.gov with a body of subscribe cm5-managers *yourfullname*.

CoCo

Contact: pecampbe@mtus5.bitnet (Paul E. Campbell)

Purpose: Discussion related to the Tandy Color Computer (any model), OS-9 Operating System, and any other topics relating to the "CoCo," as this computer is affectionately known.

Anyone wanting to be on the list should send me mail. UUCP users, please note that I need a nearby Internet or BITNET node to get things through to you reliably, so please send me a path in the following form:

zeus!yourhost!yourid@sun.com

Cogneuro

Contact: cogneuro-request@ptolemy.arc.nasa.gov

Purpose: An informal, relatively low-volume way to discuss matters at the interface of cognitive science and neuroscience.

The discussion will be scientific and academic, covering biological aspects of behavior and cognitive issues in neuroscience. Also discussable are curricula, graduate programs, and jobs in the field.

To use the list, please follow these examples exactly so that my software works.

To subscribe, send mail like this:

> To: cogneuro-request@ptolemy.arc.nasa.gov
> Subject: cogneuro: subscribe

To unsubscribe, send mail like this:

> To: cogneuro-request@ptolemy.arc.nasa.gov
> Subject: cogneuro: unsubscribe

You don't need to put anything in the body of the message. There will be no automatic confirmation, but you might get a note from me.

To change your e-mail address (also very polite to do if you know that your machine will go down for a while, or in case you leave the net), simply unsubscribe from your old address and resubscribe from your new address. This prevents error messages and prevents me from having to verify your address manually.

To post (send a message to everybody on the list), send mail to cogneuro@ptolemy.arc.nasa.gov, or follow up on an existing message. For example,

> To: cogneuro@ptolemy.arc.nasa.gov
> Subject: corpus callsosum

To ask a *metaquestion*, send it to cogneuro-request@ptolemy.arc.nasa.gov. Suggestions for improving this announcement or the list are welcome.

The following are the list guidelines:

- The language of the list is English.

- The list is meant to be low in volume and high in s/n ratio.

- Controversy and speculation are welcome, as are lack of controversy and rigor. Since the emphasis is scientific and academic, participants are expected to be extremely tolerant of other participants' opinions and choice of words. Since cogneuro is such a huge field, submission shouldn't be too off-topic or otherwise not essentially scientific or academic.

- The list is initially open to anybody who is interested. Although I don't expect ever to need to exercise it, I reserve the right to remove anybody from the list if there are problems. I want to keep a spirit of free exchange of cognitive neuroscience.

- Other than this, the list is moderated and informal.

COHOUSING-L

Contact: listserv@uci.com

Purpose: A list for discussion of *cohousing*, the name of a type of collaborative housing that has been developed primarily in Denmark since 1972 where it is known as *bofoellesskaber* (English approximation).

Cohousing is housing designed to foster community and cooperation while preserving independence. Private residences are clustered near shared facilities. The members design and manage all aspects of their community.

For automated subscription, send e-mail message to listserv@uci.com with the following command in the message body (no subject):

> SUBSCRIBE COHOUSING-L *yourfullname* (no logins please)

In response, an informative introduction will be sent. E-mail to fholson@uci.com for more information.

Coins

Contact: coins-request@iscsvax.uni.edu (Daniel J. Power)

Purpose: To provide a forum for discussions on numismatic topics including U.S. and world coins, paper money, tokens, medals, etc. The list is growing and new members are welcome.

Comix

Contact: comix-request@world.std.com
(Elizabeth Lear Newman)

Purpose: Intended for talking about non-mainstream and independent comic books. We generally don't talk about superheroes much, and we don't talk about Marvel Mutants at all.

Commodore-Amiga

Contact: subscribe@xamiga.linet.org

Purpose: For Commodore Amiga computer users. Weekly postings of hardware reviews, news briefs, system information, company progress, and information for finding out more about the Commodore and Amiga.

Send subscription requests to subscribe@xamiga.linet.org using this format:

    #commodore youraccount@yoursubdomain.yourdomain;

COMMUNE

Contact: commune-request@stealth.acf.nyu.edu (Dan Bernstein)

Purpose: To discuss the COMMUNE protocol, a telnet replacement. The list is a mail reflector, commune-list@stealth.acf.nyu.edu.

Concrete-Blonde

Contact: concrete-blonde-request@piggy.ucsb.edu (Robert Earl)

Purpose: Discussion of the rock group Concrete Blonde and related artists and issues.

Corpse/Respondents

Contact: carriec@eskimo.com

Purpose: A gothic pen-pal zine, in digest form. Small traffic mailing list. To subscribe, send e-mail to carriec@eskimo.com with the message subscribe corpse yournameandaddress.

Counterev-L

Contact: ae852@yfn.ysu.edu (Jovan Weismiller)

Purpose: A list under the aegis of l'Alliance Monarchists that is dedicated to promoting the cause of traditional monarchy and the Counter Revolution. We believe in government based on natural law principles, decentralization, sub sidiarity; an economy based on the principles of distributive justice; and the defense of traditional Western values.

We believe in a Europe united, traditional, and free from the Atlantic to the Urals, but we oppose the centralizing bureaucracy of the Maastricht Treaty. While we are based in the U.S., we are affiliated with L'Alliance pour la maintenance de la France en Europe, and we have members, as well as fraternal relations, with the monarchist organizations in most Western European countries.

We work for the strengthening of existing monarchies, the restoration in those countries with a monarchist tradition, and the building up of an infrastructure appropriate to the instauration of monarchy in those countries without a living monarchist tradition.

CP

Contact: listserv@hpl-opus.hpl.hp.com (Rick Walker)

Purpose: Topics of interest to the group include

1. Cultivation and propagation of CPs (carnivorous plants)
2. Field observations of CPs
3. Sources of CP material
4. CP trading between members

The discussion is not moderated and usually consists of short messages offering plants for trade, asking CP questions and advice, relating experiences with plant propagation, etc. The group also maintains archives of commercial plant sources and member's growing lists.

To subscribe, send a one-line message

```
SUB CP yourfirstname yourlastname
```

(substituting your own name for *yourfirstname yourlastname*) to the address listserv@hpl-opus.hpl.hp.com.

Please direct all system-related questions to Rick Walker at walker@hpl-opus.hpl.hp.com.

Croatian-News/Hrvatski-Vjesnik

Contact: croatian-news-request@andrew.cmu.edu

hrvatski-vjesnik-zamolbe@andrew.cmu.edu

Purpose: News from and related to Croatia, run by volunteers. There are actually two news distributions: one in Croatian (occasionally an article can be in some other South Slavic language) and one in English.

For subscription, please send a message with the following information: your name, your e-mail address, state/country where your account is. Please put the state/country information in the Subject line of your letter. If you would like to receive the news in Croatian as well, please indicate that in your message. If you would prefer to receive the news in Croatian *only*, please send a message to the address hrvatski-vjesnik-zamolbe@andrew.cmu.edu.

Cro-News/SCYU-Digest

Contact: cro-news-request@medphys.ucl.ac.uk
(Nino Margetic)

Purpose: *Cro-News*—a non-moderated list that is the distribution point for the news coming from Croatia. At the time of writing (Aug. 1992), the list carries articles from Novi Vjesnik, Vecernji List, Croatia Monitor, Slobodna Dalmacija, Novi Danas, Radio Free Europe/Radio Luxembourg bulletins, UPI reports, etc. The volume of news is relatively high. The languages are Croatian, English, and occasionally Slovene. For application *only*, e-mail address is required. Please send requests for subscription to the aforementioned address.

SCCro-Digest/SCYU-Digest—two moderated mailing lists that enable people without access to the USENET news groups soc.culture.croatia and soc.culture.yugoslavia to receive messages published on those forums in a digested form. The volume of the material depends on the traffic of the respective news group, but usually there is at least 700-800 lines of text daily (on each list). The topics cover wide-ranging subjects and, on occasion, one can witness *very* heated discussions between the participants. Language is mostly English. The interaction is possible through the gateway at Berkeley.

Note: These two lists are *completely* separate, and one can subscribe to one, the other, or both of them.

Crossfire

Contact: crossfire-request@ifi.uio.no
(Frank Tore Johansen)

Purpose: To discuss the development of the game Crossfire. The official anonymous ftp site is ftp.ifi.uio.no in the directory /pub/crossfire. Old mails to the list are archived there. Crossfire is a multiplayer graphical arcade and adventure game made for the X Window environment.

Cro-Views

Contact: joe@mullara.met.unimelb.edu.au (Joe Stojsic)

Purpose: An opinion service that consists of discussions relating to Croatia and other former Yugoslav republics. The main objective is to give people who cannot access the news network (e.g., via the rn command in UNIX) a chance to read and voice their own opinions about these issues. Cro-Views is a non-moderated service.

Crowes

Contact: rstewart@unex.ucla.edu

Purpose: To provide a forum for discussion about the rock band the Black Crowes. Topics could include the group's music and lyrics, but could also include topics such as the band's participation with NORML, concert dates and playlists, bootlegs (audio and video), etc.

To subscribe, mail to the address shown above with the command `subscribe` in the first line. Discussion is encouraged.

Cryonics

Contact: ...att!whscad1!kqb (Kevin Q. Brown)

kqb@whscad1.att.com

Purpose: Cryonic suspension is an experimental procedure in which patients who can no longer be kept alive with today's medical abilities are preserved at low temperatures for treatment in the future. This list is a forum for topics related to cryonics, which include biochemistry of memory, low-temperature biology, legal status of cryonics and cryonically suspended people, nanotechnology and cell repair machines, philosophy of identity, mass media coverage of cryonics, new research and publications, conferences, and local cryonics group meetings.

CSAA

Contact: announce-request@cs.ucdavis.edu
(Carlos Amezaga)

Purpose: For those folks who have no access to USENET. I provide the gate between the USENET CSAA (comp.sys.amiga.announce) news group and mail.

This group distributes announcements of importance to people using the Commodore brand Amiga computers. Announcements may contain any important information, but most likely will deal with new products, disk library releases, software updates, reports of major bugs or dangerous viruses, notices of meetings or upcoming events, and so forth. A large proportion of posts announce the upload of software packages to anonymous ftp archive sites.

To subscribe, unsubscribe, or send comments on this mailing list, send mail to announce-request@cs.ucdavis.edu and your request will be taken care of.

CTF-Discuss

Contact: ctf-discuss-request@cis.upenn.edu (Dave Farber)

Purpose: This mailing list is targeted at stimulating discussion of issues critical to the computer science community in the United States (and, by extension, the world). The Computer Science and Telecommunications Board (CSTB) of the National Research Council (NRC) is charged with identifying and initiating studies in areas critical to the health of the field. Recently one such study—"Computing the Future"— has generated a major discussion in the community and has motivated the establishment of this mailing list in order to involve broader participation. This list will be used in the future to report and discuss the activities of the CSTB and to solicit opinions in a variety of areas.

CTN News

Contact: ctn-editors@utcc.utoronto.ca

Purpose: A list covering news on Tibet.

Ctree

Contact: alberta!oha!ctree-request (Tony Olekshy)

Purpose: To provide a forum for the discussion of FairCom's C-Tree, R-Tree, and D-Tree products. This mailing list is not associated with FairCom. We have over three dozen members and cover virtually all hardware and operating system ports.

CUSSNET

Contact: cussnet-request@stat.com

Purpose: Computer Users in the Social Sciences is a discussion group devoted to issues of interest to social workers, counselors, and human service workers of all disciplines. The discussion frequently involves computer applications in treatment, agency administration, and research. Students, faculty, community-based professionals, and just good ol' plain folks join in the discussion. Software, hardware, and ethical issues associated with their use in human service generate lively and informative discussions. Please join us. Bill Allbritten, Ph.D., Moderator (Director, Counseling and Testing Center, Murray State University, Murray, KY 42071)

To join the list, send e-mail to listserv@stat.com. The first line of text should be

    subscribe cussnet

Cyber-Sleaze

Contact: request-cyber-sleaze@mtv.com

Purpose: Cyber-Sleaze is a 5-day-a-week service with all the latest dirt and celebrity soil from the entertainment biz. The list is moderated and maintained by Adam Curry, known for his work on MTV. To subscribe, send e-mail to request-cyber-sleaze@mtv.com; in the message, type subscribe CYBER-SLEAZE *your name*.

CZ

Contact: cz-request@stsci.edu (Tom Comeau)

Purpose: To discuss the Harpoon naval wargame series and related topics. This includes Harpoon, Captain's Edition Harpoon, Computer Harpoon, Harpoon SITREP, and various supplements for print and computer versions. Naval topics are discussed insofar as they are related to the game or provide useful background. Discussion is moderated. The Convergence Zone (or CZ for short) is packaged in a digest format. Listeners as well as contributors are welcome.

Dallas Stars

Contact: hamlet@u.washington.edu (Mitch McGowan)

Purpose: Discussion of the Dallas Stars of the National Hockey League and their farm clubs, the Kalamazoo Wings of the International Hockey League, the Moncton Hawks of the American Hockey League, and the Dayton Bombers of the East Coast Hockey League.

To subscribe to the list, please send e-mail to hamlet@u.washington.edu. Please include the word DSTARS in your subject line and include your name and preferred e-mail address in the body of your message.

Dark-Shadows

Contact: shadows-request@sunee.waterloo.ca (Bernie Roehl)

Purpose: *Dark Shadows* was a daily soap opera that ran on ABC in the late sixties (ending in 1971). It had a Gothic feel to it and featured storylines involving witchcraft, vampires, werewolves, and the supernatural. It was (appropriately enough) "brought back from the dead" by NBC for a single season last year. It also spawned two feature films, a series of paperback novels, and lots more. The series is celebrating its 25th anniversary this year. There are a number of international fan clubs for the series, but so far there has been no news group or (electronic) mailing list devoted to it. Now there is.

Data-Exp

Contact: stein@watson.ibm.com

Purpose: An open forum for users to discuss the Visualization Data Explorer Package. It contains three files at the moment:

faq	Frequently asked questions
summary	A summary of the software, user interface, executive, data architecture
forum	Continuing forum of questions and answers about the software

Additionally, internal forum questions and answers are also posted to it by me.

The mail server understands the following commands:

index	Send an index of available files
faq	Send the faq file
forum	Send the forum file

Each of the above commands can be preceded with send

Additional commands:

subscribe	Subscribe to any appends that are made to the forum
add	Add this mail file to the forum
remove	Remove the subscribe to the forum
help	Send help on this mail server

This has been set up to quickly disseminate information about the software. We are in the process of setting up a unmoderated USENET forum too.

Datsun-Roadsters

Contact: datsun-roadsters-request@autox.team.net (Mark J. Bradakis)

   datsun-roadsters-request@hoosier.utah.edu

Purpose: To discuss any and all aspects of owning, showing, repairing, driving, etc., Datsun roadsters.

DC-MOTSS

Contact: dc-motss-request@vector.intercon.com

Purpose: A social mailing list for the GLBO folks who live in the Washington Metropolitan Area—everything within approximately 50 miles of the Mall.

DDTs-Users

Contact: ddts-users-request@bigbird.bu.edu (automated help reply)

Purpose: For discussions of issues related to the DDTs defect tracking software from QualTrak, including (but not limited to) software, methods, mechanisms, techniques, general usage tips, policies, bugs, and bug workarounds. It is intended primarily for DDTs administrators, but that does not necessarily preclude other topics.

"DDTs" and "QualTrak" are probably both trademarks of QualTrak.

Dead-Runners

Contact: dead-runners-request@unx.sas.com (Christopher Mark Conn)

Purpose: The Dead Runners Society—a mailing list for runners who like to talk about the psychological, philosophical, and personal aspects of running. We really like to talk about anything that has to do with running, but we tend to be more interested in how it affects our lives and our brains rather than our 10K times. The group is very diverse in experience—there are marathoners and there are people who just jog around the block.

Decision Power

Contact: dp-friends-request@aiai.ed.ac.uk (Ken Johnson)

Purpose: Decision Power is a product of ICL Computers Limited, comprising a logic programming language Prolog, a constraint handling system Chip, a database interface Seduce (runs on top of Ingres), a development environment Kegi (runs on X), and an end-user graphical display environment KHS (also runs on X). It is in use for various purposes at a dozen or so sites around the United Kingdom and Ireland.

DECnews-EDU

Contact: decnews@mr4dec.enet.dec.com
(Anne Marie McDonald)

Purpose: DECNEWS for Education and Research—a monthly electronic publication from Digital Equipment Corporation's Education Business Unit for the education and research communities worldwide.

To subscribe, send a message to listserv@ubvm.cc.buffalo.edu or listserv@ubvm.bitnet. The message should be this command: SUB DECNEWS yourfirstname yourlastname (e.g., SUB DECNEWS John Jones). The command is the text of your message; the subject is ignored by LISTSERV.

DECnews-PR

Contact: decnews-pr-request@pa.dec.com (Russ Jones)

Purpose: DECnews for Press and Analysts—an Internet-based distribution of all Digital press releases. It is provided as a courtesy to analysts, members of the press, and the consulting community. This is a one-way mailing list. Approximately eight press releases per week.

To subscribe, send mail to decnews-pr@pa.dec.com with a subject line of subscribe. Please include your name and telephone number in the body of the subscription request.

DECnews-UNIX

Contact: decnews-unix-request@pa.dec.com (Russ Jones)

Purpose: DECnews for UNIX—published electronically by Digital Equipment Corporation for Internet distribution every three weeks and contains product and service information of interest to the Digital UNIX community.

To subscribe, send mail to decnews-unix@pa.dec.com with a subject line of subscribe abstract. Please include your name and telephone number in the body of the subscription request.

DECstation-Managers

Contact: decstation-managers-request@ornl.gov

   majordomo@ornl.gov

Purpose: Fast-turnaround troubleshooting tool for managers of RISC DECstations.

DECUServe-Journal

Contact: frey@eisner.decus.org (Sharon Frey)

Purpose: An alternate method of distribution for the *DECUServe Journal*, a monthly digest of technical discussions that take place on the DECUS conferencing system. The Journal (and list) is open to anyone who is interested in Digital Equipment topics, third-party topics, and connectivity topics.

Deborah Harry/Blondie Information Service

Contact: gunter@yarrow.wt.uwa.oz.au

Purpose: An information service on everything and anything regarding Deborah Harry and Blondie, including tour information, recordings/films, release information, etc.

Derby

Contact: derby-request@ekrl.com (John Wilkes)

Purpose: To discuss various aspects and strategies of horse racing, primarily dealing with, but not limited to, handicapping. Anyone is free to join.

Deryni-L

Contact: mail-server@mintir.new-orleans.la.us

    elendil@mintir.new-orleans.la.us
(Edward J. Branley)

Purpose: A list for readers and fans of Katherine Kurtz' novels and other works. While primary focus is on the Deryni universe, discussion of Kurtz's other works (the Adept series, for example) is also encouraged. To join the list, send a message to mail-server@mintir.new-orleans.la.us with the following in the body:

    SUBSCRIBE DERYNI-L

Deviants

Contact: deviants-request@csv.warwick.ac.uk

Purpose: To discuss the workings of the Great Wok and all things deviant from accepted social norm. Occasionally disgusting, but not always, it is the home of ranting, experimental reports, news clippings, and other related items. Medical curiosities, cults, murders, and other phenomena are well in place here.

DG-Users

Contact: dg-users-request@ilinx.wimsey.com

Purpose: The technical details of Data General, its OSs, and the cornucopia of hardware it supplies and supports.

The administrator e-mail address is brian@ilinx.wimsey.com or uunet!van-bc!ilinx!brian

Dinosaur

Contact: dinosaur-request@donald.wichitaks.ncr.com (John Matrow)

Purpose: Discussion of dinosaurs and other archosaurs.

Direct

Contact: direct-request@ctsx.celtech.com (Keith Gregoire)

Purpose: Discussion of the work of the musical artist Vangelis. Both "bounce" and daily digest modes are available, so you might want to specify your preference when subscribing.

Dire-Straits

Contact: dire-straits-request@merrimack.edu (Rand P. Hall)

Purpose: Discussion of the musical group Dire Straits and associated side projects.

To subscribe, send mail with a message body of this form: subscribe

Dirt-Users

Contact: dirt-users-request@ukc.ac.uk

Purpose: An X11-based UIMS.

Disney-Afternoon

Contact: ranger-list-request@taronga.com
(Stephanie da Silva)

Purpose: Discussion of the Disney Afternoon and other related topics. This is a very high-volume, low-noise mailing list. It is moderated and is also available as a digest.

Disney-Comics

Contact: disney-comics-request@student.docs.uu.se
(Per Starbuck)

Purpose: Discussion of Disney comics.

Dist-Users

Contact: shigeya@foretune.co.jp (Shigeya Suzuki)

ram@acri.fr (Raphael Manfredi)

Purpose: This list is for discussions of issues related to the dist 3.0 package and its components: metaconfig, jmake, patch tools, etc. The dist package was posted on comp.sources.misc (August 1993).

To subscribe, send a mail to majordomo@foretune.co.jp saying

```
subscribe dist-users
youraccount@yoursubdomain.yourdomain
```

or optionally specifying your e-mail address if you are not on the Internet or if the addresses in your mail headers cannot be relied upon.

Dodge Stealth/Mitsubishi 3000GT

Contact: stealth-request%jim.uucp@wupost.wustl.edu

Purpose: Discussion of anything related to these cars.

Dokken/Lynch Mob

Contact: kydeno00@ukpr.uky.edu (Kirsten DeNoyelles)

kydeno00@mik.uky.edu

Purpose: Articles, questions, and discussions on Dokken and Lynch Mob.

Domestic

Contact: domestic-request@tattoo.mti.sgi.com

Purpose: For the discussion of workplace-related issues concerning domestic partners. Topics of discussion include methods for obtaining benefits at one's place of work, methods that did not work, cost of benefits, and other related topics. University students are welcome, as are people from countries other than the U.S.A. (though most of the discussions are U.S.A.-centric). Flame wars are not allowed on this low-volume list.

Donosy

Contact: przemek@ndcvx.cc.nd.edu (Przemek Klosowski)

Purpose: Distribution of a news bulletin from Poland. English and Polish versions are both available.

Dont-Tell

Contact: `dont-tell-request@choice.princeton.edu`

Purpose: An e-mail distribution list for people concerned about the effects that the new military policy known as "don't ask/don't tell" will have at academic institutions. This new policy forbids students at the nation's service academies or enrolled in campus ROTC programs from revealing truthful information about themselves.

Down Syndrome

Contact: `wtm@bunker.afd.olivetti.com`

Purpose: For discussion of any issue related to Down Syndrome. This list is open to parents, siblings, relatives, friends, teachers, and professionals, as well as to people with Down Syndrome.

dragnet

Contact: `dragnet-request@chiller.compaq.com`

Purpose: To discuss strip drag racing from a participant's viewpoint. (Moderated.)

DSA-LGB

Contact: `dsa-lgb-request@midway.uchicago.edu`

Purpose: A mailing list for members of the Lesbian/Gay/Bisexual Commission of the Democratic Socialists of America, and for other people interested in discussing connections between sexual identity and the democratic socialist movement in the U.S. and other nations. The list is neither archived nor moderated.

Dual-Personalities

Contact: dual-personalities-request@darwin.uucp

Purpose: Discussion, maintenance/survival tips, and commercial offerings for the System/83 UNIX box made by the now-defunct DUAL Systems Corporation of Berkeley, as well as similar machines using the IEEE-696 bus (such as the CompuPro 8/16E with Root/Unisoft UNIX).

DVI-list

Contact: dvi-list-request@calvin.dgbt.doc.ca
(Andrew Patrick)

Purpose: For discussions about Intel's DVI (Digital Video Interactive) system. These discussions cover both applications and programming with DVI.

Eagles

Contact: eagles-request@flash.usc.edu

Purpose: To provide a forum for Scouts, Scouters, and former Scouts who are gay/lesbian/bisexual to discuss how they can apply pressure to the BSA to change their homophobic policies. All others who are interested are also welcome.

Earth and Sky

Contact: Majordomo@lists.utexas.edu

Purpose: This is a weekly on-line publication for the public to learn more about earth science and astronomy. It consists of transcripts of radio programs aired daily on the Earth & Sky Radio Series, which is hosted by Deborah Byrd and Joel Block. The series broadcasts on more than 500 stations in the United States and on a variety of other stations across the

globe. For more information, write to Earth & Sky at
P.O. Box 2203, Austin, TX 78768. To add yourself to the
EARTHANDSKY mailing list, send subscribe EARTHANDSKY
yourname@host.domain.name in an e-mail message to
Majordomo@lists.utexas.edu.

East Coast Hockey League

Contact: echl-news-request@andrew.cmu.edu

Purpose: For people interested in discussing and following the East Coast Hockey League.

Echoes

Contact: echoes-request@fawnya.tcs.com (H.W. Neff)

Purpose: Information and commentary on the musical group Pink Floyd as well as other projects members of the group have been involved with.

Econ-Dev

Contact: majordomo@csn.org

Purpose: To share information and network with professionals who are in economic development or are pursuing some of the same informational goals.

We here at the economic development department in Littleton, Colorado, use information as the cornerstone of our program. Littleton's New Economy Project works primarily with small, innovative companies trying to give them the sophisticated tools they need to compete in the new global environment. Rather than "hunt" for faraway companies and offer incentives to try to get them to locate in Littleton, we concentrate on adding value to existing local companies, or "garden." Services include using commercial databases to provide a variety of strategic information.

We are also actively interested in systems thinking, chaos, and complexity as they apply to economics. We look forward to hearing from those of you out there who use information and who are involved with businesses. To subscribe, send the following to majordomo@csn.org:

```
subscribe econ-dev
```

This should be sent in the body of the message. The subject is ignored.

ECTL

Contact: ectl-request@snowhite.cis.uoguelph.ca (David Leip)

Purpose: A list dedicated to researchers interested in Computer Speech Interfaces.

Ecto

Contact: ecto-request@ns1.rutgers.edu (Jessica Dembski)

Purpose: Information and discussion about singer/songwriter Happy Rhodes, and other music, art, books, films of common (or singular) interest.

Eerie, Indiana

Contact: owner-eerie-indiana@sfu.ca (Corey Kirk)

Purpose: The list is for the discussion of the critically acclaimed (but short-lived) TV series *Eerie, Indiana*, which originally aired on NBC in 1991-1992 and is now distributed internationally. The show is a strange mix of humor, fantasy, and science fiction—sort of "*The Wonder Years* meets *Twin Peaks* with a dash of Gary Larson's comic strip *The Far Side*" (*TV Guide*).

Electric Light Orchestra

Contact: elo-list-request@andrew.cmu.edu

Purpose: Discussion of the music of Electric Light Orchestra and later solo efforts by band members and former members.

Electric Vehicles

Contact: listserv@sjsuvm1.sjsu.edu (Clyde Visser)

Purpose: General list for discussion of all aspects of electric vehicles. (Flamers will be drenched.)

For additions, send mail to listserv@sjsuvm1.bitnet with a message text consisting of the line SUBSCRIBE EV *yourfirstname yourlastname*

For digest format, subscribe as above, but with the second line's being SET EV DIGEST

Electromagnetics

Contact: em-request@decwd.ece.uiuc.edu

Purpose: Discussion of issues relating to electromagnetics. This may take the form of book reviews, code problems, techniques, etc.

Elements

Contact: elements-request@alsys.com (Gary Morris KK6YB)

Purpose: The Shuttle Elements mailing list—to get Keplerian Elements out as quickly as possible during flights. We send out prelaunch elements and postlaunch elements based on either Flight Dynamics Office predictions, Shuttle computer state vector data, or on NORAD radar tracking data. Anyone may subscribe, but prior approval is required before sending submissions to the list.

E-List

Contact: vilo@cs.helsinki.fi (Jaak Vilo)

Purpose: News and discussion on Estonia.

ELP

Contact: j.arnold@bull.com (John Arnold)

Purpose: To share news, opinions, and other discussions about the musical group Emerson, Lake & Palmer and related topics.

Elvis Costello

Contact: costello-request@gnu.ai.mit.edu
(Danny Hernandez)

Purpose: For the discussion and dissemination of information of Declan Patrick Aloysius MacManus, better known as Elvis Costello. Everyone is welcome.

Embedded Digest

Contact: embed-request@synchro.com (Chuck Cox)

Purpose: A forum for the discussion of embedded computer system engineering. Suitable topics include embedded hardware and software design techniques, development and testing tool reviews, product announcements, etc.

Empire-List

Contact: empire-list-request@bbn.com

Purpose: Discussion of design and implementation issues of BSD Empire among authors and interested parties.

Emplant

Contact: subscribe@xamiga.linet.org

Purpose: For the Emplant Macintosh Hardware Emulator. Emplant is a hardware board that allows Amiga users to run any Macintosh programs, in color. The mailing list will provide any info on compatibility and software upgrades.

Send subscription requests to subscribe@xamiga.linet.org using this format:

> #emplant *youraccount@yoursubdomain.yourdomain*;

emTeX-User

Contact: emtex@chemie.fu-berlin.de (Vera Heinau and Heiko Schlichting)

> emtex-user-request@chemie.fu-berlin.de

Purpose: Information about emTeX, an implementation of TeX for MS-DOS and OS/2. This list is meant for everyone who wants to discuss problems concerning installation and/or use of the emTeX package and to be informed about bugs, fixes, and new releases. It sometimes has a traffic of about 5-10 mails per day, so if you (or your host) can't handle such a quantity of mail, please don't sign on. The list is maintained "by hand," so please be patient if a request is not answered immediately.

Conversation language: English

Endorphins

Contact: endorphins-request@taronga.com
(Stephanie da Silva)

Purpose: For people who love to attain that elusive endorphin high, whether it be by long-distance running, eating red-hot chili peppers, or being paddled on the bottom. If you feel you may be offended by discussion in the last category, please do not subscribe.

Episcopal (Anglican)

Contact: listserv@american.edu

    cms@dragon.com (Cindy Smith)

Purpose: To provide a non-hostile environment for discussion among Christians who are members of the Holy Catholic Church in the Anglican Communion, or who are simply interested in Episcopal beliefs and practices. Non-Anglicans and non-Christians may join the list and listen in, but full-blown debates between Anglicans and Protestants/Roman Catholics/non-Christians are best carried out in the soc.religion.christian and talk.religion.misc news groups. It is hoped that the availability of this list will not diminish the contributions Christians make there. Discussions on ecumenism are encouraged.

To subscribe, send a one-line message body (not subject) to the subscription address:

    SUBSCRIBE ANGLICAN *yourfullname*

Epoch Users Forum

Contact: epuf-request@mcs.anl.gov

Purpose: An ideas exchange mechanism for users of Epoch fileservers. Comments, questions, and feedback are encouraged.

es

Contact: es-request@hawkwind.utcs.toronto.edu (Chris Siebenmann)

Purpose: Discussion of the *es* shell. es is both simple and highly programmable. By exposing many of the internals and adopting constructs from functional programming languages, Paul Haahr and Byron Rakitzis have created a shell that supports new paradigms for programmers. The es shell and the mailing list archives are available on ftp.sys.utoronto.ca, directory /pub/es.

Esperanto

Contact: esperanto-request@rand.org (Mike Urban)

Purpose: A forum for people interested in the neutral international language Esperanto. Discussions about the language itself, the Esperanto movement, publications, and news are encouraged; of course, discussion *in* the language itself is especially encouraged, although English translations may be advisable when the material is of interest to beginners or non-Esperantists.

Ethology

Contact: saarikko@cc.helsinki.fi (Jarmo Saarikko)

Purpose: An unmoderated mailing list for the discussion of animal behavior and behavioral ecology. Possible topics could be, for example, new or controversial theories, new research methods, and equipment. Announcements of books, papers, conferences, new software for behavioral analysis, etc., with possible experiences, are also encouraged.

Everton

Contact: everton-request@wg.estec.esa.nl

Purpose: For any discussion concerning the Everton Football Club and anything vaguely related. In particular, it is for fixtures, results, news, and gossip, especially the kind of information that doesn't get mentioned by the international media.

Excelsior!

Contact: subscribe@xamiga.linet.org

Purpose: For users of the Amiga Excelsior! BBS system. Used for transferring small binaries, update notices, bug reports, and suggestions.

Send subscription requests to subscribe@xamiga.linet.org using this format:

```
#excelsior youraccount@yoursubdomain.yourdomain;
```

Exhibitionists

Contact: exhibitionists-request@jvnc.net

Purpose: Primarily for managers and/or projectionists, but open also to anyone working in a cinema or film society, etc. Anyone's welcome to join, but the conversation is mainly about things that only cinema workers (and in some cases only projectionists) would be interested in, so if this isn't you, think twice about joining. In short, a forum where someone can ask "So how was work at the theater today?" and then actually understand what you're talking about.

Exotic-Cars

Contact: exotic-cars-request@sol.asl.hitachi.com
(Joe Augenbraun)

Purpose: Discussion about exotic and limited-production automobiles, including maintenance, driving impressions, artistic nits, and any other aspect of the world's rarest and most desirable cars.

Extropians

Contact: extropians-request@extropy.org

Purpose: Discussion and development of Extropian ideas. The term "Extropian" was coined by the publishers of the journal *Extropy*, which is devoted to Extropian philosophy. This list is a spinoff of the journal. Extropians may be roughly described as those simultaneously interested in anarchocapitalist politics, cryonics (and other life-extension techniques), the technological extension of human intelligence and perception, nanotechnology, spontaneous orders, and a number of other related ideas. If you are an Extropian, the concept that these are all related topics will seem natural.

All Extropians (and those who suspect that they are Extropians) are invited to join.

For more information on the Extropy Institute, Inc., a not-for-profit educational foundation, send mail to exi-info@extropy.org or write Max More, c/o Extropy Institute, 11860 Magnolia Avenue, Suite R, Riverside, CA 92503.

Fairness

Contact: fairness-request@mainstream.com (automated—Craig Peterson)

Purpose: Monitoring issues of "fairness" with respect to the government. Press releases from the White House, articles from papers and journals, and opinions from individuals are included.

Fall

Contact: fall-request@wg.estec.esa.nl

Purpose: Any discussion concerning the Fall and the various offspring of it, plus any related subjects.

FASE

Contact: `fase@cs.uh.edu`

Purpose: FASE (Forum for Academic Software Engineering)—a forum for communication among academic educators who teach software engineering. Submissions are compiled and mailed to subscribers approximately monthly.

FATFREE

Contact: `fatfree-request@hustle.rahul.net`
(Michelle R. Dick)

Purpose: FATFREE, the McDougall/Ornish mailing list—for discussion about extremely low-fat vegetarianism. For this list, very low-fat indicates diets with less than 15 percent of calories as fat. Vegetarian includes milk, eggs, and honey, but excludes all meat, fish, and poultry. Two main proponents of this style of diet are John McDougall and Dean Ornish.

Members are encouraged to contribute recipes, testimonials, food news, requests, tips on dealing with family and friends, anecdotes, jokes, and questions of any sort at least mildly related to low-fat vegetarianism and living a healthy lifestyle (both McDougall and Ornish emphasize mild exercise and relaxation activities as part of a healthy lifestyle). This is not a moderated list.

This is a high-volume list; we generally get between 5 and 30 messages per day. There are two ways to receive the list: regular and digest. Regular members receive each message individually throughout the day. Digest members receive just one e-mail each day containing all the previous day's traffic. There is no difference in content.

To join, send e-mail to `fatfree-request@hustle.rahul.net`, using one of the following subjects:

`add`	To join as a regular member
`add digest`	To join as a digest member

F-Body

Contact: f-body-request@rwsys.lonestar.org

Purpose: Discussion of Camaros and Firebirds.

Fegmaniax

Contact: fegmaniax-request@gnu.ai.mit.edu

Purpose: Discussion, news, and information regarding that English eccentric and musician, Robyn Hitchcock.

Femail

Contact: femail-request@lucerne.eng.sun.com (Ellen Eades)

Purpose: To provide a forum for discussion of issues of interest to women, in a friendly atmosphere. The basic tenets of feminism and the day-to-day experiences of women do not have to be explained or defended. Men and women can join, but everyone requesting to be added to the mailing list must provide the moderator with the following:

- A full name
- A complete UUCP path to a well-known host or a fully specified Internet address
- The correspondent's gender (for records and statistics only). *No* exceptions.

Feminism-Digest

Contact: feminism-digest@ncar.ucar.edu
(Cindy Tittle Moore)

Purpose: A digest version of soc.feminism. It is intended for those who have difficulty getting soc.feminism, or who prefer to read it all at once or whatever.

Ferrets

Contact: `ferret-request@ferret.ocunix.on.ca` (Chris Lewis)

`{utzoo,utai,uunet}!cunews!latour!ecicrl!ferret-request`

Purpose: For people who have or are merely interested in ferrets (Mustela Furo). Discussions are welcome on any subject relating to ferrets—suitability as pets, health information, funny ferret stories, etc.

Filmmakers

Contact: `filmmakers-request@grissom.larc.nasa.gov`

Purpose: Deals with all aspects of motion picture production, with an emphasis on technical issues. Heavily stressed are construction and design issues for those working on tight budgets. It should be emphasized that the subject is film, not video.

Finewine

Contact: `finewine-request@world.std.com` (Eric Budke)

Purpose: A news group dedicated to the rock music group God Street Wine.

Firearms

Contact: `firearms-request@cs.cmu.edu` (Karl Kleinpaste)

Purpose: To provide an environment in which sportsmen can discuss issues of concern to them. Topics include but are not limited to hunting, firearms safety, legal issues, reloading tips, maintenance suggestions, target shooting, and dissemination of general information. Anyone is welcome to join—note that we do *not* intend to discuss the merits of gun control.

Flags

Contact: bottasini@cesi.it (Giuseppe Bottasini)

Purpose: The creation of a worldwide, real-time updated database about all kinds of flags: (inter)national, (un)official, ethnical, political, religious, movements' flags. Discussion of symbols or colors used on flags, in order to find common and/or unique meanings about them. Gathering information about flags' histories.

Flamingo

Contact: flamingo-request@lenny.corp.sgi.com

Purpose: The list is for unmoderated discussion among fans of the series *Parker Lewis* (formerly *Parker Lewis Can't Lose*) on the Fox television network. It is available both as a mail reflector and as a digest. The two formats distribute the same material; please state your preference when you subscribe.

Flashlife

Contact: flashlife-request@netcom.com (Carl Rigney)

Purpose: A mailing list for GMs of Shadowrun and other cyberpunk role-playing games to discuss rules and scenarios, ask questions, make up answers, and similar fasfax.

FL-MOTSS

Contact: fl-motss-request@pts.mot.com

Purpose: Discussion of LGB issues in Florida. Anyone can join and participate. Please include full name and e-mail address on all requests.

FM-10

Contact: fm-10-request@dg-rtp.dg.com

Purpose: To talk about modifications, enhancements, and uses of the Ramsey FM-10, other BA-1404-based FM Stereo broadcasters, also some discussion of the FM pirate radio.

Fogelberg

Contact: ai411@yfn.ysu.edu

Purpose: To discuss Dan Fogelberg and his music. To subscribe, send e-mail to ai411@yfn.ysu.edu in this form:

    subscribe fogelberg yourfullname (and)
    youraccount@yoursubdomain.yourdomain

A digest form of the list is forthcoming; write for information.

Folk-Dancing

Contact: tjw+@pitt.edu (Terry J. Wood)

    tjw@pittvms.bitnet

Purpose: Any discussion of folk dancing. Areas of dance would include but not be limited to international, contra, square, western square morris, Cajun, and barn dancing.

Please feel free to discuss such things as touring groups, artists, camps, workshops, styling, equipment, recordings, and so on. This mailing list also welcomes queries about where to find dance groups and how to get started dancing.

Please note that the Folk Dancing Mailing List (FDML) operates in conjunction with the USENET news group rec.folk-dancing. Material in rec.folk-dancing appears in the FDML. This mailing list is primarily for people who cannot (or do not want to) receive USENET.

When subscribing to the FDML, please include several computer mail addresses *and* a postal mail address (or phone number) as a last resort.

Folk_music

Contact: listserv@nysernet.org (Alan Rowoth)

Purpose: Folk_music is a moderated discussion list dealing with the music of the recent wave of American singer/songwriters. List traffic consists of tour schedules, reviews, album release info, and other information on artists like Shawn Colvin, Mary-Chapin Carpenter, David Wilcox, Nanci Griffith, Darden Smith, Cheryl Wheeler, John Gorka, Ani DiFranco, and others. There are no archives as of yet.

To subscribe, send mail to listserv@nysernet.org with this request:

    SUBSCRIBE FOLK_MUSIC yourfullname

We also maintain files for ftp at nysernet.org, including the ever popular Dirty Linen magazine monthly tour calendars. To access these files via anonymous ftp, log in as GUEST and give your *user-id@your.local.host* as a password. Files and subdirectories are contained within the directory /FOLK_MUSIC. These are also accessible via gopher on port 70. The nysernet gopher is also available via telnet by connecting to nysernet.org and typing nysernet as a login name; no password is necessary.

Fordnatics

Contact: fordnatics-request@freud.arc.nasa.gov
(Chuck Fry)

    fords-request@freud.arc.nasa.gov

Purpose: The Fordnatics mailing list is an unmoderated forum for discussing high-performance Fords or

Ford-powered vehicles, especially modifications and driving techniques for competition or track use.

Forest Management DSS

Contact: listserv@pnfi.forestry.ca (Tom Moore)

Purpose: The discussion group is a forum for rapid exchange of information, ideas, and opinions related to the topics of decision support systems and information systems for forest management planning. Also welcome are announcements of meetings, calls for papers, calls for proposals, help wanted, employment wanted, resumes, book reviews, and copies of papers or speeches.

Although this is being sponsored as part of a Canadian research program, participation from the international community is welcome. Please pass this information on to your colleagues.

To subscribe to the list, send an e-mail to listserv@pnfi.forestry.ca with the message SUBSCRIBE FMDSS-L *yourfirstname yourlastname*

FoxPro

Contact: fileserv@polarbear.rankin-inlet.nt.ca (Chris O'Neill)

Purpose: To foster information sharing between users of the FoxPro database development environment now owned and distributed by Microsoft Corporation. Both new and experienced users of FoxPro are welcome to join in the discussions.

Topics that may be discussed in the foxpro-l mailing list include (but are not necessarily limited to) the following: ideas for applications, exchanging code snippets, problem solving, product news, and just about anything else related to the FoxPro development environment.

Note: The foxpro-l mailing list is not affiliated with Microsoft Corporation in any way.

To subscribe to the foxpro-l mailing list, send an e-mail message to fileserv@polarbear.rankin-inlet.nt.ca with the following in the body:

```
JOIN FOXPRO-L
QUIT
```

Framers

Contact: framers-request@uunet.uu.net (Mark Lawrence)

Purpose: A users' forum for sharing experiences and information about the FrameMaker desktop publishing package from Frame Technology.

France-Foot

Contact: france-foot-request@inf.enst.fr
(Vincent Habchi)

Purpose: Discussions of the French football (soccer) scene. Results and news are posted regularly.

Freaks

Contact: freaks-request@bnf.com

Purpose: A list that talks about Marillion and related rock groups. To subscribe, send a message containing: subscribe freaks *yourfullname*

FREEDOM

Contact: listserv@idbsu.idbsu.edu

Purpose: Mailing list of people organizing against the Idaho Citizens Alliance anti-gay ballot initiative.

To subscribe, send a message to listserv@idbsu.idbsu.edu with one line SUB FREEDOM *yourfullname*.

Friends of Ohio State

Contact: antivirus@aol.com (Jerry Canterburg)

Purpose: To share items of interest with alumni and other friends of OSU.

Fringeware

Contact: fringeware-request@illuminati.io.com

Purpose: A moderated list devoted to cyberculture and the like.

FSP-Discussion

Contact: listmaster@germany.eu.net

Purpose: Discussion of the new FSP protocol. FSP is a set of programs that implements a public-access archive similar to an anonymous-ftp archive. The difference is that FSP is connectionless and virtually stateless. This list is open for everybody.

FSUUCP

Contact: fsuucp-request@polyslo.calpoly.edu (Christopher J. Ambler)

Purpose: For the discussion, bug hunting, feature proposing, and announcements of the availability and release dates of FSUUCP, an MS-DOS UUCP/mail/news package. FSUUCP is shareware, and includes uucico/uuxqt (with support for rmail and rnews—single, batched, and compressed batch), as well as readnews, postnews, mail, expire, uuq, uusnap, uulog, and a host of utilities.

Funky-Music

Contact: funky-music-request@athena.mit.edu

Purpose: The discussion of funk music, as well as rap, hip-hop, soul, R & B, and related varieties. Discussions of zydeco, reggae, salsa, soca, and similar gutsy street music are also welcome.

Funk music is based on the rhythmic innovations pioneered by James Brown. Other notable artists in the genre are Parliament, Funkadelic, War, Earth Wind and Fire, the Meters, and Mandrill.

Funky music has a danceable beat to it, a soulful feel, and an underlying intelligence. All the varieties of music mentioned above are funky.

Fusion

Contact: fusion-request@zorch.sf-bay.org

Purpose: E-mail redistribution of USENET sci.physics.fusion news group, for sites/users that don't have access to USENET.

Futurebus+ Users

Contact: majordomo@theus.rain.com

Purpose: A discussion group for users of Futurebus+. Topics include the design, implementation, integration, and operation of the hardware and software that are related to Futurebus+.

To subscribe, mail to majordomo@theus.rain.com with
subscribe fbus_users *youraccount@yoursubdomain.yourdomain*
in the body of the text.

Fuzzy-Ramblings

Contact: fuzzy-ramblings-request@piggy.ucsb.edu (Robert Earl)

Purpose: Discussion of the British girl group We've Got a Fuzzbox and We're Going to Use It!!!.

GAELIC-L

Contact: listserv@irlearn.ucd.ie

Purpose: A multi-disciplinary discussion list set up to facilitate the exchange of news, views, and information in Scottish Gaelic, Irish, and Manx. Read on for instructions in Scottish Gaelic (SG), Irish (IG), and Manx (MG).

To subscribe to the list, send a mail message to listserv@irlearn.ucd.ie containing the single line SUBSCRIBE GAELIC-L *yourname*, and you will be automatically added by the computer that runs GAELIC-L. For questions, contact mgunn@irlearn.ucd.ie (Marion Gunn), caoimhin@smo.ac.uk (Caoimhi/n O/ Donnai/le), or lss203@cs.napier.ac.uk (Craig Cockburn).

Gateway 2000

Contact: gateway2000-request@sei.cmu.edu (Tod Pike)

Purpose: A good source of information about Gateway 2000 products. The Gateway 2000 Mailing List is *not* owned by Gateway 2000, Inc. of North Sioux City, SD. It, in addition to the news group alt.sys.pc-clone.gateway2000, is run for and by Gateway 2000 users.

GAY-LIBN

Contact: listserv@vm.usc.edu

Purpose: Gay/Lesbian/Bisexual Librarians Network. To join the list and receive mailings from GAY-LIBN,

- At Bitnet nodes, send mail or an interactive message to `listserv@uscvm` with the text SUB GAY-LIBN *YOURFIRSTNAME YOURLASTNAME* (no punctuation, no other text).

- At other nodes, send mail to `listserv@vm.usc.edu` with the text SUB GAY-LIBN *YOURFIRSTNAME YOURLASTNAME* (no punctuation, no other text).

GayNet

Contact: gaynet-request@queernet.org (Roger B.A. Klorese)

Purpose: A list about gay, lesbian, and bisexual concerns (with a focus on college campuses), including (but not limited to) outreach programs, political action, AIDS education, dealing with school administrations, social programs, and just finding out what other support groups are doing. Items of general gay/lesbian interest are also welcome.

The list is not moderated.

Subscription/unsubscription requests are managed by an automated server called Majordomo.

To subscribe, send a mail message to

   majordomo@queernet.org

The first (not subject) line of the message should be

   subscribe gaynet

Other administrative questions and requests should be sent to the e-mail address gaynet-approval@queernet.org.

GEGSTAFF

Contact: listserv@ukcc.uky.edu (Jeff Jones)

Purpose: The discussion of all topics relating to sexuality and gender in geography. Discussions of theoretical and empirical work/issues are welcome, as are book reviews, calls for papers, and information on conferences.

To subscribe, send mail to listserv@ukcc, or on the Internet to listserv@ukcc.uky.edu, with the body containing the command SUB GEGSTAFF *yourfirstname yourlastname*

Gender

Contact: ericg@indiana.edu (Eric Garrison)

Purpose: A list created for the purpose of discussing gender issues. The intent is to provide an open-minded forum for discussion of gender stereotypes versus individuality, gender roles, and particularly how people can get beyond these restrictions. Any related topic is fair game: I won't presume to dictate the subject matter of the list, I want everyone on the list to do that. Anonymous "posting" is available.

To join, mail ericg@indiana.edu with add me mail.gender in the subject line.

GL-ASB

Contact: majordomo@queernet.org (Roger B.A. Klorese)

Purpose: For discussion of bondage and S & M topics for gay men and lesbians. It is intended to provide a forum for discussion and stories with an atmosphere of gay and lesbian culture perceived by some as being less prevalent in the alt.sex.bondage news group than they want.

The gl-asb list is administered with the assistance of an automated mailing list server called Majordomo, written by Brent Chapman. In order to be added to the list, please send a message to one of the following addresses:

>   majordomo@queernet.org
>   *wellconnectedsite*!unpc!majordomo (if you support only UUCP paths)

with the following content in the message:

```
subscribe gl-asb
end
```

Any administrative questions should be addressed to

gl-asb-approval@queernet.org
wellconnectedsite!unpc!gl-asb-approval (if you support only UUCP paths)

Glass Arts

Contact: glass-request@dixie.com

Purpose: For stained/hot glass artists.

GLBPOC

Contact: glbpoc-request@ferkel.ucsb.edu

Purpose: A mailing list for lesbian, gay, and bisexual people of color. To be added to the list, you must provide your full name and a complete Internet address.

Glove-List

Contact: listserv@boxer.nas.nasa.gov (machine)

jet@nas.nasa.gov (human) (J. Eric Townsend)

Purpose: Discussion of the Nintendo PowerGlove, a less than $100 dataglove available on the remaindered racks of Toys 'R Us and other big toy stores. To subscribe, send e-mail to listserv@boxer.nas.nasa.gov with a body of subscribe glove-list *yourfullname*.

GNU-Manual

Contact: gnu-manual-request@a.cs.uiuc.edu (Internet)

Purpose: GNU-manual members are volunteers who write, proofread, and comment on documents for a GNU Emacs Lisp programmers' manual.

GodlyGraphics

Contact: godlygraphics-request@acs.harding.edu
(Ron Pacheco)

Purpose: The GodlyGraphics mailing list is for the discussion of Christian uses of computer graphics and animations, especially using the Amiga computer, and for related trading of ideas, objects, images, and even joint projects, such as the design of a Christian computer game. The possibilities for innovative uses of computer graphics, animations, multimedia applications, and video productions in support of various Christian ministries and other endeavors are *wide open*. What better use of your technical skills or creative talents than to serve the One who gave them to you? Any interested or curious Christian is welcome to join.

Golden

Contact: golden-request@hobbes.ucsd.edu

Purpose: A mailing list for Golden Retriever enthusiasts. Suitable topics include questions and answers regarding the Golden Retriever breed in general, news bits, article summaries, discussions of particular lines and breeders, shows, activities (CCI, therapy dogs, guide dogs), show bragging, summaries of local GR club activities or newsletters, other items that might be too Golden-introverted for rec.pets.dogs, cooperation on a breed-specific FAQ for r.p.d, etc.

Gothic-Tales

Contact: carriec@eskimo.com

Purpose: Twice weekly mailings of gothic/vampire/blood stories pertaining to darkness, obscurity, and beauty. Other gothic issues (music, lifestyle) occasionally are added to the list.

GPS Digest

Contact: gps-request@esseye.si.com

Purpose: A forum for the discussion of topics related to the USAF Global Positioning System (GPS) and other satellite navigation positioning systems. The digest is moderated.

GRASS

Contact: grass-server@wharton.upenn.edu

Purpose: The Generic Religions and Secret Societies mailing list—a forum for the development of religions and secret societies for use in role-playing games. Both real-world and fictional religions and secret societies are covered. GRASS is an erratic volume, high signal-to-noise mailing list.

To subscribe, send mail to the contact address with a subject of SUBSCRIBE *yourfullname*.

Grunge-L

Contact: listserv@ubvm.cc.buffalo.edu (Jon Hilgreen)

Purpose: This list is intended for the discussion of any and all topics related to the form of music known as "grunge rock" (not just Seattle-based or Sub Pop bands). It is an open, unmoderated list with a frequently high level of traffic.

As a general guideline, the following talk is encouraged:

- Recording/concert reviews and recommendations
- Band tour dates
- Local scene reviews and news
- Record store and mail-order company recommendations
- Nose-picking techniques
- Interviews and articles, original or otherwise
- Quotes, band gossip, and insider information
- Anything else one would typically find in a music magazine

People who find "adult language and references" offensive will not want to join this list. It is also a good idea to read the grunge list with an extra dose of patience, perverse humor, and sarcasm.

To subscribe, send a message containing

    subscribe grunge-l complete real name

to listserv@ubvm (BITNET), or listserv@ubvm.cc.buffalo.edu (Internet).

GSP-List

Contact: gsp-list-request@ms.uky.edu
(David W. Rankin Jr.)

    gsp-list-request@ukma.bitnet

    {uunet, gatech, rutgers}!ukma!gsp-list-request

Purpose: To allow "alumni" (as defined by the GSPAA) of the Kentucky Governor's Scholars Program to participate in intellectual discussions on various topics, while also promoting the spirit of "community" fostered by GSP. The list maintainer requests that only GSPeople request to join the list, and that when they do, they send at least two good e-mail addresses (if possible) and the year and campus at which they attended GSP.

Gug-Sysadmins

Contact: gug-sysadmins-request@vlsivie.tuwien.ac.at

Purpose: Distributions of rumors, bug fixes, and work-arounds concerning the CAD-Tool genesil and related tools to members of the Eurochip project and other interested parties.

Gunk'l'Dunk

Contact: jeremy@stat.washington.edu (Jeremy York)

Purpose: A forum for discussing and promoting *Tales of the Beanworld*, an unusual black-and-white comic published by Eclipse comics. It is a moderated newsletter that occasionally receives input from the creator of the Beanworld, Larry Marder.

Gymn

Contact: owner-gymn@mit.edu (Robyn Kozierok)

Please specify either mailing list or digest format.

Purpose: For the discussion of all aspects of the sport of gymnastics. People of all levels of knowledge and interest are most welcome. Archive location: ftp.cac.psu.edu. Includes back issues of the digest, addresses, calendar, and other information. Ftp items may also be retrieved by sending e-mail to rachele@rice.edu.

Handicap

Contact: wtm@bunker.shel.isc-br.com

Purpose: The Handicap Digest—information/discussion exchange for issues dealing with the physically/mentally handicapped. Topics include but are not limited to medical, education, legal, technological aids, and the handicapped in society.

Note: The articles from the Handicap Digest are also posted in the USENET news group misc.handicap.

HANDS

Contact: hands@u.washington.edu

Purpose: A list compiled by Hands Off Washington-University of Washington chapter. This list tells people when our next meetings are, provides information on upcoming events such as rallies and speakers, and provides a chance for people to read selected forwarded newsbriefs from Washington state as well as other parts of the country.

The main purpose is to keep people up-to-date on activities planned by HOW-UW and to inform people about the agenda of the Citizens Alliance of Washington (CAW) and other discriminatory organizations.

Hang-Gliding

Contact: hang-gliding-request@virginia.edu
(Galen Hekhuis)

Purpose: Topics covering all aspects of hang-gliding and ballooning, for ultra-light and lighter-than-air enthusiasts.

Harleys

Contact: harley-request@thinkage.on.ca (Ken Dykes)

harley-request@thinkage.com

uunet!thinkage!harley-request

Purpose: Discussion about the bikes, politics, lifestyles, and anything else of interest to Harley-Davidson motorcycle lovers. The list is an automated digest format scheduled for twice a day Monday through Friday. Members may access an e-mail archive server for back-issues and other items of interest.

Hey-Joe

Contact: hey-joe-request@ms.uky.edu (Joel Abbott)

Purpose: Discussion and worship of Jimi Hendrix and his music. Although Jimi has been dead for about two decades, we feel that his music is still worthy to be recognized. Prerequisite to joining: appreciation for his music.

Hindu Digest

Contact: listserv@arizvm1.ccit.arizona.edu

Purpose: Hindu dharma (religious philosophy and way of life) is followed by over 650 million people in the world. Prominent among its teachings are the acceptance of various religious paths and the spirit of universal family.

The Hindu Digest is a forum to discuss various Hindu doctrines as they are applicable to day-to-day living. We also discuss various issues that affect the Hindu perspective, such as war and peace, human rights, and the participation of Hindus in political processes to promote the universal ideals mentioned above. It is also a forum for cultural news about Hindus from around the world.

To subscribe, send mail to
listserv@arizvm1.ccit.arizona.edu in this form: `SUB HINDU-D Full Name` (`Full Name` must be at least two words).

Historic Costume

Contact: h-costume-request@andrew.cmu.edu

Purpose: This list concentrates on re-creating period elegance, from the Bronze age to the mid 20th century. Its emphasis is on accurate historical reproduction of clothing, historical techniques for garment construction, and the application of those techniques for modern clothing design. Other topics appropriate for discussion include adapting historical clothing for the modern figure, clothing evolution, theatrical costumes, patterns, materials, books, and sources for supplies. Members of the SCA should note that this list discusses historic costume of all eras, not just the SCA period. General conversations about the SCA are not suitable for this list. Other topics not suitable for this list include Halloween and children's dress-up costumes, and advertisements for vintage clothing (for sale or wanted).

HIX

Contact: hix@cipher.pha.jhu.edu

Purpose: Hollosi Information Exchange—a mail server containing information about Hungarian electronic resources, i.e., discussion lists, newsletters, etc. Information is in Hungarian.

In the subject field, write only `HIX`, and make the text of the letter `HELP all`.

HOCKEY-L

Contact: listserv@maine.maine.edu

wts@maine.maine.edu (Wayne Smith)

Purpose: The discussion of collegiate ice hockey, including scores, team info, schedules, etc., allowing fans to become more involved and knowledgeable about the game.

Substantial information is available via HOCKEY-L subscription, including current year Division I team and composite schedules and scores, and other college and Olympic hockey information as assembled or created by the subscribers. In-season postings include all Division I scores and descriptions of most games. Division II, III, and Club hockey discussions are welcome.

See also `hockey3-request@hooville.mitre.org` for a list devoted to Division III college hockey.

To subscribe to HOCKEY-L, send a one-line message body (not subject) to the subscription address as follows:

> SUBSCRIBE HOCKEY-L *your name and college team(s) of interest*

Holocaust Information

Contact: `listserv@oneb.almanac.bc.ca`

Purpose: For Holocaust research and the refutation of those who deny the event. It is currently an unmoderated, public list, but I reserve the right to change status to private/moderated if the need arises.

Topics within the scope of the list include: worldwide racial supremacy organizations and activities; worldwide neo-Nazi organizations and activities; Holocaust denial via electronic networking, including but not limited to FidoNet, USENET, Internet, Prodigy, GEnie, CompuServe, etc., and the notification of all list members when a new bulletin board, fax forwarding, or voice-mail organization is identified as representing the views of the various organizations noted above, including The Institute for Historical Review (IHR), Christian Identity, Aryan Nation, America First Committee, Liberty Lobby, and activities of well-known folks like Willy Carto, David Irving, and many, many others.

To subscribe to the list, send the following command to listserv@oneb.almanac.bc.ca in this form:

    subscribe hlist yourfirstname yourlastname

    Example: subscribe hlist ken mcvay

If you do not receive confirmation from the server within 24 hours, please let me know and I will add you to the list manually.

Homebrew

Contact: homebrew-request%hpfcmr@hplabs.hp.com

    hplabs!hpfcmr!homebrew-request (Rob Gardner)

Purpose: Forum on beer, homebrewing, and related issues. Though mainly intended for discussion of beer making, also welcome are discussions on making cider, mead, wine, or any other fermented (but not distilled) beverage. Beginners are welcome, as well as experienced brewers.

Home-Ed

Contact: home-ed-request@think.com (David Mankins)

Purpose: For the discussion of all aspects and methods of home education. These include the "unschooling" approach, curricula-based home-schooling, and others. The list is currently unmoderated and welcomes everyone interested in educating their children at home, whatever the reasons.

Home-Ed-Politics

Contact: home-ed-politics-request@mainstream.com
(Craig Peterson)

Purpose: To discuss political issues dealing with home education. This includes government intrusion into families, public schooling as it influences home education, legislation in various states & the federal level, etc. This list is managed by listproc.

Horse

Contact: equestrians-request@world.std.com
(David C. Kovar)

Purpose: Discussion of things equestrian. Horse enthusiasts of all disciplines and levels of experience are welcome. Articles are distributed periodically in digest format, and also appear individually in the USENET news group rec.equestrian.

Hotrod

Contact: hotrod-request@dixie.com (Include on the Subject line the keyword subscribe and a return path to your site.)

Purpose: To provide a forum for people interested in high-performance vehicles to exchange ideas and discuss topics of current interest. This list is chartered as broadly as possible, consistent with noise suppression. Explicitly acceptable is any discussion regarding increasing the performance of any vehicle with more than three wheels.

HP Patch

Contact: hpux-patch-request@cv.ruu.nl

Purpose: The HP Patch Descriptions Mailing List—in short, the purpose of the mailing list is this:

1. If somebody receives a patch from HP, he/she can post the *description* of that patch to the mailing list.

2. Other members now know that a patch exists and can ask HP for "patch *xxxx*" if they think they have a problem.

3. The patches themselves are *never* posted!!!!!!!!

4. This list only exists as long as HP itself doesn't supply a list of available patches.

To reach all members of the list, send e-mail to hpux-patch@cv.ruu.nl. This is what you might want to do if you receive a new patch.

To subscribe, send e-mail to hpux-patch-request@cv.ruu.nl. Please include your e-mail address in the message. Not all mailers generate proper return addresses.

Problems, questions, suggestions, and the like should go to this address too. To ease searching for a patch to a specific problem, I've started to write a set of tools that I loosely call "pltools." Currently, there's one script (written in PERL) called plfind that searches through an unofficial list of patch descriptions according to user-supplied queries. Updates to this list and to the tools are posted on a semiregular basis. Also, each new member of the list receives the current distribution upon subscription.

Huskers

Contact: huskers-request@tssi.com (Michael Nolan)

Purpose: To provide coverage of University of Nebraska sports. The major in-season sports (football, basketball) will likely make up the majority of posts, but other sports are likely to be mentioned from time to time, depending on the interest. Other items likely to be of interest to NU alums or Cornhusker fans may also appear.

Hyperami

Contact: listserv@archive.oit.unc.edu

Purpose: For informal product discussion and mutual assistance concerning AmigaVision, CanDo, DeluxeVideo III,

Director 2, Foundation, Hyperbook, InterActor, PILOT, ShowMaker, TACL, Thinker, and VIVA.

To join, send a mail request to listserv@archive.oit.unc.edu and give a one-line message asking subscribe hyperami.

This list is separate from the USENET news group comp.sys.amiaga.multimedia, but material from the list may occasionally be posted to the news group.

Hyperbole, Hyperbole-Announce

Contact: hyperbole-request@cs.brown.edu (Bob Weiner)

Purpose: For discussion of the Hyperbole systems and the related topics of hypertext and information retrieval.

Hyperbole-announce announces new releases and bug fixes for Hyperbole. Anyone on Hyperbole is automatically subscribed to Hyperbole-announce, so you should request subscription to only one of the two lists.

Hyperbole is a flexible hypertext manager developed at Brown University that sits atop of GNU Emacs and provides efficient point-and-click information access and full customizability in GNU Emacs Lisp. Hyperbole allows hypertext buttons to be embedded within unstructured and structured files, mail messages, and news articles. It also provides point-and-click access to ftp archives, Wide Area Information Servers (WAIS), and the World Wide Web (WWW) hypertext system.

Use the following format on your Subject line to execute requests (include the period at the end of the line):

```
Add yourfirstname-yourlastname
<youraccount@yoursubdomain.yourdomain> to
mail-list-name-without-domain.
```

Example: Add Joe Smith <joe@mot.com> to hyperbole.

HyperChem

Contact: hyperchem-request@auto.desk.com (Mark Davies)

Purpose: Designed for, but not limited to, HyperChem users. Any and all scientific and technical issues related to the use of HyperChem are appropriate for discussion on this group.

The group is unmoderated, so any message sent to the group is sent automatically to all other members of the group. Any information on this group is to be taken "as is" without representation or warranty of any kind, either express or implied. The entire risk as to the use of this information is assumed by the user.

IAMS (Internet Amateur Mathematics Society)

Contact: iams-request@quack.kfu.com

Purpose: For discussion of math puzzles and problems.

IB

Contact: hreha@vax2.concordia.ca (Dr. Steve Hreha)

Purpose: To provide a forum for teachers, IB coordinators, and administrators involved with the International Baccalaureate Diploma Program. Discussion of all aspects of the IB program is welcome.

IBDlist

Contact: ibdlist-request%mvac23@udel.edu (Thomas Lapp)

    ...!udel !mvac23!IBDlist-request

Purpose: A moderated mailing list that discusses all aspects of Inflammatory Bowel Diseases, with particular emphasis on Crohn's disease and Ulcerative Colitis. Anyone with an interest in these diseases, whether direct or indirect, is welcome. This list will also act as a clearinghouse for information and discussion of current treatments, research, and other information related to IBDs. This list is open to any interested party and is not restricted to those with a direct link to IBD.

ICF-2010

Contact: icf-2010-request@cup.hp.com (Gary Gitzen)

    {hplabs, uunet}!cup.hp.com!icf-2010-request

Purpose: A low-volume mutual support group to discuss/share technical issues, problems, solutions, performance, and modifications related to the Sony ICF-2010 and 2001D shortwave radios.

ICI

Contact: listserv@research.canon.oz.au

Purpose: Discussion of Tim Long's ICI language and its interpreter. Also acts as an archive for the interpreter source, patches, and documentation.

ICLInfo

Contact: {obdient,tfd}!tons61!iclinfo

Purpose: To update and relay information regarding the CCI/ICL processors. Including information on product updates, product problems, service problems and information, system options, and information on CCI/ICL from "off-line" sources (i.e., inside "scoops" direct from "hidden" CCI/ICL sources).

IDOL

Contact: idol-group-request@luvthang.ori-cal.com
(David Talmage)

Purpose: An unmoderated mailing list for people interested in the Idol language. Idol, an "icon-derived object language," is "an object-oriented extension and environment for the Icon programming language." The idol-group is a forum for discussing Idol programming, object-oriented programming, and Idol implementation issues. It is also a place to exchange Idol classes and programs, contributing to the library of useful Idol code.

Igor

Contact: igor-request@pica.army.mil (Tom Coradeschi)

Purpose: To provide an easy means for users of Igor to share problems and solutions, as well as for potential users to seek opinions on the utility and performance of the application.

Imagen-L

Contact: listserv@bolis.sf-bay.org

Purpose: A discussion forum for all aspects of Imagen laser printers. Any discussion pertaining to Imagen printers is welcome, including software compatibility, hardware interfacing, LAN attachment capabilities, imPRESS programming, or methods used to create spooling and accounting software.

To subscribe, send an Internet e-mail message to listserv@bolis.sf-bay.org that contains the following:

```
subscribe Imagen-L
```

and you will be added to the list.

Imagine

Contact: imagine-request@email.sp.paramax.com
(Dave Wickard)

Purpose: Dedicated to the 3-D computer rendering package Imagine by Impulse, Inc. Currently this package is available on the Amiga computer and for MS-DOS. Subject matter spans most areas and packages in 3-D rendering, but mostly in comparison to Imagine. There are many professional artists using the IML, and the tone is light and friendly. All levels of knowledge and experience are welcome here, and everyone is encouraged to participate. We have held contests, and a frequently asked questions list and full archives since the list's inception in January 1991 are available upon request. Merely send a note to the above address with the word subscribe in the subject line.

Note: Bang-style addressing is not supported, so please include your Internet-style address in subscription request (e.g., *somebody@someplace*.edu).

Immune

Contact: immune-request@weber.ucsd.edu (Cyndi Norman)

Purpose: A support group for people with immune-system breakdowns (and their symptoms), such as Chronic Fatigue Syndrome, Lupus, Candida, Hypoglycemia, multiple allergies, learning disabilities, etc., and their SOs, medical caretakers, etc. The group is unmoderated and open to anyone anywhere in the world. (No arguments about whether these disabilities exist.)

Improv

Contact: improv-request@bmt.gun.com (Timothy Reed)

Purpose: Questions, comments, and bug-reports relating to the Improv spreadsheet for NeXTSTEP and Windows, published by Lotus Corporation. Some mail includes attachments that may be read with mail readers compatible with the NeXT Computer's NeXTmail format.

Impulse

Contact: impulse-users-request@j.cc.purdue.edu
(Kevin Braunsdorf)

Purpose: A low-volume list for users of the LPC Mpulse line of computers. The moderator does filter and journalize submissions.

INDEX-L

Contact: skuster@bingvmb.bitnet (Charlotte Skuster)

Purpose: Discussion of good indexing practice by providing a forum through which professional and aspiring indexers can share information and ideas relating to the intellectual, philosophical, and technical aspects of index preparation. Some recent participants include professional indexers, members of the American Society of Indexers (ASI), librarians, library school faculty and students, information access professionals, hypertext and database developers, and authors indexing their own work.

Indigo-Girls

Contact: indigo-girls-request@cgrg.ohio-state.edu
(Stephen Spencer)

Purpose: Discussion of Indigo Girls and related artists' music, tour dates, concert reviews, etc. Both regular and digest formats are available—please specify when sending a subscribe me message. The digest format gets you one message a day; regular gets you each message as it is sent to the list.

Info-Aids

Contact: `info-aids@rainbow.uucp`

`{pacbell,apple,hoptoad,ucbvax}!well!rainbow!info-aids`
(Ken Davis)

Purpose: To act as a clearinghouse for information and discussion about AIDS, including alternative treatments, political implications, etc. Exchanges files with `aidnews@rutvm1.bitnet`. Open to anyone with the time and inclination to participate. Mailing list will be confidential and known only to the members. Anonymous postings will be accepted. (See also "Aids" mailing list.)

Info-CCC

Contact: `uunet!xurilka!info-ccc-request` (Luigi Perrotta)

Purpose: Devoted to the Concurrent C and Concurrent C++ programming languages. However, discussions can be anything relevant to concurrent programming.

INFOCD

Contact: `mikey@perch.nosc.mil` (Michael Pawka)

Purpose: For the exchange of subjective comments about the compact audio disc medium and related hardware. Topics of discussion may include CD reviews, players, portables, import CDs, etc. Occasionally, the threads even drift off onto lyrics, video discs, etc.

Info-Encore

Contact: `info-encore-request@cs-gw.d.umn.edu`

`info-encore-request@umnd-cs.uucp` (Dan Burrows)

Purpose: Mailing list for discussion of issues involving hardware and software issues of Encore computers and EtherNet terminal servers.

This mailing list is also gatewayed into the inet list `comp.sys.encore`.

Info-GNU

Contact: `info-gnu-request@prep.ai.mit.edu`

`ucbvax!prep.ai.mit.edu!info-gnu-request`

Purpose: To distribute progress reports on the GNU Project, headed by Richard Stallman, and to ask members for various kinds of help. The list is gated both ways with the alternative news group `gnu.announce`, and is filtered (weakly moderated) by Leonard H. Tower Jr. GNU, which stands for *Gnu's Not UNIX*, is the name for a complete UNIX-compatible software system whose sources can be given away free to everyone. Major parts have already been written; major parts still remain undone. Project GNU has additional mailing lists to distribute information about specific GNU programs and to report bugs in them. Contact us at the above address for details.

Info-High-Audio

Contact: `info-high-audio-request@csd4.csd.uwm.edu` (Thomas Krueger)

Purpose: This list is for the exchange of subjective comments about high-end audio equipment and modifications performed to high-end pieces. Techniques used to modify equipment—especially, but not limited to, vacuum tube electronics—are exchanged. Some comments may be subjective or intuitive and may not yet have a measurable basis. Other topics of discussion include turntables, arms, and cartridges; preamplifiers, headamps, and cartridge matching; speakers, amplifiers, and matching; placement of speakers;

and room treatments. Any comments that prevent an open exchange of ideas and techniques are not encouraged.

Archives of projects will be maintained on csd4.csd.uwm.edu and available via anonymous ftp. Info-High-Audio is bidirectionally gatewayed with the USENET news group rec.audio.high-end.

Info-Honda

Contact: info-honda-request@cs.ucla.edu (Rich Wales)

Purpose: Discussion of Honda and Acura automobiles.

Info-Ingres

Contact: info-ingres-request@math.ams.com

Purpose: To discuss the commercial version of Ingres.

Info-LabVIEW

Contact: info-labview-request@pica.army.mil

Purpose: Discussion of the use of National Instruments' LabVIEW package for Macintosh, Windows, and Sparcstation environments.

LabVIEW is a graphical software system for developing high-performance scientific and engineering applications. LabVIEW acquires data from IEEE-488 (GPIB), RS-232/422, and modular (VXI or CAMAC) instruments and plug-in data acquisition boards.

LabVIEW programs, called *virtual instruments* (VIs), are created using icons instead of conventional, text-based code. A VI consists of a front panel and a block diagram. The front panel (with knobs, switches, graphs, and so on) is the user interface. The block diagram, which is the executable code, consists of icons that operate on data connected by wires that pass data between them.

The list is being run as a simple redistribution of all submitted messages. ftp archives are on `ftp.pica.army.mil`, directory `/pub/labview`.

Info-PGP

Contact: `info-pgp-request@lucpul.it.luc.edu`

Purpose: Discussion of Phil Zimmerman & Co.'s Pretty Good Privacy (PGP) public key encryption program for MS-DOS, UNIX, SPARC, VMS, Atari, Amiga, and other platforms. Mirror of `alt.security.pgp` and related articles on `sci.crypt`.

Info-Prime

Contact: `info-prime-request@blx-a.prime.com`

Purpose: The discussion group/mailing list for users and administrators of Prime Computer equipment: 50-series (PRIMOS) and EXL series (UNIX). This mailing list is gatewayed to the USENET news group `comp.sys.prime`.

Informix-List

Contact: `informix-list-request@rmy.emory.edu`
(Walt Hultgren)

Purpose: An unmoderated list for the discussion of Informix software and related subjects. Topics include all Informix offerings, from C-ISAM to WingZ, plus third-party products. Membership is open to anyone, including end users, vendors, and employees of Informix Software, Inc. An optional gateway service of Informix-related articles from `comp.databases` is offered. Not affiliated with Informix Software, Inc.

INFORMIX_SIG_NCA

Contact: informix_sig_nca-request@adaclabs.com

Purpose: For the INFORMIX User Group of Northern California. The purpose of this mailing list is two-fold. It is the voice for the INFORMIX User Group of Northern California. Also, it is a method of information exchange for users of Informix products. Group activities will be advertised in this mailing list and posted to comp.databases.informix.

Info-Russ

Contact: info-russ@smarty.ece.jhu.edu (Aleksander Kaplan)

Purpose: Informal communication in Russian-speaking (or having related interests) community.

Info-Solbourne

Contact: info-solbourne-request@acsu.buffalo.edu
(Paul Graham)

Purpose: Discussions and information about Solbourne computers.

Info-Stratus

Contact: info-stratus-request@mike.lrc.edu
(Richard Shuford)

Purpose: A user-centered and user-conducted forum for discussing the fault-tolerant machines produced by Stratus Computer Corporation and their cousins, the IBM System/88 and Olivetti CPS-32.

Info-Stratus is not intended to replace the vendor-provided support channels but to complement them. Subscribers to Info-Stratus will exchange technical information and tap the collective experience of a host of other professionals who use or develop software on Stratus architecture systems, or who configure and maintain hardware in the Stratus environment.

Info-Tahoe

Contact: info-tahoe-request@uwm.edu

uwm!info-tahoe-request (Jim Lowe)

Purpose: Discussions pertaining to the Tahoe type of CPU. These include the CCI Power 6/32, the Harris HCX/7, and the Sperry 7000 series computers.

The info-tahoe mailing list is set up as a mail reflector.

This mailing list is also gatewayed into the inet list comp.sys.tahoe.

Info-Tandem

Contact: info-tandem-request@zorch.sf-bay.org

Purpose: Discussion of systems from Tandem Computers, Inc. Includes both open and proprietary lines.

Info-VM

Contact: info-vm-request@uunet.uu.net
(Kyle Jones and others)

Purpose: Discussion and information exchange about the VM mail reader, which runs under GNU Emacs.

INSOFT-L

Contact: listserv@cis.vutbr.cz

insoft-l-request@cis.vutbr.cz

Purpose: Internationalized software relates to software that is written so a user can easily change the language of the interface and versions of software, such as Czech Word-Perfect, whose interface language differs from the original product.

Topics discussed on this list will include:

- Techniques for developing new software
- Techniques for converting existing software
- Internationalization tools
- Announcements of internationalized public domain software
- Announcements of foreign-language versions of commercial software
- Calls for papers
- Conference announcements
- References to documentation related to the internationalization of software

This list is moderated.

To subscribe to this list, send an electronic mail message to listserv@cis.vutbr.cz, with the body containing the following command:

```
SUB INSOFT-L yourfirstname yourlastname
```

Interest-Groups

Contact: interest-groups-request@nisc.sri.com

Purpose: A document that can be obtained by anonymous ftp from ftp.nisc.sri.com. The document contains a listing of many of the current mailing lists.

Intergraph

Contact: nik@ingr.ingr.com

Purpose: Discussion of all Intergraph CADCAM software and hardware. This mailing list is a bidirectional gateway to alt.sys.intergraph.

International Harvester

Contact: ihc-request@balltown.cma.com (Richard Welty)

Purpose: Discussion of Scouts, pickups, etc.

International Trade & Commerce

Contact: info-request@tradent.wimsey.bc.ca

Purpose: Discussions of international trade and commerce and the global economy, including postings of company profiles, trade leads, and topics pertaining to entrepreneurial ventures.

Internet Radio Journal

Contact: rrb@airwaves.chi.il.us

Purpose: A repeater for the news group rec.radio.broadcasting and, on occasion, carries independent material as well. The list is mailed as news warrants, and covers any subject related to domestic radio broadcasting. Domestic, in this case, refers to radio that is broadcast primarily for reception within the same country from which it originates. The news group and mailing list are international and frequently cover matters pertaining to nations other than the U.S. or North America. Any subject pertaining to the group's charter is encouraged, including but not limited to programming, engineering and technical matters, new trends in the field, laws and regulations, DXing, pirate radio, community and public radio, and much more. Subscriptions are open to anyone who desires one and has an Internet-compatible e-mail account. Individuals and non-commercial systems are eligible.

InterText

Contact: intertxt@network.ucsd.edu (Jason Snell)

Purpose: A bimonthly fiction magazine with over 1,000 subscribers worldwide. InterText publishes in two formats: straight ASCII and PostScript (for PostScript-compatible laser printers). For more information, to ask about subscribing, or for submission guidelines, mail intertxt@network.ucsd.edu. Back issues may be ftp-ed from network.ucsd.edu, in the /intertext directory.

intp

Contact: intp-request@satelnet.org

Purpose: This list is for sharing information and experiences between persons who are rated as INTP (Introverted iNtuitive Thinking Perceivers) on the Myers-Briggs Temperament Index.

INXS

Contact: inxs-list-request@iastate.edu

Purpose: An unmoderated forum for the discussion of the Australian rock group INXS.

iPSC-Managers

Contact: listserv@boxer.nas.nasa.gov (machine)

jet@nas.nasa.gov (human) (J. Eric Townsend)

Purpose: Discussion of administrating the Intel iPSC line of parallel computers. To subscribe, send a message to `listserv@boxer.nas.nasa.gov` with a body of `subscribe ipsc-managers` *yourfullname*.

IRChat

Contact: `irchat-request@cc.tut.fi` (Kai "Kaizzu" Keinnen)

Purpose: Discussion on irchat.el, a GNU Emacs interface to IRC, the Internet Relay Chat.

Italian-Cars

Contact: `italian-cars-request@balltown.cma.com` (Richard Welty)

Purpose: Discussion of Italian-made automobiles. Both regular and digest forms are available.

ITI151

Contact: `iti151-request@oce.orst.edu` (John Stanley)

```
{tektronix, hplabs!hp-pcd}!orstcs!oce.orst.edu!
iti151-request
```

Purpose: For users of Imaging Technology's series 150 and 151 image processing systems and ITEX151 software. The goal is to share algorithms, code, tricks, pitfalls, advice, etc., in an effort to decrease development time and increase functionality for the users of these systems.

Janes-Addiction

Contact: `janes-addiction-request@ms.uky.edu` (Joel Abbot)

Purpose: Discussion of the defunct music group Jane's Addiction and its former members' current projects.

Jargon-Helpers

Contact: jargon-helpers-request@snark.thyrsus.com

Purpose: An e-mail reflector that supplements the ongoing public discussions of hacker jargon, net.culture, and the Jargon File on alt.folklore.computers. If you have a continuing interest in these topics, you are welcome to join. The list owner is the current Jargon File editor. Members get to see new entries "in the raw" and have a hand in editorial policy.

Jewish

Contact: listserv@israel.nysernet.org (machine)

>mljewish@israel.nysernet.org (human) (Avi Feldblum)

Purpose: A non-abusive forum for discussion of Jewish topics with an emphasis on Jewish law, within the framework of the validity of the Halakhic system. Debates between Jews and non-Jews, or between various factions of Judaism, should be posted to talk.religion.misc.

Distributions are generally on a daily basis at irregular times (when contribution load is sufficient to send, or relating to the urgency of the material to be sent).

To make a subscription request, send e-mail to listserv@israel.nysernet.org with the following message body:

> subscribe mail-jewish *yourfirstname yourlastname*

For any other correspondence, send e-mail to the editor:

> mljewish@israel.nysernet.org (Avi Feldblum)

Jewishnt

Contact: listserv@bguvm.bgu.ac.il (Dov Winer)

Purpose: Jewishnt at BGUVM is a discussion forum on all things concerning the establishment of the Global Jewish Information Network. To subscribe, BITNET users should send the following command to LISTSERV@BGUVM via mail or interactive message. Internet users should send the same command to listserv@bguvm.bgu.ac.il via mail:

```
SUB JEWISHNT your full name
```

Joe-Bob

Contact: joe-bob-request@blkbox.com

Purpose: Dedicated to the humor, writings, TV and movie performances, and movie reviews of the infamous Joe Bob Briggs, b-movie critic of the Movie Channel and publisher of *The Joe Bob Report*, a biweekly rag about everything from Americana to slasher flicks.

JPop

Contact: jpop-request@ferkel.ucsb.edu (Jim Lick)

Purpose: Discussion of Japanese popular music.

JTull

Contact: jtull-request@remus.rutgers.edu (Dave Steiner)

Purpose: A mailing list for discussions about the music group Jethro Tull, including ex-members and related artists.

JudgeNet

Contact: judge-request@synchro.com
(Chuck Cox—BJCP Master Judge)

Purpose: Discussion of beer judging and competition organization. Please include your name, Internet address, and judging rank (if any) in your subscription request.

Jugo

Contact: dimitrije@buenga.bu.edu (Dimitrije Stamenovic)

Purpose: To distribute news and provide a forum for discussions about the current events in the former Yugoslavia. Also, they originate public actions related to these events.

Jump-in-the-River

Contact: jump-in-the-river-request@presto.ig.com
(Michael C. Berch)

    {apple,ames,rutgers}!bionet!ig!jump-in-the-river-request

Purpose: For the discussion of the music and recordings of Sinéad O'Connor and related matters such as lyrics and tour information. Unmoderated.

KAW

Contact: service@swi.psy.uva.nl

Purpose: For information exchange between people participating and/or interested in the knowledge acquisition workshops (EKAW, JKAW, Banff KAW, etc.) and related activities (Sisyphus, problem-solving methods workshops).

To subscribe, send mail to service@swi.psy.uva.nl with the following message:

    subscribe kaw *yourfullname*

Khoros

Contact: khoros-request@chama.eece.unm.edu

Purpose: To discuss the Khoros software package, developed by Dr. Rasure, his staff, and his students at the University of New Mexico. Khoros is an integrated software development environment for information processing and visualization, based on X11R4.

Killifish

Contact: killie-request@mejac.palo-alto.ca.us

Purpose: For people who keep and are interested in killifish (family Cyprinodontidae).

KISKEYA

Contact: listserv@conicit.ve

Purpose: Dominican mailing list oriented toward discussion of promoting and developing an efficient telecommunications network in the Dominican Republic and the rest of the Caribbean. Other topics of common interest among the subscribers are also welcome on the list. The main languages on the list are Spanish and English. To subscribe to the list, write to listserv@conicit.ve with subscribe kiskeya *youremail* as the first line in the message body.

Kitcar

Contact: kitcar-request@cs.usask.ca (John Punshon)

Purpose: To discuss purchasing, building, driving, and anything else to do with kit cars—that is, cars built using body/chassis from one source (kit manufacturer) and engine/mechanicals from another (usually a *donor* production car). List is archived and archives can be anon ftp-ed from ece.rutgers.edu.

Kites

Contact: kites-request@harvard.harvard.edu

harvard!kites-request (U.S.A./Canada/Europe)

koscvax.keio.junet!kites-request (Japan)

Purpose: This mailing list is for people interested in making, flying, or just talking about all kinds of kites. Topics will (I hope) include kite plans and construction techniques, reviews of commercially available kites and plans, timely (or otherwise) human interest notes, and flying.

Kiwimusic

Contact: kiwimusic-request@athena.mit.edu
(Katie Livingston)

Purpose: Discussion of New Zealand pop bands, particularly those on the Flying Nun, Failsafe, and Xpressway labels. Example groups include The Chills, The Bats, The Clean, Tall Dwarfs, Straitjacket Fits, and so on.

All requests for addition or deletion or correspondence with the moderator should go to kiwimusic-request@athena.mit.edu

Khush

Contact: khush-request@husc3.harvard.edu

Purpose: A mailing list for gay, lesbian, bisexual South Asians and their friends. We define South Asian as people from or descending from countries such as Bangladesh, Bhutan, India, Maldives, Nepal, Pakistan, and Sri-Lanka. The purpose of this list is to discuss South Asian gay culture/experiences/issues, as well as to form a social and support network. Currently the list is unmoderated and anybody can join or leave the list at any time.

You can join the list by sending mail to khush-request@husc3.harvard.edu. The first line in your mail *must* be of the following form:

```
subscribe khush
youraccount@yoursubdomain.yourdomain
```

Please send any questions about the list or any other administrative stuff to khush-help@husc3.harvard.edu.

KLF/Orb & Co.

Contact: klf-request@asylum.sf.ca.us (Lazlo Nibble)

Purpose: Discussion of the KLF, the Orb, and related bands (the JAMs, the Timelords, System 7/777, Fortran 5, et al.). Moderator maintains a complete discography. ftp archives available on asylum.

Kosmos

Contact: kosmos-request@athena.mit.edu

Purpose: Want to know the latest up-to-date news about the solo career of Paul "The Mod God" Weller from his foremost fanzine writers from the U.K. and the U.S.? Want to discuss his previous bands with people who actually know whom you're talking about? Just want to meet some cool people who like good music? Join Kosmos, the Paul Weller mailing list!

Previous postings are stored in monthly files and are available to all subscribers. They can be obtained from dlodge@mcs.dundee.ac.uk.

Kuharske Bukve

Contact: kuharske-bukve@krpan.arnes.si (Polona Novak and Andrej Brodnik)

```
kuharske.bukve@uni-lj.si
```

Purpose: A moderated mailing list published weekly. Each issue brings one recipe previously tested by a member of the editorial board. The recipes are formatted. Language is Slovene only. The editors are happy to receive readers' opinions.

Kundera-List

Contact: kundera-request@anat3d1.anatomy.upenn.edu

Purpose: The discussion of the works of Milan Kundera, the internationally renowned contemporary writer whose originality of imagination and clarity of prose has moved and enlightened many readers and serious writers. New subscribers will automatically receive past articles sent to the list.

Kurt Goedel Society

Contact: kgs@csdec2.tuwien.ac.at

Purpose: For members and people interested in the activities of the Kurt Goedel Society. Information about the Goedel Colloquia, Calls for Papers, the Collegium Logicum Lecture Series, the newsletter, and information from sister societies will be distributed. If you would like to be included in the mailing list, or have any questions, send an e-mail to kgs@csdec2.tuwien.ac.at.

Labrys

Contact: c._louise_vigil.osbu_north@xerox.com

Purpose: To provide a safe space for lesbians to discuss topics of interest. The membership is restricted in order to provide a space for lesbians. The forum is free form with the exception of occasional moderation should the charter be violated.

All administrative requests should be sent to

> c._louise_vigil.osbu_north@xerox.com

Please include the word `labrys` in the subject line.

LAMBDA

Contact: listserv@ukcc.uky.edu (Jeff Jones)

Purpose: This list is open to the discussion of all topics relating to gays/lesbians/bisexuals and their issues with specific focus on issues at the University of Kentucky, Lexington, and Kentucky communities.

To subscribe, send mail to listserv@ukcc or on the Internet to listserv@ukcc.uky.edu with the body containing the command `sub lambda yourfirstname yourlastname`.

LA-MOTSS, LA-MOTSS-ANNOUNCE

Contact: la-motss-request@flash.usc.edu

Purpose: On-line social and political forum for gay, lesbian, and bisexual issues in the Los Angeles and Southern California area.

Anything posted to the announcements list is automatically forwarded to the discussion list. You may choose to receive announcements only, or receive both announcements and general discussion.

Lang-Lucid

Contact: lang-lucid-request@csl.sri.com (R. Jagannathan)

Purpose: Discussions on all aspects related to the language Lucid, including (but not restricted to) language design issues, implementations for personal computers, implementations for parallel machines, language extensions, programming environments, products, bug reports, bug fixes/workarounds.

Lasnet

Contact: lasnet-request@emx.utexas.edu
(Langston James Goree VI)

Purpose: To facilitate the exchange of information among scholars doing research related to Latin America.

LDS

Contact: lds-request@decwrl.dec.com

    decwrl!lds-request

Purpose: A forum for members of the Church of Jesus Christ of Latter-day Saints (Mormons) to discuss church doctrine, Mormon culture, and life in general. Non-Mormons are welcome to join, but we're not interested in flame wars.

The Learning List

Contact: learning-request@sea.east.sun.com
(Rowan Hawthorne)

Purpose: An electronic forum for discussing child-centered learning. It is intended to provide a meeting place in cyberspace in which to advance our understanding of the processes of learning and to share personal experiences and practical suggestions to help in the great adventure we share with our children.

Members must agree with the Charter of the Learning list to subscribe. A copy of the Charter is available from the above address.

Level 42

Contact: level42-request@enterprise.bih.harvard.edu

Purpose: To support discussions of the musical artist Level 42.

Liberal-Judaism

Contact: faigin@aerospace.aero.org (Daniel Faigin)

Purpose: Non-judgmental discussions of liberal Judaism (Reform, Reconstructionist, Conservative, Secular Humanist, etc.) and liberal Jewish issues, its practices, opinions, and beliefs.

This list is moderated and is in digest format.

Libernet

Contact: libernet-request@dartmouth.edu (Barry S. Fagin)

Purpose: A Libertarian mailing list. The list is available in two modes: as a mail reflector and as a digest.

Life-Talking

Contact: life-talking-request@ferkel.ucsb.edu (Jim Lick)

Purpose: Discussion of the musical group Life Talking.

LIBFEM

Contact: libfem-request@math.uio.no (Thomas Gramstad)

Purpose: Focuses on the classical liberty and individual rights perspective as applied to feminist issues, such as issues regarding ideology, politics, culture, gender, etc., in order to establish a network for information, discourse, cooperation, encouragement, and consciousness raising. There has always been an element of individualism in the various women and feminist movements, although this element seems to have been somewhat neglected in recent movements.

Lightwave

Contact: subscribe@xamiga.linet.org

Purpose: For Video Toaster users, supporting the NewTek 3-D object modeler/ray tracer and hardware involved in video editing, such as time base correctors and VCR equipment. This mail is echoed from another site.

Send subscription requests to subscribe@xamiga.linet.org using this format:

    #lightwave youraccount@yoursubdomain.yourdomain;

Linda

Contact: linda-users-request@cs.yale.edu

    linda-users-request@yalecs.bitnet

    {cmcl2,decvax,harvard}!yale!linda-users-request

Purpose: Discussion group for users and potential users of Linda-based parallel programming systems. Linda is a set of operators that are added to various conventional programming languages to produce a parallel programming language.

Linux-Activists

Contact: linux-activists-request@niksula.hut.fi
(Ari Lemmke)

Purpose: LINUX operating system hacking. LINUX is now on a hackers-only stage. More information is available by ftp from nic.funet.fi, directory /pub/OS/Linux/README.

LIS (Lesbians in Science)

Contact: zita@ac.grin.edu

Purpose: A forum for discussions, a resource for professional and personal information sharing, and a social network and support group. (Womyn only.)

List-Managers

Contact: brent@greatcircle.com (Brent Chapman)

Purpose: There was a "Mailing Lists" workshop session at the USENIX System Administration Conference (LISA VI) in Long Beach, CA, on October 22, 1992. The participants in that workshop expressed a desire for a mailing list for discussions of issues related to managing Internet mailing lists, including (but not limited to) software, methods, mechanisms, techniques, and policies.

I've created the list as list-managers@greatcircle.com. That address is a direct mail reflector: all messages sent to that address are immediately forwarded to the list. There is a digest version of the list available as list-managers-digest@greatcircle.com. The digest version has exactly the same messages as the direct version; the messages are simply bundled into digests daily (or more frequently, if traffic warrants). Both lists are unmoderated.

To join the List-Mangers mailing list, send the command

```
subscribe list-managers
```

in the body of a message to majordomo@greatcircle.com. If you want to subscribe to something other than the account the mail is coming from, such as a local redistribution list, then append that address to the subscribe command; for example, to subscribe to "local-list-managers," send the following:

```
subscribe list-managers local-list-managers@your.domain.net
```

To subscribe to the digest version, substitute `list-managers-digest` for `list-managers` in the examples above.

Living

Contact: living-request@qiclab.scn.rain.com

Purpose: A list for women with some sort of physical handicap. It is not limited to women in wheelchairs, but is meant to be a support list for women to talk about any sort of physically challenging situation that they are living in at the moment, be it temporary or permanent. (Women only.)

Llajta

Contact: readingj@cerf.net (John Reading)

Purpose: For the discussion of any and all topics relating to Bolivia. All communication regarding the list is sent to readingj@cerf.net and messages are redistributed manually as needed.

Logo

Contact: logo-friends-request@aiai.ed.ac.uk

Purpose: Discuss the Logo computer language.

Lojban

Contact: lojban-list-request@snark.thyrsus.com (John Cowan)

Purpose: To use, discuss, and contribute to the development of the constructed human language called Lojban (known in earlier versions as Loglan). Lojban has a grammar based on predicate logic and vocabulary built from the six most widely spoken human languages. It is intended as a tool for experimental linguistics, as a medium for communication with computers, and as a possible international auxiliary language.

Lojban-list is an unmoderated mail reflector. New subscribers are asked to send their postal mailing addresses as well so that they can be placed on the mailing list of The Logical Language Group, Inc., a non-profit organization. The postal mailing list provides materials that are useful in learning about the language. Lojban-list and LLG, Inc. are in no way affiliated with The Loglan Institute, Inc., or with James Cooke Brown, the founder of Loglan.

Los Angeles Kings

Contact: kings-request@cs.stanford.edu

Purpose: Discussion on the Los Angeles Kings.

Lotus-Cars

Contact: lotus-adm%esprit.uucp@netcom.com (Alan F. Perry)

Purpose: For anyone interested in cars made by Lotus, now or in the past.

Loureed

Contact: loureed-request@cvi.hahnemann.edu (Sylvia)

Purpose: Mailing list for discussion of music, etc., related to the 30-years-and-running career of Mr. Lou Reed, including Velvet Underground matters. No digest format currently available. Unmoderated, but owner is reached at sylvia@cvi.hahnemann.edu.

Lute

Contact: lute-request@sunapee.dartmouth.edu
(Wayne B. Cripps)

Purpose: For lute players and researchers of lute music.

LymeNet-L

Contact: listserv@lehigh.edu

>mcg2@lehigh.edu (Marc Gabriel)

Purpose: The LymeNet Newsletter provides timely information on the many aspects of the Lyme disease epidemic. Published about once every 10-15 days, it includes the latest medical abstracts, support group info, and political events. Subscribers may submit questions and opinions to the newsletter for publication.

Macgyver

Contact: shari@cc.gatech.edu (Shari Feldman)

Purpose: To discuss current and previous *MacGyver* episodes. We also discuss what is currently happening with the main and recurring actors on the show.

MachTen

Contact: machten-request@tenon.com (Leonard Cuff)

Purpose: Discuss topics of interest to users of MachTen, a Mach/BSD UNIX for all Macintoshes, from Tenon Intersystems. This includes programming tips and examples, configuration questions, and discussion of problems and workarounds. People not currently using MachTen and wanting either general information or specific questions answered should not subscribe, but write to info@tenon.com.

Mac-Security

Contact: mac-security-request@world.std.com
(David C. Kovar)

Purpose: This mailing list is for people interested in Macintosh security. This can be used to

- Discuss existing security problems in various Macintosh applications
- Discuss security applications, hardware, and solutions
- Discuss potential problems and their solutions
- Discuss just about anything else related to Macintosh security and access control

With the arrival of System 7.0 and its wealth of information-sharing facilities, Macintosh security has entered a new era. Originally you only had to worry about someone getting into your Macintosh via the keyboard, or stealing it outright. Now it's much easier to browse through information on someone else's Macintosh over the network.

MAGIC

Contact: magic-request@maillist.crd.ge.com
(Bruce Barnett)

Purpose: For the discussion of sleight of hand and the art of magic. Membership to the list is restricted, as people who are merely curious are not encouraged to join. You must fill out a questionnaire to qualify.

Mailing-Lists

Contact: mailing-lists@krpan.arnes.si

Purpose: Information on mailing lists from South Slavic countries.

Mail-Men

Contact: mail-men-request@summit.novell.com

Purpose: This digested mailing list discusses "men's issues." Both women and men may join. Mail-men is a place where men and women can discuss men's issues in an atmosphere of openness and support. Men's issues are those problems and experiences that affect male humans. To join, send a message to mail-men-request@summit.novell.com that includes the word subscribe as the subject or as the first line in the body of the message. Also include your desired e-mail address *and* your full name. Pseudonymous or anonymous subscription requests will be rejected.

MAK-NEWS

Contact: listserv@uts.edu.au

Purpose: A news group for following the developments in the Republic of Macedonia. Both the Macedonian and the English languages are used, whichever the original source is in, or whichever the contributors feel most comfortable with. Discussions and submissions are primarily from contributors who inform subscribers of events, usually in their local areas, but often farther. Sources of articles from which some users extract documents are wide and varied.

MAK-NEWS is run entirely by volunteers and is reasonably well connected with outside regular sources. Translations of articles are also possible. The Macedonian Information Liaison Service (M.I.L.S.) in Brussels sends daily bulletins to MAK-NEWS from Monday to Friday. We also have individual news bulletins arriving from Skopje through a link that is fragile, but that has lately been holding up well and is improving all the time.

MAK-NEWS recently converted to run as a listserv mail group (mak-news@uts.edu.au) with the usual listserv mail commands applying. Distributions are generally on a daily basis at irregular times (when contribution load is sufficient to send, or relating to the urgency of the material to be sent), and is about 200-300 kilobytes per week.

To make subscription requests, send e-mail to listserv@uts.edu.au with the following message body:

    subscribe MAK-NEWS *yourfirstname yourlastname*

For other correspondence, send e-mail to the current editors:

    shopov@tartarus.ccsd.uts.edu.au (Sacha Shopov)

    sk@sunbim.be (Sasa Konecni) [M.I.L.S.]

Martial-Arts

Contact: martial-arts-request@dragon.cso.uiuc.edu (Steven Miller)

Purpose: For discussion on various aspects of the martial arts. This includes teaching and training techniques, martial arts philosophy, self-defense, and traditional and non-traditional styles, among other topics.

Masonic Digest

Contact: ptrei@mitre.org (Peter Trei)

Purpose: A moderated forum for discussion of Free Masonry, affiliated groups, and other fraternal orders. As moderator, I do not pass on any message that contains or purports to contain material I am obliged to conceal, or which I believe members of other orders are obliged to conceal. Within that restriction, I am as liberal as possible. Postings from non-Masons are welcome. So is criticism, as long as it is reasoned and in good taste.

MasPar

Contact: mp-users-request@thunder.mcrcim.mcgill.edu
(Lee Iverson)

Purpose: We have no restrictive charter, so we are open to any and all discussions of hardware/software issues surrounding the use of the MasPar MP-1 class of parallel SIMD machines. These machines have a full-featured data-parallel instruction set and are programmable in Fortran90 and MPL, a K&R C with parallel data types.

MATLAB

Contact: matlab-users-request@mcs.anl.gov (Chris Bischof)

Purpose: Discussion group for users and potential users of the MATLAB numeric computation software from The MathWorks. MATLAB is an interactive, matrix-oriented product for linear algebra, digital signal processing, equation solving, control system design, and other engineering and scientific applications. This mailgroup is administered by the independent MATLAB User Group.

Mayberry

Contact: listserv@bolis.sf-bay.org

Purpose: For discussion of TV shows featuring Andy Griffith, including *The Andy Griffith Show* and *Mayberry RFD*.

To subscribe, send an Internet e-mail message to listserv@bolis.sf-bay.org containing the following:

    subscribe Mayberry

and you will be added to the list.

Mazda-List

Contact: mazda-list-request@ms.uky.edu (Joel Abbott)

Purpose: Technical correspondence and discussion of Mazda-designed vehicles.

MEDGAY-L

Contact: listserv@ksuvm.ksu.edu (Robert Clark)

Purpose: The official list of the Society for the Study of Homosexuality in the Middle Ages, an affiliated society of the Medieval Institute of Western Michigan University.

To subscribe, send a one-line message, SUB MEDGAY-L *yourfullname*, to listserv@ksuvm.ksu.edu.

Medphys

Contact: medphys-request@radonc.duke.edu

Purpose: An attempt to foster electronic communication between medical physicists, open to interested others. Medical physics is a somewhat opaque but widely used synonym for radiological physics—the physics of the diagnostic and therapeutic use of radiation in medicine. At present, most of the subscribers are involved in radiotherapy.

Melissa Etheridge

Contact: etheridge-request@krylov.cnd.mcgill.ca

Purpose: To discuss Melissa Etheridge and her music.

Melrose-Place

Contact: melrose-place-request@ferkel.ucsb.edu (Jim Lick)

Purpose: Discussion of the Fox TV show *Melrose Place*.

Mensatalk

Contact: mensatalk-request@psg.com (Ed Wright)

Purpose: For members of Mensa only.

MetaCard-List

Contact: listserv@grot.starconn.com

Purpose: Discussion of the MetaCard product from Meta-Card Corporation. MetaCard is an application development system similar to Apple's HyperCard product and runs on a variety of popular platforms in a UNIX/X11/Motif environment.

To subscribe to the MetaCard-list, send mail to listserv@grot.starconn.com with the following commands in the body of the message:

```
subscribe metacard-list yourfirstname yourlastname
quit
```

Replace *yourfirstname yourlastname* with your name, not your e-mail address.

Administrative messages other than subscription and unsubscription should be sent to metacard-list-owner@grot.starconn.com.

Meteorology Students

Contact: dennis@metw3.met.fu-berlin.de

Purpose: A new mailing list, open to everyone, but particularly intended as a communication facility for meteorology students. At the moment there are 20 people from three continents subscribed to the list.

Beside the usual chatting, subjects of discussion could be student-related topics such as scholarships, summer schools, conferences, and conditions of studying meteorology at a particular university. There is also the option to ask the community for help in meteorology-related questions. There are freshman, as well as graduate students, who will be available to answer your questions in this field.

If there are enough people interested, we could organize a kind of project, too.

To come to know each other, there is a short questionnaire available. Though no obligation exists to fill it out, it would be nice if all new subscribers would at least answer the basic questions about their name, address, and university. New answered forms are posted to the list; old ones are available upon request.

Administrative mail such as subscription or questionnaire requests should be sent to

```
dennis@metw3.met.fu-berlin.de
```

Though the list is situated in Germany, the language is English. I hope for strong participation.

Miata

Contact: miata-request@jhunix.hcf.jhu.edu
(Andy S. Poling)

Purpose: Formed when it became evident that there was a growing body of enthusiastic Mazda Miata owners. There are no rules governing what you can and cannot post to the list—it is an open forum.

Middle-Eastern Music

Contact: middle-eastern-music-request@nic.funet.fi
(Juhana Kouhia)

Purpose: Discussion of the music originating in the Middle East.

Migra-List

Contact: migra-list-request@cc.utah.edu

moliva@cc.utah.edu (Maurizio Oliva)

Purpose: Mailing list on international migration.

Milieu

Contact: milieu-request@yoyo.cc.monash.edu.au

Purpose: Discussion of the works of Julian May, notably *The Saga of the Exiles* and the *Galactic Milieu* trilogy.

Mind-L

Contact: mind-l-request@asylum.sf.ca.us (John Romkey)

Purpose: Mind-L is a discussion group for people interested in mind-altering techniques in general, and mind machines (light and sound, TENS/CES, electromagnetic pulse, floatation) and biofeedback equipment in particular. Related topics include smart nutrients, hypnosis, relaxation techniques, and subliminal tapes/videos. Conversation ranges from serious research to home electronics to amateur personal observations.

This group does not cover hallucinatory drugs (such as LSD). The subject may come up from time to time, but there are other lists that already give extensive coverage of that topic.

To subscribe, send e-mail to mind-l-request@asylum.sf.ca.us with nothing in the subject line and only the words subscribe mind-l *yourname* in the text.

Some back issues and other related documents and programs are stored on Mind-L's ftp site. The address is asylum.sf.ca.us. Log in as anonymous and use your e-mail address as a password. Look in the directory /pub/mind-l.

Miniatures

Contact: minilist-request@cs.unc.edu

Purpose: An archived mailing list for discussion of painting, sculpting, converting, and displaying of miniature figurines, generally for war-gaming or fantasy role-playing games and in the smaller scales (15mm-30mm).

Minor League Baseball

Contact: minors-request@medraut.apple.com (Chuq von Rospach)

Purpose: Issues affecting the minor leagues, including new stadium standards, minor league franchise status and changes, road trips and groups, schedules, team and league status, players and teams to watch, collectibles, and anything else of importance about minor league baseball.

Miracles

Contact: perry.sills@ebay

perrys@spiritlead.sun.com

Purpose: To provide daily readings from A Course in Miracles, and other selected readings from teachers, lecturers, and A Course in Miracles centers to provide additional reflection, inspiration, and avenues of practical application.

Through the above contact address, one may also subscribe to a discussion list for A Course in Miracles, as well as a list for receiving the daily lessons from the course.

MLB Scores and Standings

Contact: jplee@cymbal.calpoly.edu (Jason Lee)

Purpose: A distributive list for people who want daily updates of scores and standings of Major League Baseball.

Model-Horse

Contact: model-horse-request@qiclab.scn.rain.com
(Darci L. Chapman)

Purpose: Discussion of the model horse hobby. All aspects of showing (live and photo), collecting, remaking/repainting for all breeds and makes are discussed. All ages and levels of experience welcome.

Modesty Blaise

Contact: modesty-blaise-request@math.uio.no
(Thomas Gramstad)

Purpose: Discussion and information exchange centered on Peter O'Donnell's Modesty Blaise books and comics, such as characters, plots, artists, relevant articles, etc.

Moms

Contact: moms-request@qiclab.scn.rain.com

Purpose: A list for lesbian mothers. (Women only.)

Morris Dancing Discussion List

Contact: listserv@suvm.acs.syr.edu

Purpose: Discussion of all things Morris. This includes Cotswold, Border, NorthWest, Rapper, LongSword, Abbots Bromley, Garland, and similar forms of English dance, along with the accompanying music and traditions. To subscribe, send mail with a message body containing

```
SUBSCRIBE MORRIS yourfullname (your-team-name)
```

If on BITNET, send this message to listserv@suvm. If on Internet, send this message to listserv@suvm.acs.syr.edu.

MR2-Interest

Contact: mr2-interest-request@validgh.com (David Hough)

Purpose: Discussion of Toyota MR2s, old and new.

MS-Access

Contact: ms-access-request@eunet.co.at (Martin Hilger)

Purpose: An unmoderated list for MS Access topics, including Access Basic questions, reviews, rumors, etc. Open to owners, users, prospective users, and the merely curious.

All requests to be added to or deleted from this list, problems, questions, etc., should be sent to ms-access-request@eunet.co.at.

MSA-Net

Contact: msa-request@htm3.ee.queensu.ca (Aalim Fevens)

Purpose: A mailing list to meet the communication needs of Muslim Student Associations in North America. Issues related to Islam and MSAs are discussed between Muslim students on the list. Only Muslims are admitted as a rule, but exceptions can be made in special cases. To subscribe, send e-mail to msa-request@hmt3.ee.queensu.ca with the following information: Name, E-mail address, Postal address, Major or Area of Research, and Religion.

Mtxinu-Users

Contact: dunike!mtxinu-users-request

mtxinu-users-request@nike.cair.du.edu

Purpose: Discussion and bug fixes for users of the 4.3+NFS release from the Mt. Xinu folks.

MUD

Contact: jwisdom@gnu.ai.mit.edu (Joseph Wisdom)

Purpose: If you are new in the MUD world, or are simply looking for new places to get into, try subscribing to Internet Games MUD-List today! Make sure to include the string mud list in the subject header.

Multicast

Contact: multicast-request@arizona.edu (Joel Snyder)

Purpose: For discussion of multicast and broadcast issues in an OSI environment. Archives of the list and a database of contributed documents are also available on arizona.edu.

Musicals

Contact: musicals-request@world.std.com
(Elizabeth Lear Newman)

Purpose: For the general discussion of musical theater, in whatever form it make take, but related non-musical theater topics are welcome too. 90 percent of the traffic is the musicals-related flow from the news group rec.arts.theatre.

Music-Research

Contact: music-research-request@prg.oxford.ac.uk
(Stephen Page)

Purpose: Established after a suggestion made at a meeting at Oxford in July 1986 to provide an effective and fast means of bringing together musicologists, music analysts, computer scientists, and others working on applications of computers in music research.

As with any forum for discussion, there are certain subject areas that are of particular interest to the group of people on this list. Initially, the list was established for people whose chief interests concern computers and their applications to music representation systems, information retrieval systems for musical scores, music printing, music analysis, musicology and ethnomusicology, and tertiary music education. The following areas are not the principal concern of this list, although overlapping subjects may well be interesting: primary and secondary education, sound generation techniques, and composition. Articles on electronic music, synthesizers, MIDI, etc., will be rejected at the request of the readers of the list.

Mustangs

Contact: mustangs-request@cup.hp.com (Gary Gitzen)

    {hplabs, uunet}!cup.hp.com!mustangs-request

Purpose: To discuss/share technical issues, problems, solutions, and modifications relating to late model (~1980+) Ford Mustangs. Some issues may also be relevant to other Fords. Flames and "my car is faster than your car" mailings are discouraged. List "noise level" is actively controlled.

Mystery

Contact: mystery-request@introl.com (Thomas Krueger)

Purpose: A mailing list for mystery and detective fiction. Reviews of works and discussions of plot, characterization, and other aspects will be discussed. The medium, whether novel, movie, or television series, is unimportant.

NA-NET

Contact: na.join@na-net.ornl.gov

Purpose: Numerical analysis discussions. To join the NA-NET, send mail and, in the message body, specify the following three fields in any order: Lastname:, Firstname:, E-mail:.

NativeNet

Contact: gst@gnosys.svle.ma.us (Gary S. Trujillo)

Purpose: To provide information about and to discuss issues relating to indigenous people around the world and current threats to their cultures and habitats (e.g., rainforests).

NAVNEWS

Contact: navnews@nctamslant.navy.mil

Purpose: E-mail distribution list for the weekly Navy News Service (NAVNEWS), published by the Navy Internal Relations Activity in Washington. NAVNEWS contains official news and information about fleet operations and exercises, personnel policies, budget actions, and more. This is the same news service that is distributed through Navy circuits to ships at sea and to shore commands around the world. Subscriptions to NAVNEWS by e-mail are available at no charge to anyone with a mailbox on any network reachable through the Internet.

NCUBE

Contact: ncube-users-request@cs.tufts.edu
(David Krumme)

Purpose: Exchange of information among people using NCUBE parallel computers.

NECI-Discuss

Contact: neci-discuss-request@pioneer.ci.net

Purpose: The general discussion forum of New England Community Internet, an organization dedicated to making USENET and Internet accessible to the public without barriers of economics or technical expertise. The group is developing ways to bring IP connectivity at low cost into homes and non-profit organizations.

To get a daily digest version, subscribe to `neci-digest`. To receive organizational announcements only, subscribe to `neci-announce`.

nedod

Contact: `nedod-request@mbunix.mitre.org` (automated LISTSERV)

`cookson@mbunix.mitre.org`

Purpose: The discussion of events, technical issues and just plain socializing related to motorcycling in the New England area of the U.S.

To subscribe, mail a single-line message to `nedod-request@mbunix.mitre.org` consisting of `subscribe nedod yourfullname` (not e-mail address).

Plain reflected and digest-type subscriptions are available. To subscribe in digest format, append `set nedod mail digest` to your subscription request.

NERaves

Contact: `ne-raves-request@silver.lcs.mit.edu` (John Adams)

Purpose: Started as a Northeastern United States/Canada equivalent of SFRaves. The list provides a forum for people to discuss the "rave" music/club/dance scene. For the purposes of the list, "Northeastern" is loosely defined as from Chicago east and from Washington D.C. north, including Ontario, Quebec, and the maritime provinces. People from outside this area are welcome, too! NERaves is an unmoderated list.

Nerdnosh

Contact: nerdnosh-request@scruz.ucsc.edu (Tim Bowden)

Purpose: Begun as a breakfast club for local nerds and writers in Santa Cruz, CA, it has expanded into an international forum about where, how, and why we live where we do. Think of it as a universal camp town meeting in M.F.K. Fisher shades and Jack Kerouac tones. Frivolous, friendly, and informative, in roughly that order.

NERO NY

Contact: lsonko@pearl.tuft.edu

Purpose: NERO is a live-action medieval role-playing game with chapters in New York, Georgia, and Massachusetts. This mailing list is for In-Game and Out-of-Game announcements about NERO NY/Ashbury. To subscribe to the list or just get information about NERO NY/Ashbury, write to lsonko@pearl.tuft.edu.

NE-Social-MOTSS

Contact: ne-social-motss-request@plts.org

Purpose: Announcements of social and other events and happenings in the Northeast (of the continental United States) of interest to lesbians, gay men, and bisexuals.

NetBlazer-Users

Contact: netblazer-users-request@telebit.com

Purpose: To provide an unmoderated forum for discussions among users of Telebit NetBlazer products. Topics include known problems and workarounds, features discussions, and configuration advice.

NetJam

Contact: netjam-request@xcf.berkeley.edu (Craig Latta)

Purpose: A means for people to collaborate on musical compositions by sending Musical Instrument Digital Interface (MIDI) and other files (such as MAX patchers and notated scores) to each other, mucking about with them, and resending them. All those with MIDI-compatible (and other interesting) equipment, access to e-mailing and compression facilities and to the Internet, and an interest in making music are encouraged to participate. Please e-mail netjam-request@xcf.berkeley.edu with the subject line request for info.

Network-Audio-Bits

Contact: murph@maine.bitnet (Michael A. Murphy)

Purpose: Network Audio Bits & Audio Software Review—a bimonthly electronic magazine that features reviews of and information about current rock, pop, new age, jazz, funk, folk, and other musical genres. A mixture of major label artists and independent recording artists can be found reviewed in these pages.

Neuron

Contact: neuron-request@cattell.psych.upenn.edu
(Peter Marvit)

Purpose: The Neuron Digest—a moderated list (in digest form) dealing with all aspects of neural networks (and any type of network or neuromorphic system). Topics include both connectionist models (artificial neural networks) and biological systems ("wetware"). Back issues and limited software is available via ftp from cattell.psych.upenn.edu. The Digest is gatewayed to USENET's comp.ai.neural-nets.

Newlists

Contact: info@vm1.nodak.edu (Marty Hoag)

Purpose: A mailing list "clearinghouse" for new mailing lists. Subscribers will get announcements of new lists that are mailed to this list.

Neworl-Dig

Contact: mail-server@mintir.new-orleans.la.us

elendil@mintir.new-orleans.la.us (Edward J. Branley)

Purpose: A digest version of the New Orleans mailing list (new-orleans@mintir.new-orleans.la.us). This digest will be distributed on a monthly basis and will include articles from the New Orleans list, minus the "noise." To subscribe, send a message to mail-server@mintir.new-orleans.la.us, with SUBSCRIBE NEW-ORLEANS in the body.

New-Orleans

Contact: mail-server@mintir.new-orleans.la.us

elendil@mintir.new-orleans.la.us (Edward J. Branley)

Purpose: A list for discussing any and all aspects of the city of New Orleans. History, politics, culture, food, restaurants, music, entertainment, Mardi Gras, etc., are all fair game. To subscribe, send a message to mail-server@mintir.new-orleans.la.us, with SUBSCRIBE NEW-ORLEANS in the body.

NewsCom

Contact: starkid@ddsw1.mcs.com (Lance Sanders)

Purpose: To make available synergies discerned in, and created from, print news media (up to a 12-year time span).

Many "facts," particularly scientific ones, have a habit of changing with time. NewsCommando shows extreme prejudice toward those articles whose contents exhibit "legs." The depth of insight possible using the information mosaic method can be staggering. A form of electronic magazine, NewsCommando can serve as a reference tool, offer unique jump-off points for Medline, PaperChase, or other searches, and, in many ways, is the "poor-man's IdeaFisher/IdeaBank." Vol. 1 will contain the following articles:

> "ChemTao: Synergies In the Life Sciences"
>
> "EarthWatch1: Defining the Scope of Environmental Destruction"
>
> "Why Euthanasia Must Never Be Legalized"

Use `NewsCom request` in the Subject field of message headers. Indicate article title(s) desired or `all` in the body of the message. Articles will be deposited in your mailbox with a `NewsCom/Vol.#` Subject header. Most will be in excess of 20K. Please group-save them to a file for later reading.

New York Islanders

Contact: `dss2k@virginia.edu` (David Strauss)

Purpose: To discuss the NYI hockey team, with emphasis on the current season. To subscribe, send mail to the contact with your e-mail address listed clearly in the message.

NeXT-GIS

Contact: `sstaton@deltos.com` (Steven R. Staton)

> `listserv@deltos.com`

Purpose: Discussion of GIS- and cartographic-related topics on the NeXT and other workstation computers. Some moderated reposting of `comp.infosys.gis` occurs as well.

To join, send a SUBSCRIBE *yourfullname* message.

NeXT-Icon

Contact: next-icon-request@bmt.gun.com (Timothy Reed)

Purpose: Distribute and receive 64-by-64 or 48-by-48 pixel icons (2-, 12-, 24-, and/or 32-bit), compatible with NeXT Computer's NeXTStep software. Nearly all mail is in NeXTmail format.

NeXT-Med

Contact: next-med-request@ms.uky.edu

Purpose: Open to end users and developers interested in medical solutions using NeXT computers and/or 486 systems running NEXTStep. Discussions on any topic related to NeXT use in the medical industry or relating to health care are encouraged.

NHL Goalie Stats

Contact: dfa@triple-i.com

Purpose: Weekday reports of NHL goalie stats.

Nissan

Contact: nissan-request@world.std.com (Rich Siegel)

Purpose: Devoted to discussion of the Nissan and Infiniti cars, with the exception of the Sentra SE-R, NX2000, and G20, which are served by the SE-R list.

NJ-MOTSS, NJ-MOTSS-ANNOUNCE

Contact: majordomo@plts.org

Purpose: *NJ-MOTSS*—mailing list for gay, lesbian, and bisexual issues, etc., in New Jersey.

NJ-MOTSS-ANNOUNCE—announcements of interest to New Jersey's finest 10 percent. Messages sent here also go to NJ-MOTSS; do *not* cross-post!

To subscribe to either list, send the message

    subscribe nj-motss

or

    subscribe nj-motss-announce

to majordomo@plts.org.

NOGLSTP

Contact: noglstp-request@elroy.jpl.nasa.gov

Purpose: A national organization of lesbigay people employed or interested in scientific or high-technology fields.

Non Serviam

Contact: solan@math.uio.no (Svein Olav Nyberg)

Purpose: An electronic newsletter centered on the philosophy of Max Stirner, author of *Der Einzige und Sein Eigentum* (*The Ego and Its Own*), and his dialectical egoism. The contents, however, are decided by the individual contributors and the censoring eye of the editor. The aim is to have somewhat more elaborate and carefully reasoned articles than are usually found on the news groups and lists.

Nordic-Skiing

Contact: nordic-ski-request@graphics.cornell.edu (Mitch Collinsworth)

Purpose: Discussion of Nordic skiing sports. This includes cross-country, biathlon, ski-orienteering, ski jumping, Nordic combined, telemark, and back-country.

NORWEAVE

Contact: listserv@nki.no

Purpose: Building on the NORWAVES success, NKI has now established NORWEAVE, an additional e-mail service for Norwegians and friends of Norway. The aim of NORWEAVE is to weave a network of people in Norway and abroad who can help each other exchange information and establish contacts across geographical boundaries. NORWEAVE is a free service available to all friends of Norway. To join the network, just e-mail the following command to listserv@nki.no:

```
SUBSCRIBE NORWEAVE your name
```

Novice MZT

Contact: novice-mzt@krpan.arnes.si

novice.mzt@uni-lj.si

Purpose: News of the Ministry for Science and Technology of the Republic of Slovenia. Provides easy access to news from science, development, universities, and innovative activities to individuals and institutions in research and development areas. The news includes the following parts:

Presentation	Brief information about individual institutions, their areas of work, departments, etc.
Achievements	Important research results, development applications, international awards and prizes, new books, etc.
Problems	Different authors present their proposals, critiques, and questions
Announcements	About seminars, symposia, conferences, different advertisements, scholarships, etc.

| Exchange of Services and Projects | Offers of and searches for research help, equipment, projects, services, etc. |

The language of publishing is Slovene. News is published at least once monthly and at most once in ten days. The volume varies.

NQTHM-Users

Contact: nqthm-users-request@cli.com

nqthm-users-request@inf.fu-berlin.de

Purpose: Discussion of theorem proving, using the Boyler-Moore theorem prover, NQTHM. Offers lore, advice, information, discussion, help, and a few flames.

NTP

Contact: ntp-request@trantor.umd.edu

Purpose: Discussion of the Network Time Protocol.

NPLC

Contact: tout@genesys.cps.msu.edu (Walid Tout)

Purpose: To establish this network for rapid communication among researchers in the field of plant lipids. This network can serve as a means to make announcements (such as post-doctoral positions) to the field. Additionally, it can be used to query co-workers regarding techniques, resources, etc. Also, we hope that research results will be disseminated more rapidly by the posting of abstracts for publications that have been accepted and are "in press." Finally, the NPLC newsletter and announcements regarding NPLC meetings, business, etc., will be posted on the network. The NPLC welcomes plant lipid researchers from anywhere in the world to make use of this network.

To subscribe, send the following message:

    SUB NPLC yourfullname

to listproc@genesys.cps.msu.edu.

Nucmed

Contact: nucmed-request@uwovax.uwo.ca

trevorc@uwovax.uwo.ca (Trevor Cradduck)

Purpose: A discussion of nuclear medicine and related issues. Of particular concern is the format of digital images.

Numeric-Interest

Contact: numeric-interest-request@validgh.com
(David Hough)

Purpose: Discussion of issues of floating-point correctness and performance with respect to hardware, operating systems, languages, and standard libraries.

NWU-Sports

Contact: nwu-sports-request@tssi.com (Michael Nolan)

Purpose: Information on Northwestern University Wildcats sports. Send requests to the contact address.

Obed-l

Contact: obed-l@reepicheep.gcn.uoknor.edu

Purpose: Discussion of dog obedience training and related working dog topics.

Objc

Contact: bunker!stpstn!objc-request (Anthony A. Datri)

Purpose: The Objective-C mailing list—for the discussion of Stepstone's Objective-C language, Objective-C compiler, Objective-C interpreter, and the ICPak-201 user interface library.

Objectivism

Contact: objectivism-request@vix.com (Paul Vixie)

Purpose: A mailing list where students of Objectivism can discuss their ideas, concrete issues, exchange news, etc. Any issue that may have some relevance to Objectivists is appropriate here.

The Observer

Contact: rwhit@cs.umu.se (Randall Whitaker)

Purpose: The central scope of the group covers the following:

- The theory of *autopoiesis* (Humberto Maturana and Francisco Varela)
- "Enactive Cognitive Science" (Varela, et al., 1991, *The Embodied Mind*)

The extended scope includes applications of the above theoretical work and linkages to other relevant work in, for example, systems theory, cognitive science, phenomenology, artificial life, etc. Started February 1993. Current format: *The Observer*, an edited electronic newsletter issued (approximately) twice monthly. ASCII research resources (e.g., bibliographies) available on request.

ODA

Contact: utzoo!trigraph!oda-request (Les Gondor)

Purpose: A mailing list for topics related to the ISO 8613 standard for Office Document Architecture, and ODIF (Office Document Interchange Format).

Offroad

Contact: offroad-request@ai.gtri.gatech.edu (Stefan Roth)

Purpose: To discuss and share experiences about 4x4 and offroad adventures, driving tips, vehicle modifications, and anything else related to four-wheeling. This list is specifically designed for owners, users, or enthusiasts of four-wheel drive vehicles. Discussions center around technical and mechanical matters, driving techniques, and trip reports. The list is unmoderated. This list is available as a real-time option (default) or as a digest option.

Oglasna Deska

Contact: oglasna-deska@krpan.arnes.si (Dean Mozetic and Marjeta Cedilnik)

    oglasna.deska@uni-lj.si

Purpose: *Oglasna Deska* (bulletin board)—transcripts taken from SLON, which is a nickname for Decnet connecting several computers in Slovenia. There is a conference similar to USENET running under SLON, and the articles and replies are occasionally saved and sent to the world. The topics cover a wide area; the language used is Slovene, Croatian, or Serbian, but some articles are in English. At the moment, interaction is limited to some "news groups" (others can only be read), but in the near future it should be possible to send articles using the mail `reply` command. The topics covered are equivalent to USENET groups `talk.politics.misc`, `rec.cars`, `rec.humor`, `comp.networks.*`, `rec.climbing`, and `misc.invest`.

OH-MOTSS

Contact: oh-motss-request@cps.udayton.edu

Purpose: The Ohio Members Of The Same Sex mailing list—for open discussion of lesbian, gay, and bisexual issues in and affecting Ohio. The mailing list is not moderated and is open to all, regardless of location or sexuality. Further, participation on the list does not necessarily indicate a person's sexual preference or orientation. The subscriber list is known only to the list owner.

OlymPuck

Contact: listserv@maine.maine.edu (Charlie Slavin)

Purpose: This list is for the discussion of Olympic ice hockey. Discussions concerning players, coaches, teams, and the games themselves are welcomed and encouraged. Related topics such as the interaction between the Olympic competition and college or NHL hockey are also acceptable. To subscribe, send e-mail to listserv@maine.maine.edu. The body of the message should contain SUBscribe OlymPuck *yourname*.

On-This-Day

Contact: geiser@pictel.com (Wayne Geiser)

Purpose: Provides a daily listing of interesting birthdays, events, religious holidays, astronomical events, etc. The messages are sent out in the wee hours of the morning, so you should have it for your morning coffee.

On-U

Contact: on-u-request@connect.com.au (Ben Golding)

Purpose: The On-U Sound mailing list—discussions related to Adrian Sherwood's On-U Sound label and the artists that record on it. They include Tack>>Head, Gary Clail, the Dub Syndicate, African Head Charge, Bim Sherman, Mark Stewart, etc.

Operlist

Contact: operlist-request@eff.org (Helen Trillian Rose)

Purpose: A discussion list for *everything* having to do with IRC. Its main purpose is IRC routing discussions, protocol discussions, and announcements of new versions (of IRC clients and servers).

Oregon-News

Contact: oregon-news-request@vector.intercon.com

Purpose: Mailing list of people organizing against the Oregon Citizens' Alliance. This list will carry news of lawsuits, rallies, events, votes, etc. that take place in the state of Oregon.

To subscribe: send a message to oregon-news-request@vector.intercon.com with one line:
SUBSCRIBE OREGON-NEWS yourfullname.

Orienteering

Contact: orienteering-request@graphics.cornell.edu (Mitch Collinsworth)

Purpose: Discuss all aspects of the sport of orienteering.

Origami

Contact: origami-l-request@nstn.ns.ca

Purpose: An unmoderated mailing list for discussion of all facets of origami, the Japanese art of paper folding. Topics include bibliographies, folding techniques, display ideas, descriptions of new folds, creativity, materials, organizations, computer representations of folds, etc.

Archives are available by anonymous ftp from rugcis.rug.nl:

1. To start ftp, enter ftp rugcis.rug.nl.
2. Log in as anonymous.
3. As your password, enter your IP address.
4. To change the directory, enter cd origami.

All requests to be added to or deleted from this list, problems, questions, etc., should be sent to origami-l-request@nstn.ns.ca.

Our-Kids

Contact: our-kids-request@oar.net

Purpose: Support for parents and others regarding care, diagnoses, and therapy for young children with developmental delays, whether or not otherwise diagnosed (e.g., CP, PDD, sensory integrative dysfunction). The name our-kids avoids labeling those who are, first and foremost, the special little ones in our lives.

OUTIL (Out in Linguistics)

Contact: outil-request@csli.stanford.edu (Arnold Zwicky)

Purpose: A list open to lesbian, gay, bisexual, dyke, queer, homosexual, etc., linguists and their friends. The only requirement is that you be willing to be out to everyone on the list as glb(-friendly); it's sort of like wearing a pink triangle.

The only official purposes of the group are to be visible and gather occasionally to enjoy one another's company; but we are all welcome to engage in any activity we can arouse interest in.

Oysters

Contact: oysters-request@blowfish.taligent.com

Purpose: For discussion of the British folk-rock band the Oyster and related topics.

Pac Ten Sports

Contact: crs@u.washington.edu (Cliff Slaughterbeck)

Purpose: The Pac Ten Sports Mailing List is an unmoderated mailing list dedicated to discussing sports of all types that are played competitively within the Pac Ten Athletic Conference.

Pagan

Contact: pagan-request@drycas.club.cc.cmu.edu
(Stacey Greenstein)

Purpose: To discuss the religions, philosophy, etc., of paganism.

PAGEMAKR

Contact: gwp@cs.purdue.edu (Geoff Peters)

Purpose: The PageMaker listserv is dedicated to the discussion of desktop publishing in general, with emphasis on the use of Aldus PageMaker. The list discusses PageMaker's use on both the PC and Macintosh realms. The list also maintains an extensive archive of help files that are extremely useful for the modern desktop publisher.

Panic

Contact: panic-request@gnu.ai.mit.edu

Purpose: A support group for panic disorders. Discussion involving phobias resulting from panic (agoraphobia and others). Also a place to meet other people who have gone through the disorder.

Papa

Contact: dgross@polyslo.calpoly.edu (Dave Gross)

Purpose: To discuss the life and works of Ernest Hemingway.

Park Rangers

Contact: 60157903@wsuvm1.csc.wsu.edu (Cynthia Dorminey)

Purpose: This list is primarily for anyone working or interested in working as a ranger (general, interpretive, etc.) for the National Park Service (U.S.A.), but rangers from state and county agencies as well as other countries are also welcome. The group discusses numerous topics related to this profession.

ParNET

Contact: parnet-list-request@ben.com (Ben Jackson)

Purpose: To discuss the installation, use, and modification of ParNET, an Amiga-to-Amiga networking program. Please direct comments and questions to parnet-list-owner@ben.com.

Partners

Contact: partners-request@cs.cmu.edu

Purpose: To advise the administration of Carnegie Mellon University, through the Vice President of Human Resources (who reads the list), of developments in Domestic Partnership benefits and make recommendations on CMU policy regarding benefits.

PBL

Contact: listserv@eng.monash.edu.au (Roger Hadgraft)

Purpose: Announcing an e-mail list for those interested in PBL. The list is an automatic way of keeping in touch with other PBLers in several countries around the world. It is an informal network that allows you to read contributions from others and to respond to their questions and comments. It is not an archive of published papers. It is most like a conversation between many participants, and consequently, it depends on enthusiastic contributions from all subscribers.

Currently, there are over 100 subscribers from the U.S.A. (50%), Australia (28%), Canada (16%), N.Z., the U.K., etc., (the rest).

To subscribe, send the following one-line e-mail message (as the body of the message, not the Subject line):

```
sub pbl-list
```

to listserv@eng.monash.edu.au.

After you are subscribed (it'll take a few minutes), send messages to

```
pbl-list@eng.monash.edu.au
```

Send problems to me:

```
roger.hadgraft@eng.monash.edu.au
```

pc532

Contact: pc532-request@bungi.com (Dave Rand)

Purpose: A mailing list for people interested in the pc532 project. This is a National Semiconductor NS32532-based system, offered for a very low cost.

PCGEOS-List

Contact: listserv@pandora.sf.ca.us

Purpose: Discussion forum for users or potential users of PC/GEOS products, including GeoWorks Ensemble, GeoWorks Pro, GeoWorks POS, and third-party products. Topics include general information, tips, techniques, applications, experiences, etc.

PD-Games

Contact: pd-games-request@math.uio.no (Thomas Gramstad)

Purpose: PD-Games is a mailing list for game theory, especially Prisoner's Dilemma type of problems. Purely technical issues and questions, as well as discussions of specific scientific applications, political and ideological aspects, and consequences of game theory are welcome, and it is a hope that the list will contribute toward the goal of elucidating and making known the nature of and the conditions for voluntary and mutual social cooperation.

PDP8-Lovers

Contact: pdp8-lovers-request@mc.lcs.mit.edu
(Robert E. Seastrom)

Purpose: To facilitate communication and cooperation between owners of vintage DEC computers, specifically, but not limited to, the PDP-8 series of minicomputers.

Discussions of all manner of hardware, software, programming techniques are invited. Ownership of an "antique" computer is not required for membership, but flames from people who feel that anything that is not cutting-edge technology is worthless are discouraged.

PDX-MOTSS

Contact: pdx-motss-request@agora.rain.com

Purpose: Discussion of LGB issues in the Portland, Oregon, metro area.

pen-pals

Contact: pen-pals-request@mainstream.com

Purpose: To provide a forum for children to correspond electronically with each other. Hopefully, this will help them improve their writing skills in a non-hostile environment. It can serve as a meeting place for them from which they can take their discussions off-line. This list is not moderated, but is monitored for content. Those who misuse the list will be sent e-mail off-line explaining their misuse and potentially bumped from the list. This list is managed by listproc.

PERQ-Fanatics

Contact: perq-fanatics-request@alchemy.com

Purpose: For users of PERQ graphics workstations. To subscribe to the list, users should post a message to perq-fanatics-request@alchemy.com. There is also an associated news group that was recently started: alt.sys.perq.

Peru

Contact: owner-peru@cs.sfsu.edu (Herbert Koller)

Purpose: For discussion of Peruvian culture and other issues. This mailing list is simply an echo site, so all posts get bounced from that address to all the people subscribed.

PH7

Contact: ph7-request@bnf.com

Purpose: To talk about Peter Hammill and related rock groups. To subscribe, send a message containing subscribe ph7 *yourfullname*.

PHOTO-CD

Contact: listmgr@info.kodak.com (Don Cox)

Purpose: The Kodak Photo-CD Mailing List provides libraries of information on Kodak CD products or technology and closely related products. Information in the library section is posted and maintained by Kodak. The mailing list is an open discussion area to talk with other Internet users interested in our CD technology and products. Kodak will participate in message conversations on occasion. Kodak does not guarantee the accuracy of information passed between mailing list users.

PHOTO-CD is a public mailing list. Those who want to subscribe to it should send mail to the address listserv@info.kodak.com with the command SUBSCRIBE PHOTO-CD *firstname lastname* on a line by itself in the body (and no other text).

Physics

Contact: physics-request@qedqcd.rye.ny.us (Mike Miskulin)

Purpose: A newly created digest to cover current developments in theoretical and experimental physics. Typical topics might include particle physics, plasmaphysics, astrophysics. Discussions related to all branches (large and small) of physics are welcome.

Picasso-Users

Contact: picasso-users@postgres.berkeley.edu

Purpose: For users of the Picasso graphical user interface development system.

Pigulka

Contact: zielinski@acfcluster.nyu.edu (Marek Zielinski)

   davep@acsu.buffalo.edu (Dave Phillips)

Purpose: Digest on the netnews from Poland, in English. Irregular.

Pipes

Contact: pipes-request@paul.rutgers.edu (Steve Masticola)

Purpose: For all those who enjoy smoking, collecting, or sharing information on pipes, tobacco, and related topics. Flames aren't allowed (except for the purpose of lighting up :-)).

Pisma Bralcev

Contact: pisma-bralcev@krpan.arnes.si (Andrej Brodnik and Srecko Vidmar)

   pisma.bralcev@uni-lj.si

Purpose: An edited (not moderated) mailing list that provides the possibility of publishing readers' opinions, questions, inquiries for help, answers, etc. There are also published travel tips and book reviews. Anybody can send a letter to the editor, and it will be published on the list under the author's name. The author can request anonymity, and it will be respected entirely. The frequency of publishing is about one issue per day or less. The language is originally Slovene, but other languages appear as well.

PKD-List

Contact: pkd-list-request@wang.com

Purpose: The discussion of the works and life of Philip K. Dick (1928-1982), one of the world's most unusual science fiction writers. Topics include his books and stories, and books and stories about him and his life; however, discussion can (of necessity) branch out into the nature of reality, consciousness, and religious experience.

POET

Contact: poet-request@scruz.ucsc.edu (Jon Luini)

Purpose: A workshop/critique forum for poetic works of all descriptions in progress.

Police

Contact: police-request@cindy.ecst.csuchico.edu (Pete Ashdown)

Purpose: Dedicated as a service to keep fans of the Police and its members—Sting, Stewart Copeland, and Andy Summers—informed and connected. To subscribe, mail to police-request@cindy.ecst.csuchico.edu, with the command subscribe in the first line. For help, send the command help to the same address.

POP

Contact: pop-request@jhunix.hcf.jhu.edu (Andy S. Poling)

Purpose: To discuss the Post Office Protocol (POP2 and POP3—described in RFCs 918, 937, 1081, and 1082) and implementations thereof.

The driving interest was lack of easily obtained knowledge of available POP2 and POP3 servers and clients. This mailing list is meant to provide this information. Anyone, whether consumer or product provider, is invited to participate.

Porschephiles

Contact: porschephiles-request@tta.com

Purpose: This list is for people who own, operate, work on, or simply lust after various models and years of Porsche automobiles. It's a good place to ask questions, talk about features and functionality, get advice on what to buy—or for how much—and, in general, sort of have a little electronic fellowship around the "driving passion" in our lives. Much like a PCA meeting, only distributed and real time.

This list is currently being run as a mail reflector, sending incoming messages to the whole list, which is currently over 350 people from all over the world. The participants include people with a variety of backgrounds, some very technical, some race/autocross/performance drivers and constructors, some owners, some admiring non-owners.

POS302-L

Contact: listserv@ilstu.edu

Purpose: POS302-L is a discussion list created for the "Race, Ethnicity, and Social Inequality" seminar offered at Illinois State University in the spring 1994 semester. The general purposes of the list are to create an electronic-mail audience for the written work of the students in the course and to invite a broad audience to participate in the seminar. Subscription to the list can be done by sending the following message to listserv@ilstu.edu:

```
SUBSCRIBE POS302-L your full name, institution
```

POSCIM

Contact: ups500@dbnrhrz1 (Markus Schlegel)

Purpose: The Political Sciences mailing list—a forum of those researching, teaching, or studying the subject, as well as the practitioners of politics.

Being a private list, POSCIM tries to be free of the "noises" common to public lists or news groups related to politics. Exchange over research programs, results, one's own projects, and the arrangement of special events or congresses are only a few of the various options of communication via POSCIM.

To join POSCIM, please contact ups500@dbnrhrz1 ups500@ibm.rhrz.uni-bonn.de markus@uni-bonn.de.

POSIX-Ada

Contact: umd5!grebyn!posix-ada-request

posix-ada-request@grebyn.com (Karl Nyberg)

Purpose: To discuss the Ada binding of the POSIX standard. This is the IEEE P1003.5 working group.

POSIX-Testing

Contact: posix-testing-request@mindcraft.com (Chuck Karish)

Purpose: To provide a forum for discussion of issues related to testing operating systems for conformance to the various POSIX standards and proposed standards (IEEE 1003.x and whatever derivative standards may emerge from the NIST, ANSI, ISO, and so on).

These issues include problems related to test suites in general, testability of various features of the standards, and portability of the test suites to the many very different POSIX implementations we expect to see in the near future. We'll focus on the test suites themselves, rather than on the standards to which they test (notably POSIX p1003.3).

Prince

Contact: prince-request@icpsr.umich.edu

Purpose: To discuss the musician Prince and related artists.

Prion

Contact: prion-request@stolaf.edu (Chris Swanson)

Purpose: To provide a resource for researchers working with prions and interested bystanders; however, all are welcome. All articles posted will be included in the next digest. If a poster feels that his or her posting is of an urgent nature, it may be distributed sooner than the regular digest.

PRL

Contact: brewer@ace.enet.dec.com (John Brewer)

Purpose: The Pirate Radio SWL list—for the distribution of questions, answers, information, and loggings of pirate radio stations. This includes SW stations, MW (AM broadcast), and FM pirates.

PROG-PUBS

Contact: prog-pubs-request@fuggles.acc.virginia.edu

Purpose: For people interested in progressive and/or alternative publications and other media.

PROG-PUBS was originally created to facilitate and encourage communication among people interested in and active with the "alternative student press" movement. However, the list's scope is now broader than this; we welcome and encourage participation from people involved in all kinds of small-scale, independent, progressive, and/or alternative media, including newspapers, newsletters, and radio and video shows, whether campus-based or not.

Progress

Contact: progress-list-request@math.niu.edu

Purpose: Discussion of the Progress RDBMS.

Project-Management

Contact: project-management-request@smtl.demon.co.uk

Purpose: The aim of the list is to discuss project management techniques generally, not just project management software and programs. You can join the list by sending e-mail to project-management-request@smtl.demon.co.uk with the subject line of subscribe.

Proof-Users

Contact: proof-request@xcf.berkeley.edu (Craig Latta)

Purpose: To discuss the left-associative natural language parser "proof." To join, e-mail proof-request@xcf.berkeley.edu with the subject line add me.

Pro-pkba-Democrats

Contact: donb@netcom.com

Purpose: For liberals/Democrats who support the Second Amendment.

Pubnet

Contact: pubnet-request@chinacat.unicom.com
(Chip Rosenthal)

Purpose: The administration and use of public access computer systems—primarily UNIX systems. The list membership includes a large number of people who run sites listed in the world-famous NIXPUB listing. If you have questions about setting up or running a public access system, this is the place to be.

Python

Contact: python-list-request@cwi.nl (Guido van Rossum)

Purpose: For discussion of and questions about all aspects of design and use of the Python programming language. This is an object-oriented, interpreted, extensible programming language. The source of the latest Python release is always available by anonymous ftp from ftp.cwi.nl, in directory /pub/python. To subscribe, send e-mail to python-list-request@cwi.nl; put your name and Internet e-mail address in the body. The list is not moderated.

QN

Contact: qn-request@queernet.org (Roger Klorese)

Purpose: A mailing list for Queer Nation activists and for all interested in Queer Nation, an activist group devoted to furthering gay rights. The purpose of QN is to network among various Queer Nation chapters, to discuss actions and tactics, and for general discussion of how to bring about Queer Liberation.

QNX2, QNX4

Contact: camz@dlogtech.cuc.ab.ca (Martin Zimmerman)

Purpose: To discuss all aspects of the QNX real-time operating systems. There are separate discussion lists for 2.15/2.20 and the 4.x POSIX versions.

Topics include compatible hardware, available third-party software, software reviews, available PD/free software, QNX platform-specific programming discussions, QNX and FLEET networking, fault-tolerance, distributed processing, process control, SCADA, and other QNX-related topics.

To subscribe, send a message to one of the following:

```
qnx2-request@dlogtech.cuc.ab.ca

qnx4-request@dlogtech.cuc.ab.ca
```

depending on which group you are interested in. The subject or body of the message should contain:

```
subscribe yourfulladdress
```

You also can send help in the subject field to get a more detailed description of how to use the list and how to post messages.

Quadraverb

Contact: qv-interest-request@swap.eng.sun.com (Bob Page)

Purpose: Discussion of the Alesis Quadraverb family of effects boxes. Unmoderated mail reflector; very light traffic.

Quanta

Contact: da1n@andrew.cmu.edu

Purpose: An electronically distributed magazine of science fiction. Published monthly, each issue contains short fiction, articles, and editorials by authors around the world and across the net. Quanta publishes in two formats: straight ASCII and PostScript for PostScript-compatible printers. To subscribe to Quanta, or just to get more info, send mail.

Quattro

Contact: quattro-request@aries.east.sun.com
(David Tahajian)

Purpose: To disuss Audi cars, and especially the AWD quattro models. All Audi-related discussion is welcome, including news, opinions, maintenance procedures, and parts sources.

Quebec Nordiques

Contact: nords-request@badaboum.ulaval.ca
(Dan Blanchard)

Purpose: This Internet mailing list will discuss topics concerning the National Hockey League's Quebec Nordiques.

Queen

Contact: qms-request@uiuc.edu (Christopher Owen Miller)

Purpose: Discussion about the rock group Queen. Please include the word SUBSCRIBE as your subject.

Race

Contact: majordomo@thumper.lerc.nasa.gov

Purpose: To discuss motorcycle racing (primarily on asphalt tracks) and associated technologies. This is a fairly broad interest group, with experience spanning motojournalism, roadracing from the perspective of the pit crew and racers, and engineering.

To subscribe to race, send the following in an e-mail message to majordomo@thumper.lerc.nasa.gov:

    subscribe race

If you feel you need to reach a human, send e-mail to

    race-approval@thumper.lerc.nasa.gov

Racefab

Contact: racefab-request@pms706.pms.ford.com

Purpose: To discuss racing fabrication and engineering. Suitable topics include suspension geometry and configurations, anti-drive, anti-squat, control arm placement, shock and strut valving, spindle design, floating rear ends, panhard bars and watts linkages, cage construction, chassis reinforcement, bearing specs, sources for information and materials, etc.

Please include the type of racing you're involved in (autox, circle track, road race) and the type of race cars/bikes you work/race on in your subscription request.

Raiders

Contact: raiders-request@super.org (Adam Fox)

Purpose: Unmoderated list; all Raider fans are welcome.

Ravenloft

Contact: raven+request@drycas.club.cc.cmu.edu

Purpose: Discussion of Gothic Horror with respect to the Ravenloft Accessory to Advanced Dungeons & Dragons.

rc

Contact: rc-request@hawkwind.utcs.toronto.edu (Chris Siebenmann)

Purpose: Discussion of the rc shell. rc is a shell designed by Tom Duff to replace the venerable Bourne shell in Plan 9. It provides similar facilities to sh, with some small additions and mostly less idiosyncratic syntax. Most of the discussion on the list is about Byron Rakitzis' free reimplementation of the shell. See the rc FAQ for more details; get it from rtfm.mit.edu as /pub/usenet/comp.unix.shell/rc-FAQ.

Reader

Contact: iskandar@u.washington.edu (Alex Khalil)

Purpose: For the support of Arabic script (Arabic, Farsi, Urdu, Sindhi, and other Pashto) on computer. The ftp site is on rama.poly.edu:/pub/reader and on u.washington.edu:/public/reader. The FAQ is in ../reader/text/faq.

Really-Deep-Thoughts

Contact: really-deep-thoughts-request@gradient.cis.upenn.edu

rdt-request@gradient.cis.upenn.edu (Anthony Kosky)

Purpose: Information and discussion on Tori Amos, her music, and other subjects that are relevant or of interest.

Recovery

Contact: recovery@wvnvm.wvnet.edu (Jeff Brooks)

Purpose: A forum and support group for survivors of childhood sexual abuse/incest and/or their SOs. Postings are published in digest format and contributors may post anonymously. The emphasis is on healing and recovery through the use of the Twelve Steps of Alcoholics Anonymous as adapted for our purpose.

REGAYN

Contact: regayn-request@csd4.csd.uwm.edu

uunet!csd4.csd.uwm.edu!regayn-request

Purpose: To serve as a contact point for discussions, opinions, meetings, personal experience sharing of addictions and recovery issues for gay, lesbian, bisexual, and transsexual people.

Any comments or suggestions are greatly appreciated. This is not a moderated mail group.

REM

Contact: valerie@athena.mit.edu (Valerie Ohm)

Purpose: Discussion of the music and lyrics by the music group R.E.M.

REND386

Contact: rend386-request@sunee.uwaterloo.ca

Purpose: Discussion by and for users of the REND386 software package (fast polygon-based graphics on 386 and 486 systems).

RENDANCE

Contact: listserver@morgan.ucs.mun.ca

Purpose: For discussion of Renaissance dance. The intended focus is dance reconstruction and related research, but discussion on any relevant topic is welcome.

RENews

Contact: nev@renews.relcom.msk.su

Purpose: Monthly digest on networking and computing in Russia.

Rockhounds

Contact: rockhounds-request@infodyn.com (Tom Corson)

Purpose: To exchange ideas, collecting sites, tips, and other information of general interest to gem and mineral collectors.

Rocky Horror

Contact: mossap@essex.ac.uk (Adam Moss)

Purpose: To distribute news and creative material concerning the film *The Rocky Horror Picture Show*, the stage shows, or anything else in any way connected with the *Rocky Horror* films or their stars. Mailings infrequent but reliable.

RokPress

Contact: ibenko@maveric0.uwaterloo.ca (Igor Benko)

rokpress@krpan.arnes.si

rokpress@uni-lj.si

Purpose: A moderated mailing list, intended primarily for news from Slovenia. Slovene is the principal language, although the articles in other languages are often included. It also covers news from the international press and important announcements related to Slovenia and Slovenes. The volume is kept as low as possible.

Role Modeling

Contact: majordomo@taskon.no

Purpose: Concerned with the use of roles as a concept in object-oriented systems design.

Topics include:

- Role modeling in OO software development
- Role models in business process modeling
- Methodologies based on role modeling such as the following:

    The OOram methodology, an object-oriented software development method that uses role modeling

    Using state machines to describe and/or specify certain aspects of an object's behavior

- Related subjects

The list is managed by cepe@taskon.no.

To subscribe to the list, send mail to majordomo@taskon.no. The body of the message should contain the line subscribe role-modeling. If you need to get in touch with a human, send mail to role-modeling-owner@taskon.no.

Romanians

Contact: romanians@sep.stanford.edu (Mihai Popovici)

Purpose: Mailing list for discussion, news, and information in the Romanian language.

ROOTS-L

Contact: listserv@vm1.nodak.edu

Purpose: ROOTS-L is a discussion list where those who have interest in genealogy may communicate via e-mail messages in hopes of finding more family history information. This discussion list is gatewayed to the USENET news group soc.roots, the intention being that all messages sent directly to ROOTS-L also appear in soc.roots, and vice versa.

To subscribe to the list, send e-mail to LISTSERV@NDSUVM1 on BITNET or listserv@vm1.nodak.edu with the body of the mail containing SUB ROOTS-L *your full name*. The Roots-L owner is alf.christophersen@nutri.uio.no (Alf Christophersen).

Rune-Quest

Contact: runequest-request@glorantha.holland.sun.com

Purpose: The RuneQuest Daily is a daily bulletin with discussion on the RuneQuest role-playing game and the fantasy world of Glorantha. RuneQuest is a trademark of Avalon Hill, Glorantha is the creation of Greg Stafford. Messages are queued daily and sent out in neat packets of up to 25K, thus facilitating users at sites with size restrictions on their mail.

Associated with the Daily is the moderated RuneQuest Digest, which appears less frequently. Messages too large or too specific for the Daily may be sent to the Digest instead. Some discussion from the Daily may find its way into the Digest.

Subscribers to the Daily will automatically receive the Digest. To subscribe to either, send e-mail to the contact address with the text subscribe list your@address fullname or subscribe digest your@address fullname.

Rush

Contact: rush-request@syrinx.umd.edu

Purpose: For fans of the Canadian rock group Rush to discuss things about the group and its music.

RX7Net E-Mail Club

Contact: rx7club@cbjjn.att.com

Purpose: An e-mail list of members who own Mazda RX7s or who are interested in gaining technical or general information about RX7s. You do not need to own an RX7 to join the list, just a love for the only rotary-powered sports car in the world. The RX7Net contains many knowledgeable people who have a lot of technical and historical information on the three generations of RX7s. The RX7Net currently has 190 members.

Saints-Best

Contact: lds-net-request@andrew.cmu.edu

Purpose: A low-volume, heavily filtered magazine featuring a few of the best messages of interest to Latter-day Saints (Mormons) from all over the Internet.

sam-Fans

Contact: sam-fans-request@hawkwind.utcs.toronto.edu (Chris Siebenmann)

Purpose: Discussion of Rob Pike's sam editor. sam is an interactive multifile text editor intended for bit-map displays. A textual command language supplements the mouse-driven, cut-and-paste interface to make complex or repetitive editing tasks easy to specify. The language is characterized by the composition of regular expressions to describe the structure of the text being modified. sam can be ftp-ed from research.att.com, directory /dist/sam; the mailing list itself is archived on ftp.sys.utoronto.ca in /pub/sam.

San Francisco Giants

Contact: giants-request@medraut.apple.com
(Chuq Von Rospach)

Purpose: Discussion and information exchange on the San Francisco Giants baseball team.

San Jose Sharks

Contact: sharks-request@medraut.apple.com (Laurie Sefton)

Purpose: Discussion and information exchange on the San Jose Sharks hockey team.

Sappho

Contact: sappho-request@mc.lcs.mit.edu
(Regis M. Donovan)

Purpose: A forum and support group for gay and bisexual women. The list is not moderated, but may become so if the volume and/or content begins to warrant it. A digest version is available; if you want it, be sure to mention it in your addition request. Men who want to "listen in," for whatever reason, are requested to use the feminist and alternates mailing lists instead; sappho membership is limited to women.

SATNEWS

Contact: listserv@orbital.demon.co.uk

Purpose: The mailing list for *Satnews*, a biweekly report of events in the satellite television industry worldwide. To subscribe to the list, write to listserv@orbital.demon.co.uk with `subscribe satnews yourfullname` as the first line in the message body, replacing `yourfullname` with your real name, not your e-mail address.

SCA

Contact: sca-request@mc.lcs.mit.edu (Danulf Donaldson, MKA Dana Groff)

Purpose: To discuss anything relating to the Society for Creative Anachronism, a worldwide medievalist organization. Anyone in the society (or interested in it) is welcome to join. Those with basic questions about the society should direct them to justin@inmet.com (Justin du Coeur, MKA Mark Waks), who will be happy to answer them. (Please note that the mailing list is not officially related to the SCA in any way; it is simply a group of talkative members.)

The SCA mailing list is gatewayed into the rec.org.sca news group.

SCA-West

Contact: sca-west-request@ecst.csuchico.edu

Purpose: To serve those persons who have a desire to discuss, share, etc., items of interest to the Society of Creative Anachronism members in the West and thereby reduce traffic on the Rialto (rec.org.sca) of subjects that might be considered too local; but there is really no restriction on any subject.

It is for those members who are in the West Kingdom, which includes northern and central California, northern Nevada, Alaska, Australia, and Japan. Anyone is welcome to join, though. This is strictly a mail list; there is no echo to a news group.

To subscribe, send a message with subscribe *yourfullname* on the first line of the message to sca-west-request@ecst.csuchico.edu.

School

Contact: school-request@balltown.cma.com (Richard Welty)

Purpose: Discussion of high-performance driving schools.

Scoann

Contact: scoann-request@xenitec.on.ca (Ed Hew)

Purpose: The SCO Announce mailing list—a moderated announcements list providing product update and new product announcements supplied by SCO or by developers offering SCO-based products.

Submissions for the list should be addressed to scoannmod@xenitec.on.ca.

The scoann mail list is bidirectionally gatewayed with the USENET biz.sco.annouce news group.

Scogen

Contact: scogen-request@xenitec.on.ca (Geoff Scully)

Purpose: For anyone interested in or currently using Santa Cruz Operation products. This mailing list is a single area where discussions and information can be exchanged regarding *all* SCO products.

The scogen mail list is bidirectionally gatewayed with the USENET biz.sco.general news group.

Scoodt

Contact: scoodt-request@xenitec.on.ca (Ed Hew)

Purpose: The SCO Open Desktop electronic mailing list—to provide a communications vehicle for interested parties to provide, request, submit, and exchange information regarding the configuration, implementation, and use of the SCO Open Desktop operating system as available from the Santa Cruz Operation.

All submissions will be posted as received with appropriate author attribution. Questions are welcome. Someone may even answer them.

The scoodt mail list is bidirectionally gatewayed with the USENET biz.sco.opendesktop news group.

Screaming in Digital

Contact: queensryche-request@pilot.njin.net

Purpose: Discussion of the band Queensryche and related topics. Caveats: Available only in weekly digest form, hand-edited.

Scribe

Contact: scribe-hacks-request@decwrl.dec.com

Purpose: For persons who perform the role of Scribe Database Administrator at their installation. Discussion will be about Scribe features, bugs, enhancements, performance, support, and other topics of interest to Scribe DBAs. The list will not be moderated, but will simply consist of a mail reflector—that is, if you send a message to the list, it will be rebroadcast to everyone on the list. Discussion at the level of

"How do I get a paragraph to indent 5 spaces instead of 3?" is specifically discouraged.

SDAnet

Contact: st0o+sda@andrew.cmu.edu (Steve Timm)

Purpose: A list for and about Seventh-Day Adventists. It is a moderated list. Anyone may post or subscribe.

SDOMINGO

Contact: listserv@enlace.bitnet

Purpose: To discuss and exchange information about the culture and events related to the Dominican Republic. Politics and sports are topics of great interest as long as the participants respect each other's opinions. Subscribers of this list are mainly college students, scientists, and Dominican professionals living overseas. The main languages on the list are Spanish and English.

To subscribe to the list, write to listserv@enlace.bitnet, with subscribe sdomingo *yourname* as the first line in the message body, replacing *yourname* with your real name, not your e-mail address.

Seattle-Mariners

Contact: seattle-mariners-request@kei.com

Purpose: The discussion of the Seattle Mariners baseball club, criticism included.

Security

Contact: uunet!zardoz!security-request (Neil Gorsuch)

security-request@cpd.com

Purpose: To notify of UNIX security flaws *before* they become public knowledge, and to provide UNIX security-enhancement programs and information. Most postings are explanations of specific UNIX security "holes," including fixes or workarounds to prevent their usage. This list is not intended for discussions of general and/or theoretical security issues. It is joined at the pleasure of the applicant's system administrator and the list administrator.

Requests to join must be mailed from a system administration account and must specify the following:

1. The full name of the recipient
2. The address to send the list to
3. The address of the contact person for that site (if different from 2)
4. Whether you want moderated digests or reflected postings

SE-R

Contact: se-r-request@world.std.com (Rich Siegel)

Purpose: Devoted to discussion of the Nissan Sentra SE-R, NX2000, and Infiniti G20 cars.

SF-LOVERS

Contact: sf-lovers-request@rutgers.edu (Saul Jaffe)

Purpose: For discussions of many topics, all of them related in some way to the theme of science fiction and fantasy. Topics have ranged very widely from rewritten stories, sci-fi and fantasy books, sci-fi movies, and sci-fi conventions to reviews of books, movies, and television shows. Anyone is welcome to submit material on these or other topics of interest in this general area.

The digest has a very large number of readers, and trivial messages are strongly discouraged due to the heavy load SF-LOVERS puts on the hosts CPU and disk space. Messages to SF-LOVERS are batched and broadcast periodically. Please be sure to read the file SFLOVERS.POLICY available from the archives.

For Internet subscribers, all requests to be added to or deleted from this list should be sent to sf-lovers-request@rutgers.edu. BITNET subscribers may issue the following command:

```
tell listserv at rutvm1 command sflovers
yourfullname
```

where *command* is either subscribe or unsubscribe as appropriate. Problems and administrative questions should always be sent to sf-lovers-request@rutgers.edu.

SFRaves

Contact: sfraves-request@soda.berkeley.edu
(Brian Behlendorf)

Purpose: About the "rave" club scene in San Francisco. Even though it's locally focused, people from all over the world are on SFRaves. It is an unmoderated list.

Shadows-Updates

Contact: shadows-update-request@sunee.uwaterloo.ca

Purpose: Regular synopses of the episodes of the television series *Dark Shadows*, currently being shown on the "Sci-Fi" cable channel. (See also Dark-Shadows in the list.)

ShadowTalk

Contact: listserv@hearn.bitnet

    listserv@hearn.nic.surfnet.nl (Robert Hayden)

Purpose: A listserv devoted to the role-playing game Shadowrun, which is published by FASA. Shadowrun takes place in the year 2054 and centers in the city of Seattle. ShadowTalk is an attempt to emulate the public communications networks presented in the game.

Contact the list owner (aq650@slc4.ins.cwru.edu) for a copy of the FAQ, which will outline many more of the details for this list, including instructions on how to subscribe.

Siege

Contact: siege-request@bransle.ucs.mun.ca

Purpose: For the discussion of pre-black powder methods of attack and defence of fortified positions. While the discussion of the downfall of the great siege engines caused by the advent of portable and powerful cannons is important, I would like this to be somewhat minimized.

Topics appropriate for discussion include physics, mechanics, materials, construction, transportation, terminology, historic evidence of use, historical reconstruction, common myths and misconceptions, and so on.

To subscribe, send mail to siege-request@bransle.ucs.mun.ca and include a single line saying subscribe siege *yourfullname*.

Sierra Club

Contact: 931rowe@merlin.nlu.edu (Eddie Rowe)

Purpose: Discussion of environmental topics with a focus on the Sierra Club's campaigns, news, and outings. A mirror of the FidoNet Sierra Club Conference (SIERRAN).

SII

Contact: owner@moumee.calstatela.edu

Purpose: To distribute news and provide a forum for discussions about the current events in the former Yugoslavia, centered around those involving or affecting Serbs. Also, they originate public actions related to these events.

SKEPTIC

Contact: listserv@jhuvm.hcf.jhu.edu

Purpose: A mailing list devoted to critical discussion of extraordinary claims. Among the paranormal topics that are commonly examined are parapsychology and psychic claims, creationism, cult archaeology, UFOs, cryptozoology, reincarnation/survival, quackery, the occult, and divination; but the discussion is not limited to any predetermined set of magical beliefs or alleged pseudosciences.

In connection with paranormal claims, issues involving science and philosophy in general are often raised. There is no policy of excluding any topic from consideration. While the common point of view expressed is skepticism about claims that go against current scientific pictures, critical approaches to science itself are also encouraged.

To subscribe, send a mail message to listserv@jhuvm.hcf.jhu.edu @jhuvm, with the line subscribe skeptic *yourfullname*.

SkillsBank

Contact: sun!kass!richard (Richard Karasik)

Purpose: To share skills with others—not just the computist ones, although those are handy to know, but some of the oddball ones that we all seem to have acquired.

Ground rules: The list is not going to be publicly available, but requests to the list for specific skills will be passed on to the people who have them, and they can decide about the level of participation they want to have. The only public piece that will be mailed around is the new skills that have been added, and the new requests for assistance.

I am open to any other suggestions for how to make this work.

Skunk-Works

Contact: skunk-works-request@harbor.ecn.purdue.edu

Purpose: To discuss Lockheed special project planes and current aviation news. We cover the Blackbird family (A-12, YF-12, and SR-71), the U-2 series, the F-117A, the B-2 (even though that's Northrop), and "Aurora."

SLLing-L

Contact: listserv@yalevm.ycc.yale.edu

Purpose: SLLING-L (formerly ASL-LING) is for discussions of Sign Language Linguistics. The discussion of deaf culture, education, medical advancements in the studies of deafness, etc., will be discouraged, except as they are pertinent to the discussion of sign linguistics. listserv@yalevm.ycc.yale.edu is the server. cromano@uconnvm.bitnet (owner) and mosko@matai.vum.ac.nz are the humans.

smail3-users

Contact: smail3-users-request@cs.athabascau.ca
(Lyndon Nerenberg)

Purpose: Targeted toward those who administer smail3.X-based mailers. Discussion of operational problems and fixes, specialized configurations, and other topics related to the day-to-day operation of smail3.X are found here. The list does not discuss smail 2.5 issues. (smail 2.5 is an unrelated piece of software that appeared in the comp.sources.unix archives under the archive name "smail3.") Questions about smail 2.5 should be directed to the news group comp.mail.misc. smail3-users deals primarily with operational issues. If you're interested in technical discussions on smail3 internals, consider joining smail3-wizards.

smail3-Wizards

Contact: smail3-wizards-request@cs.athabascau.ca (Lyndon Nerenberg)

Purpose: A discussion forum for people who are actively porting, debugging, and extending smail3.X. Discussion should be limited to topics concerning smail3 internals. Questions about smail3 installation and operation should be directed to the smail3-users list.

Smallmusic

Contact: smallmusic-request@xcf.berkeley.edu (Craig Latta)

Purpose: To discuss and develop an object-oriented software system for music. The current environment is Smalltalk 80. If you are interested in joining the discussion, e-mail smallmusic-request@xcf.berkeley.edu with the subject line add me.

Smiths-Fans

Contact: larryn@csufres.csufresno.edu

Purpose: A mailing list dedicated to the music of the rock group the Smiths. Though the group is no longer together, we feel there is a substantial enough body of work to keep a list such as this going. Topics include discussion/interpretation of lyrics, work being done currently by members, and other intellectual concerns.

Smoke-Free

Contact: maynor@ra.msstate.edu

Purpose: A support list for people recovering from addiction to cigarettes. To subscribe to the list, send the following command to listserv@ra.msstate.edu:

    subscribe smoke-free yourfullname

The list is running on UNIX listserv.

S-News

Contact: s-news-request@stat.wisc.edu (Douglas Bates)

Purpose: Information and discussion about the S language for data analysis and graphics.

Societies

Contact: societies-request@athena.mit.edu

Purpose: Discussion of Greek letter societies of all sorts, primarily those that are at American colleges. Flamage not encouraged by list owners; no affiliation with one is required. Currently unmoderated. Please include your most reliable Internet-accessible address in your subscription request.

Software Entrepreneurs

Contact: softpub-request%toolz.uucp@mathcs.emory.edu (Todd Merriman)

    ...!emory!slammer!toolz!softpub-request

Purpose: Devoted to the interests of entrepreneurial software publishing, including (but not limited to) shareware. The forum is completely open.

Soils-l

Contact: jp@unl.edu (Jerome Pier)

Purpose: A forum for the discussion of all subjects dealing with soil science. Soil physics, chemistry, genesis, classification, mineralogy, fertility, conservation, etc., may be discussed within this unmoderated group. The formation of this group has been sanctioned by The American Society of Agronomy and the Soil Science Society of America. To subscribe, send e-mail to listserv@unl.edu containing the one-line message sub soils-l *yourname*.

SOMWPS

Contact: SOMWPS-Info@knex.via.mind.org

Purpose: SOMWPS is a mailing list for people interested in the technical aspects of IBM's System Object Model and associated object technologies like CORBA and the OS/2 WorkPlace Shell. It is primarily aimed at developers, but it may be interesting for technically advanced users as well.

IBM's System Object Model is a language neutral framework for object-oriented programming. The first implementation is part of IBM's OS/2 operating system. SOM is compliant with the Object Management Group's (OMG) Common Object Request Broker Architecture. There are also extensions to SOM for distributed object-oriented design, DSOM.

The OS/2 WorkPlace Shell is the most famous application of SOM. As such, we will be discussing its technical underpinnings, as well as discussing WPS programming techniques. For the most part, if it is related to SOM, we are interested in discussing it.

To subscribe, send the following commands to Mail-Server@knex.via.mind.org:

```
SUBSCRIBE SOMWPS FirstName LastName
OPTION SOMWPS ALIAS your_email_address
```

Note that the Subject header line is ignored. The commands must appear in the body of the e-mail text.

SONIC-LIFE-L

Contact: rtv1@cornell.edu

Purpose: The discussion of the music and other work of Sonic Youth. It is a private mailing list with restricted membership determined by the list owner.

To subscribe to SONIC-LIFE-L, send the following command in the body of a message via electronic mail to listserv@cornell.edu:

```
SUB SONIC-LIFE-L yourfirstname yourlastname
```

Please use your real first and last name. Nicknames and aliases may not be accepted. Lurkers (people who do not post on a regular basis) are always welcome.

If you have any questions about SONIC-LIFE-L, contact Rob Vaughn, the list owner, at rtv1@cornell.ed.

If you have any questions about listserv, contact the listserv manager, at listmgr@cornell.edu.

Soundtracks

Contact: soundtracks-request@ifi.unizh.ch (Michel Hafner)

Purpose: For people with general sound-track interests; the list includes the following:

- Discussions and reviews of new and older sound tracks (musical and technical aspects)

- Information about availability of specific sound tracks on different formats in different parts of the world

- Publication of trading lists so members can swap stuff and complete their collections

- Compiling of lists on different subjects with entries collected via the list (for example, passages in sound tracks "lifted" from other sound tracks, classical compositions with detailed data, discographies, etc.)
- Discussions and reviews of books, fanzines, etc., about sound tracks/music for films
- Discussions and reviews of hardware for (film) music reproduction

Please don't join if you are just looking for some sound track(s) but have no general interest in the field!

Sovokinform

Contact: burkov@drfmc.ceng.cea.fr

Purpose: CIS news, events, general information; usually in transliterated Russian. To subscribe, send the message SUB SOVOKINFORM *yourfullname*.

Space: 1999

Contact: space-1999-request@quack.kfu.com

Purpose: For discussion on almost any subject of interest to fans of the 1975-1976 TV show *Space: 1999*.

Spojrzenia

Contact: krzystek@u.washington.edu (Jerzy Krzystek)

Purpose: A weekly e-journal, devoted to Polish culture, history, politics, etc. In Polish.

Sports-Cards

Contact: cards-request@tanstaafl.uchicago.edu (Keane Arase)

Purpose: For people interested in collection, speculation, and investing in baseball, football, basketball, hockey, and other trading cards and/or memorabilia. Discussion and want/sell lists are welcome. Open to anyone.

SQL-Sybase

Contact: sybase-request@apple.com

Purpose: A semi-unmoderated mailing list for sharing information about the Sybase SQL server and related products.

Sri Lanka Net (SLNet)

Contact: pkd@fed.frb.gov

slnetad@ganu.colorado.edu

Purpose: A moderated mailing list that carries news and other articles about Sri Lanka. Wire service (AP, UPI, Reuters, etc.) news is obtained for exclusive use of SLNet members. Newspaper clippings from Sri Lanka are also carried (in electronic form) on a regular basis. SLNet is not a discussion group. Members may request information from others.

SSI_Mail

Contact: listprocessor@link.com

Purpose: A moderated list for space development topics related to Space Studies Institute programs past, present, and future. Space Studies Institute is a non-profit organization founded in 1977 by Gerard and Tasha O'Neill for the purpose of opening the high frontier of space for the benefit of all humanity.

SSI_Mail list has been created by members of SSI to increase member communication and is also available to non-members who are interested in the high frontier. Information on accessing the archives and using the list pro-cessor is available by sending help as the only word in the body to listprocessor@link.com. To subscribe, send to listprocessor@link.com the message subscribe ssi_mail *your name*. Please use your real name, not a handle or e-mail address.

List owner: Mitchell James (mjames@link.com, mitchellj@aol.com)

Stagecraft

Contact: stagecraft-request@jaguar.cs.utah.edu (Brad Davis)

Purpose: For the discussion of all aspects of stage work, including (but not limited to) special effects, sound effects, sound reinforcement, stage management, set design and building, lighting design, company management, hall management, hall design, and show production. This is not a forum for the discussion of various stage productions (unless the discussion pertains to the stagecraft of a production), acting or directing methods (unless you know of ways to get actors to stand in the right spots), or film or video production (unless the techniques can be used on the stage). The list will not be moderated unless problems crop up. Archives will be kept of the discussion (send mail to stagecraft-request for copies).

Star Fleet Battles

Contact: hcobb@fly2.berkeley.edu (Henry J. Cobb)

Purpose: The SFB Tacticsline—for discussion of tactics of the SFB game, and as a contact point for SFB PBeM games.

Starserver

Contact: starserver-request@engr.uky.edu (Wes Morgan)

Purpose: For owners, operators, and administrators of AT&T StarServer systems. While all interested parties are invited to join, the list is dedicated to matters of system administration/operation; many "UNIX questions and answers" resources are available, and we ask that you utilize them. Several ATT/NCR technical support personnel participate in the discussion. The list is not currently moderated.

St. Louis Blues

Contact: blues@medicine.wustl.edu (Joe Ashkar)

Purpose: For information, game reports, stats, discussion, etc., about the St. Louis Blues of the National Hockey League.

Stock Market Secrets

Contact: smi-request@world.std.com

Purpose: A stock-market-related daily comment. In addition, we answer questions on a wide variety of investment and financial topics.

This is a moderated list in order to keep confidential information.

Stonewall25

Contact: stonewall25-request@queernet.org

    wellconnectedsite!unpc!stonewall25-request

Purpose: For discussion and planning of the "Stonewall 25" international gay/lesbian/bi rights march in New York City on Sunday, June 26, 1994, and the events accompanying it.

Stormcock

Contact: stormcock-request@dcs.qmw.ac.uk (Paul Davison)

Purpose: For general discussion and news concerning the music of Roy Harper, a folk-rock musician with a conscience. Recommendations and news concerning similar artists are encouraged. The list is set up as a mail reflector.

Note: Some Internet sites may have to route mail through the U.K. Internet gateway nsfnet-relay.ac.uk. Also, in some exceptional circumstances, we may have to refuse membership because we get charged for mail to certain addresses in the UUCP domain.

Strathspey

Contact: strathspey-request@math.uni-frankfurt.de

Purpose: A forum for the discussion of all aspects of Scottish Country Dancing, e.g., dance descriptions, dancing technique, the history of dances and dancing, learning or teaching how to dance. We also welcome descriptions of new dances, announcements of events like courses or balls, or anything the subscribers might find interesting.

The mailing list is unmoderated, i.e., everything that is submitted is forwarded directly to the subscribers of the list. We hope to be able to offer an archive of past traffic if the demand should arise.

Subscription/unsubscription/info requests should be directed to

    strathspey-request@math.uni-frankfurt.de

Just send a message with the word subscribe in the Subject header to subscribe to the list. Similarly, send a Subject of unsubscribe to unsubscribe, or a Subject of help to get a copy of the help message (which is very much like this posting).

Most (un)subscription requests are processed automatically without human intervention. To reach a human for special requests or problems, send mail to owner-strathspey@math.uni-frankfurt.de.

ST Viruses

Contact: r.c.karsmakers@stud.let.ruu.nl

Purpose: To provide fast and efficient help where infection with computer viruses is concerned—Atari ST/TT/Falcon only, no MS-DOS or compatibles! Also, it's the electronic helpline for registered users of the "Ultimate Virus Killer" program. Questions about virus symptoms or any other general questions of Atari 16/32-bit viral nature may be directed to the above address. No digest format available (at least not yet).

The Sugarcubes

Contact: glocke@morgan.ucs.mun.ca (Gord Locke)

Purpose: The blue-eyed-pop mailing list—for discussion of the now-defunct (though-not-necessarily-for-good) Icelandic band the Sugarcubes. Also acceptable fodder for discussion: the solo career of their lead singer, Bjork Gudmundsdottir, other Icelandic bands, trading/selling of sundry paraphernalia, what you like to take with your tea...you get the idea.

To subscribe to this list, send a message to listserver@morgan.ucs.mun.ca, with the message body consisting only of

```
subscribe blue-eyed-pop yourfullname
```

(yourfullname is not your e-mail address, just your name—like Gord Locke.) The account you send this message from determines where mail from the list will be sent.

There is no blue-eyed-pop-request address; mail administrative stuff to the list owner (me, Gord Locke):
glocke@morgan.ucs.mun.ca.

Sun-386i

Contact: sun-386i-request@ssg.com (Rick Emerson)

Purpose: Discussion and information about the 386i-based Sun machines.

Sunflash (aka The Florida SunFlash)

Contact: flash@sun.com (John J. McLaughlin)

Purpose: To keep Sun users informed about Sun via press releases, product announcements, and technical articles. This is a one-way mailing list. Each month, 25 to 35 articles are posted. Over 110,000 Sun users subscribe. Requests to be added to the list should go to sunflash-request@sun.com. For more information, send mail to info-sunflash@sun.com.

Sun-Managers

Contact: sun-managers-request@eecs.nwu.edu

Purpose: Information of special interest to managers of sites with Sun workstations or servers.

Sun-Nets

Contact: sun-nets-request@umiacs.umd.edu

Purpose: Discussion and information on networks using Sun hardware and/or software.

SupraFAX

Contact: subscribe@xamiga.linet.org (David Tiberio)

Purpose: To help people who have been having trouble using the SupraFAX v.32bis modem. Topics include what some common problems are, where to get support, what bugs are found in the current ROM revisions, and how to follow basic setup and usage of the Supra command set (Hayes compatible).

To subscribe to the list, send e-mail to subscribe@xamiga.linet.org, with a line in the body of the text like:

    #supra username@domain

where your *username* is the name mail is sent to and *domain* is your IP address for your machine. For example, I would subscribe by writing #supra dtiberio@xamiga.linet.org in the body. We run multiple lists, and users may subscribe to multiple lists in one posting. On receipt of your welcome letter, please respond to become an activated subscriber.

Supercomputing Sites

Contact: gunter@yarrow.wt.uwa.oz.au

Purpose: Weekly mailing of the list of the world's most powerful computing sites.

Sysops

Contact: {harpo,bellcore,cmcl2}!cucard!dasys1!sysops-request

    {allegra,cmcl2,philabs}!phri!dasys1!sysops-request

Purpose: To facilitate communication among operators of computerized bulletin board systems. Topics will include, but are certainly not limited to, applications, security, legal issues, and software.

Szemle

Contact: ujsagker@vuhepx.phy.vanderbilt.edu

Purpose: Discussion and distribution of news about Hungary, in digest form. Information is mainly in Hungarian.

To receive the digest, write to the contact address, with the Subject KELL.

Tadream

Contact: tadream-request@vacs.uwp.edu (Dave Datta)

    ...uwm!uwpvacs!tadream-request

    uwpvacs!tadream-request@uwm.edu

Purpose: A forum for discussions about Tangerine Dream and related artists. The discussions are not moderated, but discussions should have some small relation to Tangerine Dream (solo works and instrumentation discussions are welcome). The list is set up both as a mail relay and a daily digest.

Talon-Eclipse-Laser

Contact: todd@di.com (Todd Day)

Purpose: For owners and admirers of Talon, Eclipse, or Laser automobiles.

Tandem

Contact: tandem-request@hobbes.ucsd.edu

Purpose: A mailing list for tandem bicycle enthusiasts. Suitable topics include questions and answers related to tandem componentry, riding technique, brands and equipment selection, prices, clubs, rides, and other activities; cooperating on a section on tandems for the rec.bicycles.* FAQ, etc.

Tandy4k

Contact: `...!{psu-cs,reed,ogcvax}!qiclab!tandy4k-users` (Steven Neighorn)

Purpose: A mailing list for owners, users, and other interested parties of the Intel 80386-based Tandy 4000 Microcomputer. The list will contain problems encountered, hints, program source code, and anything else related to the operation of Tandy's newest entry into the world of microcomputers.

TBI-Sprt

Contact: `listserv@sjuvm.stjohns.edu`

Purpose: The St. Johns University Traumatic Brain Injury Support List—for the exchange of information by survivors, supporters, and professionals concerned with traumatic brain injury and other neurological impairments that currently lack a forum. We know from our own experience that one of the difficulties people dealing with TBI face is that their time is often dominated by the survivor's recovery process. Accessing support groups or networking of any kind can seem like one more thing to add to an already packed schedule. A forum such as this is available at all hours of the day or night and does not need to become one more event that must be scheduled.

The postings to the list are archived and made available monthly through the listserv. A file containing introductions submitted by subscribers is also available along with files relevant to topics of the list. Additions to these resources are welcome.

To subscribe to tbi-sprt, send mail to `listserv@sjuvm.bitnet` or `listserv@sjuvm.stjohns.edu`. Leave the subject line blank and in the body of the message put the line `tbi-sprt` *yourfullname*.

List owners: Len Burns (lburns@cats.ucsc.edu) and Tapati Amber Sarasvati (labyris@gorn.echo.com).

TCAD

Contact: tcad-request@iec.ufl.edu (Mark Law)

Purpose: To serve the needs of users and software developers of TCAD (technology computer-aided design) codes. These codes typically aid the IC process designer in developing, debugging, and optimizing new and old processes. The group discusses software such as PISCES, SUPREM, FABRICS, SAMPLE, SIMPL, and MINIMOS.

TCP-Group

Contact: tcp-group-request@ucsd.edu

Purpose: Discussion about promoting TCP/IP use on Ham packet radio.

Tears4-Fears

Contact: tears4-fears-request@ms.uky.edu (Joel Abbot)

Purpose: Discussion of the music group Tears For Fears.

TeleUSErs

Contact: teleusers-request@telesoft.com (Charlie Counts)

Purpose: To promote the interchange of technical information, examples, tips, etc., among the users of Tele-USE. The TeleUSErs mailing list is unmoderated. (Mail for TeleSoft TeleUSE Technical Support should *not* be sent to the list; technical support e-mail should be sent to guisupport@telesoft.com).

Testing-Research

Contact: testing-research-request@cs.uiuc.edu
(Brian Marick)

Purpose: A forum for testing researchers to discuss current and future research. Since testing is one of the most down-to-earth kinds of software engineering research, testing practitioners are welcome. Messages about practice should be the kind that can guide or improve research; messages that can improve practice should go in comp.software-eng. This list is unmoderated.

Theatre

Contact: theatre-request@world.std.com
(Elizabeth Lear Newman)

Purpose: For the general discussion of theater, in whatever form it may take. This list is primarily a gateway for the traffic in the news group rec.arts.theatre.

They-Might-Be

Contact: they-might-be-request@gnu.ai.mit.edu

Purpose: Discussion of the musical group They Might Be Giants.

TheWho

Contact: majordomo@cisco.com

Purpose: An unmoderated mailing list for discussion of the band The Who, its individual members, lyrics, etc. To subscribe, send e-mail to majordomo@cisco.com, with the following line in the body of the message (NOT the subject line):

    subscribe thewho

Think-C

Contact: think-c-request@ics.uci.edu (Mark Nagel)

Purpose: To discuss the Think C compiler for the Macintosh. Acceptable topics include discussion of compiler problems and solutions/workarounds, discussion of object-oriented programming and Macintosh programming, and the sharing of source code. Associated with this list is an archive stored on ics.uci.edu accessible via ftp and a mail archive server (archive-server@ics.uci.edu). Submissions to the archive should go to think-c-request.

Thunderbird

Contact: htunca@ncsa.uiuc.edu (Han Tunca)

Purpose: To discuss all aspects of Ford Thunderbird automobiles. The mailing list is not limited to any model year.

TinyMUCK-Sloggers

Contact: tinymuck-sloggers-request@piggy.ucsb.edu (Robert Earl)

Purpose: Forum for programmers, wizards, and users of the extensible, programmable TinyMUD derivative known as TinyMUCK (current version: 2.2).

TinyMUSH-Programmers

Contact: tinymush-programmers-request@cygnus.com

Purpose: Discussion devoted to the programming language integral to the TinyMUSH subfamily of mud servers. (See the rec.games.mud FAQ for more general information about muds.)

Tolkien-Czech

Contact: tolkien-request@pub.vse.cz

Purpose: Discussion, held in Czech and Slovak languages only, concerning works of J.R.R. Tolkien, especially the Czech (and Slovak) translations.

To subscribe, send SUBSCRIBE TOLKIEN *yourfirstname yourlastname* mail to listserver@pub.vse.cz.

TolkLang

Contact: tolklang-request@lfcs.ed.ac.uk (Julian Bradfield)

Purpose: Discussions of the linguistic aspects of J.R.R. Tolkien's works. This covers everything from Elvish vocabulary and grammar to his use of Old English. The list is (lightly) moderated.

TOP

Contact: top-request@cv.ruu.nl (Ger Timmens)

Purpose: Discussion of the musical group Tower of Power and associated side projects.

TopSoft

Contact: ts-request@atlas.chem.utah.edu (Tony Jacobs)

Purpose: TopSoft is a worldwide network Macintosh Programming User Group developing high quality free software. FilterTop is a batch processing program with an iconic/graphical programming interface. It lets you pass the files selected through an assembly line process of objects called *filters*. Each filter performs a separate operation on the file or data.

Torg

Contact: torg-request@cool.vortech.com (Clay Luther)

Purpose: The mailing list dedicated to the infiniverse of West End Game's "Torg, the Possibility Wars" role-playing game. Please put HELP on the subject line, as this is an automated request.

Toronto Blue Jays

Contact: stlouis@unixg.ubc.ca (Phill St-Louis)

Purpose: Discussion of the Toronto Blue Jays baseball club, including player transactions, predictions, game commentary, etc. Everyone welcome!

Towers

Contact: bill@wrangler.wlk.com (Bill Kennedy)

Purpose: General discussion on the subject of NCR tower computers. Gatewayed with comp.sys.ncr.

Toyota

Contact: toyota-request@quack.kfu.com

Purpose: The discussion of almost any subject for owners and prospective owners of all models of Toyota consumer passenger vehicles and light trucks.

Toyota Corolla

Contact: corolla-request@mcs.com

Purpose: The discussion of Toyota Corollas. From 1970-1994 models, all engines, even the Chevy Nova and Geo Prism twins.

TRANSGEN

Contact: listserv@brownvm.brown.edu

Purpose: A list specifically for and about people who are transsexual, transgendered, and/or transvestites. The list is open to the public.

TRANSGEN may be received in two formats. For setting TRANSGEN to post by post format, the proper command is SET TRANSGEN MAIL. For setting it to digest format, the command is SET TRANSGEN DIGEST. The proper address to which to send these commands is one of the following:

```
listserv@brownvm.brown.edu
listserv@brownvm.bitnet
```

Transputer

Contact: transputer-request@tcgould.tn.cornell.edu

Purpose: To enhance the communication among those who are interested in the Transputer and Transputer-based systems.

Submissions should be of non-proprietary nature and be concerned with, but not limited to, the following:

- Algorithms
- Current development efforts (hardware and software)
- INMOS and third-party systems (Meiko, FPS, etc.)
- Interfaces
- Dedicated computational resources
- Occam and non-Occam language development

Archives of submissions are available by anonymous ftp from the host tcgould.tn.cornell.edu (user ID anonymous; password is of the form *user@host*) and through UUCP on a per-request basis.

The list is maintained as a mail reflector. Submissions are therefore sent out as they are received.

Traveller

Contact: `traveller-request@engrg.uwo.ca` (James T. Perkins)

Purpose: To discuss the Traveller science fiction role-playing game, published by Game Designers' Workshop. All variants of Traveller (Traveller 2300, MegaTraveller) and Traveller games (Snapshot, Trillion Credit Squadron, etc.) are included, too. Discussion is unmoderated and open to all facets and levels of Traveller discussion. Listeners as well as contributors are welcome.

TREK-REVIEW-L

Contact: `listserv@cornell.edu` (Michael Scott Shappe)

Purpose: A noise-free forum for reviews of *Star Trek* material. This category includes, but is not limited to, television programs, feature films, novels and novelizations, comic books, games, and parodies of *Star Trek*.

The list is not rooted in any specific generation of *Trek*. Original Series, Animated Series, Movie Era, *Next Generation*, and *Deep Space Nine* materials are all valid.

To subscribe to the list, send the following command in mail to `listserv@cornell.edu`:

```
SUBSCRIBE TREK-REVIEW-L yourfirstname yourlastname
```

Triples

Contact: `triples-request@hal.com` (Howard A. Landman)

Purpose: To discuss non-monogamous relationships, polyfidelity, group marriage, and the various issues that arise in that context, like jealousy, shared housing, marriage laws, sex, etc. Not moderated.

TurboVision

Contact: listserv@vtvm1.cc.vt.edu

Purpose: For TurboVision programmers (a library that comes with Borland C++ and Pascal compilers). Both languages are discussed. You can subscribe by sending the message subscribe turbvis *yourfullname* to listserv@vtvm1.cc.vt.edu.

Twilight Zone

Contact: r.c.karsmakers@stud.let.ruu.nl

Purpose: A fiction-only on-line magazine. It's published quarterly and is available only in ASCII. Fiction featured in it is primarily fantasy, science fiction, and (hopefully) humor. Subscriptions may be acquired by sending mail. Writers welcome, as long as they don't like carnivorous plants.

Twins

Contact: owner-twins@athena.mit.edu

Purpose: Even though the term "twins" is used, it is meant to represent twins, triplets, etc. The purpose of this mailing list is to provide an open forum for the discussion of issues related to twins. This might include research on twin-related issues, parenting issues, and issues concerning adult twins.

To join, send mail to owner-twins@athena.mit.edu, with Twins Subscription on the subject line, and a brief note asking to be added to (or deleted from) the list.

Two-Strokes

Contact: 2strokes-request@microunity.com

Purpose: For the discussion of two-stroke motorcycle technology, maintenance, and riding. It is primarily oriented toward street and road-racing two-strokes, but discussion about two-stroke dirt bikes is fine.

TX-Firearms

Contact: tx-firearms-request@frontier.lonestar.org

Purpose: To keep interested parties aware of Texas firearms laws, hunting seasons, and regulations, pending legislation, group meetings, competition schedules—basically anything related to firearms in the State of Texas. The list is not moderated and is available to anyone.

UK-DANCE

Contact: listserv@orbital.demon.co.uk

Purpose: For discussion about all aspects of dance music culture in the U.K.: clubs, raves, record shops, radio, records, and anything else to do with the underground dance music scene.

To subscribe to the list, write to listserv@orbital.demon.co.uk with subscribe uk-dance *yourfullname* as the first line in the message body, replacing *yourfullname* with your real name, not your e-mail address.

UK-Hockey

Contact: uk-hockey-request@cee.hw.ac.uk (Steve Salvini)

Purpose: This is an open invitation to followers of hockey in the U.K. to join a mailing list dedicated to the discussion of (ice!) hockey in Britain. At present, we are mailing out news, gossip, league tables, match reports, and results on a fairly regular basis.

UKlegal

Contact: lsg001@uk.ac.coventry.cck

Purpose: The objective of this mailing group is to consider and discuss matters of a legal nature relating to English—and to some respects, Scottish—law. People may join the group by mailing to lsg001@uk.ac.coventry.cck. People should put the word uklegal as the header and put their e-mail address on the next line.

UK-MOTSS

Contact: uk-motss-request@pyra.co.uk (Internet)

uk-motss-request@uk.co.pyra (JANet)

uk-motss-request%pyrltd.uknet (Brain-dead JANet mailers)

Purpose: For gay people in the U.K., or those who are interested in the U.K. gay scene/politics. It is a supportive environment for those unwilling or unable to read the soc.motss news group, and confidentiality is assured. Anonymous posting is available.

UltraLite-List

Contact: listserv@grot.starconn.com

Purpose: Discussion forum for users or potential users of the original NEC UltraLite PC1701 and PC1702 computers (the V30-based notebook computer with a 1M or 2M silicon hard disk, not the newer 80X86-based models). Topics include general information, tips, techniques, applications, experiences, and sources for hardware, software, accessories, and information.

To subscribe, send a message to listserv@grot.starconn.com with the following commands in the body of the message:

```
subscribe ultralite-list yourfirstname yourlastname
quit
```

Replace *yourfirstname yourlastname* with your name, not your e-mail address.

Administrative messages other than subscription and unsubscription may be sent to ultralite-list-owner@grot.starconn.com.

Undercover

Contact: undercover-request@snowhite.cis.uoguelph.ca (Steve Portigal)

Purpose: An unmoderated mailing list for the discussion of the Rolling Stones. Discussion topics may include bootleg trading; how-to guitar-playing advice; information about recent books, such as Wyman's *Stone Alone* and others; perspectives on recent solo albums by Watts, Richards, and Wood; and the upcoming album by Jagger (and the rarely released "Stuff" by Wyman).

To be added to (or removed from) the list, send mail to undercover-request@snowhite.cis.uoguelph.ca. Note that this is a human (me), so requests like SUB LIST JOHN@TOADY are kind of annoying. Please include your e-mail address in the message. If you don't get any messages, please get back in touch because I will drop bouncing addresses from the list.

This list (Rolling Stones discussion) is now a digest.

Unisys

Contact: unisys-request@bcm.tmc.edu (Richard H. Miller)

Purpose: Discussion of all Unisys products and equipment.

Univel

Contact: univel-request@telly.on.ca

Purpose: To provide a forum for users, developers, and others interested in the products of Univel, the Novell subsidiary that produces UNIX system software for PC-architecture systems. This list is gatewayed to/from the news group biz.univel.misc.

To subscribe, send mail to univel-request@telly.on.ca with a message body of this form:

    subscribe univel yourfullname

UPS-Alumni

Contact: ups_alumni-request@stephsf.com (Bill England)

Purpose: Ostensibly for the purpose of linking graduates of the University of Puget Sound. This list will also help those interested keep abreast of current events and changes at the university. Commercial postings are prohibited.

Uruguay

Contact: uruguay-request@db.toronto.edu
(Mariano Consens)

Purpose: A mailing list for general discussions and information on topics related to Uruguay. To subscribe, please send name, e-mail, topics of interest, and (optionally) address and phone number. Spanish is the dominant language in this group.

USENET-Oracle

Contact: oracle-admin@cs.indiana.edu (Steve Kinzler)

Purpose: An active, cooperative effort for creative humor. The USENET Oracle answers any questions posed to it. Send mail to oracle@cs.indiana.edu with the word help in the subject line for complete details on how to participate.

A distribution list is available for receiving compilations of the best USENET Oracle answers (the USENET Oracularities, also posted to rec.humor.oracle).

Note: This is wholly unrelated to the Oracle database software or company.

Utne-Salon-List

Contact: utne-salon-request@netcom.com (Bill Sheppard)

Purpose: Discussion relating to the Utne Reader Neighborhoood Salon Association, a group facilitating community discussion groups around the country where interested citizens can meet with other neighbors and community members to discuss any topics of interest, be they deeply philosophical or trivially important.

UUG-Dist

Contact: uug-dist-request@dsi.com (Syd Weinstein)

Purpose: Discussion of Unify Corporations Database products including Unify, Accell/IDS, Accell/SQl, and Accell/"generic database engine."

UUs-L

Contact: uus-l@info.terraluna.org (Automated Info Server)

uus-lman@terraluna.org (Steve Traugott)

Purpose: A global meeting place for Unitarian Universalists and anyone going our way. The list's intent is to provide a forum for sharing of UU-related information across district and regional boundaries, to bring into contact people and ideas who normally would never have met, and to foster discussion of functional and structural innovations that we can make in our organizations and world.

To subscribe to UUs-L, send the following in the body of a message to `listserv@ubvm.cc.buffalo.edu`:

```
SUBSCRIBE UUs-L yourfullname
```

Valiant Visions

Contact: `cvitek@drew.drew.edu`

Purpose: A forum for discussing and promoting Valiant comics. It is a moderated newsletter (hopefully biweekly). The first part (Visions # X.X.a) will consist of reviews and summaries. The second part (Visions # X.X.b) will consist of comments, questions, and anything else. This is also where the editorial will appear. We will discuss characters, plot, artists, relevant articles, etc.

Vampire

Contact: `vampire-request@math.ufl.edu`

Purpose: A mailing list dedicated to the White Wolf role-playing game, Vampire.

Those who may be interested in the subject but are not familiar with the game itself are also invited to join. To subscribe, send `sub vampire` as the first line of a message to `vampire-request@math.ufl.edu`.

Vancouver Canucks

Contact: `boey@sfu.ca`

Purpose: Discussion of anything related to the Canucks. Trips and activities are occasionally arranged for subscribers. There are also hockey pools.

VEGGIE

Contact: listserv@gibbs.oit.unc.edu

Purpose: If you are interested in vegetarianism, veganism, fruitarianism, macrobiotics, whole/natural foods, health/fitness, cooking, etc., this new mailing list may be for you. (We are a "dissident" spin-off of Granola, another vegetarian mailing list.) Our list is called VEGGIE to be inclusive of vegans, fruitarians, lacto-, ovo-, ovo-lacto-vegetarians, vegetable lovers, those simply interested in vegetarianism or veggie recipes, etc. You do not have to be a vegetarian to join.

Articles, recipes, discussions, your thoughts, etc., on vegetarianism or veganism are warmly welcomed. Flames are not.

Here's how to join—it's so easy! Send a message to listserv@gibbs.oit.unc.edu with this line:

    SUB VEGGIE yourfirstname yourlastname

That's all!

For more information about VEGGIE (why we began an alternative to Granola, or anything else), feel free to contact any of the following people:

Penny Ward (crunchy@gibbs.oit.unc.edu)

Michael Blackmore (michaelb@ksgrsch.harvard.edu)

Johnn Tan (atan@cc.weber.edu)

Vettes

Contact: vettes-request@compaq.com

Purpose: For Corvette owners and enthusiasts to share their ideas and experiences about their cars.

Vintage

Contact: vintage-request@presto.ig.com

Purpose: Vintage clothing and costume jewelry.

Vision

Contact: pruss@math.ubc.ca

Purpose: To discuss, in a charitable and Christian context, visions, prophecies, and spiritual gifts; to discuss any visions, dreams, and other manifestations that people may have received, to seek their significance in the spirit of truth. Non-Christians are invited, though it should be noted that the moderator may well not post any postings that are offensive. Postings may be done anonymously upon request, and efforts will be taken in the future to ensure anonymity in the membership.

Vizantija

Contact: dimitrije@buenga.bu.edu (Dimitrije Stamenovic)

Purpose: To distribute news and provide a forum for discussions about the current events in the former Yugoslavia, centered around those involving or affecting Serbs. Also, they originate public actions related to these events.

VMEbus

Contact: att!houxl!mlh (Marc Harrison)

Purpose: A users' group for the AT&T VMEbus products to provide a two-way USENET conduit for the open exchange of information, both within and outside of AT&T. There's very little data that's proprietary about the products (other than the source code for UNIX System V/VME), so the list is open to suggestions as to items of interest.

If you're interested, please send your name, e-mail path (via att preferred), affiliation, and use of WE 321SB (if you have one). Suggestions for items of interest are also encouraged.

Volvo

Contact: swedishbricks-request@me.rochester.edu (Tim Takahashi)

Purpose: A meeting place for Volvo automotive enthusiasts around the world. It is an open forum for discussion of Volvo-related topics, such as, but not limited to, ownership, maintenance, repairs, mechanics, fix-it yourself, competition driving, and preparation.

Vreme

Contact: p00981@psilink.com

Purpose: Carries *Vreme* and VND (selected articles from *Vreme* translated into English). Since the fall of 1989, *Vreme* has been the major independent newspaper in Yugoslavia and neighboring countries. It is published weekly on Monday, and the electronic mail edition of VND is usually available on the same day. Please keep in mind that due to the situation in the country, the distribution of VND is not always smooth. Further, VND is published by a professional news agency that makes this material available to us by a special agreement. The proper credit to VND should be given whenever this material is cited or used in any way.

Vreme News Digest

Contact: dimitrije@buenga.bu.edu (Dimitrije Stamenovic)

Purpose: Vreme News Digest (VND) is an English-language newsletter published by the Vreme News Digest Agency (VNDA) from Belgrade.

WAIS-Discussion

Contact: wais-discussion-request@think.com

Purpose: WAIS stands for Wide Area Information Servers, an electronic publishing project led by Thinking Machines.

The WAIS-discussion is a digested, moderated list on electronic publishing issues in general and Wide Area Information Servers in particular. There are postings every week or two.

WAIS-Talk

Contact: wais-talk-request@think.com

Purpose: WAIS stands for Wide Area Information Servers, an electronic publishing project led by Thinking Machines.

WAIS-talk is an open list (interactive, not moderated) for implementors and developers. This is a techie list that is not meant as a support list. Please use the alt.wais news group for support, and send bug fixes and the like to bug-wais@think.com.

Walkers-in-Darkness

Contact: walkers-request@world.std.com (David Harmon)

Purpose: For sufferers from depression and/or bipolar disorder, and affected friends. This includes both "novices" and those who have learned to cope.

Warhammer

Contact: wfrp-request@morticia.cnns.unt.edu

Purpose: For the discussion of Games Workshop's Warhammer Universe, the Old World, Warhammer Fantasy Role Play, and Warhammer Fantasy Battle.

The Warhammer mailing list is running ListMan 1.0b List Manager software. To subscribe, send e-mail to the above request address, and as the first word on the subject line or any line in the text of the message put the word sub. You may also include a parameter with the sub command. This parameter will be treated as your real name, not your address (which is determined from your mail headers). You may also send wfrp-request other commands, not the least of which is help.

Waterski

Contact: waterski-request@nda.com

Purpose: Discussion topics open to anything of interest to water-skiers, from absolute beginners to competitors. This includes any activity that involves being pulled behind a boat, such as barefooting, kneeboarding, wakeboarding, and even tubing. Discussion of boats, equipment, techniques, safety, courtesy, rules of competition, tournament results, site negotiation, and club organization is encouraged.

Weather-Users

Contact: weather-users-request@zorch.sf-bay.org

Purpose: Updates from the maintainer of the Weather Underground at the University Michigan, exchange of programming hints and tips among weather client developers, and related discussion.

Weights

Contact: weights-request@mickey.disney.com
(Michael Sullivan)

Purpose: The discussion of all aspects of using weights in exercise. Includes bodybuilding (competitive and non-competitive), sport-related weight training, "stay in shape" weight training—basically, anything to do with lifting weights.

Western Hockey League

Contact: `klootzak@u.washington.edu` (Michael A. Stuyt)

Purpose: To discuss matters relevant to the Western Hockey League: game results, standings, and occasionally player statistics. To subscribe, send e-mail `klootzak@u.washington.edu` with the words WHL SUB in the subject line of your message.

Wetleather

Contact: `wetleather-request@frigg.isc-br.com` (automated LISTSERV)

`carlp@mail.isc-br.com` (Carl Paukstis)

Purpose: For discussion, chatter, ride reports, socializing, and announcements of upcoming motorcycle events in the Greater Pacific Northwest. The definition of that geographic term is flexible, but is generally taken to include the Cascadia subduction zone and all areas within a one-day ride from it, which naturally includes southwestern Canada. Anyone is free to subscribe, and topic limitations are not enforced. The list is not moderated, but is intended for socialization among the area riders—not to supplant `rec.motorcycles`.

Mail-geek tip: We're running LISTSERV 5.5, and `wetleather-request` is just aliased to `listserv`, so those familiar with LISTSERV services may use any of the usual commands. Both reflected and digest subscription modes are available, along with a small set of archive files.

Automated subscription information: send a single-line mail message to `wetleather-request@frigg.isc-br.com` consisting only of `subscribe WETLEATHER` *yourfullname*.

Wheel-to-Wheel

Contact: wheeltowheel-request@abingon.Eng.Sun.COM
(Andy Banta)

Purpose: For people interested in participation in auto racing as driver, worker, or crew. People interested in all types of wheel-to-wheel racing are welcome, but the majority of the discussion centers on road courses.

Whitewater

Contact: whitewater-request@gynko.circ.upenn.edu

Purpose: To discuss whitewater sports, experiences, and information. Includes kayak and canoeing enthusiasts. Please note that this mailing list is partially bidirectionally gatewayed to the USENET group rec.boats.paddle. Whitewater-specific postings are culled and sent to the mailing list, and mailing list traffic is sent to the news group. This mailing list is moderated and is probably only useful to those who do not receive rec.boats.paddle, or are only interested in the whitewater traffic in that group.

Wildnet

Contact: zaphod!pnwc!wildnet-request@access.usask.ca

wildnet-request@access.usask.ca (Eric Woodsworth)

Purpose: Concerned with computing and statistics in fisheries and wildlife biology. Relevant topics include G.I.S., ecological modelling, software, etc.

Windsurfing

Contact: windsurfing-request@gcm.com

...uunet!gcm!windsurfing-request

Purpose: To provide a discussion forum for boardsailing enthusiasts all over the world. While non-windsurfers are welcome to join, the primary purpose is to enhance the enjoyment of our sport by discussing windsurfing-related topics such as equipment, technique, sailing spots, weather, competition, etc. We welcome you to join and share your windsurfing experiences and thoughts. The list is unmoderated.

WITSENDO

Contact: listserv@dartcms1.dartmouth.edu

Purpose: A moderated mailing list that discusses all aspects of endometriosis with particular emphasis on coping with the disease and its treatment. Anyone with an interest in this disease is welcome to participate, whether or not they actually suffer from the disease. The list will act as a clearinghouse for information exchange and to promote discussion of current treatments, research, and educational literature. Professional (medical) comments are, of course, most welcome. However, the list is primarily dedicated to the women who suffer from this painful and often demoralizing disease; therefore, any information should be expressed in lay terms and attempt to exclude professional jargon (or, at the very least, provide adequate references and/or definitions of terms).

To subscribe to the list, send mail to
listserv@dartcms1.bitnet or
listserv@dartcms1.dartmouth.edu with the body of the mail (*not* subject) containing the following command:

    SUB WITSENDO yourfullname

Owner: David Avery (david.avery@dartmouth.edu)

Word-Mac

Contact: word-mac-request@alsvid.une.edu.au
(Roger Debreceny)

Purpose: To serve users of the Microsoft Word package in its various versions on the Apple Macintosh platform. The list is available in digest form and archives of all digests are available by anonymous ftp from /pub/archives/word-mac/digests on alsvid.une.edu.au. Gopher access is also available by pointing your Gopher to alsvid.une.edu.au (port 70).

To subscribe, mail to listserv@alsvid.une.edu.au with the text subscribe word-mac yourfirstname yourlastname in the body of the e-mail.

Wxsat

Contact: wxsat-request@ssg.com (Richard B. Emerson)

Purpose: Two functions: The primary function is the distribution of NOAA status and prediction bulletins for the GOES and polar weather satellites. This data is the same data available via SCIENCEnet NOAA.SAT bulletin board area. The mail list also acts as a reflector for subscribers' comments and discussion of matters related to weather satellites, ground stations, and associated topics.

X-Ada

Contact: x-ada-request@expo.lcs.mit.edu

Purpose: To discuss the interfaces and bindings for an Ada interface to the X Window system.

XGKS

Contact: xgks-request@unidata.ucar.edu (Steve Emmerson)

Purpose: A mailing list for the maintenance, enhancement, and evolution of the XGKS package, created by the

University of Illinois under contract with IBM and distributed as part of X11R4. The XGKS package is a full 2C GKS implementation and allows GKS applications to operate in an X Window system environment.

XOPEN-Testing

Contact: xopen-testing-request@uel.co.uk (Andrew Josey)

Purpose: A forum for discussion of issues related to testing operating systems for conformance to the X/OPEN Portability Guide (XPG), including Issue 3 (XPG3) and later.

The scope of this newsletter is the discussion of items associated with the testing of the X/Open Portability Guide—including, but not limited to, test suite technology (X/Open's VSX and other third-party test suites for the XPG), latest news on X/Open Branding, and other related issues. These issues can include problems related to test suites in general, testability of various features of the XPG, and portability of the test suites.

XPress-List

Contact: listserv@grot.starconn.com

Purpose: Discussion of the X*Press X*Change data service, which is available on some cable television systems in the U.S. and Canada and on some satellite television channels.

To subscribe to the xpress-list, send mail to listserv@grot.starconn.com with the following commands in the body of the message:

```
subscribe xpress-list yourfirstname yourlastname

quit
```

Replace *yourfirstname yourlastname* with your name, not your e-mail address.

Administrative messages other than subscription and unsubscription should be sent to xpress-list-owner@grot.starconn.com.

XVT

Contact: tim@qedbbs.com (Tim Capps)

Purpose: XVT is a multiplatform window environment development tool. Interested parties should send mail with HELP XVTDEV as the body of the letter to listserv@qedbbs.com.

Yello

Contact: yello-request@overpass.calpoly.edu (Cliff Tuel)

Purpose: A forum for discussing anything about the group Yello or any solo works by the band's members. An extensive discography is available, as are several other files of interest.

Y-RIGHTS

Contact: listserv@sjuvm.bitnet

Purpose: Discussion group on the rights of kids and teens. Broad spectrum of discussion topics, with individual liberty being one of the main focuses. Open to kids, teens, young adults, adults, senior citizens, teachers, students, grade schools, middle schools, high schools, colleges, and university networks, gatewaying to other networks.

Digest/notebook version available, as well as past discussions. E-mail to listserv@sjuvm.bitnet, using the following commands as needed:

- To subscribe to the list, use SUB Y-RIGHTS *yourfirstname yourlastname*.

- To receive the weekly digest of the list, use AFD Y-RIGHTS DIGEST.

- To receive a list of previous discussion logs, use GET Y-RIGHTS FILELIST.

List owner: Kenneth Udut (kudut@hamp.hampshire.edu)

YSN

Contact: ysn-adm@zoyd.ee.washington.edu (John Sahr)

Purpose: Activism on employment issues for scientists just beginning their careers. The Young Scientists' Network attempts to inform the press, the public, and government officials that there is no shortage of scientists; we hope to find traditional and non-traditional employment for scientists. Stories about the Young Scientists' Network have appeared in *Science*, in *Physics Today*, and on National Public Radio; we've met with officials from the National Science Foundation and other agencies.

Zang Tuum Tumb

Contact: ztt-request@asylum.sf.ca.us (Lazlo Nibble)

Purpose: Discussion of artists, releases, and other issues related to Trevor Horn's U.K. record label Zang Tuum Tumb. (Frankie Goes to Hollywood, Art of Noise, Propaganda, 808 State, Seal, and others.) Moderator maintains a complete discography. ftp archives available on asylum.

Z-Cars

Contact: z-car-request@dixie.com (John De Armond)

Purpose: For those interested in Datsun/Nissan Z cars. The interest base is primarily for the original Z, though all discussion regarding the Z line of cars is welcome.

Zeppelin

Contact: zeppelin-l@cornell.edu

Purpose: For fans of the rock group Led Zeppelin. For further information about this list, send e-mail to listserv@cornell.edu with info zeppelin-l as the body of the message.

ZForum

Contact: zforum-request@comlab.ox.ac.uk (Jonathan Bowen)

Purpose: To handle messages concerned with the formal specification notation Z. Based on set theory and first order predicate logic, Z has been developed at the Programming Research Group (PRG) at Oxford University for well over a decade. It is now used by industry as part of the software (and hardware) development process in both the U.K. and the U.S. It is currently undergoing standardization. ZForum provides a convenient forum for messages and queries concerned with recent developments and the use of Z. ZForum is gatewayed to the USENET news group comp.specification.z.

Zoomer-List

Contact: listserv@grot.starconn.com (Brian Smithson)

Purpose: Discussion forum for users or potential users of the Zoomer personal digital assistant products from Casio, Tandy, and others. Topics include general information, tips, techniques, applications, experiences, and sources for hardware, software, accessories, and information. To subscribe, send mail to the LISTSERV address with the following commands in the message body:

```
subscribe zoomer-list yourfirstname yourlastname
quit
```

Part III

Host Resource Guide

This part describes a few sites on the Internet that provide services such as anonymous ftp or Gopher. The sites are organized by the type of service they provide (ftp, Gopher, and so on). Each listing gives the name of the site (and the Internet address, in case your system doesn't understand the name) and a list of the information that's available there. If a specific contact person is available at the site for questions about the material there, that name is also listed. If no specific contact name is given, you can send mail to that site's postmaster address for more information.

Following the list of sites is some of the information available on the Internet that's related to special interests (professional, hobby, and so on). Some of the information is available via anonymous ftp, Gopher, or some other information retrieval service; the individual sections outline the best way to find the information you are looking for.

Internet ftp Sites

In this section, individual sites on the Internet providing anonymous ftp services are listed, with details on what can be found there. You can locate specific information by browsing large anonymous ftp sites. This section lists some large sites that are a good starting place in your search for programs or information.

The file locations for directories and files are given from the top of the anonymous ftp area for each site. The directories are shown in UNIX format (/directory), and subdirectories are indented under upper-level directories.

ftp.uu.net

Site name: ftp.uu.net (192.48.96.9)

Contact: archive@uunet.uu.net or tale@uunet.uu.net

Description: UUNET, an Internet services provider, is also one of the central distribution sites for all netnews traffic across the Internet. The ftp archive at ftp.uu.net is one of the largest and most complete on the Internet—almost everything can be found here! It has a very broad collection of programs and informational files.

Location	Description
/index	Lists of what files are available
/systems	Software for various types of systems
/amiga	Software for Amiga computers
/next	Software for NeXT computers
/apple2	Software for Apple II computers
/gnu	Free Software Foundation software
/pyramid	Fixes for Pyramid system software
/sun	Software and documentation for Sun systems
/vms	Software for VMS systems
/iris	Software for SGI Iris systems
/mac	Info-mac mailing list archives, mainly
/msdos	Lots of software for MS-DOS machines
/unix	Software for UNIX systems (LINUX and so on)
/simtel20	Copy of the Simtel20 PC software archive

Location	Description
/mach	Software for systems running MACH
/apollo	Software for Apollo computers
/vendor	Information from many computer vendors
/info	Information about UUNET and the ftp area
/index	Index files for this ftp site
/news	Software for netnews transport and reading
/published	Information from publishers
/mail	Software for mail reading and transport
/pub	Miscellaneous software and information
/ai	AI (artificial intelligence) journals and information
/archiving	Compression and archiving software
/database	Information on different databases
/economics	Information on economics
/games	Game software for various computers
/linguistics	Linguistic information
/physics	Software for physicists
/security	Security software packages (COPS and so on)
/shells	Shell software for UNIX systems
/text-processing	Editors and text processing systems

(continues)

Location	Description
/window-sys	Window system software (X Window and so on)
/inet	Information on the Internet
/aups	Acceptable use policies from sites
/ddn-news	DDN management bulletin archives
/doc	General network documentation
/ien	IEN documents
/iesg	Internet Engineering Steering Group documents
/ietf	Internet Engineering Task Force documents
/internet-drafts	IETF draft documents
/isoc	Internet Society documents
/maps	Maps of the Internet and subnets
/netinfo	General network information
/nren	NREN documents and information
/protocols	Information about different network protocols
/resource-guide	The Internet Resource Guide
/rfc	All Internet RFC documents
/networking	Different network software packages
/doc	Documents of general interest
/dictionaries	Various language dictionaries
/libraries	Lists of libraries on the Internet
/music	Musical scores for various instruments

Location	Description
/patents	Patent documents
/political	Political documents (U.S. Constitution, for example)
/security	Computer security related documents
/standards	Standards documents (IEEE, ISO, and so on)
/style	Written style documents
/supreme-court	U.S. Supreme Court decisions
/graphics	Graphics software and documentation
/languages	Computer language software

wuarchive.wustl.edu

Site name: wuarchive.wustl.edu (128.252.135.4)

Description: This site, at Washington University at St. Louis, is one of the biggest ftp sites on the Internet. It holds copies of software archived at many different Internet sites. It holds very large collections of IBM PC and Apple Macintosh software, as well as software and documents covering almost every topic.

Location	Description
/decus	DEC User's Society tapes
/systems	Software for different computer systems
/aix	IBM AIX software (large collection)
/amiga	Amiga computer software

(continues)

Location	Description
/apple2	Software for Apple II computers
/atari	Software for Atari computers
/aux	Apple AUX software (large collection)
/cpm	Software for CPM machines
/gnu	All Free Software Foundation software
/hp	Software for Hewlett-Packard machines and calculators
/ibmpc	Huge amount of IBM PC software
/linux	Software for machines running LINUX
/mac	Huge amount of Macintosh software
/minix	Software for systems running Minix
/misc	Miscellaneous software for various systems
/next	Software for NeXT machines
/novell	Software specifically for Novell NetWare
/os9	Information and software for OS/9 systems
/penpoint	Software and information on PenPoint
/sinclair	Software for Sinclair systems
/sun	Software from Sun Exchange
/svr4-pc	UNIX System V.R4 for PC systems
/unix	Software for UNIX systems

Internet ftp Sites

Location	Description
/vax-vms	Software for people running VAX VMS
/xenix	Software for Xenix systems
/mirrors	Copies of information on different sites across the Internet
/info	Information about this site
/languages	Information about the Ada language
/packages	Different software packages
/TeX	The TeX document formatting system
/X11R5	The X11R5 windowing system
/benchmarks	Different computer benchmark software
/compression	Compression and archiving software
/dialslip	Serial Line IP dialup software
/dist	Software distribution software
/gopher	Gopher client and server software
/mail	Mail-reading software
/news	Netnews software
/wuarchive-ftpd	The special ftp daemon written here
/www	The World Wide Web software system
/graphics	Different computer graphics packages
/usenet	Archives of some USENET groups
/doc	General documents

(continues)

Location	Description
/EFF	Electronic Frontier Foundation information
/bible	The Bible in electronic form
/graphics-formats	Different graphics formats
/ietf	Internet Engineering Task Force documents
/nsfnet	NSFNET network-related documents
/nsfnet-stats	Network statistics collected by NSF
/rfc	Network Request For Comments (RFC) documents
/techreports	Reports from various universities
/edu	Software and information for educational sites
/multimedia	Multimedia data files
/audio	Internet Talk Radio files
/images	Pictures in different formats

sunsite.unc.edu

Site name: sunsite.unc.edu (152.2.22.81)

Contact: ftpkeeper@sunsite.unc.edu

Description: Sunsite is run by the University of North Carolina as a major site for academic information. It contains collections of software and information for many academic areas, and also is a central site for information about computers manufactured by Sun Microsystems, Inc.

> **Note**
>
> All directories listed for this site are under the /pub directory. You should issue a cd /pub command after logging in.

Location	Description
/Linux	Software for sites running LINUX
/X11	Distribution and information about X11
/academic	Software for academic use, arranged by area of knowledge
/agriculture	
/astronomy	
/athletics	
/biology	
/business	
/chemistry	
/computer-science	
/data_analysis	
/economics	
/education	
/engineering	
/environment	
/fine-arts	
/geography	
/geology	

(continues)

Location	Description
/history	
/languages	
/library	
/mathematics	
/medicine	
/physics	
/political-science	
/psychology	
/religious_studies	
/russian-studies	
/archives	Archives of mailing lists, USENET news groups, and publications
/docs	Written materials, Internet documents, computers, literature, politics
/gnu	All Free Software Foundation software
/languages	Compilers and interpreters of computer languages
/micro	Software for microcomputers
/mac-stuff	Archives of Mac software
/mips-pc	Archives of MIPS PC software
/pc-stuff	Archives of IBM PC software
/multimedia	Software and information about computer-based video and sound
/packages	Large source distributions for UNIX

Location	Description
/TeX	The TeX document production system (sources)
/bbs	Bulletin board systems
/cygnus	Software from Cygnus Corporation
/gopher	Gopher client and server software
/infosystems	Different information retrieval systems
/Mosaic	Mosaic clients
/WWW	World Wide Web system
/Z39.50	Software implementation of Z39.50
/archie	archie clients for different machines
/ftp-archive	Software to run an ftp archive
/gopher	Gopher client and server software
/wais	WAIS client and server software
/mail	Different mail packages
/news	Different news software
/pctelnet	telnet protocol for PC systems
/terminal-emulators	Terminal emulation software
/sun-info	Information about Sun computer systems
/catalyst	Copies of Sun's Catalyst catalog
/development-tools	Tools for software development
/sun-dist	Sun-distributed patches for its software
/sun-fixes	Security fixes from Sun

(continues)

Location	Description
/sun-managers	Archives of Sun-Managers mailing list
/sunenergy	Archives of SunEnergy bulletins
/sunflash	Archives of SunFlash newsletters
/sunspots	Archives of SunSpots mailings
/white-papers	Copies of different Sun white papers
/talk-radio	Audio files from Internet Talk Radio

oak.oakland.edu

Site name: oak.oakland.edu (141.210.10.117)

Description: oak.oakland.edu is a major mirror site. Because Oak is very well connected to the Internet, this makes retrieving the software easier.

Location	Description
/pub	
/ada	Simtel20 Ada language archives
/misc	Simtel20 miscellaneous software (lots!)
/msdos	Very large archive of MS-DOS software
/pc-blue	PC-BLUE archive of PD and user-contributed PC software
/pub2	
/cpm	Software for CPM machines (lots!)

Location	Description
/cpmug	CPM User's Group software
/macintosh	Very large Macintosh software archive
/unix-c	Very large archive of UNIX software

rtfm.mit.edu

Site name: rtfm.mit.edu (18.70.0.224)

Description: This important site holds the archives of all the Frequently Asked Questions (FAQ) informational postings made to various netnews groups. If you have a question about a topic covered by a netnews group, check here to see whether it's covered by one of the FAQ postings.

> **Note**
>
> All directories listed for this site are under the /pub directory. You should issue a cd /pub command after logging in.

Location	Description
/pcm	A PC emulator package
/popmail	The Post Office Protocol mail package
/usenet-by-group	FAQ postings organized by news group
/usenet-by-hierarchy	FAQ postings organized by news hierarchy
/usenet-addressed	Database and information on the USENET address server

ftp.cica.indiana.edu

Site name: ftp.cica.indiana.edu (129.79.26.102)

Description: This archive, a central site for Microsoft Windows applications, is run by the Center for Innovative Computer Applications at Indiana University. If you are looking for a Windows application, check here first.

> **Note**
>
> All directories listed for this site are under the /pub directory. You should issue a cd /pub command after logging in.

Location	Description
/laser	Information on Laser Sailboating
/next	Software and information on NeXT machines
/pc	IBM PC software
/borland	Software and information from Borland International
/misc	Miscellaneous PC software and information
/starter	Important first software (UNZIP, uudecode, and so on)
/win3	Microsoft Windows applications
/unix	Miscellaneous UNIX software
/wx	Weather files (GIF images and so on)

ds.internic.net

Site name: ds.internic.net (198.49.45.10)

Description: The InterNIC sites (ds, is, and rs) collectively form the InterNIC services. They provide different types of information, but ds is the most useful for new users. This site has collections of all Internet documents and information.

Location	Description
/dirofdirs	Pointers to information at different sites, organized by category
/fyi	Internet FYI documents
/iesg	Internet Engineering Steering Group documents
/ietf	Internet Engineering Task Force documents
/internet-drafts	Drafts of common Internet documents
/internic.info	Information about the InterNIC
/isoc	Internet Society documents
/nsf	National Science Foundation documents
/policies-procedures	Network policies and procedures from sites
/pub	Other information
/conf.announce	Conference announcements
/current-ietf-docs	Documents under IETF review
/internet-doc	General Internet documents (zen, EARN)
/netpolicies	NSFNET acceptable use policy
/the-scientist	On-line issues of *The Scientist*

(continues)

Location	Description
/z39.50	Databases available using the Z39.50 protocol
/resource-guide	The Internet Resource Guide
/rfc	Internet Request For Comments (RFC) standards
/std	Internet Activities Board standards

ftp.eff.org

Site name: ftp.eff.org (192.88.144.4)

Description: This site is maintained by the Electronic Frontier Foundation, an organization interested in exploring the legal aspects of computers and networks.

> **Note**
>
> All directories listed for this site are under the /pub directory. You should issue a cd /pub command after logging in.

Location	Description
/EFF	Electronic Frontier Foundation information
/SJG	Notes on the Steve Jackson Games case, in which a bulletin board system was impounded because of alleged illegal material on the system
/academic	Information from academic sites
/cpsr	Notes from the Boston chapter of Computer Professionals for Social Responsibility

Location	Description
/cud	Archives of the Computer Underground Digest
/internet-info	Copies of Internet documents
/journals	Various journals on-line

ftp.cso.uiuc.edu

Site name: ftp.cso.uiuc.edu (128.174.5.61)

Description: This large, general-purpose site, run by the University of Illinois at Champaign-Urbana, holds a good variety of programs and information, but an especially large collection of software for Amiga, IBM PC, and Macintosh computers.

Location	Description
/ACM	UIUC's student Association for Computing Machinery information
/pgsi	Power glove serial interface project documentation and software
/amiga	
/amoner	On-line *Amoner* magazine
/cucug	Champaign-Urbana Commodore User Group
/fish	Fred Fish collection—500 disks' worth!
/virus	Virus scanners for Amiga systems
/bbs	Information on local bulletin board systems
/doc	General computing-related documentation

(continues)

Location	Description
/pcnet	Lists of compression and network software
/mac	
/MUG	Champaign-Urbana Macintosh User Group collection of software
/eudora	E-mail package for Macintosh computers
/virus	Antivirus software for Macintosh
/mail	sendmail and smail packages
/math	PD math software and source code
/mrc	Index to materials available at the CSO resource center
/pc	
/adf	IBM Adapter Description Files and other PS/2-related items
/exec-pc	Index and sample files from Exec-PC BBS
/local	Collection of local files and software
/pbs	Disks from Public Brand Software
/pcmag	*PC Magazine* files from Exec-PC or PC-Magnet
/pcsig	Files from the largest PC-SIG (Special Interest Group) CD-ROM
/scripts	Kermit and other login scripts
/virus	UIUC collection of antivirus files
/tandy	Tandy Model 100/102 laptop files
/uiuc	MOTIF and X11R4 for various systems

Location	Description
/unix/virus	UNIX information and patches, Internet worm information, Sun sendmail and ftp

wiretap.spies.com

Site name: wiretap.spies.com (130.43.43.43)

Contact: archive@wiretap.spies.com

Description: This site collects interesting information that flows over the Internet. It has a large and eclectic collection of documents ranging from jokes to White House press releases. If you are looking for an official document, such as a government charter or report, this is the place to look.

Location	Description
/Clinton	White House press releases
/Economic_Plan	Clinton's economic plan
/GAO_Reports	General Accounting Office reports
/Gov	Government and civics archives from around the world
/Aussie	Australian Law Documents
/Canada	Canadian documents
/Copyright	Copyright laws
/Economic	Clinton's economic plan
/Forfeit	Civil Forfeiture of Assets laws
/GAO-Report	GAO miscellaneous reports
/GAO-Risk	GAO high-risk reports

(continues)

Location	Description
/GAO-Tech	GAO technical reports
/GAO-Trans	GAO transition reports
/Maast	Maastricht Treaty of European Union
/NAFTA	North American Free Trade Agreement document
/NATO	NATO press releases
/NATO-HB	NATO handbook
/Other	Miscellaneous world documents
/Patent	Patent office reform panel final report
/Platform	Political platforms of the United States
/Treaties	Treaties and international covenants
/UCMJ	Uniform code of military justice
/UN	United Nations resolutions (selected)
/US-Docs	U.S. miscellaneous documents
/US-GOV	U.S. government today
/US-History	U.S. historical documents
/US-Speech	U.S. speeches and addresses
/US-State	Various U.S. state laws
/World	World constitutions
/Library	Wiretap on-line library of articles
/Articles	Various articles

Location	Description
/Classics	Classic literature
/Cyber	Cyberspace documents
/Document	Miscellaneous documents
/Fringe	Fringes of reason
/Humor	Funny material of all types
/Media	Mass media
/Misc	Miscellaneous unclassified documents
/Music	Music scores and lyrics
/Religion	Religious articles and documents
/Techdoc	Technical information of all sorts
/Untech	Non-technical information
/Zines	Magazines

Internet Gopher Sites

Because Gopher is based in a hierarchical structure, you can easily browse among many sites. This section lists a few of the major Gopher sites to get you started.

In addition to the sites that provide access using a Gopher client program (listed in the next sections), the following sites allow telnet access to Gopher. These sites let you access the Gopher system without you having any client software on your end, just the telnet program.

Host Name	Address	Login	Area
consultant.micro.umn.edu	134.84.132.4	gopher	U.S.
ux1.cso.uiuc.edu	128.174.5.59	gopher	U.S.
panda.uiowa.edu	128.255.40.201	panda	U.S.
gopher.msu.edu	35.8.2.61	gopher	U.S.
gopher.ebone.net	192.36.125.2	gopher	Europe
info.anu.edu.au	150.203.84.20	info	Australia
gopher.chalmers.se	129.16.221.40	gopher	Sweden
tolten.puc.cl	146.155.1.16	gopher	Chile
ecnet.ec	157.100.45.2	gopher	Ecuador
gan.ncc.go.jp	160.190.10.1	gopher	Japan

gopher.micro.umn.edu

Site name: gopher.micro.umn.edu (128.101.62.12)

Description: This is the Gopher home site, where the Gopher software was developed. As such, it has the complete list of all available Gopher sites around the world and keeps the most recent information about Gopher on-line.

Menu Items
Information about Gopher
> Gopher FAQ
> comp.infosystems.gopher archive
> New stuff in Gopher
> Computer Information
> Other Gopher and information servers (complete list)

boombox.micro.umn.edu

Site name: boombox.micro.umn.edu (134.84.132.2)

Description: This site, also run by the University of Minnesota, holds the source code for most of the Gopher servers and clients. If you don't already have Gopher client code running, you can anonymous ftp to this machine to retrieve the current versions.

wiretap.spies.com

Site name: wiretap.spies.com (130.43.43.43)

Description: Also described under the earlier anonymous ftp section, wiretap contains many interesting documents that have moved over the Internet. All the following headings have more categories under them—there are too many interesting files to list.

> **Menu Items**
> About the Internet Wiretap
> Clinton press releases
> Electronic books at Wiretap
> GAO transition reports
> Government documents (U.S. and world)
> North American Free Trade Agreement
> Usenet alt.etext Archives
> Usenet ba.internet Archives
> Various ETEXT resources on the Internet
> Video game archive
> Waffle BBS software
> Wiretap on-line library
> Worldwide Gopher and WAIS servers

gopher.internic.net

Site name: gopher.internic.net (198.49.45.10)

Description: The InterNIC site is the central Network Information Center for the Internet. The site allows you to find easily information about the Internet and many of its resources.

> **Menu Items**
> Information about the InterNIC
> InterNIC Information Services
> > Welcome to the InfoSource
> > Getting connected to the Internet
> > InterNIC store
> > About the InterNIC Information Services
> > Getting started on the Internet
> > Internet information for everybody
> > Just for NICs
> > NSFNET, NREN, national information infrastructure information
> > Beyond InterNIC: Virtual treasures of the Internet
> > Searching the InfoSource by keyword
>
> InterNIC Registration Services
> > InterNIC registration archives
> > WHOIS searches for InterNIC registries
> > WHOIS searches for non-MILNET individuals
>
> InterNIC directory and database services
> > InterNIC directory of directories
> > InterNIC directory services ("White Pages")
> > InterNIC database services (public databases)
> > Additional Internet resource information
> > Internet documentation (RFCs, FYIs, and so on)
> > National Science Foundation information

gopher.nsf.gov

Site name: gopher.nsf.gov (128.150.195.40)

Description: This server—the main Gopher server run by the National Science Foundation—is a central clearinghouse for many scientific reports and documents. This server also provides pointers to many other government Gopher servers; if you are looking for information from a government office or department, look here.

Menu Items
NSF publications
BIO—Director for Biological Sciences
CISE—Director for Computer and Information Science and Technology
EHR—Director for Education and Human Resources
ENG—Director for Engineering
GEO—Director for Geosciences
MPS—Director for Math and Physical Sciences
NSB—National Science Board
OIG—Office of the Inspector General
Office of the Director
SBE—Director for Social, Behavioral, and Economic Sciences
SRS—Science Resources Studies Division
Other US Government Gopher Services
    Extension Service, USDA
    Federal Information Exchange (FEDIX)
    LANL Physics Information Service
    Library of Congress MARVEL
    NASA Goddard Space Flight Center
    NASA Mid-Continent Technology Transfer Center
    NASA Network Application and Information Center
    National Institute of Standards and Technology (NIST)
    National Institutes of Health (NIH)
    National Science Foundation (NSF)
    Protein Data Bank—Brookhaven National Lab
    US Environmental Protection Agency (EPA)
    USDA National Agricultural Library Plant Genome
    USDA-ARS GRIN National Genetic Resources Program

Special Interest Topics

This section lists a few of the many special interest topics that have information available on the Internet. In some cases, the information is available via anonymous ftp; in other cases, you can use telnet to log in to a host and get information on the topic. Each individual entry lists the method of access and all the information necessary to get access to your topic.

> **Note**
>
> This section is by no means complete; it is intended to give a feel for the types of information available and how to access them.

Agriculture

Several different services offer agricultural information on the Internet. Some services are weather- and crop-related; others provide information related to health.

Access method: telnet caticsuf.csufresno.edu (129.8.100.15)

    Log in: super

Description: This service, the Advanced Technology Information Network, provides information about agriculture and biotechnology. Because it's located in California, the information is somewhat biased toward that area; but it's useful for people in other areas also. Information offered includes daily agricultural market reports; weather, labor, and job reports; safety information; and schedules of events.

Access method: telnet psupen.psu.edu (128.118.36.5)

    Log in: state_code

Description: This service, PENpages, is provided by Penn State University. It provides access to agricultural prices and commodity reports, as well as USDA and 4-H information. Also available is the International Food & Nutrition Database, as well as a rich assortment of weather information.

Access method: gopher esusda.gov (192.73.224.100)

Description: This Gopher server, run by the Extension Service of the USDA, provides access to various educational and information services of the Cooperative Extension System, as well as providing links to other agricultural Gopher servers around the country. This Gopher also provides information such as White House press releases, the Clinton health plan, the federal budget, and more.

Access method: ftp ftp.sura.net (128.167.254.179)
get file /pub/nic/agricultural.list

Description: This document, titled "Not Just Cows—A Guide to Internet/Bitnet Resources in Agriculture and Related Sciences," contains pointers to many resources on BITNET and the Internet for the agricultural sciences. This document is fairly large (about 2,700 lines), so you should peruse it on-line when you retrieve it.

Access methods: mail almanac@esusda.gov

mail almanac@ecn.purdue.edu

mail almanac@oes.orst.edu

mail almanac@ces.ncsu.edu

mail almanac@silo.ucdavis.edu

mail almanac@joe.uwex.edu

mail almanac@wisplan.uwex.edu

Description: The almanac servers provide e-mail access to different agricultural information based on the server. You should send a mail message with send guide in the message body to one of these addresses to receive a guide on how to use the server. A mail message with send catalog returns the list of available information.

Aviation

The following services offer aviation information on the Internet. These services provide a repository and weather and flight-planning information.

Access method: gopher av.eecs.nwu.edu

Description: This site is run by Northwestern University as a repository for aviation information. Some information is from the USENET rec.aviation group, but quite a bit is contributed from individual pilots on the Internet. Stories, pictures, and flight-planning information are available.

Access method: telnet duat.gtefsd.com (131.131.7.105)

or telnet duats.gtefsd.com (131.131.7.106)

Description: The DUAT service (Direct User Access Terminal) is provided by the FAA to give aviation weather and flight-planning information for pilots. The first address is for certified pilots, the second one is for uncertified ones.

> **Note**
>
> Although this service is provided under contract from the FAA, it's now being reviewed and may be terminated.

Books

Access method: ftp mrcnext.cso.uiuc.edu
(128.174.201.12)
cd /pub/etext

Description: This site maintains an archive of the Project Gutenberg files. Project Gutenberg is aimed at producing 10,000 of the most widely read books in electronic form. Some books already available at this site are *Alice in Wonderland*, *The CIA World Fact Book*, *Roget's Thesaurus*, and *Moby Dick*.

Calculators

Access method: telnet hpcvbbs.cv.hp.com (15.225.72.16)

    Log in: new

Description: This bulletin board system is for owners of Hewlett-Packard calculators. It features conferences with information and programs for HP calculators, plus real-time conversations with other HP users.

Computer Security

Access method: ftp ftp.cert.org (192.88.209.5)
                     cd /pub

Description: The Computer Emergency Response Team (CERT) is a federally funded organization that acts as a clearinghouse for computer security information. On its ftp site are archives of all its security bulletins, some computer security tools, computer virus information, and other computer security-related items.

Databases

For access to databases, check out the following sites. You can tap into databases on libraries, compact discs, and education, among others.

Access method: telnet echo.lu (158.64.1.36)

    Log in: echo

Description: This system, run by the European Commission Host Organization, provides databases on scientific and R & D projects, business, economy, languages, and others. Because the server is located in Europe, it's most useful to sites there, but anyone can find interesting material.

Access method: telnet pac.carl.org (192.54.81.128)

Description: CARL, run by the Colorado Alliance of Research Libraries, provides access to various library catalogs, indexes to current articles, and an information database. Access to many library databases is available.

Access method: telnet columbia.ilc.com (38.145.77.221)

Log in: cas

Description: The ILC server provides a search and purchase database for bookstores, VHS video cassettes, music CDs, laser disks, and UNIX software. You must have a verified account to order merchandise, but browsing the database is open to anyone.

Access method: telnet holonet.net (157.151.0.1)

Log in: cdc

Description: This system provides an on-line search and purchase database for compact disks of all types. If you have a credit card, you can order disks.

Education

Access method: gopher nysernet.org (192.77.173.2)

or   telnet nysernet.org

Log in: empire

Description: The Empire Schoolhouse is one option under the Nysernet Gopher server (under the K-12 special collection), but is accessed directly via telnet. This server has information about education from grades kindergarten through 12, including the Educational Resource Information Center and the Empire Internet Schoolhouse.

Games

The Internet isn't all seriousness. You still can have fun, as the following sites will show.

Access method: telnet coot.lcs.mit.edu 5000

or telnet 18.52.0.70 5000

Description: This is the Chess server; it allows you to play a game of chess, or watch others play. Type **help** for information about the available commands and how to play.

Access method: telnet astro.temple.edu 12345
(129.32.1.100)

or telnet argo.temple.edu 12345
(129.32.32.102)

Description: Both of these sites provide a *fortune cookie*—a random quote from a large database of quotes. You get a different quote each time you connect.

Access method: telnet castor.tat.physik.uni-tuebingen.de (134.2.72.153)

Log in: games

Description: This site (in Germany) provides access to several different on-line games, such as Tetris, NetHack, and Multiuser Dungeons.

> **Note**
>
> Because this site is in Europe, your response time may be very slow, because the Internet connection between the United States and Europe is fairly slow.

Genealogy

If you are looking up your roots and need some help, the following sites may be just what you need. They provide information on genealogy, including database programs.

Access method: ftp wood.cebaf.gov (129.57.32.165)
cd genealogy

Description: This site contains a large amount of information on genealogy, including information on the PAF genealogy program, genealogy database programs, and text files relating to genealogy.

Access method: ftp vm1.nodak.edu (134.129.111.1)
   cd roots-l

Description: This site contains a large number of text files relating to genealogy.

Geography

If you want to access information about populations, ZIP codes, and other geographical data from the United States and around the world, try the following sites.

Access method: telnet martini.eecs.umich.edu 3000 (141.212.99.9)

Description: This server holds U.S. Geological Survey and U.S. Postal Service information about U.S. cities, counties, and states. You can perform searches by ZIP code or city name, and the server returns information such as population data, latitude, longitude, ZIP code, and so on.

Access method: telnet glis.cr.usgs.gov (152.61.192.54)

   Log in: guest

Description: The Global Land Information System offers land use maps of the United States, along with graphs and data. Using a PC client or X Window client, you can display maps and information on your local system.

Government

You can access data provided by the Federal Information Exchange and the Food and Drug Administration, as described in the following sites.

Access method: telnet fedix.fie.com (192.111.228.33)

Description: The Federal Information Exchange offers information on federal opportunities, minority college and university capability information, and higher education opportunities for minorities and women.

Access method: telnet fdabbs.fda.gov (150.148.8.48)

Log in: bbs

Description: This site, run by the Food and Drug Administration, contains information about drug enforcement reports, drug and device approvals, the center for devices and radiological health, current information about AIDS, the FDA consumer magazine index (with selected articles), and other information. You can search the FDA files for summaries of FDA information and also retrieve the text of testimony at FDA congressional hearings. Even veterinary medicine news is available!

Health

Access method: gopher gopher.nih.gov

Description: Run by the National Institutes of Health, this Gopher site has health and clinical information, grants and research information, molecular biology databases, and links to the National Institute of Allergy and Infectious Disease and National Institute of Mental Health Gopher sites. This site also features information relating to cancer (CancerNet information) and AIDS. Access to the National Library of Medicine is also available.

History

Several different servers provide information of interest to historians. Information about the history of the United States, as well as the rest of the world, is represented.

Access method: telnet ukanaix.cc.ukans.edu
(129.237.1.30)

Log in: history

Description: The University of Kansas HNSource is a central information server for historians. From the main menu, you can get information on ftp sites with historical information and databases, information about discussion lists, and bibliographic information.

Access method: ftp byrd.mu.wvnet.edu (129.71.32.152)
cd /pub/history

Description: This site offers documents on many different historic categories, including diplomatic, ethnic, maritime, and U.S. history.

Access method: telnet clus1.ulcc.ac.uk (192.12.72.60)

Log in: ihr-uk

Password: ihr-uk

Description: This site gives on-line resources for historians in the London area, as well as on-line resources for historians in the United Kingdom and the rest of the world. It uses a very well organized hypertext system to allow you to locate resources and information easily.

Law

Several law schools offer extensive resources on the Internet for lawyers and others interested in the law. Some of these are discussed in the following sections.

Access method: gopher fatty.law.cornell.edu
(132.236.108.5)

Description: This site, run by the Cornell University law school, features information such as a directory of legal academia; discussion and LISTSERV archives; U.S. law (primary documents and commentary); foreign and international law (primary documents and commentary); and other legal resources (such as government agencies and Internet sources). This site is very complete and valuable for all legal references.

Access method: gopher gopher.law.csuohio.edu
(137.148.22.51)

Description: This site, run by the Cleveland State University law school, features information such as electronic forms of many legal sources, legal sources on the Internet, course schedules, and links to other Gopher sites.

Libraries

Libraries are very well represented on the Internet. They have historically been a major user of the Internet, and many university and public libraries are connected to the Internet. The sites below are only a fraction of the libraries available.

Access method: telnet library.dartmouth.edu
(129.170.16.11)

Description: The Dartmouth library server offers the capability to search for text in several on-line literary works. Use the command connect dante to search through Dante's *Divine Comedy*. Use the command select file bible to search the Bible. The commands select file s plays and select file s sonnets allow you to search Shakespeare's plays and sonnets, respectively.

Access method: telnet access.usask.ca (128.233.3.1)

        Log in: hytelnet

or   telnet info.ccit.arizona.edu
        (129.196.76.201)

        Log in: hytelnet

or   telnet laguna.epcc.edu (192.94.29.3)

        Log in: library

Description: The hytelnet servers (additional ones are available in other countries) provide links to many libraries and other information services around the world. Services include library catalogs, other resources (such as archie, electronic books, and others), an Internet glossary, and help on the library catalogs.

Access method: telnet liberty.uc.wlu.edu
(137.113.10.35)

Log in: lawlib

or gopher liberty.uc.wlu.edu

or ftp liberty.uc.wlu.edu
cd /pub/lawlib

Description: Run by Washington and Lee University, this site is very well run and set up. It not only provides access to W & L's law library (with a very large amount of information on-line), but also has connections to a great number of other libraries and information sources on the Internet. The Gopher interface is easier to work with, but the telnet interface is usable also, if you don't have access to Gopher.

Access method: ftp ariel.unm.edu (129.24.8.1)
get file /library/internet.library

Description: This document lists all the libraries accessible from the Internet. It's very large (more than 8,800 lines) and should be viewed on-line if possible—it's too big to print easily!

Access method: telnet marvel.loc.gov (140.147.254.3)

Log in: marvel

or gopher marvel.loc.gov

Description: This site, run by the Library of Congress, has information about the library, the U.S. Congress, the federal government, and copyright and employee information. It also has the Global Electronic Library, with information on many subjects such as library science, philosophy, religion, the arts, social sciences, law, economics, and others.

Mailing Lists

Access method: ftp ftp.nisc.sri.com (192.33.33.22)
get file /netinfo/interest-groups

Description: This file contains a complete listing of all available electronic mailing lists on the Internet. Updated quarterly, it has mailing lists from A.Rice (discussing Anne Rice books) to YUNUS (the Turkish TeX Users Group).

> **Note**
> This file is *enormous*—please don't print it if you can avoid it.

Mathematics

Access method: gopher e-math.ams.com (130.44.1.100)

or telnet e-math.ams.com

Log in: e-math

Password: e-math

Description: This site is run by the American Mathematics Society to provide an electronic forum for AMS members and others interested in mathematics. Topics include mathematical publications, mathematical preprints, mathematical discussion lists and bulletin boards, general information of interest to mathematicians, and professional information for mathematicians.

Music

Musicians have access to several archives of information, including scores, guitar tablature, and lyrics of popular songs.

Access method: ftp ftp.nevada.edu (131.216.1.11)
cd /pub/guitar

Description: This directory contains tablature or chords written for guitar. People from all over the world submit songs that they have transcribed into tablature form; if you submit something, however, please make sure that it's not copyrighted.

Access method: ftp ftp.uwp.edu (131.210.1.4)
cd /pub/music

or   gopher ftp.uwp.edu

Description: This server has archives of information about music, including articles about music composition, archives of music by artists' name, classical music buying guide, folk music files and pointers, lyrics archives, and more.

Networking

Access method: ftp dhvx20.csudh.edu (155.135.1.1)
cd global_net

Description: This site maintains an archive of documents pertaining to the effort to bring network access to lesser-developed nations and the poorer parts of developed nations.

> **Note**
>
> Many other networking documents are available, as described in the host-specific section earlier. The site ds.internic.net is a primary source for all documents and information about the Internet and networking in general.

Recipes

Several Internet mailing lists and USENET groups are devoted to cooking and recipes. Over quite a few years, these recipes have been collected into several archives on the Internet.

Access method: ftp gatekeeper.dec.com (16.1.0.2)
cd /pub/recipes

Description: The archive at gatekeeper.dec.com has many different items of interest. The recipes area has hundreds of items submitted by users over a period of several years. This archive is organized by recipe title.

Access method: ftp mthvax.cs.miami.edu (129.171.32.5)
cd /pub/recipes

Description: This site holds the archives for the USENET group rec.food.recipes. Recipes here are organized by food type—that is, fish, chicken, and so on. Programs for indexing and reading the rec.food.recipes archives are also available on this site (for the Macintosh and IBM PC computers); see the file /pub/recipes/readme for information.

Religion

Many different religious texts and informational files are available on Internet servers. These sites are a good place to find many of these texts.

Access method: ftp wuarchive.wustl.edu (128.252.135.4)
cd /doc/bible

Description: A complete edition of the King James Version of the Bible, including cross-references, are available for the IBM PC and Macintosh computers. You probably want to get the README file first to understand how to use the files.

Access method: ftp quake.think.com (192.31.181.1)
cd /pub/etext/koran

Description: This directory contains an electronically scanned version of M.H. Shakir's translation of the Holy Qur'an, as published by Tahrike Tarsile Qur'an, Inc. There are files for each chapter, and you can retrieve each one individually.

Access method: ftp nic.funet.fi (128.214.6.100)
cd /pub/doc/bible/hebrew

Description: This directory contains the Torah from the Tanach in Hebrew, the Prophets from the Tanach in Hebrew, and the Writings from the Tanach in Hebrew. Also included is a program to display Hebrew letters on an IBM PC monitor and a Hebrew quiz with biblical Hebrew language tutor. This site is in Europe, so you may want to limit your file transfers somewhat.

Roller Coasters

Access method: ftp gboro.rowan.edu
cd /pub/Coasters

Description: The anonymous ftp site gboro.rowan.edu has roller-coaster-related information in /pub/Coasters. More than 100 GIF format pictures of roller coasters are available, as are almost 100 reviews of amusement parks and/or roller coasters. There's also a coaster census, the rec.roller-coaster news group FAQ article, and several AVI (Video for Windows) full-motion animations of the Top Gun roller coaster at Paramount Great America amusement park in California.

Science (General)

Access method: gopher gopher.hs.jhu.edu

Description: This server is run by the History of Science Department at Johns Hopkins University. Available topics include "scientists on disk"—that is, a collection of important documents by scientists—the history of science (including departmental information such as memos and correspondence), classes about the history of science, and other information in the "grab bag" category. The scientists on disk collection includes papers by Darwin and Oppenheimer and information about the Royal Society of Science.

Seismology

For various information on earthquakes—including dates, times, and magnitudes—the following sites may yield the data you need.

Access method: telnet geophys.washington.edu

   Log in: quake

   Password: quake

Description: This server gives recent earthquake information, either reported by the USGS National Earthquake Information Center or by the University of Washington. Information includes the date, time, and magnitude of the earthquake, and the latitude, longitude, and description of the location.

Access method: telnet bison.cc.buffalo.edu

   select INDX followed by QKLN

Description: This site offers the NCEER Quakeline Earthquake resource database. You can search for information on earthquakes, earthquake engineering, natural hazards mitigation, and related topics.

Space

Space flight in general, and information from NASA in particular, has been extremely popular on the Internet for quite a few years. Many NASA sites are directly on the Internet; the sites listed here are only a sampling of the ones available.

Access method: telnet spacelink.msfc.nasa.gov
   (192.149.89.61)

Description: This site, run by NASA, provides the latest NASA news, including schedules of space shuttle launches and information about satellites and other topics. You are asked for information and assigned a login name and password that you can use for future login sessions.

Access method: finger nasanews@space.mit.edu
(18.75.0.10)

Description: This site provides a daily news summary from NASA headquarters in Washington, D.C. It gives information on current and planned shuttle flights and other NASA projects.

Access method: telnet stinfo.hq.eso.org (134.171.8.4)

Log in: stinfo

Description: This site is run by the European Space Organization and provides status reports on the Hubble Space Telescope and European HST news.

Access method: telnet lpi.jsc.nasa.gov
(192.101.147.11)

Log in: envnet

Password: henniker

Description: This site, run by the NASA Lunar and Planetary Institute (LPI), contains information about the LPI, including the Lunar and Planetary Bibliography database, the image retrieval and processing system (IRPS), and the Mars exploration bulletin board system.

Access method: telnet ned.ipac.caltech.edu
(134.4.10.118)

Log in: ned

Description: This site offers access to the NASA Extragalactic Database. It provides search capabilities into the database of more than 200,000 astronomical objects and also information about astronomical publications.

Sports

Access method: `telnet culine.colorado.edu`
             (128.138.129.83)

Description: The telnet command lets you specify a port number to connect to, and this server takes advantage of that capability. There are actually four different sports servers at this machine, each of which works at a different telnet port. To get schedules for NBA teams, connect to port 859. Others are listed as follows:

Port	Sport
859	National Basketball Association
860	National Hockey League
862	Major league baseball
863	National Football League

Stock Market Reports

Access method: `telnet a2i.rahul.net` (192.160.13.1)

    Log in: guest

    Select n and set your terminal characteristics

Description: This site is an Internet access provider and has many interesting items available. The stock market reports are under the current system information menu. Other information is also available about the Internet and the A2I site.

Television

Television—a major part of modern culture—is well represented on the Internet. Information about many current and past television shows is available; the following is a small sample.

Access method: ftp ftp.cs.widener.edu (147.31.254.132)
cd /pub/simpsons

Description: This directory contains information about the television show *The Simpsons*. Information includes plot summaries, an episode guide, air dates for each episode, and even information about *The Simpsons* pinball game.

Access method: ftp ftp.uu.net (192.48.96.9)
cd /usenet/rec.arts.startrek

Description: This directory contains archives of information about the *Star Trek* television show. Information here includes parodies written by fans, information about the various *Star Trek* spin-off shows, archive of articles posted to the USENET rec.arts.startrek group, and other information.

> **Note**
>
> The directory /usenet/rec.arts.tv on ftp.uu.net contains information about hundreds of television shows. Everything from the *A-Team* through *The Young and the Restless* is represented here. Most of the files are compressed using the UNIX compress program, so you should have an uncompress program ready.

Weather

Everyone is interested in the weather, and you can find out current weather information at several sites on the Internet. Weather maps, forecasts, and historical data are among the data you can find.

Access method: telnet exnet.iastate.edu
(129.186.20.200)

Log in: flood

Description: This server, run by the Iowa State University Extension, contains articles on flooding and dealing with the results of floods. The server allows you to read or download the information.

Access method: `finger forecast@typhoon.atmos.colostate.edu`

Description: This server returns the seasonal forecast for the Atlantic ocean. It also reports how the current season compares with previous years.

Access method: `telnet downwind.sprl.umich.edu 3000`

or `telnet 141.212.196.177 3000`

Description: This server returns the current forecast for given cities. If you know the city code for the desired location, you can enter it at the prompt; otherwise, you should press Enter and use the menu system. Other information available are a national weather summary, ski conditions, and severe weather and hurricane advisories.

Access method: `telnet wind.atmos.uah.edu 3000`

or `telnet 146.229.8.2 3000`

Description: This server is similar to the `downwind` site in the preceding description, but it doesn't have the initial prompt for your city code. In addition to the general information available above, it also allows access to the "wx" weather system, which can display weather maps and other information on your local computer if you are running the X Window system.

Access method: `gopher wx.atmos.uiuc.edu` (128.174.80.10)

Description: This server is the University of Illinois Weather Machine. It gives Gopher access to weather information for many different regions, including many major cities in the United States. It also allows access to image files from different satellites. These images are in GIF format and may be displayed on your local machine after you retrieve them.

ZIP Codes

Access method: ftp oes.orst.edu (128.193.124.2)
cd /pub/almanac/misc
get zipcode

Description: This file gives a list of all postal ZIP codes for the United States (and territories) as of the current date of the file. The file is of the form *zipcode:city* (that is, 15001:Aliquippa, PA), which allows for easy searching.

Part IV

Special Internet Connections List

Like the SURAnet Guide, the Special Internet Connections list provides a useful index to Internet hosts that provide information on specific topics. Suppose that you are interested in finding sources of information on geology. The Special Internet Connections list contains the following:

```
*GEOPHYSICAL/GEOGRAPHICAL/GEOLOGICAL-----------------------------------------
 -Earthquake Info.    finger quake@geophys.washington.edu or 128.95.16.50
                      telnet geophys.washington.edu (Login/password: quake)
   offers: Recent quake info (location, time, magnitude, etc.)

 -Geographic Server    telnet martini.eecs.umich.edu 3000 or 141.212.99.9 3000
   offers: Info by city or area code (Population, Lat./Long., Elevation, etc).

 -Global Land Info Sys telnet glis.cr.usgs.gov or telnet 152.61.192.54
   offers:Land use maps of U.S., graphs/data of geological info (Login: guest)
-----------------------------------------------------------------------------
```

For each connection listed, the name, login/password, and IP address are given, along with a brief description of what is available from that connection. The connection type (finger, ftp, telnet, and so forth) is also given.

Although the Special Internet Connections list contains some of the same material found in the SURAnet Guide, it provides additional information on some important topics. One example is more extensive listings of hosts that provide access to network search tools such as archie and Gopher.

426 The Internet Resource Quick Reference

```
     * A + by an entry designates new entries/changes since last update *

* Type "finger yanoff@csd4.csd.uwm.edu" to find ways to receive this list!

* HTML versions of this list are produced bi-weekly, FTPable from csd4.csd...

-Agricultural Info.,   telnet psupen.psu.edu or telnet 128.118.36.5
   Family Issues,         PENpages (Login: Enter your two-letter state abbrev.)
   Food & Nutrition,   telnet caticsuf.csufresno.edu or telnet 129.8.100.15
   and Environment        CSU Fresno ATI-NET              (Login: super)
                       telnet eureka.clemson.edu or telnet 130.127.8.3
                          CUFAN (Clemson U Forestry & Ag. Net.) (Login: PUBLIC)
                       telnet empire.cce.cornell.edu or telnet 132.236.89.2
                          CENET (Cornell Extension NETwork)    (Login: guest)
                       ftp ftp.sura.net (get file pub/nic/agricultural.list,
                          it contains agricultural email lists & services.)
                       telnet idea.ag.uiuc.edu (Login: flood) See FLOOD Below
   offers: Agricultural info (livestock reports, current market prices, etc.)


-Almanac mail servers  mail almanac@esusda.gov or mail almanac@ecn.purdue.edu
                       mail almanac@oes.orst.edu or mail almanac@ces.ncsu.edu
                       mail almanac@silo.ucdavis.edu
                       mail almanac@joe.uwex.edu or almanac@wisplan.uwex.edu
   offers: USDA market news, articles about use of computer in agricultural
      science, and Extension Computing Technology Newsletters.
   In body of letter: send guide Other cmds: send catalog, send help haylist

-Almanac of Events     finger copi@oddjob.uchicago.edu
                       mail geiser@pictel.com to join the mailing list!
   offers: Daily list of events and b-days in history, and sports schedules.


-Am. Philos. Assoc.    gopher apa.oxy.edu
   offers: BBS for philosophers.


-Amateur Radio         mail info@arrl.org or ftp world.std.com (pub/hamradio)
   offers: Ascii files about Amateur Radio and electronics.
   In Body of letter: help, info, send <filename> or quit (ie send prospect)


-Archeological Dbase   telnet cast.uark.edu or telnet 130.184.71.44
   offers: National Arch. Database information management system. (Login: nadb)

*AVIATION----------------------------------------------------------------
 -Aviation Gophers     gopher av.eecs.nwu.edu
                       telnet gopher.unomaha.edu (Select UNO Student Org...)
   offers: Acts as a repository for things on rec.aviation. (pics, stories...)

 -DUATS                telnet duat.gtefsd.com or telnet 131.131.7.105
                       telnet duats.gtefsd.com or telnet 131.131.7.106
    offers: Aviation weather, flight planning. (Login: <last name>)
    The first address is for certified pilots, the second for uncertified.
```

```
-------------------------------------------------------------------------------

-Career Centers Online gopher gopher.msen.com
                      mail occ-info@mail.msen.com
   offers: Jobs database, resume listing service, search by location/keyword
         H.E.A.R.T.    telnet career.com or telnet 157.151.160.1
   offers: Search for jobs by company, position, or state.


-CARL                  telnet pac.carl.org or 192.54.81.128
   offers: Online database, book reviews, magazine fax delivery service.


*COMPUTERS---------------------------------------------------------------------
 -Amiga User Area      gopher gopher.unomaha.edu (Select UNO Student Org...)
   offers: Lots of useful information for Amiga owners.


 -Macintosh Usergroup  telnet amdalinz.edvz.uni-linz.ac.at or 140.78.5.55
   offers: Austrian Mac group. UserID/Password (hit return).
-------------------------------------------------------------------------------


-Consumer Access Serv. telnet columbia.ilc.com or 38.145.77.221 (Login: cas)
                       telnet holonet.net or telnet 157.151.0.1 (Login: cdc)
                       telnet books.com or telnet 192.148.240.9 (press return)
                       telnet netmark.com or telnet 192.246.101.1
                       telnet orders.sales.digital.com or 192.208.36.2
                       telnet cio.cisco.com or 131.108.89.33 (Login: cio)
   offers: Search for/buy CDs, books, software, and video tapes online!


-Dartmouth Library     telnet library.dartmouth.edu or 129.170.16.11
   offers: Divine Comedy and reviews.                (connect dante)
           Read/Find passages in the King James Bible (select file bible)
           Read/Find passages in Shakespeare's plays  (select file s plays)
           Read/Find passages in Shakespeare's sonnets (select file s sonnets)


-DataBase Via Finger   finger help@dir.su.oz.au
   offers: Query databases, find newsgroups, access archie, etc., via finger.


-ECHO                  telnet echo.lu or telnet 158.64.1.36
   offers: European Commission Host Organization, free databases! (Login: echo)


*ECONOMICS/BUSINESS------------------------------------------------------------
 -Econ. Working Papers telnet netec.mcc.ac.uk   (Login: netec)

 -Economic BBS         telnet infopath.ucsd.edu or gopher infopath.ucsd.edu
     Choose: News & Services ¦ Economic Bulletin Board   (Login: infopath)

 -Stock Market Reports telnet a2i.rahul.net or telnet 192.160.13.1
     offers: Select n, "Menu: Current Info", then "Market Report" (Login: guest)
   Vienna Stock Exchange telnet fiivs01.tu-graz.ac.at  (Login: BOERSE)
-------------------------------------------------------------------------------
```

```
*EDUCATION/TEACHING/LEARNING------------------------------------------------
 -Distance Ed. Dbase   telnet acsvax.open.ac.uk or telnet 137.108.48.24
   (Username: ICDL  Account Code: USA  Password: aaa)

 -Education Gophers     gopher ernest.ccs.carleton.ca 419  (Canada's SchoolNet)
                        gopher gopher.ed.gov             (U.S. Dept. of Education)
                        gopher chronicle.merit.edu       (Merit Computer Network)
    Empire Schoolhouse telnet nysernet.org or 192.77.173.2 (Login: empire)
   offers: Provides K-12 resources, discussion groups, etc.

 -FEDIX/MOLIS/HERO     telnet fedix.fie.com or telnet 192.111.228.33
   offers: info. on scholarships, minority assistance, etc.

 -IKE                   telnet isaac.engr.washington.edu or 128.95.32.61
   offers: IBM Kiosk for Education User Discussion Forums. (Login: register)

 -KidLink Gopher       telnet kids.ccit.duq.edu or 165.190.8.35
   offers: Telecomm. project aimed at 10-15 year olds.  (Login: gopher)

 -Learning Link        telnet sierra.fwl.edu or telnet 198.49.171.2
   offers: Electronic info. & communication service (Login/password: newuser)

 -MicroMUSE             telnet michael.ai.mit.edu or telnet 18.43.0.177
  MariMUSE              telnet pc2.pc.maricopa.edu 4228 or 140.198.16.12 4228
   offers: Educational Multi-User Simulated Environments.  (Login: guest).

 -Nat'l Education BBS  telnet nebbs.nersc.gov or telnet 128.55.128.90
   offers: A limited-access system for NESP educators. (Login: new)

 -Nanaimo SchoolsNET   telnet crc.sd68.nanaimo.bc.ca or telnet 134.87.120.1
   offers: Education-based BBS  (Login: GUEST)    (See also: NICOL)

 -Newton                telnet newton.dep.anl.gov or telnet 130.202.92.50
   offers: BBS for those teaching/studying sci., CS, math. (Login: bbs)

 -QUERRI               telnet isn.rdns.iastate.edu or telnet 129.186.99.13
   offers: Questions on Univ. Extension. Regional Research Info (Login: querri)
----------------------------------------------------------------------------

 -Fax via Internet    mail info@awa.com ("HELP" in body of message)
                      ftp ftp.pandora.sf.ca.us (get pub/elvis/faxgate.help)

 -Finger via Telnet   telnet site 79   (example: telnet csd4.csd.uwm.edu 79)
    "site" is the place you are fingering.  Once connected, type the username.
         via Mail     mail b.liddicott@ic.ac.uk w/ subj. "#finger user@site"

*FTP------------------------------------------------------------------------
 -Archie                telnet archie.au or 139.130.4.6               (Aussie)
                        telnet archie.edvz.uni-linz.ac.at or 140.78.3.8
                        telnet archie.univie.ac.at or 131.130.1.23   (Austria)
```

```
                    telnet archie.funet.fi or 28.214.6.102         (Finland)
                    telnet archie.th-darmstadt.de or 130.83.128.111 (Ger.)
                    telnet archie.kuis.kyoto-u.ac.jp or 130.54.20.1 (Japan)
                    telnet archie.sogang.ac.kr or 163.239.1.11      (Korea)
                    telnet archie.nz or telnet 130.195.9.4     (New Zealand)
                    telnet archie.inesc.pt or 146.193.0.153        (Portugal)
                    telnet archie.luth.se or telnet 130.240.18.4   (Sweden)
                    telnet archie.ncu.edu.tw or telnet 140.115.19.24 (TWN)
                    telnet archie.doc.ic.ac.uk or 146.169.11.3  (UK/Ireland)
                    telnet archie.hensa.ac.uk or 129.12.21.25   (UK/Ireland)
                    telnet archie.sura.net or 128.167.254.194     (USA [MD])
                    telnet archie.unl.edu or 129.93.1.14          (USA [NE])
                    telnet archie.ans.net or 147.225.1.10         (USA [NY])
                    telnet archie.rutgers.edu or 128.6.18.15      (USA [NJ])
                    telnet ds.internic.net or 198.49.45.10           (AT&T)
  offers: Searches all ftp sites for any program you want.  (Login: archie)


-Archie Mail Servers  mail archie@<INSERT ONE OF ABOVE ADDRESSES HERE>
  Subject: help offers: alternative Archie access to those w/o ftp or telnet.


-FTP via EMail        mail ftpmail@decwrl.dec.com
    Subject: (hit return) Body-of-letter: help (return) quit
                    mail ftpmail@grasp.insa-lyon.fr
    Body-of-letter: help.   Please, European users only.
                    mail bitftp@pucc.princeton.edu
                    mail ftpmail@doc.ic.ak.uk
                    mail BITFTP@DEARN or to BITFTP@vm.gmd.de (Europe only)
                    mail ftpmail@ftp.uni-stuttgart.de
  Body-of-letter: help or ftplist for a list of anon. ftp sites.


-FTP Sites/Archives    ftp ocf.berkeley.edu or ftp 128.32.184.254
    offers: cd /pub/Library for great lib. of docs, bible, lyrics, etc.
                    ftp wuarchive.wustl.edu or ftp sunset.cse.nau.edu
    offers: Gifs, Sights, & Sounds!  ftp sounds.sdsu.edu for the sounds archive
                    ftp ftp.uu.net or ftp rtfm.mit.edu
    offers: You name it, it's here! (Archives, FAQs, how-to's, etc.)
                    ftp archive.umich.edu or sumex-aim.stanford.edu
    offers: Software for MS-Dos computers, Mac, Amiga, Apple2, Apollo...
                    ftp oak.oakland.edu
    offers: A huge software archive for PCs and UNIX.
                    ftp ftp.sura.net (/pub/nic) or ftp quartz.rutgers.edu
    offers: How-to's about internet (email, ftp, telnet, etc.) (/pub/internet)
                    ftp quartz.rutgers.edu or ftp cathouse.org
    offers: All the text/humor files you'd want (tv, sex..) cd pub/humor


-FTP via Telnet        telnet grind.isca.uiowa.edu or telnet 128.255.200.3
    offers: Access UIowa's huge FTP site via telnet!
-------------------------------------------------------------------------------
```

```
*GAMES/RECREATIONAL/FUN/CHAT------------------------------------------------
 -Backgammon Servers   telnet fraggel65.mdstud.chalmers.se 4321 (Login: guest)
                       mail ldb-help@midnight.wpi.edu w/ subject "help"

 -Bridge Server        telnet 140.117.11.33 (Login: okbridge)

 -Bolo Tracker         telnet gwis.circ.gwu.edu 1234 or 128.164.140.37 1234
    offers: Location of current bolo games.

 -Chat Clients         ftp ftp.santafe.edu    (4M Chat Service: /pub/SIG/4m)
                       ftp csd4.csd.uwm.edu   (ICB Chat Service: cd pub/tjk)
                       ftp cs.bu.edu          (IRC Chat Service: cd /irc/clients)
    Get chat client program from ftp sites, compile program (make) and execute.
                       telnet sci.dixie.edu 1 ¦ sh or 144.38.16.2 1 ¦ sh
                       telnet rush.cc.edu 1 ¦ sh
    NEW! The above gets AND compiles automagically an IRC client for UNIX.

 -Chat Servers - IRC   telnet sci.dixie.edu 6677 or telnet 144.38.16.2 6677
                       telnet exuokmax.ecn.uoknor.edu 6677 or 129.15.20.11
                       telnet irc.tuzvo.sk 6668 or telnet 192.108.157.3 6668
                       telnet irc.nsysu.edu.tw (Password: irc)
    TRY compiling own client rather than using these. (See above) (Login: irc)

 -Chat Services        telnet 128.112.4.12 1420
    Somewhere          telnet 129.118.41.9 2010
    FootHills          telnet marble.bu.edu 2010 or telnet 128.197.10.75 2010
    The Coffee House   telnet 128.198.1.116 2525
    Olohof's BBS       telnet morra.et.tudelft.nl 2993
    DS9                telnet 128.8.11.201 3000
   +Starship           telnet 129.108.3.7 3000
    Mansion II         telnet 163.200.97.1 4000
                      ?telnet 128.250.20.3 4000
   +Elec. Night Club   telnet 129.215.162.64 4001 (Evenings Only)
    Leaky House        telnet upsun.up.edu 4000 or telnet 192.102.10.63 4000
    CyberEden          telnet rivendel.slip.umd.edu 5000 or 128.8.11.201 5000
    Virtual Campus     telnet indigo.lut.ac.uk 5000 or 158.125.102.4 5000
   +Davenport Beach    telnet 129.74.80/116 7777
    Tele-Chat          telnet speedway.net 7777

 -Chess Server         telnet rafael.metiu.ucsb.edu 5000 or 128.111.246.2 5000

 -Chinese Chess        telnet coolidge.harvard.edu 5555 or 128.103.28.15 5555
                       telnet hippolytos.ud.chalmers.se 5555 or 129.16.79.39

 -Cookie Server        telnet astro.temple.edu 12345 or telnet 129.32.1.100
                       telnet argo.temple.edu 12345 or telnet 129.32.32.102
    offers: Funny quote or saying everytime you telnet there.

 -Cyber-Sleaze Report  finger hotlist or adam@mtv.com (Also: gopher mtv.com)
    offers: Daily reports on entertainers and such.
```

Special Internet Connections List

```
-Diplomacy            mail judge@morrolan.eff.org or judge@dipvax.dsto.gov.au
                      mail judge@shrike.und.ac.za or judge@u.washington.edu
   offers: Play the Avalon Hill game Diplomacy via email. Body-of-letter: help
   Note:   No new games are forming on the u.washington Judge, but substitute
           players are still needed.


-Fingers for Fun      finger info or graph@drink.csh.rit.edu
                      finger coke@cs.cmu.edu
   offers: Status of drink and candy machines for fun.
                      finger franklin@ug.cs.dal.ca
   offers: Random Star Trek/TNG quotes, and Almanac Information.
                      finger cyndiw@magnus1.com or cyndiw@198.242.50.4
   offers: Weekly Trivia


-Game Server          telnet castor.tat.physik.uni-tuebingen.de
   offers: Tetris, Moria, Nethack, MUDs, Text Adventures, etc.  (Login: GAMES)


-GO Server            telnet hellspark.wharton.upenn.edu 6969


-Othello/Reversi      telnet faust.uni-paderborn.de 5000 or 131.234.28.29
-----------------------------------------------------------------------------

*GEOPHYSICAL/GEOGRAPHICAL/GEOLOGICAL------------------------------------------
-Earthquake Info.     finger quake@geophys.washington.edu or 128.95.16.50
                      telnet geophys.washington.edu (Login/password: quake)
                      telnet bison.cc.buffalo.edu (select INDX 4 Bib. server)
   offers: Recent quake info (location, time, magnitude, etc.)


-Geographic Server    telnet martini.eecs.umich.edu 3000 or 141.212.99.9 3000
   offers: Info by city or area code (Population, Lat./Long., Elevation, etc).


-Global Land Info Sys telnet glis.cr.usgs.gov or telnet 152.61.192.54
   offers:Land use maps of U.S., graphs/data of geological info (Login: guest)
-----------------------------------------------------------------------------

-Gopher               telnet consultant.micro.umn.edu or telnet 134.84.132.4
                      telnet seymour.md.gov or telnet 128.8.10.46
                      telnet gopher.msu.edu or telnet 35.8.2.61
                      telnet twosocks.ces.ncsu.edu or telnet 152.1.45.21
                      telnet cat.ohiolink.edu or telnet 130.108.120.25
                      telnet ENVIROLINK.hss.cmu.edu (Password: envirolink)
                      telnet wsuaix.csc.wsu.edu / 134.121.1.40(Logn: wsuinfo)
                      telnet telnet.wiscinfo.wisc.edu    (Login: wiscinfo)
                      telnet infoslug.ucsc.edu or 128.114.143.25   (INFOSLUG)
                      telnet infopath.ucsd.edu           (Login: infopath)
                      telnet sunsite.unc.edu or telnet 152.2.22.81
                      telnet ux1.cso.uiuc.edu or telnet 128.174.5.59
                      telnet panda.uiowa.edu or telnet 128.255.40.201
                      telnet inform.umd.edu or telnet 128.8.10.29
```

```
                    telnet grits.valdosta.peachnet.edu or 131.144.8.206
                    telnet gopher.virginia.edu / 128.143.22.36(Login: gwis)
                    telnet ecosys.drdr.virginia.edu or 128.143.86.233
                    telnet gopher.ORA.com or telnet 140.186.65.25
                    telnet nicol.jvnc.net or 128.121.50.2    (Login: NICOL)
                    telnet finfo.tu-graz.ac.at or 129.27.2.4 (Login: info)
                    telnet info.anu.edu.au or 150.203.84.20   (Login: info)
                    telnet tolten.puc.cl or telnet 146.155.1.16      (Chile)
                    telnet gopher.denet.dk or telnet 129.142.6.66 (Denmark)
                    telnet gopher.th-darmstadt.de or telnet 130.83.55.75
                    telnet ecnet.ec or telnet 157.100.45.2            (Ecuador)
                    telnet gopher.uv.es or telnet 147.156.1.12         (Spain)
                    telnet gopher.isnet.is or telnet 130.208.165.63   (Iclnd)
                    telnet siam.mi.cnr.it or telnet 155.253.1.40       (Italy)
                    telnet gopher.torun.edu.pl or 158.75.2.5         (Poland)
                    telnet info.sunet.se or telnet 192.36.125.10     (Sweden)
                    telnet gopher.chalmers.se or 129.16.221.40       (Sweden)
                    telnet hugin.ub2.lu.se or telnet 130.235.162.12(Sweden)
                    telnet gopher.brad.ac.uk or 143.53.2.5       (Login: info)
  offers: Access to other services, gophers, documents, etc.   (Login: gopher)


-Gopher             gopher english-server.hss.cmu.edu
  offers: Most comprehensive gopher I've seen so far, it gets its own entry!


-GopherMail         mail gophermail@ncc.go.jp or mail gophermail@calvin.edu
  offers: Email access to gopher for those with mail-only access to Internet.


-Ham Radio Callbooks   telnet callsign.cs.buffalo.edu 2000 / 128.205.32.2 2000
                    telnet ns.risc.net or 155.212.2.2 (Login: hamradio)
  offers: National ham radio call-sign callbook.  (Also: Amateur Radio above)


-History Databases  telnet ukanaix.cc.ukans.edu or telnet 129.237.1.30
  offers:  History databases (Login: history) and CIS info (Login: ex-ussr)
                    ftp byrd.mu.wvnet.edu / ftp 129.71.32.152(/pub/history)
                    telnet clus1.ulcc.ac.uk or telnet 192.12.72.60
  offers: Docs, archives, comprehensive history server(Login/Password: ihr-uk)


-HP Calculator BBS  telnet hpcvbbs.cv.hp.com or telnet 15.255.72.16
  offers:  BBS for HP Calc. users, with chat mode.  (Login: new)


-Hpcwire            telnet hpcwire.ans.net or telnet 147.225.1.51
  offers: Excellent menu-driven information searches. (Login: hpcwire)


-Hytelnet Server    telnet access.usask.ca or telnet 128.233.3.1
                    telnet info.ccit.arizona.edu or 129.196.76.201
                    telnet laguna.epcc.edu or 192.94.29.3   (Login: library)
                    telnet info.anu.edu.au or 150.203.84.20 (Login:library)
                    telnet library.adelaide.edu.au (Login: access)
```

Special Internet Connections List

```
                    telnet nctuccca.edu.tw or 140.111.1.10          (TAIWAN)
                    telnet info.mcc.ac.uk or telnet 130.88.200.15
                    telnet rsl.ox.ac.uk or telnet 129.67.16.31
  offers: univ. & library catalogues around the world. (Login: hytelnet)

-IEEE SPAsystem     telnet stdsbbs.ieee.org or telnet 140.98.1.11
  offers: Standards Process Automation System. (Login: guest)


-Internet Guides/Docs  gopher una.hh.lib.umich.edu (Select: inetdirs)


-InterNIC           telnet rs.internic.net or telnet 198.41.0.5
  offers: Gopher, WAIS, Whois, finger, TONS of Internet info, book orders, etc


-IP Address Resolver  mail resolve@cs.widener.edu
                      mail dns@grasp.insa-lyon.fr (body of letter: help)
  usage: in body-of-letter: site <address here>  Mails you IP address of site.

*LAW------------------------------------------------------------------------
 -Access            telnet access.uhcc.hawaii.edu or telnet 128.171.7.167
   offers: Legislative Info. Service, Hawaii State Legislature.


 -Gopher LAW Servers  telnet fatty.LAW.cornell.edu or telnet 132.236.108.5
                      telnet gopher.LAW.csuohio.edu or telnet 137.148.22.51
                      telnet acc.wuacc.edu or 192.104.1.2   (Login: washlaw)
   offers: Law info. via gopher.  (Login: gopher)


 -Law Library       telnet liberty.uc.wlu.edu or telnet 137.113.10.35
                    ftp sulaw.law.su.oz.au (cd /pub/law)
   offers: Law libraries and legal research. (Login: lawlib)
           Offers copies of laws for each state/computer laws, and more!


 -LawNet            telnet lawnet.law.columbia.edu or telnet 128.59.176.83
   offers: Law/Judicial info and catalogs access.  (Login: lawnet)


 -Supreme Court Rulings ftp ftp.cwru.edu
   offers: ASCII files of Supreme Court rulings in directory /hermes


 -WWW Law Servers   telnet www.LAW.indiana.edu or telnet 129.79.131.170
                    telnet fatty.LAW.cornell.edu or telnet 132.236.108.5
   offers: Hypertext access to legal documents (Login: www)
-----------------------------------------------------------------------------

-Library Catalogs   ftp dla.ucop.edu (pub/internet/libcat-guide)
  offers: "Library Catalogs on the Internet: Strategies for Selection
    and Use" document (how, but not where; also get one of the following).
                    ftp ftp.unt.edu (library/libraries.txt)
  offers: "Accessing Bibliographic Databases" document.
                    ftp ariel.unm.edu (library/internet.library)
```

offers: "Internet-Accessible Catalogs and Databases" document.

-Library of Congress   telnet locis.loc.gov or telnet 140.147.254.3
  offers: Library of Congress Information System (LOCIS) Offers access
          to lib. of congress, legislative info, and copyright info.
                    telnet marvel.loc.gov or telnet 140.147.2.15
  offers: LOC gopher, with access to lots of gov't docs. (Login: marvel)

-LIBS   telnet nessie.cc.wwu.edu or telnet 140.160.240.11
                        telnet info.anu.edu.au or telnet 150.203.84.20
                        telnet garam.kreonet.re.kr or 134.75.30.11 (Login: nic)
  offers: Access to nearly all online services seen in this list.(Login: LIBS)

-List of Lists   ftp crvax.sri.com or ftp 128.18.30.65
  offers: List of interest groups/email lists in /netinfo/interest-groups.

?Matchmaker by Email   mail perfect@match.com with "SEND FORM" in body of msg
  offers: Will reply with instructions and questionnaire.

*MEDICAL/HEALTH/BIOLOGY/GENETICS--
 -Anesthesiology Gopher gopher eja.anes.hscsyr.edu
    offers: Lots of medical info, archives, and positions.

 -Biological Services mail grail@ornl.gov ("help" in body of message)
    offers: Service predicting intron-exon splice sites in vertebrate genes.
                    telnet atcc.nih.gov or telnet 156.40.144.248
    offers: American Type Culture Collection (Login: search Password: common)
                    gopher life.anu.edu.au
    offers: Access to lots of biological sciences information.

 -CancerNets   mail cancernet@icicb.nci.nih.gov
    offers: Cancer info. statements thru email. Body-of-letter:help or spanish
                    gopher gopher.nih.gov (Health & Clinical Information/)
                    gopher gan.ncc.go.jp
                    telnet txcancer.mda.uth.tmc.edu or telnet 129.106.60.97
    offers: Texas Cancer Data Center.   (Login: TCDC) (See also: NICOL)

 -CHAT   telnet debra.dgbt.doc.ca or telnet 142.92.36.15
    offers:Interactive AIDS & Epilepsy docs,simulated conversation(Login: chat)

 -Educational Tech Net telnet etnet.nlm.nih.gov or telnet 130.14.10.123
    offers:Forums and discussion groups on medical tech. and edu.(Login: etnet)

 -Genetics Banks   mail gene-server@bchs.uh.edu
                       mail retrieve@ncbi.nlm.nih.gov
                       mail blast@ncbi.nlm.nih.gov ("help" in body of message)
                       mail genmark@ford.gatech.edu
                       mail blocks@howard.fhcrc.org
                       mail cbrg@inf.ethz.ch ("help" in body of message)

```
                        mail QUICK@EMBL-Heidelberg.DE
                        mail NETSERV@EMBL-Heidelberg.DE
    Subject: help offers: genetic database/nucleic acid/protein sequence.


 -Genomic Database      telnet morgan.jax.org or telnet 192.43.249.17
    offers: Genomic Database of the Mouse.  (Login: guest)


 -Handicap/Med. Sites ftp handicap.shel.isc-br.com or ftp 129.189.4.184
    offers: anonymous ftp of software and medical info.
                        telnet bongo.cc.utexas.edu or telnet 128.83.186.13
    offers: Aids user in finding disability assist. equip. & serv.(Login: tatp)
-----------------------------------------------------------------------------

-Monochrome            telnet mono.city.ac.uk or telnet 138.40.17.1
   offers: Multi-user messaging system (w/ chat) (Login/Password: mono)


-Movie Database Request movie@ibmpcug.co.uk with "HELP" in body of message
   offers: Info on actors, directors, movies, etc.

*MUSIC-----------------------------------------------------------------------
 -Billboard Charts     finger buckmr@rpi.edu
   offers: U.S. Top Pop singles for the week.

 -Guitar Chords/TAB    ftp ftp.nevada.edu or ftp 131.216.1.11
    offers: Tablature/Chords for guitar in /pub/guitar. Also at ftp.uu.net

 -Lyric/Music Server   ftp ftp.uwp.edu
    offers: Lyrics, chords/tablature, and music pictures. (/pub/music/...)

 -Music & Brain D-base telnet mila.ps.uci.edu or telnet 128.200.29.81
    offers: Research on music related to behavior.(Login: mbi Password: nammbi)

 -Music Newsletter     mail listserv@vm.marist.edu (internet) or
                        mail listserv@marist (bitnet)
    Body-of-letter: SUBSCRIBE UPNEWS <your full name>  offers: Reviews, intviews

 -Sid's Music Server   mail mwilkenf@silver.ucs.indiana.edu
    Subject: BOOTHELP  offers: Lists of rare live recordings, cd's for sale.

 -Used Music Server    mail used-music-server@wang.com w/ subject: help
    offers: Users can buy/sell/trade CDs/LPs/Tapes or subscribe to the list.

 -Music List of Lists  mail mlol-request@wariat.org (music list of lists)
-----------------------------------------------------------------------------

*NEWS------------------------------------------------------------------------
 -Electronic Journals  gopher gopher.cic.net or gopher 192.131.22.5
                        telnet enews.com or telnet 192.215.1.51 (Login: gopher)
    offers: Access to MANY electronic journals (Select Elec. Serials)
```

```
+Global News Navig.    URL for http://nearnet.gnn.com/GNN-ORA.html
   offers: O'Reilly's GNN, accessible with URL above via Mosaic or Lynx.

-List-Periodic Posts  finger nichol@stavanger.sgp.slb.com
   offers: Listing of all FAQs, lists, and periodic postings to Usenet news.

-News Mail Servers    mail [newsgroup]@cs.utexas.edu
   offers: Post to Usenet news via email. (eg. [newsgroup] = alt-bbs)

-NNTP Server List     finger lesikar@tigger.stcloud.msus.edu
   offers: A list of publicly accessible NNTP news servers.

-NNTP Usenet News     telnet kufacts.cc.ukans.edu or 129.237.1.30
   Select: Reference Shelf (Login: kufacts) (See Also: UNC BBS, Panda Gopher)

-USA Today            telnet freenet-in-[a,b,c].cwru.edu or 129.22.8.38
                      telnet yfn.ysu.edu or 192.55.234.27 (Login: visitor)
   offers: USA Today Headline News, Sports, etc... (Also avail. via gopher)
-----------------------------------------------------------------------------

-Nielsen TV Ratings   finger normg@halcyon.halcyon.com
   offers: Weekly TV ratings according to the Nielsen rating system.

-Oracle               mail oracle@cs.indiana.edu w/ subject: help
   offers: The Usenet Oracle answers all your questions!

-OSS-IS               ftp soaf1.ssa.gov
                      mail info@soaf1.ssa.gov with "send index" as your msg.
   offers: Many FAQ's, ftp lists, library and service lists, gov't documents.

*POLITICS/GOVERNMENT---------------------------------------------------------
 -Air Pollution BBS   telnet ttnbbs.rtpnc.epa.gov or telnet 134.67.208.177
   offers: Various BBS' that cover a wide range of Air Pollution information

 -ACE                 mail info@ace.esusda.gov w/ "send help" in body of msg
   offers: Americans Communicating Electronically.  (Gov't docs via email)

 -FedWorld Gateway    telnet fedworld.doc.gov or telnet 192.239.92.201
   offers: Access to lots of gov't databases, files, libraries, etc.

 -Iowa Polit. Stk Mkt telnet iem.biz.uiowa.edu or 128.255.44.2
   offers: Buy & sell shares in political candidates and other stuff.

 -White House Releases mail Clinton-Info@Campaign92.Org with the subject: Help
   offers: Subscribe to White House press releases (news, speeches, etc.)

 -White House Summaries mail almanac@esusda.gov (in msg: subscribe wh-summary)
   offers: Daily mailing of summary of White House press releases.
```

Special Internet Connections List

-Window on Gov't   telnet window.texas.gov or telnet 192.198.66.186
  offers: Government-related info, and lots of info on state of Texas.

-Project Gutenberg   ftp mrcnext.cso.uiuc.edu or ftp 128.174.201.12
  offers: Many books in print and almanac files.   cd pub/etext

-Psychology Gopher   gopher panda1.uottawa.ca 4010
  offers: Psychology-related gopher.

-Public-Access Unix   telnet nyx.cs.du.edu or 130.253.192.68
  offers: Free account, with access to various UNIX features. (login: new)

-Public-Access Unix   telnet hermes.merit.edu or telnet 35.1.48.150
                      telnet m-net.ann-arbor.mi.us or telnet 35.208.17.4
  (Which host: um-m-net Enter 'g' for guest. login: newuser)

-Queer Resource Dir. ftp vector.intercon.com or ftp 149.52.1.130
  offers: AIDS info/gay rights info. Recommend get file: README (cd pub/QRD)

-Recipe Archives   ftp gatekeeper.dec.com   (cd pub/recipes)
                      ftp mthvax.cs.miami.edu   (cd pub/recipes)
                      ftp ftp.neosoft.com   (cd pub/rec.food/recipes)
                      ftp cs.ubc.ca   (cd pub/local/RECIPES)
  offers: Anonymous ftp site for MANY food recipes.

*RELIGION/BIBLE RELATED---
  -Gabriel's Horn   telnet 138.26.65.78 7777 (Also see Dartmouth above)
    offers: Returns a Bible verse from the Old or New Testament

  -JewishNet   telnet vms.huji.ac.il or telnet 128.139.4.3
    offers: WWW w/ info. on mailing lists, restaurants, etc. (Login: JEWISHNET)

  -NY-Israel Gopher   gopher israel.nysernet.org 71
    offers: Jewish libraries, lists, projects, holocaust info, etc.
---

*SCIENCE/MATH/STATISTICS--
  -ASCinfo   telnet asc.harvard.edu or telnet 128.103.41.101
    offers: Info. relating to Advanced XRay Astrophy. Facility (Login: ascinfo)

  -E-Math   telnet e-math.ams.com or 130.44.1.100
    offers:Am. Math. Soc. bbs w/ software and reviews. (Login/Password: e-math)

  -Math Gopher   gopher archives.math.utk.edu
    offers: Math archives (software, teaching materials, other gophers)

  -NetLib   mail netlib@ornl.gov or mail netlib@uunet.uu.net
    offers:Math (usually Fortran) programs via email Body-of-letter: send index

-Nuclear Data Center telnet bnlnd2.dne.bnl.gov or telnet 130.199.112.132
  offers: National nuclear data. (Login: nndc)

-Particle Information telnet muse.lbl.gov or telnet 131.243.48.11
  offers: Lookup information on any particle! (Login: pdg_public)

-Periodic Table   telnet camms2.caos.kun.nl 2034 or 131.174.82.239 2034
  offers: electronic periodic table of elements.

-StatLib Server   mail statlib@lib.stat.cmu.edu
  Mail with line: send index. offers:Prgms, Datasets, etc. for statisticians.

-STIS   telnet stis.nsf.gov or 128.150.195.40
  offers: Science & Technology Information System. (Login: public)

-The Scientist   ftp ds.internic.net (cd pub/the-scientist)
  offers: Biweekly paper targeted at science professionals

-SERVICES   telnet library.wustl.edu or telnet 128.252.173.4
  offers: Access to nearly every listed service! (Login: hit return)

-SFI BBS   telnet bbs.santafe.edu (login: bbs)
  offers: Research BBS provides access to info. on Complex Systems.

*SOFTWARE/Information SERVERS---
 -Info/Software Server telnet rusinfo.rus.uni-stuttgart.de or 129.69.1.12
   offers: journals, unix stuff, recipes, online cookbook, etc. login: info

 -Software Server(ASK) telnet askhp.ask.uni-karlsruhe.de or 129.13.200.33
   offers: On-line software search.   (Login/password: ask)

 -ZIB Electronic Libr. telnet elib.zib-berlin.de or telnet 130.73.108.11
   offers: Library of software, links to other libraries. (Login: elib)
----

*SPACE/ASTRONOMY--
 -EnviroNet   telnet envnet.gsfc.nasa.gov or telnet 128.183.104.16
   offers: Space environment resource.   (Login: envnet Password: henniker)

 -Europe Space Agency telnet esrin.esa.it or telnet 192.106.252.1
   offers: Access ESA PID (Prototype Info Dir) & ESIS (Eur. Space Info System)

 -FIFE   telnet pldsg3.gsfc.nasa.gov or telnet 128.183.36.16
   offers: Science, etc. databases from satellites, etc. (Login: FIFEUSER)

 -Lunar/Planet Instit. telnet lpi.jsc.nasa.gov or telnet 192.101.147.11
   offers: Resources on Geology, Geophys, Astron., Astrophys. (Login: lpi)

 -NASA Headline News   finger nasanews@space.mit.edu
   offers: Recent press releases from NASA. (See also SpaceNews)

```
-NASA SpaceLink      telnet spacelink.msfc.nasa.gov or telnet 192.149.89.61
   offers: Latest NASA news, including shuttle launches and satellite updates.

-NASDA               telnet nsaeoc.eoc.nasda.go.jp or telnet 133.56.72.1
   offers: National Space Development Agency of Japan (Login: nasdadir)

-NED                 telnet ned.ipac.caltech.edu or telnet 134.4.10.118
   offers: NASA Extragalactic Database. Bibliographies, info. (Login: ned)

-NODIS               telnet nssdc.gsfc.nasa.gov or telnet 128.183.36.25
                     telnet nssdca.gsfc.nasa.gov or telnet 128.183.36.23
   offers:Menu-driven access to Nat'l Space Science Data Center (Login: nodis)

-SDDAS               telnet espsun.space.swri.edu 540 or 129.162.150.99 540
   offers: SW Research Data Display & Analysis Center.

-SpaceMet            telnet spacemet.phast.umass.edu or 128.119.50.48
   offers: Science/space bbs about space exploration w/ info from NASA.

-SpaceNews           finger magliaco@pilot.njin.net
   offers: Weekly publication of space news. (See also Nasa Headline News)

-STInfo              telnet stinfo.hq.eso.org or tenet 134.171.8.4
   offers: Reports about Hubble Telescope, press releases (Login: stinfo)
-------------------------------------------------------------------------------
*SPORTS------------------------------------------------------------------------
 -Sports Schedules NBA: telnet culine.colorado.edu 859 / 128.138.129.83 859
                   NHL: telnet culine.colorado.edu 860 / 128.138.129.83 860
                   MLB: telnet culine.colorado.edu 862 / 128.138.129.83 862
                   NFL: telnet culine.colorado.edu 863 / 128.138.129.83 863
                        finger copi@oddjob.uchicago.edu for sports schedules
   offers: Sports schedules on-line. help for help, return for today's games.

 -NFL Scores/Standings finger nfl@spam.wicat.com or nfl@192.150.148.62
                       finger nflline@spam.wicat.com (NFL Line Spreads)
   offers: Football scores, standings, and next week's schedule.
-------------------------------------------------------------------------------
*TRAVEL------------------------------------------------------------------------
 -Subway Navigator    telnet metro.jussieu.fr 10000 or 134.157.0.132 10000
   offers: Search subway routes of major cities, in French or English.

 -Travel Info. Library  ftp ftp.cc.umanitoba.ca or ftp 130.179.16.24
   offers: Travelogues, guides, FAQs. cd to the directory "rec-travel"
-------------------------------------------------------------------------------
-UNC BBS             telnet launchpad.unc.edu or telnet 152.2.22.80
   offers: Usenet News, Lib. of Congress, nationwide libs.  (Login: launch)
```

```
*USER LOOKUP SERVICES/WHOIS SERVICES------------------------------------------
-Mail Srvr/Usr Lookup  mail mail-server@rtfm.mit.edu
   in body of mail message: send usenet-addresses/[name searching for]

 -Netfind User Lookup   telnet bruno.cs.colorado.edu or telnet 128.138.243.151
                        telnet cobber.cord.edu or telnet 138.129.1.32
                        telnet pascal.sjsu.edu or telnet 130.65.86.15
                        telnet mudhoney.micro.umn.edu or telnet 134.84.132.7
                        telnet redmont.cis.uab.edu or telnet 138.26.64.4
                        telnet athe.wustl.edu or telnet 128.252.122.173
                        telnet ds.internic.net or telnet 198.49.45.10
                        telnet netfind.oc.com or telnet 192.82.215.88
                        telnet archie.au or telnet 139.130.4.6
                        telnet netfind.anu.edu.au or telnet 150.203.2.14
                        telnet netfind.if.usp.br or telnet 143.107.249.132
                        telnet macs.ee.mcgill.ca or 132.206.61.15
                        telnet malloco.ing.puc.cl or telnet 146.155.1.43
                        telnet netfind.vslib.cz or telnet 147.230.16.1
                        telnet nic.nm.kr or telnet 143.248.1.100
                        telnet lincoln.technet.sg or telnet 192.169.33.6
                        telnet nic.uakom.sk or telnet 192.108.131.12
                        telnet monolith.cc.ic.ac.uk or telnet 155.198.5.3
                        telnet lust.mrrl.lut.ac.uk or telnet 158.125.220.7
                        telnet dino.conicit.ve or telnet 150.188.1.10
    offers: Given a name and org./school, finds a user for you (login: netfind)

 -Whois Services        telnet rs.internic.net or telnet 198.41.0.5
                        mail service@rs.internic.net  (w/ subject: help  OR
                          send RFC-xxxx.TXT, with xxxx being the RFC number)
                        telnet info.cnri.reston.va.us 185  (Knowbot Info Serv.)
                        telnet garam.kreonet.re.kr or 134.75.30.11 (Login: nic)
                        telnet paradise.ulcc.ac.uk or 128.86.8.56  (Login: dua)
                        ftp sipb.mit.edu (pub/whois/whois-servers.list)
    offers: Way to find internet address given a keyword. To access type: whois
-----------------------------------------------------------------------------

-UUCP map entries by mail:   mail dns@grasp.insa-lyon.fr (body: help)
  usage: in body-of-letter: uucp uucp_site Mails you UUCP map entry

-WAIStation             telnet quake.think.com or telnet 192.31.181.1
                        telnet wais.com or telnet 192.216.46.98
                        telnet swais.cwis.uci.edu or 128.200.15.2
                        telnet sunsite.unc.edu or telnet 152.2.22.81
                        telnet info.funet.fi or 128.214.6.100 (Login: info)
                        telnet wais.nis.garr.it or 192.12.192.10 (Login: wais)
     offers: Wide Area Info. Service. (Login: swais)
```

```
*WEATHER/ATMOSPHERIC/OCEANIC------------------------------------------------
 -Auroral/Solar Report finger aurora@xi.uleth.ca or finger aurora@142.66.3.29
                      finger solar@xi.uleth.ca or finger solar@142.66.3.29
                      finger daily@xi.uleth.ca or finger daily@142.66.3.29
    offers: Auroral activity warnings/watches/sightings, updated hourly.
            Solar = 3-Hourly solar & Geophysical report, daily is the daily one

 +Avalanche Forecast   mail snowfall@dcs.glasgow.ac.uk  with a blank message

 -Emergency Info.      telnet oes1.oes.ca.gov 5501 or 134.186.127.1 5501
    offers: State of Cali. - Governor's Office of Emergency Services
                      gopher vita.org
    offers: Disaster Information Center with disaster reports and data.

 -Flood Gopher/Info    telnet idea.ag.uiuc.edu or telnet 128.174.123.126
                      telnet exnet.iastate.edu or telnet 129.186.20.200
    offers: Tons of files for coping with floods and hurricanes (Login: flood)

 -NOAA                 telnet esdim1.nodc.noaa.gov or telnet 140.90.235.168
    offers: Nat'l Oceanic and Atmos. Admin.  Lots of data!  (Login: noaadir)

 -Oceanic Info. Center telnet delocn.udel.edu or telnet 128.175.24.1
    (Login: info)

 -Tropicl Strm Forecst finger forecast@typhoon.atmos.colostate.edu
    offers: Seasonal forecast for Atl. Ocn. Also: finger forecast@129.82.107.24

 -Weather Account      telnet aeolus.rap.ucar.edu or telnet 128.117.192.73
    offers: (Login: weather Password: orknot  type: weather or man weather)

 -Weather Services     telnet downwind.sprl.umich.edu 3000 or 141.212.196.177
                      telnet wind.atmos.uah.edu 3000 or 146.229.8.2 3000
                      telnet nevado.SRCC.lsu.edu     (Login: srcc)
                      gopher wx.atmos.uiuc.edu or gopher 128.174.80.10
    offers: City/State forecasts, ski conditions, earthquake reports, etc.
                      telnet vicbeta.vic.bom.gov.au 55555 or 134.178.130.2
    offers: Weather service for Australia.
-----------------------------------------------------------------------------

-Dictionary Servers    telnet cs.indiana.edu 2627 or 129.79.254.191 2627
                      telnet chem.ucsd.edu or 132.239.68.1 (login: webster)
                      telnet/gopher wombat.doc.ic.ac.uk (login: guest)
    offers: Dictionary/Spelling service.  Type "HELP" for info.  (ALL CAPS!)

-World-Wide Web        telnet www.njit.edu or telnet 128.235.163.2   (USA [NJ])
                      telnet ukanaix.cc.ukans.edu or 129.237.1.30    (USA[KA])
                      telnet www.twi.tudelft.nl    (Login: lynx) (NETHERLANDS)
                      telnet millbrook.lib.rmit.edu.au (Login: lynx) (AUSSIE)
                      telnet info.cern.ch or telnet 128.141.201.74    (SWISS)
```

```
                    telnet vms.huji.ac.il or telnet 128.139.4.3      (ISRAEL)
                    telnet sun.uakom.sk or telnet 192.108.131.11 (SLOVAKIA)
   offers: Access to various documents, lists, and services. (Login: www)
```

* NOTE: NO LOGIN NAMES OR PASSWORDS ARE REQUIRED UNLESS STATED OTHERWISE! *
  NOTE: FOR FTP SITES, LOGIN AS anonymous, Password is your email address.

Part V

The Inter-Network Mail Guide

The Internet is commonly referred to as a *global network of networks*. The majority of networks participating in the Internet were designed to use the same means for communicating information as the Internet itself uses (the transmission control protocol with the Internet protocol, or TCP/IP for short). They were also designed to use a common means of addressing users, called the Domain Name Service (DNS).

But many well established networks, such as CompuServe and America Online, also can be reached through the Internet, but their user addressing scheme does not conform to the DNS. Thus, figuring out just how to construct a proper address for a user of one of these networks becomes difficult.

To help ease the problem of determining the means for addressing users of these other networks, the Inter-Network Mail Guide (INMG) was developed. The INMG lists address formats and instructions for more than 40 different networks. Each entry in the list contains several fields:

FROM: The network you are sending mail from

TO: The network you are sending mail to

RECIPIENT: The address of the recipient as specified in the format for his or her network

CONTACT: A point of contact for assistance or more information

INSTR: Instructions on how to send your mail

Suppose that you are using the America Online (AOL) service and want to know how to address users of CompuServe, GEnie, and other Internet users in general. By looking for the places where aol is listed in the FROM field, you would find

```
#FROM: aol
#TO: compuserve
#RECIPIENT: 71234,567
#CONTACT: Internet
#INSTR: send to '71234.567@cis'

#FROM: aol
#TO: genie
#RECIPIENT: user
#CONTACT: Internet
#INSTR: send to 'user@genie'

#FROM: aol
#TO: internet
#RECIPIENT: user@domain
#CONTACT: Internet
#INSTR: send to 'user@domain'
```

Thus, sending a mail message to a GEnie user would simply require that you add **@genie** to the end of that user's GEnie address when sending your message from AOL.

Conversely, if an Internet user wanted to send mail to your AOL address, he would find the following:

```
#FROM: internet
#TO: aol
#RECIPIENT: A User
#CONTACT: postmaster@aol.com
#INSTR: send to auser@aol.com (all lower-case, remove spaces)
#INSTR: msgs are truncated to 32K (8K for PCs), all characters except newline
#-     & printable ASCII characters are mapped to spaces, users are limited to
#-     75 pieces of Internet mail in their mailbox at a time.
```

Notice that here, some limitations on the content and number of messages that an AOL user can receive have been pointed out.

The following names and descriptions of the possible FROM and TO fields are available:

The Inter-Network Mail Guide

```
N: aol            ; America Online; America Online, Inc.; commercial;
N: alternex       ; AlterNex; IBASE; non-profit;
N: applelink      ; AppleLink; Apple Computer, Inc.; commercial;
N: arcom          ; ArCom; Swiss PTT; commercial; X.400 only
N: att            ; AT&T Mail; AT&T; commercial;
N: bitnet         ; BITNET; none; academic;
N: bix            ; Byte Information eXchange; Byte magazine; commercial;
N: bmug           ; BMUG ; Berkeley Macintosh Users Group; in-house;
N: calvacom       ; Calvacom;
   Reseau & Communication Informatique (RCI-Calvacom); commercial;
N: chasque        ; Chasque; Instituto del Tercer Mundo; non-profit;
N: comlink        ; ComLink; ? ; non-profit;
N: compuserve     ; CompuServe; CompuServe Inc.; commercial;
N: connect        ; Connect Professional Information Network; ?; commercial;
N: easylink       ; Easylink; AT&T; commercial;
N: easynet        ; Easynet; DEC; in-house;
N: econet         ; EcoNet; Institute for Global Communications; non-profit;
N: ecuanex        ; EcuaNex; ? ; non-profit;
N: envoy          ; Envoy-100; Telecom Canada; commercial; X.400
N: fax            ; Facsimile document transmission; none; none;
N: fidonet        ; FidoNet; none; bbs;
N: genie          ; GEnie; GE Information Services; commercial;
N: geonet         ; GeoNet Mailbox Systems;
   Geonet Mailbox Services GmbH/Systems Inc.; commercial;
N: glasnet        ; GlasNet; ? ; non-profit;
N: gold-400       ; GNS Gold 400; British Telecom; commercial; X.400
N: goldgate       ; GoldGate Telcom Gold; Net-Tel Computer Systems; ?;
N: greennet       ; GreenNet; Soft Solutions Ltd; commercial;
N: gsfcmail       ; GSFCmail; NASA/Goddard Space Flight Center; in-house;
N: ibm            ; VNET; IBM; in-house;
N: ibmmail        ; ?; IBM; commercial;
N: internet       ; Internet; none; academic;
N: keylink        ; KeyLink; Telecom Australia; commercial; X.400
N: mailnet        ; X.400; ?; ?;
N: mausnet        ; Mausnet; Mausnet; non-profit;
N: mci            ; MCIMail; MCI; commercial;
N: nasamail       ; NASAMail; NASA; in-house;
N: nicarao        ; Nicarao; CRIES; non-profit;
N: nordnet        ; NordNet; ? ; non-profit;
N: nsi            ; NASA Science Internet; NASA; government;
   Dual-protocol: instructions given here pertain only to NSI-DECnet addresses
   (NSI-TCP/IP addresses should be treated as shown for 'internet')
N: omnet          ; OMNET; OMNET; commercial;
N: peacenet       ; PeaceNet/EcoNet; Institute for Global Communications;
   non-profit;
N: pegasus        ; Pegasus; Pegasus Networks; non-profit;
N: prodigy        ; PRODIGY; commercial; ?;
N: pronet         ; Pro-Net Australia; National Info. Resource Gateway; ?;
```

```
N: sinet         ; Schlumberger Information NETwork; ?; ?;
N: sprintmail    ; SprintMail; Sprint; commercial;
N: telecom       ; Telecom Australia; National Videotex Network; ?;
N: thenet        ; Texas Higher Education Network; University of Texas;
   academic ;
N: web           ; The Web; Nirv Community Resource Centre; non-profit;
N: wwivnet       ; WWIVnet; WWIVnet; non-profit;
```

In the following list, the RECIPIENT field gives an example of an address on the destination network, to make it clear in subsequent lines what text requires subsitution. The CONTACT field gives an address for inquiries concerning the gateway, expressed as an address reachable from the source (FROM) network. The INSTR field—which may contain several lines—tells you how you can send mail to someone on the destination network. Text that represents variables (which you replace with the pertinent information) appears in double quotation marks (" ").

> **Note**
>
> Presumably, if you can't get the gateway to work at all, knowing an unreachable address on another network won't be of great help.

Instructions that consist simply of mailing to a certain address will be indicated by the words send to followed by an address in single quotation marks. Alternative addresses (if any) will be marked or to.

```
FROM: aol
TO: applelink
RECIPIENT: user
CONTACT: Internet
INSTR: send to 'user@applelink'

FROM: aol
TO: compuserve
RECIPIENT: 71234,567
CONTACT: Internet
INSTR: send to '71234.567@cis'

FROM: aol
TO: genie
```

The Inter-Network Mail Guide

```
RECIPIENT: user
CONTACT: Internet
INSTR: send to 'user@genie'

FROM: aol
TO: internet
RECIPIENT: user@domain
CONTACT: Internet
INSTR: send to 'user@domain'

FROM: applelink
TO: bitnet
RECIPIENT: user@site
INSTR: send to 'user@site.bitnet@internet#'

FROM: applelink
TO: internet
RECIPIENT: user@domain
INSTR: send to 'user@domain@internet#' (address must be < 35 characters)

FROM: arcom
TO: internet
RECIPIENT: fred@Domain.dd.uu.us
INSTR: send to:
  PN=/C=ch/O=inet/ADMD=SWITCHgate/DDA=RFC-822=fred(a)Domain.dd.uu.us

FROM: att
TO: bitnet
RECIPIENT: user@site
INSTR: send to 'internet!site.bitnet!user'

FROM: att
TO: internet
RECIPIENT: user@domain
INSTR: send to 'internet!domain!user'

FROM: bitnet
TO: internet
RECIPIENT: user@domain
INSTR: Methods for sending mail from Bitnet to the Internet vary depending on
  what mail software is running at the Bitnet site in question. In the
  best case, you should simply be able to send mail to 'user@domain'.
  If this doesn't work, try 'user%domain@gateway' where 'gateway' is a
  Bitnet-Internet gateway site nearby. Finally, if neither of these
  works, you may have to try hand-coding an SMTP envelope for your mail.

FROM: calvacom
TO: fax
RECIPIENT: (1) 41 08 11 99
INSTR: send to 'TLC/41081199'
INSTR: use standard phone numbers as calling from Paris, France.
```

```
FROM: calvacom
TO: internet
RECIPIENT: user@domain
CONTACT: postmaster@calvacom.fr
INSTR: send to 'EM/user@domain'

FROM: calvacom
TO: easylink
RECIPIENT: number
CONTACT: 19000600
INSTR: send to 'ML/number'
INSTR: Calvacom professional account needed.

FROM: compuserve
TO: fax
RECIPIENT: +1 415 555 1212
INSTR: send to '>FAX 14155551212'
INSTR: not transitive - message must originate from a CompuServe user
INSTR: for calls outside the NANP, use '011' as the international prefix

FROM: compuserve
TO: internet
RECIPIENT: user@domain
INSTR: send to '>INTERNET:user@domain' (only from CompuServe users)

FROM: compuserve
TO: mci
RECIPIENT: 123-4567
INSTR: send to '>MCIMAIL:123-4567' (only from CompuServe users)

FROM: connect
TO: internet
RECIPIENT: user@domain
INSTR: send to 'DASN'
       and set the first line of message: '"user@domain"@DASN'

FROM: easylink
TO: calvacom
RECIPIENT: JS10 (John Smith)
INSTR: send to '19000600 /ATTN JS10 SMITH+'

FROM: easynet
TO: bitnet
RECIPIENT: user@site
CONTACT: DECWRL::ADMIN
INSTR: send to 'nm%DECWRL::"user@site.bitnet"' (from VMS using NMAIL)
INSTR: send to 'user@site.bitnet' (from Ultrix)
INSTR:    or to 'user%site.bitnet@decwrl.dec.com' (from Ultrix via IP)
INSTR:    or to 'DECWRL::"user@site.bitnet"' (from Ultrix via DECN)
```

```
FROM: easynet
TO: fidonet
RECIPIENT: john smith at 1:2/3.4
CONTACT: DECWRL::ADMIN
INSTR: send to 'nm%DECWRL::"john.smith@p4.f3.n2.z1.fidonet.org"'
       (from VMS using NMAIL)
INSTR: send to 'john.smith@p4.f3.n2.z1.fidonet.org'
       (from Ultrix)
INSTR: or to '"john.smith%p4.f3.n2.z1.fidonet.org"@decwrl.dec.com'
       (from Ultrix via IP)
INSTR: or to 'DECWRL::"john.smith@p4.f3.n2.z1.fidonet.org"'
       (from Ultrix via DECN)

FROM: easynet
TO: internet
RECIPIENT: user@domain
CONTACT: DECWRL::ADMIN
INSTR: send to 'nm%DECWRL::"user@domain"' (from VMS using NMAIL)
INSTR: send to 'user@domain' (from Ultrix)
INSTR:   or to 'user%domain@decwrl.dec.com' (from Ultrix via IP)
INSTR:   or to 'DECWRL::"user@domain"' (from Ultrix via DECN)
INSTR:   or to 'user@domain @Internet' (using ALL-IN-1)

FROM: envoy
TO: internet
RECIPIENT: user@domain
CONTACT: ICS.TEST or ICS.BOARD
INSTR: send to '[RFC-822="user(a)domain"]INTERNET/TELEMAIL/US'
INSTR: for special characters, use @=(a), !=(b), _=(u),
INSTR:             any=(three octal digits)

FROM: fax
TO: calvacom
RECIPIENT: JS10 (John Smith)
INSTR: send to '+33 1 41 08 11 99'
INSTR: and write on every page 'ATTN JS10 SMITH'
INSTR: faxes are manually processed.

FROM: fidonet
TO: internet
RECIPIENT: user@machine.site.domain
INSTR: convert to 'user@machine.site.domain ON 1:1/31'

FROM: fidonet
TO: wwivnet
RECIPIENT: number@node
CONTACT: Kevin C. ON 1:100/215
INSTR: convert to '#number @node ON 1:100/215'
```

```
INSTR: WWIVgate; LOW TRAFFIC SITE, USE SPARINGLY.  Gateway is modem-based,
       they absorb cost of long-distance connects to pickup and deliver.
       Keep messages under 10K, use infrequently, do NOT use mail-lists or
       file/list-server commands.

FROM: genie
TO: internet
RECIPIENT: user@domain
CONTACT: postmaster@genie.geis.com
INSTR: send to 'user@domain@INET#'

FROM: geonet
TO: internet
RECIPIENT: user@domain
INSTR: send to 'DASN'
INSTR: set subject line to 'user@domain!subject'

FROM: gold-400
TO: internet
RECIPIENT: user@host
INSTR: send to '/DD.RFC-822=user(a)host/O=uknet/PRMD=uk.ac/ADMD=gold 400/C=GB/'
INSTR: for special characters, use @=(a), %=(p), !=(b), "=(q)

FROM: gsfcmail
TO: internet
RECIPIENT: user@domain
CONTACT: cust.svc
INSTR: send to '(SITE:SMTPMAIL,ID:<user(a)domain>)'
INSTR: or to '(C:USA,A:TELEMAIL,P:SMTPMAIL,ID:<user(a)domain>)'
INSTR: or send to 'POSTMAN'
       and set the first line of message to 'To: user@domain'
INSTR: Help is also available by phoning +1 800 858 9947.

FROM: gsfcmail
TO: nsi
RECIPIENT: host::user
CONTACT: cust.svc
INSTR: send to '(SITE:SMTPMAIL,ID:<user(a)host.DN.NASA.GOV>)'
INSTR: or to '(C:USA,A:TELEMAIL,P:SMTPMAIL,ID:<user(a)host.DN.NASA.GOV>)'
INSTR: or send to 'POSTMAN'
       and set the first line of message to 'To: user@host.DN.NASA.GOV'

FROM: ibmmail
TO: internet
RECIPIENT: "userid@domain"
INSTR: imbed the following lines in messages sent from IBMMAIL and address
  the message to IBMMAIL(INTERNET)
  /INTERNET
```

The Inter-Network Mail Guide

```
/TO userid1@domain
/CC userid2@domain
/REPORT
/END
```

```
FROM: internet
TO: alternex
RECIPIENT: user
CONTACT: suporte@ax.apc.org or +55 (21) 286-0348
INSTR: send to 'user@ax.apc.org'
```

```
FROM: internet
TO: aol
RECIPIENT: A User
CONTACT: postmaster@aol.com
INSTR: send to auser@aol.com (all lowercase, remove spaces)
INSTR: msgs are truncated to 32K (8K for PCs), all characters except newline
       & printable ASCII characters are mapped to spaces, users are limited to
       75 pieces of Internet mail in their mailbox at a time.
```

```
FROM: internet
TO: applelink
RECIPIENT: user
INSTR: send to 'user@applelink.apple.com'
```

```
FROM: internet
TO: arcom
RECIPIENT: fred@swissbox.inet.ch
INSTR: send to:
  /DDA=SYS=11000/DDA=UFD=TSC000/G=/PN=fred/O=swissbox/A=arCom/C=CH/
```

```
FROM: internet
TO: att
RECIPIENT: user
INSTR: send to 'user@attmail.com'
```

```
FROM: internet
TO: bitnet
RECIPIENT: user@site
INSTR: send to 'user%site.bitnet@gateway' where 'gateway' is a gateway host
       that is on both the internet and bitnet.  Some examples of gateways
       are: cunyvm.cuny.edu mitvma.mit.edu.  Check first to see what local
       policies are concerning inter-network forwarding.
```

```
FROM: internet
TO: bix
RECIPIENT: user
INSTR: send to 'user@bix.com'
```

```
FROM: internet
TO: bmug
RECIPIENT: John Smith or John J. Smith
CONTACT: Email the director: Steve_Costa@bmug.org or phone (510)849-BMUG
INSTR: send to 'John.Smith@bmug.org'  or 'John_J_Smith@bmug.org'

FROM: internet
TO: calvacom
RECIPIENT: JS10 (John Smith)
INSTR: send to 'js10@calvacom.fr'
INSTR: msgs are limited to 100 000 chars each.

FROM: internet
TO: chasque
RECIPIENT: user
CONTACT: apoyo@chasque.apc.org or +598 (2) 496192
INSTR: send to 'user@chasque.apc.org'

FROM: internet
TO: comlink
RECIPIENT: user
CONTACT: support@oln.comlink.apc.org or +49 (511) 350-3081
INSTR: send to 'user@oln.comlink.apc.org'

FROM: internet
TO: compuserve
RECIPIENT: 71234,567
INSTR: send to '71234.567@CompuServe.com'
INSTR:   Ordinary Compuserve account IDs are pairs of octal numbers

FROM: internet
TO: compuserve
RECIPIENT: organization:department:user
INSTR: send to 'user@department.organization.compuserve.com'
INSTR:   This syntax is for use with members of organizations which have a
        private CompuServe mail area.  'department' may not always be present.

FROM: internet
TO: connect
RECIPIENT: NAME
INSTR: send to 'NAME@connectinc.com'

FROM: internet
TO: easylink
RECIPIENT: user mail number 1234567
INSTR: send to: 1234567@eln.attmail.com

FROM: internet
TO: easynet
RECIPIENT: HOST::USER
CONTACT: admin@decwrl.dec.com
```

```
INSTR: send to 'user@host.enet.dec.com'
INSTR:   or to 'user%host.enet@decwrl.dec.com'

FROM: internet
TO: easynet
RECIPIENT: John Smith @ABC
CONTACT: admin@decwrl.dec.com
INSTR: send to 'John.Smith@ABC.MTS.DEC.COM'
INSTR:   this syntax is for sending mail to ALL-IN-1 users

FROM: internet
TO: econet
RECIPIENT: user
CONTACT: support@igc.apc.org or +1 (415) 442-0220
INSTR: send to 'user@igc.apc.org

FROM: internet
TO: ecuanex
RECIPIENT: user
CONTACT: intercom@ecuanex.apc.org or +593 (2) 505 074
INSTR: send to 'user@ecuanex.apc.org'

FROM: internet
TO: envoy
RECIPIENT: John Smith (ID=userid)
INSTR: send to 'uunet.uu.net!att!attmail!mhs!envoy!userid'

FROM: internet
TO: fidonet
RECIPIENT: john smith at 1:2/3.4
INSTR: send to 'john.smith@p4.f3.n2.z1.fidonet.org'

FROM: internet
TO: genie
RECIPIENT: user
CONTACT: postmaster@genie.geis.com
INSTR: send to 'user@genie.geis.com'

FROM: internet
TO: geonet
RECIPIENT: user at host
INSTR: send to 'user@host.geonet.de'
INSTR: geo1 (Europe), geo2 (UK), geo4 (USA)

FROM: internet
TO: glasnet
RECIPIENT: user
CONTACT: support@glas.apc.org or +7 (095) 217-6182
INSTR: send to 'user@glas.apc.org'
```

```
FROM: internet
TO: gold-400
RECIPIENT: (G:John, I:Q, S:Smith, OU: org_unit, O:organization, PRMD:prmd)
INSTR: send to 'john.q.smith@org_unit.org.prmd.gold-400.gb'
INSTR:   or to
  '"/G=John/I=Q/S=Smith/OU=org_unit/O=org/PRMD=prmd/ADMD=gold 400/C=GB/"
  @mhs-relay.ac.uk'

FROM: internet
TO: goldgate
RECIPIENT: 10087:CQQ061
INSTR: send to '10087.CQQ061@goldgate.ac.uk'
INSTR:   or to '/G=10087/S=CQQ061/P=uk.ac/O=GoldGate/C=GB/'

FROM: internet
TO: greennet
RECIPIENT: user
CONTACT: support@gn.apc.org or +44 (71) 608-3040
INSTR: user@gn.apc.org     (or user@gn.uucp if mailing from JANET)

FROM: internet
TO: gsfcmail
RECIPIENT: user
CONTACT: naic@nasa.gov
INSTR: send to 'user@gsfcmail.nasa.gov'
INSTR:   or to '/PN=user/ADMD=TELEMAIL/PRMD=GSFC/O=GSFCMAIL/C=US/
          @x400.msfc.nasa.gov'

FROM: internet
TO: ibm
RECIPIENT: user@vmnode.tertiary_domain (syntax?)
CONTACT: nic@vnet.ibm.com
INSTR: send to 'user@vmnode.tertiary_domain.ibm.com'
INSTR: To look up a user's mailbox name, mail to nic@vnet.ibm.com with
  the line 'WHOIS name' in the message body.

FROM: internet
TO: ibmmail
RECIPIENT: ccsssuuu@IBMMAIL.COM
CONTACT: IBMMAIL(ccsssuuu)
INSTR: send to ccsssuuu@ibmmail.com
  cc=country code, sss=company site, uuu=unique number (alphanumeric base 35
  <36?> number) together this form the "userid" for ibmmail.

FROM: internet
TO: keylink
RECIPIENT: (G:John, I:Q, S:Smith, O:MyOrg, A:Telememo, C:au)
CONTACT: aarnet@aarnet.edu.au
INSTR: send to John.Q.Smith@MyO~g.telememo.au
```

```
INSTR: for keylink Private Mail Domains such as
INSTR:   (G:John, S:Smith, O:MyDept, P:AusGov, A:Telememo, C:au)
INSTR:   send to John.Smith@MyDept.AusGov.telememo.au

FROM: internet
TO: mausnet
RECIPIENT: hans schmidt @ box
CONTACT: postmaster@hb.maus.de
INSTR: send to 'hans_schmidt@box.maus.de'

FROM: internet
TO: mci
RECIPIENT: John Smith (123-4567)
INSTR: send to '1234567@mcimail.com'
INSTR: or to 'JSmith@mcimail.com' (if 'JSmith' is unique)
INSTR: or to 'John_Smith@mcimail.com' (if 'John Smith' is unique - note the
       underscore!)
INSTR: or to 'John_Smith/1234567@mcimail.com' (if 'John Smith' is NOT unique)

FROM: internet
TO: nasamail
RECIPIENT: user
CONTACT: naic@nasa.gov
INSTR: send to 'user@nasamail.nasa.gov'
INSTR: Help is available by phoning +1 205 544 1771 or +1 800 858 9947.
INSTR: Also get the document: ftp.jsc.nasa.gov:/pub/emaddr.txt

FROM: internet
TO: nicarao
RECIPIENT: user
CONTACT: support@nicarao.apc.org or +505 (2) 26228
INSTR: send to 'user@nicarao.apc.org'

FROM: internet
TO: nordnet
RECIPIENT: user
CONTACT: support@pns.apc.org or +46 (8) 600-0331
INSTR: send to 'user@pns.apc.org'

FROM: internet
TO: nsi
RECIPIENT: host::user
CONTACT: naic@nasa.gov
INSTR: send to 'user@host.dnet.nasa.gov'
INSTR:   or to 'user%host.dnet@ames.arc.nasa.gov'
INSTR:   or to 'user%host.dnet@east.gsfc.nasa.gov'
INSTR: Help is also available by phoning +1 800 858 9947.
```

```
FROM: internet
TO: omnet
RECIPIENT: user
CONTACT: /dd.un=omnet.service/c=us/admd=telemail/o=omnet/@sprint.com
INSTR: send to '/dd.un=user/o=omnet/admd=telemail/c=us/@sprint.com'
INSTR: Help is available by phoning +1 617 244 4333

FROM: internet
TO: peacenet
RECIPIENT: user
CONTACT: support@igc.org
INSTR: send to 'user@igc.apc.org'

FROM: internet
TO: pegasus
RECIPIENT: user
CONTACT: support@peg.apc.org or +61 (7) 2571111
INSTR: send to 'user@peg.apc.org'

FROM: internet
TO: prodigy
RECIPIENT: user
CONTACT: postmaster@prodigy.com
INSTR: send to 'userid@prodigy.com'         For example: abcd01a@prodigy.com

FROM: internet
TO: pronet
RECIPIENT: user
CONTACT: support@pronet.com or +61 3 349-1719 (Brian Evans)
INSTR: send to 'user@tanus.oz.au'

FROM: internet
TO: sinet
RECIPIENT: node::user or node1::node::user
INSTR: send to 'user@node.SINet.SLB.COM'
INSTR:   or to 'user%node@node1.SINet.SLB.COM'

FROM: internet
TO: sprintmail
RECIPIENT: John Smith at SomeOrganization
INSTR: send to
  '/G=John/S=Smith/O=SomeOrganization/ADMD=TELEMAIL/C=US/@Sprint.COM'
  Help is available by phoning +1 800 827 4685

FROM: internet
TO: telecom
RECIPIENT: user
CONTACT: support@pronet.com or +61 3 349-1719 (Brian Evans)
INSTR: send to 'user@viatel.pronet.com'
INSTR: User mailboxes consist of a 9 digit number.
INSTR: Eg: the postmaster at viatel could be reached
```

The Inter-Network Mail Guide

```
INSTR: at 010000003@viatel.pronet.com. User mailbox
INSTR: queries can be directed to: postmaster@viatel.pronet.com

FROM: internet
TO: thenet
RECIPIENT: user@host
INSTR: send to 'user%host.decnet@utadnx.cc.utexas.edu'

FROM: internet
TO: web
RECIPIENT: user
CONTACT: spider@web.apc.org or +1 (416) 596-0212
INSTR: send to 'user@web.apc.org

FROM: internet
TO: wwivnet
RECIPIENT: number@node
CONTACT: faq-request@tfsquad.mn.org or bryen@tfsquad.mn.org
INSTR: convert to 'number-node@wwiv.tfsquad.mn.org'
INSTR: WWCPgate; LOW TRAFFIC SITE, USE SPARINGLY. Gateway is modem-based,
       they absorb cost of long distance connects to pick-up and deliver.
       Keep messages under 10K, use infrequently, do NOT use mail-lists or
       file/list-server commands.

FROM: keylink
TO: internet
RECIPIENT: John Smith <user@domain>
CONTACT: (G:CUSTOMER, S:SERVICE, O:CUST.SERVICE, P:telememo, C:au)
INSTR: send to '(C:au, A:telememo, P:oz.au, "RFC-822":"John Smith
   <user(a)domain>")'
INSTR: special characters must be mapped: @->(a), %->(p), !->(b), "->(q)

FROM: mausnet
TO: internet
RECIPIENT: user@domain
CONTACT: sysop@k2
INSTR: send to 'user@domain'

FROM: mci
TO: compuserve
RECIPIENT: John Smith (71234,567)
CONTACT: 267-1163 (MCI Help)
INSTR: at the 'To:' prompt type 'John Smith (EMS)'
INSTR: at the 'EMS:' prompt type 'compuserve'
INSTR: at the 'Mbx:' prompt type '71234,567'

FROM: mci
TO: internet
RECIPIENT: John Smith <user@domain>
CONTACT: 267-1163 (MCI Help)
INSTR: at the 'To:' prompt type 'John Smith (EMS)'
```

```
INSTR: at the 'EMS:' prompt type 'INTERNET'
INSTR: at the 'Mbx:' prompt type 'user@domain'

FROM: nasamail
TO: internet
RECIPIENT: user@domain
CONTACT: admin
INSTR: send to '(site:smtpmail,id:<user(a)domain>)'
INSTR: Help is also available by phoning +1 205 544 1771 and at 'admin/nasa'.

FROM: nasamail
TO: nsi
RECIPIENT: host::user
CONTACT: admin
INSTR: send to '(site:smtpmail,id:<user(a)host.DN.NASA.GOV>)'
INSTR: Help is also available by phoning +1 205 544 1771 and at 'admin/nasa'.

FROM: nsi
TO: gsfcmail
RECIPIENT: user
CONTACT: naic@nasa.gov
INSTR: send to 'east::"user@gsfcmail.nasa.gov"'
INSTR: or to 'east::"/PN=user/ADMD=TELEMAIL/PRMD=GSFC/O=GSFCMAIL/C=US/
       @x400.msfc.nasa.gov'
INSTR: Help is also available by phoning +1 800 858 9947.

FROM: nsi
TO: internet
RECIPIENT: user@domain
CONTACT: east::"naic@nasa.gov"
INSTR: send to 'east::"user@domain"'
INSTR: or to 'dftnic::"user@domain"'
INSTR: or to 'nssdca::in%"user@domain"'
INSTR: or to 'jpllsi::"user@domain"'
INSTR: Help is also available by phoning +1 800 858 9947.

FROM: nsi
TO: omnet
RECIPIENT: user
CONTACT: omnet.service
INSTR: send to 'east::"user@omnet.nasa.gov"'
INSTR: Help also available by phoning +1 617 244 4333 (OMN customers only)

FROM: nsi
TO: sprintmail
RECIPIENT: John Smith at SomeOrganization
CONTACT: east::"naic@nasa.gov"
INSTR: send to
   '/G=John/S=Smith/O=SomeOrganization/ADMD=TELEMAIL/C=US/@Sprint.COM'
INSTR: Help is also available by phoning +1 800 858 9947.
```

The Inter-Network Mail Guide

```
FROM: omnet
TO: internet
RECIPIENT: user@domain
CONTACT: omnet.service
INSTR: send to '(site:internet, id:<user(a)domain>)'
INSTR: Or, enter 'compose manual' at the command prompt. Choose the Internet
       address option from the menu that appears. (Option 3.)
INSTR: Help also available by phoning +1 617 244 4333

FROM: sinet
TO: internet
RECIPIENT: user@domain
INSTR: send to 'M_MAILNOW::M_INTERNET::"user@domain"'
INSTR:    or to 'M_MAILNOW::M_INTERNET::domain::user'

FROM: sprintmail
TO: internet
RECIPIENT: user@domain
INSTR: send to '(C:USA,A:TELEMAIL,P:INTERNET,"RFC-822":<user(a)domain>) DEL'
INSTR: Help available within the United States by phoning +1 800 336 0437 and
       pressing '2' on a TouchTone phone.

FROM: sprintmail
TO: nsi
RECIPIENT: host::user
INSTR: send to
       '(C:USA,A:TELEMAIL,P:INTERNET,"RFC-822":<user(a)host.DNET.NASA.GOV>) DEL'
INSTR: Help available within the United States by phoning +1 800 336 0437 and
       pressing '2' on a TouchTone phone.

FROM: thenet
TO: internet
RECIPIENT: user@domain
INSTR: send to 'UTADNX::WINS%" user@domain "'

FROM: wwivnet
TO: fidonet
RECIPIENT: First Last ON zone:node/fnet
CONTACT: 1@3469
INSTR: convert to 'First Last ON zone:node/fnet @656'
INSTR: WWIVgate; LOW TRAFFIC SITE, USE SPARINGLY. Gateway is modem-based,
       they absorb cost of long distance connects to pick-up and deliver.
       Keep messages under 10K, use infrequently, do NOT use mail-lists or
       file/list-servers commands.

FROM: wwivnet
TO: internet
RECIPIENT: user@machine.site.domain
CONTACT: faq-request@9702 or 1@9702
```

INSTR: convert to 'user#machine.site.domain@506'
       If 'user' begins with digits, begin address with a quote.
INSTR: WWCPgate; LOW TRAFFIC SITE, USE SPARINGLY. Gateway is modem-based,
       they absorb cost of long distance connects to pick-up and deliver.
       Keep messages under 10K, use infrequently, do NOT use mail-lists or
       file/list-server commands.

Index

Symbols

12-step programs, 150
3-D photography, 151
30 something, 151
80386-based computers, 151
900 telephone numbers, 151
90210, 151

A

A Course in Miracles, 284
ABC programming language, 152
abortion, 61, 144
abuse, 34
AC/DC, 29
ACA, 150
academics, 387
accordion, 152
Acorn computers, 82-84
activism, 9, 108, 153
    AR-News, 164
    AR-Talk, 164
    bisexuality, 172
    environment, 387
    feminism, 20
    gay rights, 437
    homosexuality, 153
    individualism, 23
Ada language, 385, 390
Adams, Douglas, 18
addictions, 338
addresses
    lookup services, 440
    whois services, 440
    ZIP codes, 410, 424
adoption, 9, 154, 175
Advanced Dungeons & Dragons, 321
Advanced XRay Astrophy, 437
adventure games, 87
aeronautics, 155
aerospace industry, 66
affirmative action, 16
Afghan society, 139
Africa, 154
Afro-Latin music, 122
Agenda hand-held computer, 155
Agent Orange, 35
aging, 136
agriculture, 155, 387, 404-405, 426
agroforestry, 38
AI (artificial intelligence), 66, 98, 381
AIDS, 66, 136, 156, 251, 411, 434
Aikido, 156
air pollution, 436
aircraft, 156, 406, 426
Al-Anon, 150
Alaskan culture, 15
Alcoholics Anonymous, 150
Alesis Quadraverb, 318

Allen, Woody, 19
The Allman Brothers, 157
Almanac of Events, 426
almanacs, 437
alt news groups, 6
alternative music, 24, 123
amateur radio, 28, 426, 432
America Online, 444
American culture, 143
American Mathematics Society, 415
American Philosophy Association, 426
American Stock Exchange, 54
Americans with Disabilities Act (ADA), 153
AmeriCast, 51
Amiga, 35, 45, 82, 84, 427
    Amiga Excelsior! BBS system, 218
    CD-ROM, 161
    software, 380, 383, 429
    source code, 33
Amoner magazine, 395
AMOS programming language, 161
Amos, Tori, 321
amusement parks, 418
anarchy, 32
The Andy Griffith Show, 279
anesthesiology, 434
Angband, 120
Anglicanism, 216
animals, 62, 144
    animal rights, 164
    aquariums, 10
    birds, 116, 124
    cats, 125
    chinchillas, 13
    cows, 15
    dogs, 125, 234, 299
    ferrets, 222
    fish, 112
    golden retrievers, 234
    killifish, 264
    lemmings, 23
    lemurs, 19
    pets, 124
    reptiles, 125
    veterinary medicine, 411
    wolves, 38

Animaniacs, 36
annealing, 162
Anthony, Piers, 19
antiques, 112
antivirus software (Macintosh), 396
Apollo computer systems, 85, 429
Apple Computer, 85
    Apple AUX software, 384
    Apple II software, 380, 384
    Apple2 software, 429
Application Visualization System, 71
Arabic, 321
arcade-style games, 86
archaeology, 426
archery, 10
archie, 428
    clients, 389
architecture, 10
archived software, 383-386
archives
    civics, 397
    ftp, 389
    government, 397
    Simtel 20 Ada language, 390
    USENET, 385, 388
Argentina, 15, 139, 163
artificial intelligence, 66, 98, 381
artificial life, 157
artists, 165
arts, 10, 18, 113
    fine arts, 387
    handcrafts, 117
    miniatures, 284
    model horses, 285
    origami, 304
    pictures, 12
    stage craft, 343
    stained glass, 233
    theater, 352
    woodworking, 128
Asia, 48
Asian Indians, 15
Asian-Americans, 139
assassinations, 15
Association for Computing Machinery, 75

astrology, 10, 18
astronomy, 30, 66, 134, 210, 387, 438
  Europe Space Agency, 438
  Hubble telescope, 439
  NASA, 438-439
  National Space Development Agency, 439
  National Space Science Data Center, 439
  satellite databases, 438
  space environment, 438
  space exploration, 439
astrophysics, 438
AT&T 3B systems, 145
AT&T StarServer systems, 344
Atari
  Atari Explorer Online magazine, 38
  Atari ST, 82
  Lynx, 21
  software, 384
atheism, 10
Attention Deficit Disorder, 154
audio equipment, 252
audio systems, 115, 155
Australia
  Australian National University, 111
  Australian rules football, 127
  culture, 139
  law, 397
  weather information, 441
  World Wide Web, 441
autographs, 14
automobiles, 10
  Acura, 253
  Audi, 319
  audio systems, 115
  BMW, 178
  British cars, 180
  Camaros, 221
  Corvettes, 365
  Datsun, 202
  Dodge Stealth, 208
  driving schools, 329
  Eclipse, 349
  electric vehicles, 213
  exotic automobiles, 218
  Firebirds, 221
  Fords, 225
  Honda, 253
  hot rods, 22, 243
  Infiniti, 295
  International Harvester, 258
  Italian automobiles, 260
  kit cars, 264
  Laser, 349
  Lotus, 274
  Mazda, 280
    Mazda RX7, 326
    Miata, 282
  Mitsubishi 3000GT, 208
  Mustangs, 288
  Nissan, 295, 376
  Porsche, 313
  racing, 371
  Talon, 349
  Thunderbird, 353
  Toyota
    Corolla, 355
    MR2, 286
  Volkswagens, 115
  Volvo, 367
avalanche forecasts, 441
aviation, 59, 115, 156, 336, 406, 426

B

Babylon-5, 36
backbones, 170
backgammon, 118, 430
bagpipes, 168
baking, 118
Bangladesh, 139
Banyan Vines, 42
Barney the dinosaur, 10, 36
Barry, Dave, 17
baseball, 33-34, 65, 126, 421
  major league, 284
  minor league, 284
  San Francisco Giants, 327
  Seattle Mariners, 331
  Toronto Blue Jays, 355
basketball, 126, 421
  NBA schedules, 439
Batman, 14

BBSs, 10-11, 68, 129, 348, 389
    Amiga Excelsior!, 218
    information, 395
    SFI, 438
    UNIC, 439
Beatles, 122
Beavis and Butthead, 36
beer, 11, 117, 242, 263
behavioral relationships, 435
Belgium, 141
Beverly Hills 90210, 36, 151
Bible, 143, 386, 413, 417, 427, 437
bibliographies, 433
bicycling, 116, 171-173
Bigfoot, 11
Billboard charts, 435
binary-only postings, 68
biodiversity network, 174
biofeedback, 283
biology, 38-41, 134, 371, 387, 434-435
biomechanics, 174
bionet news groups, 7
Biosym Technologies, 175
bipolar disorder, 368
bird watching, 116
birds, 124
bisexuality, 172, 175-176
bit news groups, 7
biz news groups, 7
Biz Usenet, 51
Black Crowes, 196
blindness, 42, 177
Blondie, 205
blues music, 122
boats, 117
Bolivia, 273
bolo games, 25, 430
Bond, James, 18
bondage, 232
books, 59, 112, 406, 427
    Adams, Douglas, 18
    Anthony, Piers, 19
    Bible, 143, 413, 417, 437
    Dick, Philip K., 312
    Eddings, David, 18
    Gallaci, Steve, 18
    gothic tales, 235
    Hemingway, Ernest, 306
    Holy Qur'an, 417
    in print, 437
    Kundera, Milan, 267
    Kurtz, Katherine, 12, 205
    literature, 399
    May, Julian, 283
    McCaffery, Anne, 19
    mysteries, 288
    Pratchett, Terry, 19
    reviews, 12
    Rice, Anne, 12
    technical, 13, 108
    Tolkien, J.R.R., 19, 112, 354
    Torah, 418
    Wodehouse, P.G., 19
boombox.micro.umn.edu (Gopher site), 401
Borland International software, 392
Bosnia-Hercegovina, 16, 139
Boston, 176
bowling, 33
Boy Scouts, 210
Boyler-Moore theorem prover, 298
brain injury, 350
Brazil, 139, 179
bridge, 118, 430
Briggs, Joe Bob, 262
Britain, *see* United Kingdom
Brooklyn Technical High School, 180
Bruce Springsteen, 168
Brunvand, Jan Harold, 20
Buddha, 13
Buffett, Jimmy, 18
Builder Xcessory, 181
Bulgaria, 139
Bush, Kate, 123
business, 387
    cooperatives, 13
    economics, 427
    feature stories, 53
    lawsuits, 53
    stock market, 421, 427

C

C programming language, 188
Cabot, Sebastian, 181
CADCAM, 258
Cadence Design Systems, 69
caffeine, 17

calculators, 384, 407, 432
California, 13, 441
Canada, 24, 54, 140, 397
cancer, 35, 411, 434
capital punishment, 9
careers, 427
    job openings, 52
    scientific job opportunities, 39
    see also employment
CARL (Colorado Alliance of Research Libraries) databases, 408
Carnegie Mellon University, 307
carnivorous plants, 194
cartoons
    Beavis and Butthead, 36
    Disney, 18
    Ren and Stimpy, 37
    The Simpsons, 37, 422
    Tiny Toon Adventures, 37
Catholicism, 42, 183, 184
cats, 125
caving, 184
CD-ROM, 87, 184
CDs, 122, 251, 427
    for sale, 435
    Kodak Photo CD, 310
celebrities, 63
    Allen, Woody, 19
    Buffett, Jimmy, 18
    Costello, Elvis, 214
    Elvis, 17
    Etheridge, Melissa, 280
    Harry, Deborah, 205
    Letterman, David, 19
    Limbaugh, Rush, 19, 30
    Madonna, 19
    Prince, 25
    Quayle, Dan, 17
    Stern, Howard, 18
    Zappa, Frank, 18
Celtic music, 122
censorship, 13
Center for Innovative Computer Applications, 392
Central Intelligence Agency (CIA), 27
CERT (Computer Emergency Response Team), 407
chat services, 23, 430, 434
chemical engineering, 186
chemistry, 134, 186, 387
chess, 118, 187, 409, 430
child support, 13
children, 60, 132, 304
    adoption, 9, 154
    Attention Deficit Disorder, 154
    behavior, 109
    chat service, 23
    Hyperactivity Disorder, 154
    missing, 24
    pen pals, 309
    rights, 375
Chile, 140
China, 140, 145
chinchillas, 13
Chinese, 13
Chinese chess, 430
Christian music, 122
Christianity, 43, 143, 187, 366
chronic fatigue syndrome, 24, 43
Church of Jesus Christ of Latter-day Saints, 269, 326
Church of Scientology, 13
CIA (Central Intelligence Agency), 27
Cincinnati Reds, 33
cinema, 112, 218
civics, 397
civil engineering, 135
Civil Forfeiture of Assets, 397
civil liberties, 32
civil rights, 62
Civil War, 37
clari news groups, 7
ClariNet, 51
classifieds, 108
client/server technology, 69
clients (archie), 389
Clinton administration press releases, 397, 401, 436
Clinton, Bill, 27-28
    economic plan, 397
    press releases, 401
Clipper, 14
clothing, 366
codependency, 29
The Coffee House chat service, 430
cognitive engineering, 69

cognitive science, 190-191, 300
cohousing, 191
coins, 192
collectors
    autographs, 14
    postcards, 48
Colorado Alliance of Research Libraries (CARL), 408
Colorado Rockies, 33
comedy, 399, 429
    British, 14
    Firesign Theatre, 14
    Seinfeld, Jerry, 37
comic books, 112, 192
    Batman, 14
    Cerebus, 185
    Disney, 207
    Japanese comic fanzines, 112
    Marvel Comics, 113
    O'Donnell, Peter, 285
    Superman, 14
    Tales of the Beanworld, 237
    Valiant, 364
Commodore, 395
comp news groups, 6
compact audio disc, 251
Complex Systems, 438
compression software, 381, 385, 396
CompuServe, 444
Computer Emergency Response Team, 104, 407
computer jobs in Israel, 188
computer science, 198, 387
The Computer Underground Digest, 81
computer-aided design, 13
computers, 91
    386bsd, 180
    80386-based, 151
    academic freedom, 14
    Agenda hand-held computer, 155
    Alspa, 158
    Amiga, 192, 427
    Amiga CD-ROM, 161
    anecdotes, 20
    Apollo, 85
    Apple, 85
    architecture, 67
    artificial life, 157
    AT&T, 166
    AT&T StarServer systems, 344
    AUC-TeX, 166
    Cadence Design Systems, 69
    Commodore, 395
    computer speech interfaces, 212
    Confederation of Future Computer Professionals, 185
    consultants, 14
    Cray, 101
    Data General, 206
    Decision Power, 203
    Digital Equipment Corporation, 75, 94, 203-204, 308
    Digital Signal Processing, 71
    DUAL Systems Corporation, 210
    Eastern Europe, 44
    Electronic Frontier Foundation, 394-395
    Emplant Macintosh Hardware Emulator, 215
    Encore, 252
    Epoch fileservers, 216
    Futurebus+, 229
    games, 45
    Gates, Bill, 17
    Gateway 2000, 230
    GNU, 96
    hackers, 22
    hardware, 129
    Harris systems, 86
    Hewlett-Packard, 243
    human-computer interaction, 72
    Hyperbole systems, 245
    Igor, 248
    imaging, 9
    Intel, 210
    IRC, 303
    languages, 73
    laptop computers, 89
    legal issues, 394-395
    Logo language, 273
    Macintosh, 427
    microcomputers, 388

multimedia, 75
music, 99, 287
NCR tower computers, 355
NCUBE parallel computers, 289
neural networks, 292
NeXT, 90, 100, 294
object-oriented programming, 339
PC/GEOS products, 308
Power Glove, 395
public-access computer systems, 317
sam editor, 327
security, 30, 407
Solbourne, 105, 255
storage systems, 67
Stratus Computer Corporation, 255
Sun, 91, 105, 347, 386-390
Tandem Computers, Inc., 256
Tandy, 92, 189, 350
Telebit NetBlazer products, 291
Thinking Machines, 189
Unisys products, 361
UNIX, 388, 437
user support, 9
vendors, 381
viruses, 346
Zoomer personal digital assistants, 377
see also software
Concurrent C programming language, 251
Concurrent C++ programming language, 251
Confederation of Future Computer Professionals, 185
conservatism, 32
conspiracy, 15
constitutions, 398
construction, 129
consumer issues, 60, 108
conventions, 20
cooking, *see* food
cooperatives, 13
copyrights, 397, 414
cosmetics, 129
Cosmic Encounter, 118

Costello, Elvis, 214
costume design, 240
country music, 122
cows, 15
CPM software, 384, 390
Cray computers, 101
cricket, 126
crimes, 62
    assassinations, 15
    capital punishment, 9
    missing children, 24
    prisons, 28
    sexual abuse, 32
    stolen merchandise postings, 53
Croatia, 140
Croatian, 301
cryonics, 134, 197
CSAA, 197
CSI MacForth programming environment, 98
cults (movies), 15
Cyber-Sleaze Report, 430
cyberculture, 228
CyberEden, 430
cyberpunk, 223
cyberspace, 16, 28, 399
Cygnus Corporation software, 389
Czechoslovakia, 354, 442

D

daily events, 302
Dall'Agata, Michele, 17
dance music, 359
dancing, 117, 169
Dark Shadows, 333
Dartmouth Library, 427
darts, 33
data analysis, 387
data compression, 69
databases, 173
    bibliographies, 433
    CARL, 408
    Clipper, 14
    ECHO, 407
    Extragalactic Database (NASA), 420, 439
    government, 436
    ILC, 408

information, 381
satellites, 438
dating services
    Matchmaker by E-mail, 434
    personals, 26
Davenport Beach chat service, 430
DECathena, 16, 52
DECNews, 52
defense, 66, 334
Democrats, 317
dentistry, 136
dependency, 29
depression, 368
Desert Storm, 16
desktop publishing
    CD-ROM, 184
    FrameMaker, 92, 227
    PageMaker, 305
deviants, 206
diabetes, 109
Dick, Philip K., 312
dictionaries, 382, 441
Digex, 52
Digital Equipment Corporation, 43, 75, 94, 308
Digital Imaging and Communcations, 80
dining out, 117
dinosaurs, 206
Diplomacy game, 118, 431
disaster information, 441
discrimination, 16
diseases
    AIDS, 156, 411
    cancer, 434
    multiple sclerosis, 35
    see also medicine
Disney, 113, 207
Disney, Walt, 18
distribution software, 385
DNS (Domain Name Service), 443
dogs, 38, 125, 234, 299
Domain Name Service, *see* DNS
domestic partners, 208
Dominican Republic, 264, 331
Down Syndrome, 209
Dr. Who, 113
drag racing, 209
dreams, 17
driving schools, 329

drugs, 17, 109, 145
    caffeine, 17
    crime, 63
    endorphins, 215
    Food and Drug Administration, 411
    marijuana, 22
drum and bugle corps, 113
ds.internic.net (Internet ftp site), 393
Dutch literature, 41
Dylan, Bob, 123

E

e-mail, 146
    ftp, 429
    GopherMail, 432
    Macintosh, 396
    Matchmaker by E-mail, 434
E-Math, 437
earth science, 210
earthquakes, 419, 425, 431, 441
Eastern Europe, 44
Eastern religions, 144
ECHO (European Commission Host Organization)
    databases, 407, 427
ecology, 134, 135
economics, 53, 134, 211, 381, 387, 427
    Clinton, Bill, 397
    NAFTA (North American Free Trade Agreement), 398
    politics, 27
    stock market, 421, 427
editors, 381
education, 17, 44, 106-108, 135, 387, 408, 428
    academic software, 386-390
    artificial intelligence, 98
    driving schools, 329
    English grammar, 37
    graduate schools, 138
    history, 432
    home education, 242
    International Baccalaureate Diploma Program, 246
    law schools, 46
    learning processes, 269

library catalogues, 432
mathematics, 428, 437
medical, 434
physics, 48
religion, 388
Russian studies, 388
scholarships, 428
student government, 49
telecommunications, 428
Eiffel language, 73
electric vehicles, 213
electromagnetics, 213
Electronic Frontier Foundation, 75, 386, 394-395
Electronic Library, 414
Electronic Night Club, 430
electronics, 66, 135
amateur radio, 28, 426, 432
Elvis, 17
embedded computer system engineering, 214
Emerson, Lake & Palmer, 214
Emplant Macintosh Hardware Emulator, 215
employment, 109
domestic partners, 208
homosexuality, 296
job listings, 129, 146, 427
strikes, 62
Encore computers, 252
endometriosis, 372
endorphins, 215
energy, 438
engineering, 10, 135, 387
England, *see* United Kingdom
English, 50
English grammar, 37
entertainment industry, 60
environment, 16, 30, 66, 135, 144, 334, 387
air pollution, 436
nuclear energy, 438
space, 438
epilepsy, 434
equestrians, 117, 243
Escher, M.C., 18
Esperanto, 102
Estonia, 214
Etheridge, Melissa, 280
ethics, 145
ethology, 217
etiquette advice, 55

Europe, 47
Europe Space Agency, 438
European Commission Host Organization (ECHO), 427
European Space Organization, 420
Maastricht Treaty of European Union, 398
satellite TV, 30
Everton Football Club, 217
evolution, 144
exercise, 108
explosives, 17
Extragalactic database (NASA), 439
Extropian philosophy, 219

F

FairCom, 198
family, 9, 426
adoptions, 9
child-support, 13
genealogy, 409-410
parent/teen relationships, 26
paternal rights, 16, 44
stepparents, 35
farming, 387, 404-405, 426
FASE (Forum for Academic Software Engineering), 220
fashion, 20, 63
pantyhose, 26
supermodels, 34
faxes, 70, 428
Federal Information Exchange, 410
feminism, 20, 143, 221, 270
ferrets, 222
fiction, 113
FidoNet area, 130
film production, 222
finances, 53-54, 109
fine arts, 387
finger database, 427
firearms, 103, 121, 145, 181, 222, 359
Firesign Theatre, 14
fishing, 20, 124
flags, 223

flight simulation, 87, 167
floods, 422, 441
Florida, 223
folk dancing, 224
folk music, 123, 225
folklore, 20
food, 117, 129, 426
    baking, 118
    cereal, 13
    dining out, 117
    fat-free, 20
    ketchup, 23
    McDonald's, 20, 24
    recipes, 21, 416-417, 437-438
    universities, 14
    vegetarianism, 118, 220, 365
Food and Drug Administration, 410
football, 34, 65, 421
    Australian rules, 127
    collegiate, 65, 127
    Everton Football Club, 217
    NFL scores, 439
    Raiders, 320
FootHills chat service, 430
forest management planning, 226
forestry, 38
FORTRAN, 73
four-wheeling, 301
FrameMaker, 92, 227
France, 140
Franz Lisp programming language, 99
Free Software Foundation, 380, 384, 388
French, 107
Frequently Asked Questions, 391
ftp, 428-429
ftp sites, 380-399
fun, 399
    practical jokes, 32
    quotes, 409
    tasteless jokes, 35
    see also recreation
funk music, 123, 229
Futurebus+, 229

G

Galactic Bloodshed, 21
Gallacci, Steve, 18
games
    adventure, 87
    Angband, 120
    arcade-style, 86
    Atari Lynx, 21
    backgammon, 118, 430
    bolo, 25, 430
    bridge, 118, 430
    Chaosium, 186
    chess, 118, 187, 409, 430
    Chinese chess, 430
    computer, 45
    Cosmic Encounter, 118
    Crossfire, 196
    cyberpunk, 223
    Diplomacy, 118, 431
    Galactic Bloodshed, 21
    game theory, 308
    Harpoon, 199
    juggling, 121
    math puzzles, 246
    Moria, 119, 431
    Mortal Kombat!, 21
    Multiuser Dungeons, 409
    NetHack, 409, 431
    Netrek, 120
    Nintendo, 120
    Nintendo PowerGlove, 233
    Omega, 21
    Othello, 431
    Paintball, 127
    pinball, 120
    Play by Mail, 120
    poker, 169
    robot, 119
    Rogue, 120
    role-playing, 87, 118, 235, 291, 325, 334, 355-357, 364
    Sega, 120
    Sega Genesis, 30
    SFB, 343
    software, 381
    Street Fighter 2, 21
    Tetris, 409, 431
    Text Adventures, 431
    TORG, 21
    VGA Planets, 21

Warhammer Universe, 368
Xpilot, 21
see also sports
GAO, 397-398, 401
gardening, 121
    bonsai trees, 112, 178
    carnivorous plants, 194
Gates, Bill, 17
Gay/Lesbian/Bisexual Librarians Network, 230
gender issues, 143, 176, 184, 221, 231-232, 270, 277, 356
genealogy, 144, 325, 409-410
General Accounting Office, 397
generation X, 32
genetics, 39, 435
GEnie, 444
Genomic Database, 435
Geographic Information Systems, 72
geography, 231, 387, 410, 425, 431
geology, 135, 387, 425, 431
geophysics, 438, 441
German, 106, 140
ghost stories, 20
Global Jewish Information Network, 262
Global News Navigator, 436
GNU, 95
GNU Emacs Lisp programmers' manual, 234
gnu news groups, 7
GNU Project, 252
God Street Wine, 222
Godel, 18
golf, 127
Gopher, 21, 31-43
    client/server software, 146, 385, 389
    information service, 72
    Gopher sites, 399-400
GopherMail, 432
gophers (psychology), 437
gothic issues, 235, 321
gothic movement, 21
government, 45, 398, 414
    CIA, 27
    Clinton press releases, 401
    Clinton's economic plan, 397
    databases, 436
    departments, 403
    document access, 436
    environment, 16, 30, 387, 436
    fairness, 219
    Federal Information Exchange, 410
    Food and Drug Administration, 410
    international constitutions, 398
    Library of Congress, 439
    NAFTA (North American Free Trade Agreement), 398, 401
    NATO press releases, 398
    nuclear energy, 438
    offices, 403
    policies, 160
    political candidates (Iowa), 436
    political platforms, 398
    press releases, 436
    resistance, 32
    speeches, 398
    student government, 49
    Supreme Court rulings, 383
    taxes, 61
    Texas, 437
    United Nations resolutions, 398
    White House press releases, 397, 436
GPS (USAF Global Positioning System), 235
grammar, 37
graphics, 91, 383
GRASS geographic information system, 103
Grateful Dead, 123
Great Lakes, 21
Greece, 140
Greek letter societies, 338
Green party, 27
grunge rock, 235
GUIs
    Builder Xcessory, 181
    Motif, 101
    Open Look, 95
    Picasso, 311
guitars, 22, 123, 416, 435
Guns 'n' Roses, 29
gymnastics, 237

H

hackers, 22
ham radio, 426, 432
Hammill, Peter, 310
handcrafts, 117
hang gliding, 238
hardware, 67, 74, 87, 129
    Amiga, 84
    Applebus, 80
    CADCAM, 258
    compact audio disc, 251
    floating-point correctness, 299
    microchannel hardware, 88
    networks, 87
    publishing, 80
Harley-Davidson motorcycles, 122, 239
Harper, Roy, 345
Harpoon, 199
Harris computer systems, 86
Harry, Deborah, 205
Hawaii
    culture, 15
    legislative information, 433
health, 411, 426
Hemingway, Ernest, 306
Hendrix, Jimi, 239
hep news groups, 7
herbs, 20
Hermes language, 73
Hewlett-Packard, 243
    calculators, 407, 432
    software, 384
Hinduism, 22, 45, 239
history, 45, 134, 143, 388, 411, 432
    Civil War, 37
    Desert Storm, 16
    genealogy, 409-410
    Holocaust, 241, 437
    living history, 22
    treaties, 398
    U.S. documents, 398
    U.S. speeches, 398
    United Kingdom, 412
    Vietnam War, 37
    wars, 37
Hitchcock, Robyn, 221
hobbies
    aquariums, 10
    autographs, 14
    automobiles, 10
    comics, 14
    fishing, 20
    postcards, 48
    sewing, 31
    see also recreation
hockey, 65, 127, 161, 421
    Boston Bruins, 179
    collegiate hockey, 241
    Dallas Stars, 200
    East Coast Hockey League, 211
    goalie stats, 295
    Los Angeles Kings, 274
    New York Islanders, 294
    Olympic hockey, 302
    Quebec Nordiques, 319
    San Jose Sharks, 327
    St. Louis Blues, 344
    United Kingdom, 359
    Vancouver Canucks, 364
    Western Hockey League, 370
Hofstadter, Douglas, 18
holistic health care, 109
Holmes, Sherlock, 18
Holocaust, 241, 437
Holy Qur'an, 417
home education, 242
home video, 120
home-owning, 108
Homolka, Karla, 18
homosexuality, 22, 27, 45, 61, 138, 143, 153, 158, 175, 187, 209-210, 304
    addictions, 322
    AIDS, 156, 251, 437
    Australia, 166
    bears, 171
    bondage, 232
    gay rights, 437
    Gay/Lesbian/Bisexual Librarians Network, 230
    geography, 231
    Idaho Citizens Alliance, 227
    lesbianism, 169, 267, 272, 285, 327

Los Angeles, 268
Middle Ages, 280
minorities, 233, 265
New Jersey, 295
Northeast, 291
Ohio, 302
Queer Nation, 317
Stonewall 25 march, 344
United Kingdom, 360
University of Kentucky, 268
workforce, 296
Hong Kong, 140
horror, 22
horse racing, 205
hot rods, 243
housewares, 129
Houston Astros, 33
Hpcwire, 432
Hubble telescope, 134, 420, 439
human rights, 144
human-computer interaction, 72
humor, 22, 121, 132, 362, 399, 429-430
    Barry, Dave, 17
    collegiate, 20
    Seinfeld, Jerry, 37
    tasteless jokes, 35
    Wodehouse, P.G., 19
Hungarian electronic resources, 240
Hungary, 141, 349
hunting, 121
hurricanes, 441
Hyperactivity Disorder, 154
Hyperbole systems, 245
hypertext, 22
hypnosis, 22
hytelnet server, 432

I

IBM, 48
    education, 45, 428
    mainframes, 45
    software, 383-386, 388, 392
    word processing, 51
ICON programming language, 98
Idaho Citizens Alliance, 227
IEEE, 97
ieee news groups, 7
IEEE SPA system, 433
IETF (Internet Engineering Task Force), 103
ILC database, 408
Illinois State University, 313
imaging, 9
immune-system breakdowns, 249
indexing, 250
India, 23, 45, 140
Indiana University Center for Innovative Computer Applications, 392
individualism, 23
Indonesia, 15, 140
industrial music, 123
inet news groups, 7
inflammatory bowel diseases, 246
info news groups, 7
information sciences, 46
Informix database management, 69
Informix software, 254
Ingres software, 253
INMG (Inter-Network Mail Guide), 3, 443
Instrument Flight Rules, 116
instruments, *see* musical instruments
Integrated Services Digital Network (ISDN), 70
Inter-Network Mail Guide, 3, 443
interactive fiction, 113
Intergraph, 35
international
    constitutions, 398
    Maastricht Treaty of European Union, 398
    movies, 10
    music, 25
    newsletter, 50
    trade, 258
    treaties, 398
    see also world politics
International Association of Business and Commerce Students, 138
International Baccalaureate Diploma Program, 246
International Harvester, 258

International Student Society
for Neural Networks, 76
internationalized software, 257
Internet
    culture, 15
    ftp sites, 380-399
    FYI documents, 393
    Gopher sites, 399-400
    information, 382, 393-394
    Internet Engineering Task
        Force (IETF), 103
    Internet Radio Journal, 258
    Internet Resource Guide,
        382, 394
    Internet Society, 99
    libraries, 382, 414
    mailing lists, 415
    maps, 382
    Talk Radio, 386, 390
InterNIC, 402, 433
interracial relationships, 139
InterText, 259
investment, 53
INXS, 259
Iowa, 436
IP Address Resolver, 433
Iran, 140
Irish, 230
ISDN (Integrated Services
    Digital Network), 70
ISEK (International Society of
    Electrophysiological
    Kinesiology), 174
Islam, 144
Israel, 140, 442
Italian automobiles, 260
Italy, 141

J

Jane's Addiction, 260
Japan, 80, 141
    Japanese animation, 112
    Japanese popular music,
        262
    language, 136
    National Space Develop-
        ment Agency, 439
Jargon File, 261
Jarvis, Brian, 187
Jethro Tull, 104, 262
Jittlov, Mike, 19
Jo-MAAN, 103
job listings, 109, 129, 146
    see also employment
journals, 438
    AI (artificial intelligence),
        381
    biology, 39
    electronic, 435
Judaism, 61, 141, 261, 270, 437
    Holocaust, 241, 437
    music, 24
juggling, 121

K

k12 news groups, 7
Karnataka culture, 15
Kennedy, John, 15
Kentucky Governor's Scholars
    Program, 236
Keralites, 15
Kermit, 80, 396
Khoros software, 264
kites, 121, 265
knowledge acquisition
    workshops, 263
Kodak Photo CD, 310
Korea, 141
Kundera, Milan, 267
Kurt Goedel Society, 267
Kurtz, Katherine, 12, 205

L

L.A. Law, 36
labor unions, 54
languages, 388
    Ada, 385
    Chinese, 13
    computer, 73
    Croatian, 301
    Czech, 354
    dictionaries, 382
    Dutch, 41
    Esperanto, 102, 217
    French, 107
    German, 106
    Hungarian, 240, 349
    interpreters, 388

Irish, 230
Japanese, 136
Lojban, 273
Macedonian, 277
Manx, 230
Norwegian, 297
Polish, 341
Russian, 107, 129, 255, 341
Scottish Gaelic, 230
Serbian, 301
sign language, 336
Slovak, 354
Slovene, 298, 301, 311
Spanish, 107, 264, 331
see also programming
languages
Laos, 141
laptop computers, 89
laser printers, 74
laserdiscs, 37
lasertag, 33
Latin America, 141
law, 110, 360, 412-413, 433
Australia, 397
Civil Forfeiture of Assets, 397
copyright, 397
education, 46
Electronic Frontier Foundation, 394-395
enforcement, 23
Hawaii, 433
libraries, 433
state, 398
Supreme Court rulings, 383, 433
law enforcement, 63
LawNet, 433
lawsuits, 53
Leaky House chat service, 430
Lebanon, 141
Led Zeppelin, 377
legislation, 159
Americans with Disabilities Act (ADA), 153
Legos, 36
lemmings, 23
lemurs, 19
lesbianism, *see* homosexuality
Letterman, David, 19
Level 42, 270
libertarianism, 27, 182, 270

libraries, 143, 388, 413-415, 439
catalogs, 414, 432-433
Internet, 382, 414
law, 433
software, 438
Library of Congress, 414, 434
library science, 46
Liddy, G. Gordon, 18
Life Talking, 270
lifestyles, 158
Limbaugh, Rush, 19, 30
linguistics, 381
LINUX, 76
operating system, 271
software, 384, 387
Liquid TV, 36
literature, 399
Dutch, 41
Shakespeare, 413
local area networks, 70, 132
local news, 55
Lockheed special project planes, 336
locksmiths, 23
Logo language, 73, 273
Lojban, 273
lookup services, 440
Los Angeles, 268
Dodgers, 33
Kings, 274
Lucid programming language, 268
Lunar and Planetary Institute, 420
Lyme disease, 275
Lynx Real-Time Systems, 77

M

Maastricht Treaty of European Union, 398
Macedonia, 25
MacGyver, 275
MACH
operating system, 104
software, 381
Macintosh, 58, 82, 88, 108, 472
e-mail, 396
object-oriented programming, 89
security, 276

software, 383-386, 388, 391, 429
Think C compiler, 353
TopSoft user group, 354
word processing, 51
Madonna, 19
magazines, 38, 259, 399
magic, 23-24, 276
mail, 75
multimedia mail, 99
sending to/from non-Internet addresses, 444-460
mail-reading software, 385
mailing lists, 257, 415
Malaysia, 141
managing mailing lists, 272-273
Mansion II chat service, 430
Manx, 230
maps, 431
Internet, 382
weather, 423
marijuana, 22
Marillion, 227
Married...With Children, 36
martial arts, 121, 156, 278
M*A*S*H, 36
Masons, 278
Matchmaker by E-mail, 434
materials engineering, 136
mathematics, 49, 388, 415
calculators, 407
E-Math, 437
education, 428, 437
Hewlett-Packard calculators, 432
puzzles, 246
MathWorks, 81
MATLAB software, 279
May, Julian, 283
McCaffery, Anne, 19
McDonald's, 20, 24
mechanical engineering, 135
media, 25, 399
censorship, 13
telecommunications, 16
medicine, 23, 47, 66, 388
Advanced XRay Astrophy, 437
aging, 136
AIDS, 66, 136, 251, 411, 434, 437
anesthesiology, 434
biomedical engineering, 135
brain injury, 350
cancer, 35, 411, 434
chronic fatigue syndrome, 24, 43
dentistry, 136
dependency, 29
diabetes, 109
Digital Imaging and Communcations, 80
drugs, 17
education, 434
endometriosis, 372
epilepsy, 434
Food and Drug Administration, 410
genetics banks, 435
health care, 145
herbs, 20
holistic health care, 109
immune-system breakdowns, 249
inflammatory bowel diseases, 246
Lyme disease, 275
medical physics, 280
nuclear medicine, 299
nutrition, 426
paramedics, 108
veterinary medicine, 411
weight loss, 35
meditation, 24
Melrose Place, 36, 280
memetics, 24
men's issues, 143, 277
Mensa, 281
mental disabilities
children, 304
Handicap Digest, 238
mental disorders
depression, 368
panic disorders, 306
sexual abuse, 322
messages, 430
messaging systems, 435
Metallica, 29
meteorology, 281
Mexico, 141
microchannel hardware, 88
microcomputer software, 388

Microsoft
    Word, 373
    Windows applications, 50, 392
Middle Ages, 280
Middle Eastern music, 282
military, 16, 24, 63, 116, 137, 144, 209
Milwaukee Brewers, 34
mind-altering techniques, 283
miniatures, 284
MINIX, 77
Minix software, 384
Minnesota Twins, 34
Minnesota Vikings, 34
minorities, 139, 313
    discrimination, 16
    homosexuality, 233, 265
    Muslim Student Associations, 286
MIPS PC software, 388
misc news groups, 6
missing childen, 24
modeling, 121
modems, 71, 87, 348
Modesty Blaise, 285
monarchism, 193
monitors, 87
Montreal Expos, 34
Monty Python, 19
Moria, 119, 431
Mormons, 269, 326
Morris dancing, 285
Mortal Kombat!, 21
motherhood, 285
Motif GUI, 101
motorcycles, 358, 370
    BMW, 178
    British motorcycles, 180
    Harley-Davidson, 122, 239
    New England, 290
    racing, 122, 320
movies, 10, 112-113, 435
    Allen, Woody, 19
    Briggs, Joe Bob, 262
    celebrities, 63
    cults, 15
    international, 10
    James Bond, 18
    Monty Python, 19
    mysteries, 288
    reviews, 113
    The Rocky Horror Picture Show, 15, 323
    sexuality, 31
    Star Wars, 114
MS-DOS, 132
    programmers, 24
    software, 380, 390, 429
multimedia, 11, 75, 388
multimedia mail, 99
multiple sclerosis, 35
Multiuser Dungeons, 409
multiuser message systems, 435
Muppets, 36
music, 12, 24, 29, 382, 399, 415-416
    a cappella, 24, 122
    Afro-Latin, 122
    alternative, 24, 123
    bass, 170
    behavioral relationships, 435
    Billboard charts, 435
    blues, 122, 177
    Canada, 24
    Celtic, 122
    Christian, 122
    classical, 122
    collaborations, 292
    computers, 99, 287
    country and western, 122
    dance music, 359
    drum and bugle corps, 113
    European, 123
    exotic, 17
    folk music, 123, 225
    funk music, 123, 229
    grunge rock, 235
    heavy metal, 29
    homosexuality, 187
    Indian, 123
    industrial, 123
    international, 25
    Japanese popular music, 262
    Jewish, 24
    live recordings, 435
    Middle Eastern music, 282
    music videos, 124
    musical theater, 287
    New Age, 124
    newsletters, 435
    oldies, 30

rap, 28
  rave scene, 290
  reggae, 124
  reviews, 63, 292
  selling equipment, 124
  software, 337
  soundtracks, 340
musical groups
  AC/DC, 29
  Allman Brothers, 157
  Amos, Tori, 321
  Beatles, 122
  Bel Canto, 171
  Black Crowes, 196
  Blondie, 205
  Bolton, Michael, 178
  Buffett, Jimmy, 18
  Bush, Kate, 123
  Concrete Blond, 193
  Costello, Elvis, 214
  Dire Straits, 207
  Dokken, 208
  Dylan, Bob, 123
  Electric Light Orchestra, 213
  Elvis, 17
  Emerson, Lake & Palmer, 214
  Etheridge, Melissa, 280
  Gibson, Debbie, 172
  God Street Wine, 222
  Grateful Dead, 123
  Guns 'n' Roses, 29
  Hammill, Peter, 310
  Harper, Roy, 345
  Hendrix, Jimi, 239
  Hitchcock, Robyn, 221
  Indigo Girls, 250
  INXS, 259
  Jane's Addiction, 260
  Jethro Tull, 104, 262
  KLF, 266
  Led Zeppelin, 377
  Level 42, 270
  Life Talking, 270
  Lynch Mob, 208
  Madonna, 19
  Marillion, 227
  Metallica, 29
  New Zealand pop bands, 265
  O'Connor, Sinéad, 263
  On-U Sound label, 303
  Oyster, 305
  Phish, 124
  Pink Floyd, 211
  Police, 312
  Prince, 25, 315
  Queen, 25, 319
  Queensryche, 330
  Reed, Lou, 274
  REM, 322
  Rhodes, Happy, 212
  Rolling Stones, 30, 361
  Rush, 25, 326
  Smiths, 337
  Sonic Youth, 340
  Springsteen, Bruce, 168
  Sugarcubes, 346
  Tangerine Dream, 349
  Tears for Fears, 351
  They Might Be Giants, 352
  Tower of Power, 354
  Vangelis, 206
  Weller, Paul, 266
  We've Got a Fuzzbox and We're Going to Use It!!!, 230
  The Who, 352
  XTC, 186
  Yello, 375
  Zang Tuum Tumb label, 376
musical instruments, 382
  accordions, 152
  bagpipes, 168
  bass guitars, 22
  brass instruments, 179
  guitars, 22, 123, 435
  lutes, 275
  percussion, 124
Muslim Student Associations, 286
mysteries, 18
mythology, 25

N

NAFTA (North American Free Trade Agreement), 398, 401
NASA, 420
  Extragalactic Database, 420, 439
  Hubble telescope, 420

Lunar and Planetary
Institute, 420
press releases, 438-439
space exploration, 439
space shuttle launches, 419
NASDAQ reports, 54
National Park Service, 306
National Public Radio, 28
National Science Foundation,
393, 402-403
National Space Development
Agency (Japan), 439
National Space Science Data
Center, 439
NATO press releases, 398
natural disasters, 60
Navy, 289
NBA, 421, 439
NCR tower computers, 355
NCUBE parallel computers, 289
Nepal, 141
Netfind user lookup services,
440
NetHack, 409, 431
Netherlands, 141, 441
netnews
frequently asked questions,
391
software, 385
Netrek, 120
NetWare, 384
network news systems, 111
Network News Transfer
Protocol, 102
network Request For Comments
documents, 386
Network Time Protocol, 298
network trainers, 47
networks, 416
Cisco Systems, 188
hardware, 87
ParNET, 306
protocols, 382
Russia, 323
software, 382, 396
SysOp, 10
testing software, 110
wireless networks, 83
neural networks, 67, 292
International Student
Society for Neural
Networks, 76

neuroscience, 190-191
New Age music, 124
New England
motorcycles, 290
New England Community
Internet, 289
New Jersey, 174, 295
New Orleans, 293
New York
culture, 15
Islanders, 294
Mets, 34
New York State Institute for
Sebastian Cabot Studies,
181
New Zealand, 141, 265
news
electronic journals, 435
Global News Navigator,
436
NASA, 438-439
NNTP servers, 436
software, 389
USA Today, 436
USENET, 436, 439
White House press releases,
436
news groups, 5
categories, 6-7
Internet Radio Journal, 258
listings, 111
NewsCommando, 293
newsletters, 435
NeXT, 47, 90, 294
new products, 52
NeXTstep computing
environment, 100
software, 380, 384, 392
NFL (National Football League),
421, 439
NHL (National Hockey League),
421
Nielsen ratings, 436
Nintendo, 120
Nintendo PowerGlove, 233
Nixon, Richard, 25
NNTP news servers, 436
NOC tools, 99
non-monogamous
relationships, 357
Nordic skiing, 296
North Africa, 141

Northern Exposure, 36
Northwestern University, 104, 299
Norwegian, 297
Notesfile software, 111
Novell LAN, 47
Novell NetWare software, 384
NSF statistics, 386
nuclear energy, 438
nuclear medicine, 299
nuclear power, 66
nudism, 124
nutrition, 426
  fat-free foods, 20
  Food and Drug Administration, 410
NYSE reports, 54

O

oak.oakland.edu, 390-391
object-oriented programming, 73-75, 89, 324, 339
Objective-C programming language, 300
Objectivism, 300
Oceanic Information Center, 441
O'Connor, Sinéad, 263
O'Donnell, Peter, 285
Ohio, 302
Ohio State University, 228
Olohof's BBS chat service, 430
Olympic games, 65, 127, 302
Omega, 21
On-U Sound label, 303
Open Look GUI, 95
Open Software Foundation, 93
operating systems
  LINUX, 271
  Mach, 104
  QNX, 318
  UNIX, 204
  VxWorks, 79
  XINU, 79
Oracle (USENET), 436
Oregon, 15, 309
Oregon Citizens' Alliance, 303
O'Reilly and Associates, 52

organizations
  American Philosophy Association, 426
  Association for Computing Machinery, 75
  Computer Science and Telecommunciations Board, 198
  Computer Users in the Social Sciences, 199
  Confederation of Future Computer Professionals, 185
  Dead Runners Society, 203
  Electronic Frontier Foundation, 75
  Global Jewish Information Network, 262
  Greek letter societies, 338
  IEEE, 97
  IETF (Internet Engineering Task Force), 103
  Kurt Goedel Society, 267
  Masons, 278
  Muslim Student Associations, 286
  New England Community Internet, 289
  New York State Institute for Sebastian Cabot Studies, 181
  Oregon Citizens' Alliance, 303
  Society for Creative Anachronism, 124, 328
  Space Studies Institute, 342
  Women in Science and Engineering, 105
  Young Scientists' Network, 376
orienteering, 303
origami, 304
OS/2, 47, 78
OS/9 software, 384
Othello, 431
Overeaters Anonymous, 150
Oyster, 305
OZONE, 47

P

Pac Ten sports, 305
paganism, 26, 305
PageMaker, 48, 305
Paintball, 127
Pakistan, 142
Palestine, 142
panic disorders, 306
pantyhose, 26
paramedics, 108
parapsychology, 335
  out-of-body experiences, 25
parenting, 35, 154
park rangers, 306
Parker Lewis, 223
ParNET, 306
particles, 438
Pascal programming language, 130
patents, 383, 398
PBL, 307
PC Magazine, 396
PC/GEOS products, 308
PCs, 429
peace corps, 51
pen pals, 143, 309
PenPoint software, 384
periodic tables, 438
Perot, Ross, 27
PERQ graphics workstations, 309
personal digital assistants, 377
Peru, 142, 310
pet peeves, 26
pets, *see* animals
Philadelphia Phillies, 34
Philippines, 140
philosophy, 144
  Extropian philosophy, 219
  Objectivism, 300
Phish, 124
photography, 125, 151
physical disabilities, 44, 109
  assistance, 435
  blindness, 42, 177
  Down Syndrome, 209
  epilepsy, 434
  Handicap Digest, 238
  multiple sclerosis, 35
  women, 273
physics, 30, 136, 229, 311, 388
  Dall'Agata, Michele, 17
  education, 48
  software, 381
Picasso Graphical User Interface Development System, 311
pictures, 11-12
pinball, 120
Pink Floyd, 211
pipes, 311
pirate radio stations, 315
Pittsburgh Pirates, 34
Pixar Typestry, 27
planets, 10, 30
Play by Mail games, 120
plays, 427
poetry, 113, 312
Poland, 142, 209, 311, 341
Police, 312
political science, 314
politics, 48, 63, 132, 143, 317, 383, 388
  candidates (Iowa), 436
  Clinton, Bill, 27
    economic plan, 397
    press releases, 401
  economics, 27
  environment, 16, 30, 387, 436
  government documents, 436
  Green party, 27
  NAFTA (North American Free Trade Agreement), 398, 401
  Perot, Ross, 27
  platforms, 398
  reform, 27
  Republican party, 27
  Supreme Court rulings, 383
  U.S. Bureau of Alcohol, Tobacco, and Firearms, 27
  U.S. Constitution, 27
  U.S. National Security Agency, 27
  United Kingdom, 27
  White House press releases, 397

pollution, 16, 30
pool, 33
ports, 33
Portugal, 142
postcards, 48
PowerHouse, 48
A Prairie Home Companion, 115
Pratchett, Terry, 19
presidents
    Clinton, Bill, *see* Clinton, Bill
    Kennedy, John, 15
    Nixon, Richard, 25
    Reagan, Ronald, 19
press releases
    Clinton, Bill, 401
    Hubble telescope, 439
    NASA, 438-439
    NATO, 398
    White House, 397, 436
Prince, 25, 315
printers, 248
prions, 315
The Prisoner, 36
prisons, 28, 63
professions
    editors, 381
    engineering, 387
    law enforcement, 23
    locksmiths, 23
programming
    CSI MacForth environment, 98
    GNU Emacs Lisp programmers' manual, 234
    languages
        ABC, 152
        AMOS, 161
        BETA, 172
        C, 83, 188
        C++, 83
        Concurrent C, 251
        Concurrent C++, 251
        Franz Lisp, 99
        ICON, 98
        Idol, 248
        Lucid, 268
        Objective-C, 300
        Pascal, 130
        Prolog, 203
        Python, 317
        Scheme, 74, 99
    Linda, 271
    object-oriented programming, 73, 89
    TurboVision, 358
    visual programming, 99
    Z specification notation, 83, 377
programs, 181
Progress RDBMS, 316
Project Gutenberg, 406, 437
project management, 316
Prolog programming language, 203
protocols, 382, 389
pseudoscience, 138
PSION computers, 91
psychology, 15, 46, 49, 134, 388, 437
Public Brand Software, 396
public-access computer systems, 317
publications, 28
    Adams, Douglas, 18
    Amoner magazine, 395
    Atari Explorer Online, 38
    books, 406
        Anthony, Piers, 19
        Gallaci, Steve, 18
        Kurtz, Katherine, 12
        McCaffery, Anne, 19
        Pratchett, Terry, 19
        reviews, 12
        Rice, Anne, 12
        Tolkien, J.R.R., 19
    copyright laws, 397, 414
    Eddings, David, 18
    magazines, 38, 399
    PC Magazine, 396
    Wired magazine, 38
    see also books
Publicly Accessible Mailing List, 3
puzzles, 125
Pyramid, 380
Python programming language, 317

Q

QNX real-time operating systems, 318
Quakers, 144
Quayle, Dan, 17
Quebec Nordiques, 319
Queen, 25, 319
Queensryche, 330
Queer Nation, 317
quotations, 28

R

racing fabrication, 320
racing motorcycles, 122
racism, 62
radio, 28, 161
Radio Free Europe, 110
radios, 125
Rainbow Gathering, 21
rap music, 28
rape, 145
rave scene, 290, 333, 359
Reagan, Ronald, 19
real estate, 129
rec news groups, 6
recipes, 21, 416-417, 437-438
recovery
    abuse partners, 34
    cancer, 35
    emotional support, 34
    sexual abuse, 32
recreation, 430
    Ars Magica role playing game, 164
    bird watching, 116
    brewing beer, 117, 242
    chat services, 430
    cinema, 112, 218
    costume design, 240
    Cyber-Sleaze, 199
    dancing, 117
    film production, 222
    folk dancing, 224
    home video, 120
    kit cars, 264
    kites, 121, 265
    magic, 276
    modeling, 121
    Morris dancing, 285
    musical theater, 287
    Nielsen ratings, 436
    nudism, 124
    photography, 125
    pipes, 311
    poker, 169
    puzzles, 125
    rave scene, 290, 333, 359
    Renaissance dance, 323
    Scottish Country Dancing, 345
    Star Trek, 431
    stereos, 224
    tandem bicycles, 349
    theme parks, 124
    trading cards, 342
    travel, 128, 439
    trivia, 120, 431
    vintage clothing, 366
    see also arts, books, games, movies, sports, television, theater
recreational software, 82
Reed, Lou, 274
reggae music, 124
relationships, 144
    couples, 139
    interracial, 139
    Matchmaker by E-mail, 434
    non-monogamous relationships, 357
    parent/teen, 26
    personals, 26
    polyamory, 28
    romance, 30
    weddings, 37
relcom news groups, 7
religion, 63, 145, 167, 388, 399, 417-418
    Anglicanism, 216
    atheism, 10
    Bahai-Faith, 168
    Bible, 386, 413, 417, 427, 437
    Buddha, 13
    Catholicism, 42, 183, 184
    Christian use of graphics, 234
    Christianity, 43, 143, 187, 366

Church of Jesus Christ of
  Latter-day Saints, 269,
  326
Church of Scientology, 13
Eastern religions, 144
Hinduism, 22, 45, 239
Holy Qur'an, 417
Islam, 144
Judaism, 61, 141, 261, 270,
  437
minority religions, 145
paganism, 305
Quakers, 144
scientology, 29
Seventh-Day Adventists,
  331
shamanism, 144
Torah, 418
REM, 322
Ren and Stimpy, 37
Renaissance dance, 323
reptiles, 125
Republic of Macedonia, 277
Republic of South Siberia, 15
Republican party, 27
research, 163
retrieval systems, 389
reviews, 12
rftm.mit.edu, 391
Rhodes, Happy, 212
Rice, Anne, 12
Robbins, Tom, 19
robotics, 81, 119
Rockford Files, 37
The Rocky Horror Picture Show,
  15, 323
Rogue, 120
role-playing games, 87, 118,
  235, 291, 325, 334, 355,
  357, 364
roller coasters, 418
Rolling Stones, 30, 361
romance, 30, 48, 434
Romania, 142, 325
RSCS modifications, 48
rugby, 127
rumors, 145
RuneQuest, 325
running, 126
  Dead Runners Society, 203
rural living, 110

Rush, 25, 326
Russia, 323, 388
Russian, 107, 129, 255, 341

S

S & P market reports, 54
sam editor, 327
San Francisco, 64
  rave scene, 333
  Giants, 34, 327
San Jose Sharks, 327
SAS statistics package, 81
satanism, 30
satellite television, 128, 328
satellites
  databases, 438
  NASA, 419
Scheme programming
  language, 74, 99
scholarships, 428
Schrag, John, 187
sci news groups, 6
science fiction, 113, 319, 332,
  357-358
  Anthony, Piers, 19
  McCaffery, Anne, 19
  Pratchett, Terry, 19
sciences, 418, 438
  aeronautics, 155
  astronomy, 66, 134, 387
  biology, 134, 387
  chemistry, 134, 387
  cognitive science, 300
  ecology, 134, 135
  electromagnetics, 213
  electronics, 135
  ethology, 217
  geography, 231
  geology, 135
  medical physics, 280
  meteorology, 281
  National Science Foundation, 393, 402-403
  nuclear energy, 438
  particle information, 438
  periodic tables, 438
  physics, 136, 229, 311, 381
  plant lipids, 298
  pseudoscience, 138

Index

satellite databases, 438
soil science, 339
space, 342
speech science, 83
wildlife biology, 371
Young Scientists' Network, 376
scientology, 29
Scottish country dancing, 345
Scottish Gaelic, 230
Scribe Database Administrator, 330
scuba diving, 48, 126
searches, 438
seasons, 219
Seattle Mariners, 331
Sega, 120
    Genesis, 30
Seinfeld, Jerry, 37
seismology, 419
self-improvement, 31
sending mail to/from non-Internet addresses, 444-460
Serbian, 301
Serial Line IP software, 385
servers, 436
Seventh-Day Adventists, 331
sewing, 31
sexual abuse, 32, 322
sexuality, 31-32, 158, 166
    Australia, 166
    bisexuality, 172
    movies, 31
    non-monogamous relationships, 357
    see also homosexuality
SFI BBS, 438
SGI Iris software, 380
Shadowrun, 334
Shakespeare, 413, 427
shamanism, 144
shortwave radio, 28, 126, 247, 426, 432
Sierra Club, 334
sign language, 336
Simple Network Management Protocol, 100
The Simpsons, 37, 422
Simtel20 PC
    Ada language, 390
    software, 380

SIMULA language, 49
simulation, 81
Sinclair software, 384
Singapore, 142
skateboarding, 32
skating, 126
skinheads, 32
skydiving, 126
SLA research, 49
Slovenia, 297, 301, 311, 324
smail3.X, 336
Smiths, 337
smoking, 338
SNA network management, 49
snow skiing, 126
soap operas, 115
soc news groups, 6
soccer, 33, 128, 227
social sciences, 199
    economics, 60, 134
    genealogy, 144, 325
    history, 134, 143
    parapsychology, 335
    political science, 314
    psychology, 134
    sociology, 30
Societies for Biomechanics, 174
Society for Creative Anachronism, 124, 328
sociology, 30
soft drinks, 20
software, 67, 74, 130, 383, 427, 438
    academic, 386-390
    Amiga, 380, 383, 429
    apE, 162
    Apollo, 429
    Apple AUX, 384
    Apple II, 380, 384
    Apple2, 429
    Applebus, 80
    archived, 383-386
    archivists, 385
    artists, 165
    Atari, 384
    Biosym Technologies, 175
    Borland International, 392
    bugs, 82
    CADCAM, 258
    compression, 381, 385, 396
    CPM, 384, 390

Cygnus Corporation, 389
DDTs, 202
development, 389
distribution, 385
e-mail, 146
E-Math, 437
educational sites, 386
engineering, 81
FASE (Forum for Academic Software Engineering), 220
flight simulators, 167
FrameMaker, 92, 227
Free Software Foundation, 380, 384, 388
ftp archives, 389
games, 381
Gopher, 146
Gopher client/server, 385, 389
graphics, 91, 383
Hewlett-Packard, 384
IBM, 383-386, 388, 392
Imagine, 249
Improv spreadsheet, 249
Informix, 254
Ingres, 253
internationalized software, 257
Khoros, 264
LavVIEW, 253
libraries, 438
licensing, 46
LINUX, 384, 387
MACH, 381
Macintosh, 82, 383-386, 388, 391, 396, 429
mail-reading, 385
mathematics, 437
MATLAB, 279
microcomputers, 388
Microsoft Word, 373
Minix, 384
MIPS PC, 388
miscellaneous, 381, 384-385, 392
MS-DOS, 132, 380, 390, 429
multimedia, 388
music, 337
netnews, 385
networks, 110, 382, 396
news, 389
NeXT, 380, 384, 392
NOC, 99
Notesfile, 111
Novell NetWare, 384
Open Software Foundation, 93
OS/9, 384
PageMaker, 305
PCs, 429
PenPoint, 384
physics, 381
Public Brand Software, 396
publishing, 80, 338
Pyramid, 380
recreational, 82, 148
searches, 438
security, 381
Serial Line IP, 385
SGI Iris, 380
Simtel20 PC, 380
Sinclair, 384
spreadsheets, 67
Sun Exchange, 384
terminal emulation, 389
testing research, 352
UNIX, 381, 384, 391-392, 429
VAX VMS, 385
VMS, 380
WAIS client/server, 389
World Wide Web, 385
Xenix, 385
soil science, 339
Solbourne computers, 105, 255
Somalia, 61
Somewhere chat service, 430
Sonic Youth, 340
sounds, 12
soundtracks, 340
source codes, 33
South Asia, 265
Soviet politics, 145
Soviet Union, 61
space, 66, 145, 342
    aliens, 9
    environment, 438
    Europe Space Agency, 438
    European Space Organization, 420

exploration, 439
Extragalactic Database (NASA), 420
Hubble telescope, 420, 439
Lunar and Planetary Institute, 420
NASA, 420
    press releases, 438-439
    space shuttle launches, 419
National Space Development Agency, 439
National Space Science Data Center, 439
planets, 438
Space: 1999, 341
Spanish, 107
Special Internet Connections list, 3, 425-442
Spielberg, Steven, 36
sports, 121, 387, 421
    archery, 10
    auto racing, 371
    ballooning, 168
    baseball, 33-34, 65, 126, 421
        Atlanta Braves, 33
        Baltimore Orioles, 33
        Chicago Cubs, 33
        major league, 284
        minor league, 284
        San Francisco Giants, 327
        Seattle Mariners, 331
        Toronto Blue Jays, 355
    basketball, 126, 421
    bicycling, 116, 171-173
    bowling, 33
    caving, 184
    Cleveland, 189
    crew, 127
    cricket, 126
    dancing, 169
    darts, 33
    drag racing, 209
    equestrians, 117, 243
    exercise, 108
    fishing, 20, 124
    football, 34, 65, 421
        Australian rules, 127
        collegiate, 65, 127
        Everton Football Club, 217
        Los Angeles Raiders, 320
    four-wheeling, 301
    golf, 127
    gymnastics, 237
    hang-gliding, 116, 238
    hockey, 65, 127, 161, 421
        Boston Bruins, 179
        collegiate hockey, 241
        Dallas Stars, 200
        East Coast Hockey League, 211
        goalie stats, 295
        Los Angeles Kings, 274
        New York Islanders, 294
        Olympic hockey, 302
        Quebec Nordiques, 319
        San Jose Sharks, 327
        St. Louis Blues, 344
        United Kingdom, 359
        Vancouver Canucks, 364
        Western Hockey League, 370
    horse racing, 205
    hunting, 121
    martial arts, 121, 156, 278
    motorcycle racing, 320
    NBA schedules, 439
    NFL scores, 439
    Nordic skiing, 296
    Northwestern University, 299
    officiating, 33
    Olympic games, 65, 127
    orienteering, 303
    Pac Ten, 305
    racing, 65
    racing motorcycles, 122
    rugby, 127
    running, 126
        Dead Runners Society, 203
    scuba diving, 48, 126
    skateboarding, 32
    skating, 126
    skydiving, 126
    snow skiing, 126

soccer, 33, 128, 227
surfing, 35
swimming, 128
table tennis, 128
tennis, 65, 128
trading cards, 182, 342
University of Nebraska, 244
volleyball, 128
water skiing, 369
weights, 369
whitewater sports, 371
windsurfing, 128, 372
wrestling, 127
spreadsheets, 67
Sri Lanka, 142, 342
St. Johns University Traumatic Brain Injury Support List, 350
St. Louis Blues, 344
St. Louis Cardinals, 34
stage craft, 114, 343
stained glass, 233
standards documents, 383
Star Trek, 34, 114, 357, 422, 431
Star Wars, 114
Starship chat service, 430
state laws, 398
statistics, 386, 438
stepparents, 35
stereos, 224, 252
Stern, Howard, 18
Stirner, Max, 296
stock market, 54, 344, 421, 427
Stonewall 25 march, 344
Stoney, Graham, 181
Stratus Computer Corporation, 255
Street Fighter 2, 21
student issues
    Canada, 182
    Kentucky Governor's Scholars Program, 236
    Muslim Student Associations, 286
subways, 439
Sugarcubes, 346
suicides, 34
Sun Microsystems, 35, 91, 105, 347, 386-390
Sun Exchange software, 384
sunsite.unc.edu, 386-390
SuperComputers, 48
Superman, 14
supermodels, 34
superstitions
    Bigfoot, 11
    ghost stories, 20
    vampires, 37
    werewolves, 22
SupraFAX v.32 bis modem, 348
Supreme Court, 63
    rulings, 383, 433
surfing, 35
surveys, 64
swimming, 128
Switzerland, 441
Sybase SQL servers, 342
SysOp, 10
system down times, 111

T

table tennis, 128
Tahoe CPU, 256
Taiwan, 142
Tales of the Beanworld, 237
talk news groups, 6
tandem bicycles, 349
Tandem Computers, Inc., 256
Tandy computers, 92
    Tandy 4000, 350
    Tandy Color Computer, 189
Tangerine Dream, 349
tattoos, 112
teaching, 428
Tears for Fears, 351
technology, 399, 438
    architecture, 10
    mathematics, 49
    patents, 383, 398
teenagers, 26
Tele-Chat, 430
Telebit, 51
Telebit NetBlazer products, 291
telecommunications, 16, 66, 71, 428
TeleUSE, 351
television, 421-422
    30 something, 151
    The Andy Griffith Show, 279
    Beavis and Butthead, 36

Beverly Hills 90210, 36
cable television, 128
celebrities, 64
Clarissa Explains It All, 189
Dark Shadows, 200, 333
Eerie, Indiana, 212
European satellites, 30
history, 114
L.A. Law, 36
Letterman, David, 19
Liquid TV, 36
MacGyver, 275
Married...With Children, 36
M*A*S*H, 36
Melrose Place, 36, 280
Muppets, 36
music videos, 124
Nielsen ratings, 436
Northern Exposure, 36
Parker Lewis, 223
The Prisoner, 36
Ren and Stimpy, 37
Rockford Files, 37
satellite television, 128, 328
Seinfeld, 37
The Simpsons, 37, 422
soap operas, 115
Space: 1999, 341
Star Trek, 114, 357, 422
Stern, Howard, 18
Tiny Toon Adventures, 37
Twin Peaks, 37
United Kingdom, 37, 115
X*Press X*Change data service, 374
telnet
finger, 428
Gopher sites, 399-400
protocols, 389
tennis, 65, 128
terminal emulation software, 389
terrorism, 64, 109
testing research, 352
Tetris, 409, 431
TeX, 389
Texas, 359, 437
Texas Instruments, 92, 101
Text Adventures, 431
theater, 34, 59, 352
costume design, 240
musical theater, 287

stage craft, 343
stage work, 114
theme parks, 124
theorems, 298
They Might be Giants, 25, 352
Think C compiler, 353
Thinking Machines, 189, 368
Tibet, 145, 198
Tiny Toon Adventures, 37
TinyMUCK, 353
Tolkien, J.R.R., 19, 112, 354
Torah, 418
"Torg, The Possibility Wars", 355
TORG, 21
Toronto Blue Jays, 355
tourism, 130
Tower of Power, 354
toys
Legos, 36
Transformers, 36
Tracht, Doug, 18
trade, 258
trading cards, 182, 342
transportation, 406, 426
transsexualism, *see* gender issues
travel, 128, 439
Great Lakes, 21
subways, 439
visas, 37
Traveller, 357
treaties, 398
trivia, 120, 431
tropical storm forecasts, 441
Turkey, 142
Twilight Zone magazine, 358
Twin Peaks, 37
twins, 358
Typestry, 27
typhoons, 441

U

U.S. Bureau of Alcohol, Tobacco, and Firearms, 27
U.S. Constitution, 27
U.S. National Security Agency, 27
U2, 19, 25
u3b news groups, 7

UFOs, 26
UNIC BBS, 439
Unisys, 361
Unitarian Universalists, 363
United Kingdom, 139, 359
    comedy, 14
    history, 412
    politics, 27
    television, 37, 115
United Nations resolutions, 398
universities, 138
    Australian National University, 111
    Carnegie Mellon University, 307
    collegiate humor, 20
    food, 14
    Greek letter societies, 338
    Illinois State University, 313
    library catalogues, 432
    Northwestern University, 104, 299
    Ohio State, 228
    reports, 386
    St. Johns University, 350
    University of Michigan, 369
    University of Illinois, 111, 373
    University of Kentucky, 268
    University of Nebraska, 244
    University of Puget Sound, 362
    University of Washington, 238
    Western Michigan University, 280
UNIX, 59, 68, 81, 93, 204, 332, 381, 384, 388, 391-392, 429, 437
Uruguay, 142, 362
USA Today, 436
USAF Global Positioning System, 235
USENET, 197
    archives, 388
    groups, 385
    news groups categories, 2, 6-7, 436, 439
    Oracle, 436

user groups
    Informix, 255
    TopSoft, 354
Utne Reader, 363
UUNET Internet ftp site, 380-383

V

vampires, 37, 364
Vancouver Canucks, 364
Vangelis, 206
VAX VMS, 385
vegetarianism, 118, 220, 365
vendors
    computers, 381
    ILC database, 408
Venezuela, 143
veterans, 144
VGA planets, 21
video cards, 87
videotapes, 427
Vietnam War, 37
Vietnamese, 143
virtual campus, 430
Virtual Reality, 138
viruses, 50, 346
visas, 37
visual programming, 99
Vizualization Data Explorer, 201
VMS, 146, 380
vmsnet news groups, 7
volleyball, 128
Vreme, 367
VxWorks real-time operating system, 79

W

WAIS client/server software, 389
WAIStation, 440
War Lord of the West Preservation Fan Club, 19
Warhammer Universe, 368
wars, 37
    Civil War, 37
    Desert Storm, 16
    Vietnam War, 37

Washington, D.C., 202
Washington Redskins, 34
water skiing, 369
weather, 50, 64, 369, 373, 392, 422-423, 441
    Atlantic Ocean, 423
    Australia, 441
    avalanche forecasts, 441
    California emergency information, 441
    flight information, 426
    floods, 422, 441
    forecasts, 423, 441
    hurricanes, 441
    maps, 423
    Oceanic Information Center, 441
    solar reports, 441
    tropical storm forecasts, 441
    typhoons, 441
weddings, 37
weight loss, 35
Weller, Paul, 266
werewolves, 22
Western Hockey League, 370
Western Michigan University, 280
western music, 122
White House
    Clinton's economic plan, 397
    press releases, 397, 401, 436
whitewater sports, 371
The Who, 352
whois services, 440
Wide Area Information Servers, 368, 440
Windows, 70, 77
windows, 94
windsurfing, 128, 372
wine, 117
Wired magazine, 38
wireless networks, 83
wiretap.spies.com
    Gopher site, 401
    Internet ftp site, 397-399
Wisseman, Tim, 21
Wodehouse, P.G., 19
wolves, 38

Women in Science and Engineering, 105
women's issues, 61, 144, 159, 221
    lesbianism, 327
    motherhood, 285
    physical disabilities, 273
    rape, 145
    Women in Science and Engineering, 105
woodworking, 128
word processing
    IBM, 51
    Macintosh, 51
WordPerfect, 50
work environments, *see* employment
workstations, 309
world politics, 60, 110
    Argentina, 139
    Australia, 139
    Bangladesh, 139
    Bolivia, 273
    Bosnia, 139, 178
    Brazil, 139
    China, 140, 145
    Croatia, 140, 195-196
    Dominican Republic, 331
    Estonia, 214
    Holocaust, 241
    Hungary, 349
    international trade, 258
    Iran, 140
    Israel, 140
    Japan, 141
    Korea, 141
    Latin America, 141
    Lebanon, 141
    Mexico, 141
    Middle East, 145
    Pakistan, 142
    Palestine, 142
    Peru, 310
    Poland, 142, 209, 311, 341
    Republic of Macedonia, 277
    Romania, 142, 325
    Slovenia, 297, 301, 311, 324
    Somalia, 61
    Soviet politics, 145
    Soviet Union, 61

Sri Lanka, 342
Tibet, 145, 198
United Kingdom, 139
Uruguay, 362
Vietnamese, 143
Yugoslavia, 143, 263, 335, 366, 367
World Wide Web, 389, 441
software, 385
wrestling, 127
wuarchive.wustl.edu
Internet ftp site, 383-386

X

X Window system environment, 133, 373
X*Press X*Change data service, 374
Xenix software, 385
Xerox, 51
XINU operating system, 79
Xpilot, 21
XTC, 186

Y

Yello, 375
Young Scientists' Network, 376
youth rights, 375
Yugoslavia, 143, 263, 335, 366, 367

Z

Zang Tuum Tumb label, 376
Zappa, Frank, 18
Zeos, 53
ZIP codes, 410, 424

EXPLORE THE INTERNET AT LIGHT SPEED.

Atlantis Internet CD-ROM: a new frontier for Internet users, providing a wealth of software and documentation acquired from the Internet in a single, easy to use package for the DOS, Windows, Mac and UNIX environments.

The CD-ROM provides an extensive collection of communications software, demonstration programs, computer-based tutorials and many other utilities to help you get the most from the Internet, whether you are a novice user or an experienced professional.

The **Atlantis Internet CD-ROM** features all the most widely used Internet documents including the complete series of Request For Comments (RFCs), For Your Information (FYIs) and Standards Documents (STDs). Valuable lists of network providers and Internet services are included on the CD-ROM as well, saving you time and effort in finding such information yourself. With regular CD-ROM updates available, you will always be able to fly through a galaxy of information at warp speed.

Accelerate your Internet explorations for just **$39.95. Call 1-800-285-4680 today for fastest ordering service.** Fax and e-mail orders are also accepted.

Atlantis
INTERNET CD-ROM

YES, send me the Atlantis Internet CD-ROM at $39.95 each plus $4.95 for U.S. shipping & handling. ($9.95 S&H outside of U.S.) Georgia residents add 4% sales tax.

Please check one: ☐ Check   ☐ VISA   ☐ MasterCard

Credit Card # _____ Expiration Date _____

Signature _____
Name _____
(please print name as it appears on credit card)
Address _____
City/State/Zip _____
Day Phone _____

ATLANTA INNOVATION, INC.
P.O. Box 767849 • Roswell, Georgia 30076
404 642-8402 • FAX 404 640-8769 • cdrom-info@atlinv.com